ENEMIES OF THE LATER ROMAN ORDER

JAGIELLONIAN STUDIES IN HISTORY

Editor in chief
Jan Jacek Bruski

Vol. 10

Michał Stachura

ENEMIES OF THE LATER ROMAN ORDER

A STUDY OF THE PHENOMENON OF LANGUAGE AGGRESSION IN THE THEODOSIAN CODE, POST-THEODOSIAN NOVELS, AND THE SIRMONDIAN CONSTITUTIONS

Translated by Marcin Fijak

Jagiellonian University Press

The publication of this volume was financed by the Jagiellonian University in Kraków – Faculty of History.

REVIEVER
prof. dr hab. Maciej Salamon

SERIES COVER DESIGN
Jan Jacek Bruski

COVER DESIGN
Agnieszka Winciorek

Front cover:
© Zastavkin – Dreamstime.com

ISBN 978-83-233-4505-3
ISBN 978-83-233-9871-4 (e-book)

JAGIELLONIAN
UNIVERSITY
PRESS

www.wuj.pl

Jagiellonian University Press
Editorial Offices: Michałowskiego 9/2, 31-126 Krakow
Phone: +48 12 663 23 80, Fax: +48 12 663 23 83
Distribution: Phone: +48 12 631 01 97, Fax: +48 12 631 01 98
Cell Phone: + 48 506 006 674, e-mail: sprzedaz@wuj.pl
Bank: PEKAO SA, IBAN PL 80 1240 4722 1111 0000 4856 3325

To My Parents

Contents

Abbreviations 11

Introduction 15

Part I: Method

Chapter I: Invective in the world of Classical Antiquity – the problem of definition 27

The tradition of language aggression 27
The concepts of invective and the language of invective 35
Essential features of analyzed statements 37

Chapter II: The position of the "language of invective" in the ideological message of the Imperial documents 43

Imperial documents of Late Antiquity 43
Criticism of the post-classical law in terms of language 50
Three *genera dicendi* vs. the language of post-classical law 53
Education- and propaganda-related functions of the law in Antiquity... 55
The position of the language of invective in the ideological message of the Late Antique constitutions 59

Chapter III: The possibility of researching the "language of invective" in the Imperial documents of Late Antiquity 63

Methods used to formulate the "language of invective" – amplification 63
Relevant documents: the actual state of preservation 65
The research method and its limitations 72

Part II: Analysis

Chapter IV: Composition of invective in documents of Late Antiquity – examples **79**

C.Th. 1.16.7 81
C.Th. 6.4.22 83
C.Th. 9.16.5 89
C.Th. 9.38.6 91
C.Th. 9.40.17 94
C.Th. 12.1.85 98
C.Th. 16.5.6 100
C.Th. 16.5.24 104
Nov. Theod. 15.2 105
Nov. Valent. 18 110

Chapter V: Terms indicating the nature of the opposition to Roman or ecclesiastical communities **117**

Hostis, inimicus, adversarius 117
Barbarus, barbaricus 124
Tyrannus 128
Praedo, latro, rebellis, desertor 130
Haereticus 134
Paganus 140
Maleficus 142

Chapter VI: Terms indicating the perpetrator's attitude **145**

Avaritia, cupiditas, desidia, invidia 145
Audacia 149
Furor 163
Pertinacia, obstinatio 172
Subreptio 173
Features contrary to *humanitas* 174
Perfidia 180
Impietas 182
Improbitas 184

Chapter VII: Terms indicating the nature of a criminal act 187

Terms describing offences in amplificatory manner 188
Piaculum 195
Profanatio 196
Contagium 198
Adjectives ending with *-bilis* as terms of invective 206
Terms indicating disturbances of public order 209

Chapter VIII: Terms indicating deviation (particularly in relation to religion) 219

Superstitio 219
Error, devio, pravitas, depravatio, perversitas, scaevus 226

Part III: Synthesis

Chapter IX: Categories of enemies 233

Sacrilegium 233
Hostes rei publicae 237
Inimici ecclesiae 242
Corrupted officials 248
Criminosi 252

Chapter X: Conclusions. The hierarchy of "enemies" in Imperial documents 257

A listing of the relevant terms with possibly negative emotional content as present in the individual constitutions 263

Bibliography 289

Index of Latin terms 311

Abbreviations

AAntHung	*Acta antiqua Academiae Scientiarum Hungaricae*
AARC	*Atti dell' Accademia Romanistica Costantiniana*
ACD	*Acta classica Universitatis Scientiarum Debrecenensis*
AClass	*Acta classica*
ACO	*Acta conciliorum oecumenicorum*, ed. E. Schwartz, Berolini 1914–
AG	*Archivo giuridico*
AJPh	*American Journal of Philology*
AncSoc	*Ancient Society*
AncW	*The Ancient World: A Scholarly Journal for the Study of Antiquity*
Annales(ESC)	*Annales. Economies, Sociétés, Civilisations*
ANRW	*Aufstieg und Niedergang der römischen Welt*, Berlin–New York 1972–
AntTard	*Antiquité Tardive: revue internationale d'histoire et d'archéologie (IVe – VIIIe siècle)*
APF	*Archiv für Papyrusforschung und verwandte Gebiete*
AUB(class)	*Annales Universitatis Budapestiensis de Rolande Eötvös nominatae, Sectio classica*
AUFG	*Annali dell'Università di Ferrara. Nuove serie. Sezione V, Scienze Giuridiche*
BAGB	*Bulletin de l'Association Guillaume Budé*
BIDR	*Bulletino dell'Istituto di Diritto Romano*
BStudLat	*Bolletino di Studi Latini: periodico semestrale d'informazione bibliografica*
BRL	*Bulletin of the John Rylands University Library of Manchester*
CCSL	*Corpus Christianorum. Series Latina*
CE	*Chronique d'Égypte*
CIL	*Corpus Inscriptionum Latinarum*, Berolini 1862–
CJ	*The Classical Journal*
C.J.	*Codex Justinianus*
CLCLT-6	*Library of Latin Texts CLCLT-6*, mod. P. Tombeur, Turnhout 2005 (digital database)
Coll.	*Collatio Legum Mosaicarum et Romanarum* = *FIRA* 2: 541–589
Coll. Avell.	*Collectio Avellana* = *Epistulae imperatorum pontificum aliorum*, rec. O. Guenther, *CSEL* 35, Vindobonae 1895
Const. Sirm.	*Constitutio Sirmondiana*
CPh	*Classical Philology: A Journal Devoted to Research in Classical Antiquity*

CQ	*Classical Quarterly*
CrSt	*Cristianesimo nella storia: ricerche storiche, esegetiche, teologiche*
CSEL	*Corpus Scriptorum Ecclesiasticorum Latinorum*
C.Th.	*Codex Theodosianus*
CW	*Classical World*
D.	*Digesta*
FIRA	*Fontes Iuris Romani Anteiustiniani*, 1–3, ed. S. Riccobono, Florentiae 1940–1943
FMS	*Frühmittelalterliche Studien. Jahrbuch des Instituts für Frühmittelalterforschung der Universität Münster*
GRBS	*Greek, Roman and Byzantine Studies*
GCS	*Die Griechische Christliche Schriftsteller*
GWU	*Geschichte in Wissenschaft und Unterricht*
HE	*Historia Ecclesiastica*
HPTh	*History of Political Thought*
HThR	*Harvard Theological Review*
ICS	*Illinois Classical Studies*
ILS	*Inscriptiones Latinae selectae*, ed. H. Dessau, Berolini 1954–1955
JbAC	*Jahrbuch für Antike und Christentum*
JESHO	*Journal of the economic and social history of the Orient*
JRS	*The Journal of Roman Studies*
MD	*Materiali e discussioni per l'analisi die testi classici*
Nov. Anth.	*Novella Anthemii*
Nov. Majo.	*Novella Majoriani*
Nov. Marc.	*Novella Marciani*
Nov. Sev.	*Novella Sevariani*
Nov. Theod.	*Novella Theodosii*
Nov. Valent.	*Novella Valentiniani*
OSAPh	*Oxford Studies in Ancient Philosophy*
P&P	*Past and Present: A Journal of Historical Studies*
PHist	*Przegląd Historyczny*
PLRE 1	Jones, Martindale, Morris 1971
PLRE 2	Martindale 1980
RAC	*Reallexikon für Antike und Christentum*, Stuttgart 1950–
RAL	*Rendiconti dell'Accademia Nazionale dei Lincei: Classe di Scienze Morale, Storiche e Philologiche*
RE	*Realenzyklopädie der classischen Altertumswissenschaft*, Stuttgart 1894–
REL	*Revue des études latines*
RG	*Rhetores Graeci*, rec. L. Spengel, 1–3, Lipsiae 1853–1856
RHR	*Revue de l'histoire des religions*
RIDA	*Revue internationale de droits de l'antiquité*
RJ	*Rechtshistorisches Journal*
SChr	*Sources Chrétiennes*

SDHI	*Studia et documenta historiae et iuris*
SHHA	*Studia historica. Historia Antigua*
SR	*Studies in religion = Sciences religieuses*
TAPhA	*Transactions and Proceedings of the American Philological Association*
ThLL	*Thesaurus Linguae Latinae*, Lipsiae 1900–
VChr	*Vigiliae Christianae: a review of early Christian life and languages*
ZRG	*Zeitschrift der Savigny Stiftung für Rechtsgeschichte. Romanistische Abteilung*
ZSS KA	*Zeitschrift der Savigny-Stiftung für Rechtsgeschichte. Kanonistische Abteilung*

Number of constitution and verse recorded as according to Gradenwitz 1925.

Introduction

In 1966, Ramsay MacMullen published an important book on "the enemies of the Roman order."[1] It lists the social groups that had stood in actual opposition to the order reigning in the Roman Empire from the first up to the fifth century AD: senatorial opposition, philosophers, magicians, astrologers, rebellious inhabitants of cities, country brigands, even anachoretic hermits migrating outside the boundaries of the Roman community. At first glance, this varied assortment of figures appears to be collected at random. In fact, however, all these "characters" as assembled by MacMullen share one feature: their intense reluctance to conform to some aspect of the Roman order, which was constituted and defended by the Roman Empire.

The work which I hereby present to the reader states the question of the "enemies" in exactly the opposite way. The question that I ask of the sources is: "Who did the rulers of the Later Roman Empire, the guarantors of the Roman order, treat as 'enemies'?" The most appropriate way to start searching for answers to this question, it seems to me, are the documents issued at the behest of the emperors themselves, products of the Imperial bureaux, and therefore – in particular – Imperial laws. Nonetheless, the criterion on which I have sought and categorized the "enemies" of the emperor-lawgiver is not the sanctions administered by the said laws but the language in which these "enemies" are described. In my opinion, the right method to build such a hostile relation was to use a condemnatory language towards a given group – the language suitable for the phenomenon described, beginning from Antiquity, as "invective."

Like nowadays, language aggression in ancient times served as one of the fundamental means of expression of political propaganda.[2] Its role seems to be quite easy to comprehend in the context of political rivalry among various parties, i.e., in speeches delivered before the Popular Assembly of the Athenian

---

1 MacMullen 1966.

2 Kamińska-Szmaj 2007: 7.

democracy or the Senate of the late Roman Republic. Yet even after the Roman Empire had been established, the importance of the political propaganda, and its accompanying language aggression, did not cease to exist. Each new law was the effect of the ruler's solicitude for the well-being of the Roman people; stern decisions had required proper justification as well. In that way, the terms shaped within the sphere of politically-oriented invective had found their way into the language of Imperial documents.[3] In a world without mass media, where circles of readers of literary works were strongly limited, the Imperial law, which was duplicated for application by consecutive offices, and promulgated publicly in cities,[4] became the best vehicle to communicate the desired ideological message to the subjects.[5]

As early as Plato's writings, there existed a demand postulating that the law should not only prescribe and impose its authority by force, but also educate. Roman emperors supplemented it with some elements of propaganda. The proper place to present this sort of justification was the *praefatio* of a law. Yet in the Dominate period elements of justification, which we now tend to see as expressions of the legislator's emotion, had also found their way into the part of the law containing the imperial disposition.[6] The instructions that were formulated successively during the works on the *C.Th.* and *C.J.* provided for the removal from the copied laws of any "superfluous" contents, "irrelevant for the sanction."[7] But if we now find so many of these "superfluous" ideological contents in the Codes, it is not so much the result of the compilers' negligence as rather of the filling of just about every single section of the promulgated laws with such a particular content.

The task which I have set for myself is to find the traces of the language of invective applied in imperial documents, both the ones that are completely preserved and those much more numerous, stripped of a major part of such "superfluous" rhetoric by compilers. In the latter case, in particular, there is not much of a chance to encounter anything more than individual terms specific for describing an "enemy" in a given source. This compels one to exercise much caution in selecting a research method, suitable for a large body of smaller texts

---

3 For more on the subject, see Chapter II.

4 On promulgating Imperial laws, see Matthews 2000: 187–190; Millar 2006: 169.

5 Let us remember that the texts in question are normally Latin letters addressed directly to a specific Imperial official, and for this reason they are an element of the discourse within the power structure; only at a later stage, an Imperial order was to be published in the form of an edict in Latin or Greek, depending on the part of the Empire (cf. Millar 2006: 20–23, 84–93 on the role of Latin in the Eastern part of the Empire as the language of discourse within the authority structure).

6 Ries 1983: 184, 187. The terminology used here is further explained in Chapter II: 43–62.

7 *C.Th.* 1.1.5 (429); 1.1.6 (435); constitution *Haec* (528).

that are usually preserved in an incomplete form, that would – at the same time – take into consideration the fact that only one of the present messages contained therein is analyzed, and not the one that was preferred at the time they had been abridged.[8]

This work is composed of three parts: methodological, analytical, synthetic. The methodological part contains three chapters: Chapter I defines the "language of invective," Chapter II explains the role it played in the documents under consideration, while Chapter III enumerates assumptions and limitations of the proposed method of study. The analytical part contains results of the search for the "language of invective" in the relevant material. Chapter IV, the first one in this part, uses analysis of some individual documents to demonstrate where and how that language functions in a given source studied. The subsequent chapters compile and analyze instances of individual terms with negative content. I have attempted to select all the terms characterized by definitely negative content that appear more than once in the source material, although, as the reader shall notice in Chapter IV, the list could be extended by the words which acquire a negative overtone in a suitable context. As a footnote-based presentation of the evidence material, on the basis of which I have built up this "dictionary of invective," would have disrupted the framework of narration (as there are often dozens of instances of each specific term in the analyzed material), I have decided to supplement each entry with an annex in which all the instances of respective terms in the material are listed; if necessary, I also take into account boundary and ambiguous cases. Finally, the third synthetic part is an attempt to form a taxonomy of "enemies of the Empire," according to how they are depicted by use of the "language of invective" in Imperial documents. In Chapter X, the last one, I shall present some conclusions for our study resulting from a quantity analysis of the instances of the investigated terms in the aforementioned evidence material. An appendix is attached thereto in the form of an index in which all the instances of the analyzed terms are mentioned for each individual document.

For the purpose of the present study, I have decided to embrace three sets of laws from the fifth century: Theodosian Code, Post-Theodosian Novels issued within 30 years after the completion of the Code, and the so-called Sirmondian Constitutions. Just as each selection, this one also requires some justification. There is no doubt these three collections of constitutions contain an overwhelming majority of the fourth and fifth-century documents, which is the best critically evaluated set thanks to the edition by Theodor Mommsen

---

[8] Cf. Chapter III: 65–76.

and Paul Meyer,[9] a complementary translation by Clyde Pharr[10] and an index by Otto Gradenwitz.[11] All of the documents in these collections are preserved in Latin (only one constitution of the Theodosian Code in Greek as well).[12] This allows us to avoid unnecessary deliberations over rendering Greek terms into Latin.[13] All of them also contain directives of a general character, *leges generales*, and thus they may be defined as Imperial constitutions.[14]

A fundamental problem was the question of using some constitutions of the Code of Justinian. The entire texts of the *Codex Iustinianus* from the years 311–437 come probably from the Theodosian Code (also from the parts which are now lost).[15] Those texts were, unfortunately, altered by Justinian's compilers, in the years 528–534.[16] It would be logical, for this reason, to reach for all, not just some, documents of this Code, i.e., from Hadrian to Justinian, yet the work would have lost, in that way, its character of a monographic study of the fourth- and fifth-century documents. An additional problem is the presence in the Code of Justinian of the texts written

[9] *Theodosiani Libri XVI cum Constitutionibus Sirmondianis et Leges Novellae ad Theodosianum Pertinentes*, ed. Th. Mommsen, P. M. Meyer, Berlin 1905.

[10] *The Theodosian Code and Novels and the Sirmondian Constitutions. A Translation with Commentary, Glossary and Bibliography* by C. Pharr, Princeton 1952.

[11] Gradenwitz 1925.

[12] *C.Th.* 9.45.4, cf. Stolte 2008.

[13] Such a problem would turn up during analysis of many texts of the Code of Justinian (see below), Imperial letters, as well as the documents contained in the acts of the Council, which are translated back into Latin from Greek (Millar 2006: 166, 237).

[14] Cf. Chapter II: 43–47.

[15] Matthews (2000: 90) indicates that there has never been any doubt cast on the fact that all the laws from the years 312–437 contained in the Code of Justinian had been incorporated there by way of the Theodosian Code. Cf. also Sirks 2007: 84.

[16] The constitution *Haec* (February 13, 428), which served as an instruction for creating the first version of the Code, permitted to use one operation that had not existed for the Theodosian Code: merging several constitutions concerning the same subject into one provision (dated the same as the last one of the individual constitutions). Moreover, the compilers of the Code of Justinian could not find in their instructions any permission to include provisions that were no longer valid. It would ordinarily have resulted in the omission of the already outdated constitutions. But, in at least several cases, it is possible to show how the content of the law incorporated in the Code of Justinian was modified in order to reflect the then-current state of laws. For instance, the *C.J.* 1.5.5.9–10[2] adds *et ultimo supplicio tradendis* to the words from the *C.Th.* 16.5.65 (428), in accordance with the Justinian-era, but not Theodosian, sanction of death penalty for Manichaeans. In turn, the *C.J.* 9.17.1 omits the words of the *C.Th.* 9.16.1.7–8: *superstitioni enim suae servire cupientes poterunt publice ritum proprium exercere* (319), as in the time of Justinian's reign, unlike that of Constantine, no public haruspicies were allowed. Cf. also Delmaire 2012.

in Greek, the so-called *leges restitutae*.[17] There are definitely more of them especially throughout the period of the last half-century prior to the creation of this Code, even though the Emperor Zeno's reign (474–491) does not form any strict dividing line here.[18] It seems then that the studies of the use of invective in the documents of the *Codex Iustinianus* should be given a separate treatment. In any case, it would be an undertaking of a comparable extent.

It is notable that not only the aggressive aspect but also the ideological message in the Late Antique documents have long been neglected as subjects of historical study. The rhetorical side of the contemporary laws had indeed continued to remain within the sphere of Romanists' interest, but primarily as a proof of the decadence of the post-classical law. A departure from the professional language of classical jurists was viewed with much attention, the guilty were sought, yet the autonomous function of these documents – as vehicles of not only Imperial dispositions but also of a significant ideological message – was not considered.[19] A change in this respect was brought in thanks to Åke Fridh's work on the style of Cassiodorus' bureau,[20] followed up by Richard Honig, who was the first one to have ventured to turn that ideological message into the chief subject of his research studies.[21] The German scholar decided to analyze the meaning of the term *humanitas* in the language of the Late Antique law, yet he did not treat it as a technical legal term but as a key word in the ideology that the emperors used to validate their legislation activity. At the same time, Honig contests the traditional views,

17 These texts were omitted, as incomprehensible, by copyists; only in modern times were some of them restored in the Code on the basis of Byzantine sources (Wenger 1953: 651). As far as the authenticity of the words used in it, one cannot prove it with certainty. Those which come from the later Byzantine codes are reckoned as genuine, but it is clear we cannot presume the authenticity of the terms used in the case of the texts restored from Byzantine commentaries (Van der Wal 1980: 18–19, n. 34).

18 Sirks argues that the first known constitution written in Greek comes from Zeno. Before that, we could only deal with some Greek versions of the constitutions issued in Latin. Still, he does not justify his view exhaustively (Sirks 2007: 96). For the period 311–437, I have found 4 Greek constitutions in the Code of Justinian (*C.J.* 1.9.2; 1.12.3; 8.11.3; 9.36.1), out of which two (*C.J.* 1.12.3; 8.11.3) are present in the Theodosian Code in Latin; for the period 338–474 – 7 constitutions (*C.J.* 1.1.3; 1.3.29; 1.4.14; 1.5.9; 1.14.10; 4.49.1; 11.41.7); in addition, undated constitutions *C.J.* 1.40.12 from 412–471 and *C.J.* 4.20.13 from 423–486; whereas for the reign of Zeno – 13 constitutions (*C.J.* 1.2.15; 1.3.35; 1.5.11; 1.51.13; 2.7.18; 2.7.19; 3.3.6; 3.10.1; 6.34.4; 7.50.5; 8.10.12; 10.3.7; 10.32.65).

19 This criticism is discussed extensively in Voß 1982: 4–5, 8; more briefly, Turpin 1985: 351.

20 Fridh 1956.

21 Honig 1960. Yet it should be noted that Fichtenau had studied, somewhat earlier, the issue of the continuation of the ancient ideological watchwords in the *arengae* of some early medieval documents (1957: 30–88).

even evaluating positively the presence in the Imperial laws of that other, ideological, message which would complement the legal disposition proper. In his view, this attests to the emperors' resignation of exerting the sheer coercion upon their subjects, to a transformation from the nihilism of the "Crisis of the Third Century" to an epoch where the emperor treats his obligations towards subjects so seriously that he must communicate them on the occasion of promulgating his dispositions.

These somewhat naive raptures on Honig's part are not reflected in the later studies' more mitigated approach. For example, in his important work on the role of the preface in the legislations of Antiquity as well as of the ancient Near East, Gerhard Ries notes that the more despotic an authority is and the less it has to take heed of the voice of the subjects, the more it feels obliged to explain the motives for its decisions.[22]

The most important and in many aspects the only one that throws light on the role of the ideological message in the Late Antique constitutions is Wulf Eckart Voß's book. Devoted, as a matter of fact, to the language of the law regulating sales and transfers of property in Late Antiquity, it is preceded by an extensive chapter in which the author explains the reasons why the language of Imperial constitutions had succumbed to a far-reaching "rhetorization."[23] He argues that those reasons did not lie in low legal abilities of the authors of these texts but in a prevailing requirement that the texts of laws should encompass admonition. It was expressed by means of the style which had required that technical terms be replaced with synonyms, metaphors, and descriptions.

As much as the German scholars have focused on the ideological message itself, the Anglophones have contributed greatly to the understanding of its historical context. Particularly important here is the recently published work by Fergus Millar, which analyzes the legal documents in question as a medium of communication between the Imperial power and its officials.[24] The role of laws as a medium rather conveying an ideological message than truly reflecting the actual contemporary problems was appreciated a little earlier by Jill Harries.[25]

If the role of the ideological message in the Late Antique laws has been the subject of study for half a century, it cannot be said that the negative side of that message, i.e., the language of invective discussed in the present work, has

---

22 Ries 1983: 220–222.

23 Voß 1982: 15–81.

24 Millar 2006.

25 Harries 1999a.

been investigated exhaustively. Honig devoted only one chapter to one of its many aspects, which is the presence in the Late Antique constitutions of verbal adjectives ending with *-bilis*, characterized by their intense level of negative emotions. Since then, a number of studies have been published dealing with some individual aspects of the issue. The language of invective in the laws on usurpers was discussed in the articles written by Spanish scholars: Maria Vittoria Escribano and José Luis Cañizar Palacios,[26] while the term *superstitio* as used in the anti-pagan laws was described by Michèlle Renée Salzman.[27] The rhetoric used by the authority towards imperial officials has been analyzed by Jill Harries.[28] It is also worth mentioning the works of the Italian scholar Maria Pia Baccari, who studied the issue of the exclusion from the Roman community in the Late Antique laws, from the language perspective as well.[29] Certain observations referring to invective can also be found in the studies dealing with heretics[30], and barbarians[31] in the period of the Later Roman Empire. Apparently, a fresh perspective can be found in an article by Sylvie Crogiez-Pétrequin and Pierre Jaillet on deserters, revealing the presence of the same metaphorical representations of the soldier deserting his post in various constitutions dealing with many different themes, as well as an article by Béatrice Caseau that attempts to explain the negative contents conveyed by the term *profanes* used in the constitutions.[32]

I would like to draw particular attention to Fernando Zuccotti's work on the "madness of heretics." The author takes note of a majority of the terms which are also the subject of this present study; therein, he has noticed the amplification,[33] i.e., the rhetorical technique characteristic of the invective structure. He is primarily occupied with an evident wish to separate "the mad" and "the contaminated" from the "healthy" part of the Roman community; simultaneously, he draws far-reaching conclusions regarding fears of an individual in Late Antiquity. His most quaint idea is his recognition of the laws

---

26 Escribano 1997; Cañizar Palacios 2006.

27 Salzman 1987.

28 Harries 1999a: 97–98; Harries 1999b.

29 Baccari 1991; Baccari 1996.

30 Harmening 1979; De Giovanni 1980; Hunt 1993; Maceratini 1994: 50–56; Stemberger 2002; Zinser 2002; Zeddies 2003: 47–68; Coyle 2004. It is worthwhile taking note of the more recent articles by Escribano Paño (Escribano Paño 2008, Escribano Paño 2009), which aim to discuss the composition of the image of a heretic in Theodosius I's constitutions; especially in the second one of the aforementioned texts, there is a more broadly drawn attempt at a typology of invectives targeting this particular group.

31 Ohnacker 2003; Rugullis 1992.

32 Crogiez-Pétrequin, Jaillet 2009; Caseau 2008.

33 Zuccotti 1992: 143–155.

as a sort of exorcism through which the emperors chased away demons from the Roman world subordinated to their rule.[34]

Another work that deserves a separate mention is Maria Teresa Fögen's book on the prohibition of prophecies in Late Antiquity.[35] The author refers to the appearance of a common idea in the legislations of Diocletian and Constantine, directed against astrologers, haruspices, diviners, but also magicians and Manichaeans – the idea that had underpinned, among other things, the formulation of invectives. She also devotes several subchapters to an analysis of those invectives, but this is only a secondary theme in the book, as its major objective is to prove that the way the divination practices had been condemned in Late Antiquity was an absolute *novum* in the Roman world.[36]

I must stress here that none of the above-mentioned works defines the stigmatizing language of the laws explicitly as a language of invective. The placement of the phenomenon in question within the classical tradition of invective is my own idea, which, I hope, shall be convincingly substantiated in the methodology chapter.

There have been numerous important works on the classical invective in literature. A fundamental study is Severin Koster's book attempting to embrace the phenomenon in the entire history of Greco-Roman literature.[37] This study is of particular importance, as it endeavours to provide theoretical foundations for the study of invective, especially as regards defining the phenomenon itself. On the other hand, Ilona Opelt has limited her scope of investigation to the sources written in Latin, and, unlike Koster, focused her study on the basic constituent of an invective, i.e., an "offensive word" (*Schimpfwort*).[38] Means of expression specific for the phenomenon of invective are characterized briefly by Heinrich Lausberg,[39] yet specific examples of their usage in practice can be found in some more detailed studies, which I list as part of a brief discussion of the tradition of invective at the close of Chapter I.

---

34 Zuccotti 1992: 117, 126, 188. Even a superficial knowledge of exorcism would be sufficient to reject this view of the Italian scholar, cf. Stachura 2004: 245, n. 127.

35 Fögen 1993.

36 This statement is expressed in very radical terms (before Diocletian, there had been no legal proscription at all on clairvoyance practices) and in opposition to practically all the earlier scholars involved in the study of this subject (cf. Fögen 1993: 54); I have not found, in the more recent literature, any acceptance of Fögen's statement in its radical form, along with suggestions on deliberate forgery, by the adherents of the new outlook, of the texts such as *D.* 47.10.15.13, *D.* 10.2.4.1, *D.* 48.8.13, *Coll.* 15.2 (*FIRA* 2: 579–580).

37 Koster 1980.

38 Opelt 1965a. The author focused on the invective in the Patristic literature over the years, cf. Opelt 1967; Opelt 1972; Opelt 1973; Opelt 1974; Opelt 1980.

39 Lausberg 1960.

The idea behind this work had been taking its shape for quite some time. It first appeared in connection with the research on the vocabulary of the laws concerning non-Catholics, which was carried out as part of the grant by the State Committee for Scientific Research (0158/H01/2001/20). At that time, I noticed that an analysis of the vocabulary used in the laws would offer some surprising opportunities for enriching our knowledge of the ideas at the foundations of the religious/penal legislation. Extending these studies into the whole of the invective question in the language of the Late Antique legislation was, in turn, made possible thanks to the scholarship grant assigned by the Polish Science Foundation following my return from a scholarship visit at Mainz in 2005. It turned out to be a necessary complement to the research conducted as part of the project of the Polish Science Foundation Scholarship for Young Scholars with a Doctoral Degree, which is dedicated to "The Policy of Religious Unification of the Roman Empire in the Light of the Late Antique Historiography." I believe that the present book is the most significant publication that has originated from the said project.

Thanks to the aforementioned Foundation grant, I was able to continue my research in Poland, obtain the indispensable publications, as well as ensure access to the electronic databases. In turn, my foreign trips necessary for collecting the remaining material were possible thanks to the resources obtained from the Lanckoronski Foundation (a month-long visit to London, 2007), the History Institute of the Jagiellonian University (short trips to Belgium, Germany, Great Britain, and Italy, in the years 2007–2010), and a foreign exchange with the University of Vienna (2008, 2010). I would like to express my heartfelt thanks to all the institutions without whose assistance this book would not have been possible. Special thanks are also due to my colleague Jochen Walter from the University of Mainz, whose hospitality made it possible for me to visit the University on a number of occasions.

I also owe my acknowledgements to those institutions whose libraries I had visited during my research trips – first of all, the libraries of the Institute of Classical Studies and the Warburg Institute in London, the Gutenberg University at Mainz, as well as the libraries of the Universities at Vienna, Leuven, Padova, and the École Française at Rome.

The first Polish edition of the present book was published in 2010. The work on preparing an English translation would not have been possible without yet another visit to the specialist academic centre Max-Planck-Institut für europäische Rechtsgeschichte in Frankfurt am Main. I would like to take this opportunity to extend thanks to the Institute for granting me a scholarship for a two-month-long research visit in 2012, as well as to the Institute associates, in particular Professor Thomas Duve, Director of the Institute, my supervisor,

Professor Wolfram Brandes, Dr Lorena Atzeri, whose comments proved to be very useful at this stage of my work, and my friend Dr Lars Hoffman, who has played a key role in making the English edition possible.

Unfortunately, the publication of the present book has been delayed by several years due to various objective reasons. The excellent opportunity has appeared only recently, with the inauguration of the English language series of historical monographs by the Jagiellonian University Press, under the general supervision of Professor Jan Jacek Bruski. Considering the circumstances, I was confronted with the difficult task of submitting the previously completed text for publication on a short notice or, alternatively, spending perhaps as many as several months on revising the current version of the work, with the risk of missing the deadline and losing the publishing opportunity. A swift survey of the recent publications concerning the relevant subject matter allowed me to determine that there was no significant amount of new findings that would have essentially altered or questioned the conclusions contained in the present study. I have therefore decided to choose the first of the two options. Despite the passing of a few years, it is my hope that *The Enemies of the Roman Order* shall be a welcome contribution to the current state of our knowledge of Late Antiquity.

This study would not have been written without the kindness of many people I met at various stages of my research work. I owe my particular acknowledgements to my Mentor, Professor Maria Dzielska (†), whose academic achievements, noted for their eloquence and outstanding writing talent, remained an unmatched example to be followed in the course of my work on this book. I would also like to thank Professor Ewa Wipszycka, on whose advice and assistance I could always rely on despite the distance to Warsaw. I owe a debt of gratitude to my original reviewers, Professors Maciej Salamon and Przemysław Nehring, for their valuable comments and advice, all contributing to the final shape this book has taken. I also wish to thank all my friends and colleagues whose kind advice has enriched this study; in particular, I would like to mention those of them whose contributions have been most helpful: Kazimierz Ilski, Sławomir Bralewski, Rafał Kosiński, Maciej Jońca, Sławomir Sprawski, Jacek Wiewiorowski, and Robert Wiśniewski. Of course, the author bears the sole responsibility for any controversial statements in this book.

Part I: Method

Chapter I: Invective in the world of Classical Antiquity – the problem of definition

The tradition of language aggression

"The rapacious hands of the apparitors shall immediately cease, they shall cease, I say; for if after due warning they do not cease, they shall be cut off by the sword" (*Cessent iam nunc rapaces officialium manus, cessent, inquam: nam nisi moniti cessaverint, gladiis praecidentur*).[1] "The contamination of the Photinian pestilence, the poison of the Arian sacrilege, the crime of the Eunomian perfidy, and the sectarian monstrosities, abominable because of the ill-omened names of their authors, shall be abolished even from the hearing of men" (*Fotinianae labis contaminatio, Arriani sacrilegii venenum, Eunomianae perfidiae crimen et nefanda monstruosis nominibus auctorum prodigia sectarum ab ipso etiam aboleantur auditu*).[2] These instances of language aggression quoted from the texts of the Late Antique Imperial constitutions are good illustrations of the phenomenon which is the subject of our study. It is not difficult to notice where the rhetorical strength of these two condemnatory sentences is located. In the both cases, one is faced here with accumulations of aggressive, closely related, formulas – reinforcing the sense of anger and indignation with which the author states his condemnation.

Yet this rhetorical figure is not an accidental invention by the compilers of these two particular constitutions. "Accumulation" (*congeries*) was one of the methods of amplification, recommended in composing speeches intended to condemn a specific person or an act.[3] As a result, the compilers of the Imperial constitutions had made use of a variety of means already

---

1 *C.Th.* 1.16.7 (331).

2 *C.Th.* 16.5.6–(381).

3 See Chapter III: 63–76.

elaborated by the ancient art of rhetoric for the purpose of drawing up the so-called epideictic speeches. They placed themselves, consciously rather than unwittingly, within the long tradition of formulating verbally aggressive statements, nowadays often known as "invective."

But what is the meaning of the word? The term *invectiva* had taken shape as a word of Latin derivation, from the beginning clearly denoting a "verbal assault."[4] It had not yielded to the further narrowing of the sense that would have turned the "invective" into a technical term which could be used only with some specific literary structures and forms. The *Thesaurus Linguae Latinae* states two meanings of the term: one referring to "verbal assault" in general and the other to a specific composition.[5] As a matter of fact, let us note, this is a late word, appearing in literature at the close of Antiquity.[6]

In Polish, for instance, the term "invective" is now present in the former meaning.[7] The scholars who have studied its existence in the twentieth-century Polish language point to several dictionary definitions of invective, all of which come down to the meaning "insulting accusation, verbal abuse, offence."[8] The invective is therefore treated here as a relatively broad notion, encompassing a whole gamut of occurrences consisting in verbally insulting another person. According to Ewa Kołodziejek, one could also speak of the conduct "aiming to offend, demean, or insult a person or a group of people,"[9] that is of a deliberate, intentional action, which appears to be the only narrowing of this term.

---

4 The noun *invectiva* is a derivative of the verb *inveho* (intransitive). Nonetheless, although the meaning "to attack verbally" is only one of the possible meanings of this verb (alongside "to attack" and "to enter in"), the noun *invectiva* does not possess meanings other than those connected with a "verbal assault" (*ThLL* 7.2: 125).

5 *ThLL* 7.2: 125.

6 Augustine of Hippo on Cicero's aggressive statements (*Contra Iulianum* 1.22, *De Civ. Dei* 3.15), Rufinus of Aquilaea on Jerome's writings addressed against him (*Apol.* 2.33, 2.43), Ammianus Marcellinus on Julian the Apostate's letter against Constantius, addressed to the Senate (Amm. Marc. 21.10.7), the same Emperor's composition *Misopogon* as an invective against the Antiochians (Amm. Marc. 22.14.2) and on Himentius' letter slandering the Emperor Valentinian I (Amm. Marc. 28.1.20). Moreover, *ThLL* 7.2: 125 refers primarily to the Late Antique grammars and commentaries.

7 In respect of the modern meaning of "invective," my view is in opposition to that of Neumann, who argues that the term can be used in a "terminologically valid" way only with regard to the classical literature (Neumann 1998: 556).

8 Kołodziejek 1994: 70; Stępień 2000: 312–313; Preisert 2004: 35–36; in turn, Kamińska-Szmaj (2007: 54) defines "invective" as a verbal offence, insult, or affront.

9 Kołodziejek 1994: 70. Likewise, Kamińska-Szmaj (2007: 57) defines political invective as deliberate verbal behaviour.

Antiquity had known, nevertheless, a certain type of literary compositions in which the art of verbal aggression was particularly recommended and elaborated. In the Classical period, the Greek theory of rhetoric (the *Rhetoric for Alexander*, once attributed to Aristotle, and Aristotle's own *Rhetoric*), mentions – among six or seven types of oratories – one which it calls *psogos* (ψόγος, "oratory of blame").[10] In fact, this genre is so closely connected with the phenomenon of language aggression that modern scholars are inclined to render its name as "invective."[11] It is not fully justified, as classical authors used the Latin term *vituperatio* to refer to such a genre of orations.[12]

Oratories of "blame" (*psogoi*) and "praise" (*epainoi*[13]) both constitute the type of orations of epideictic nature,[14] which the two aforementioned fourth-century BC works contrast with judicial and deliberative orations (the ones that were delivered at the Assembly).[15] Aristotle mentions praise and blame in themselves as a "goal" of these speeches,[16] whereas the author of the *Rhetoric for Alexander* indicates that the goal is not, in principle, an argument, but a demonstration.[17] For this reason, it could be assumed that there is no place for blame or praise at the court or the Assembly. Nothing could be more misleading! The division outlined by these two treatises (and also by many others following them) is purely theoretical; as a matter of fact, in both judicial and deliberative speeches there are extensive passages of "praise" and "blame" oratories.[18]

---

10 *Rhet. ad Alex.* 3, 1425B, 35, 1440B, 1441B; Aristot., *Rhet.* I.3, 1358B, I.9, 1366A.

11 Cf. Kennedy 1983: 63.

12 Cic., *De Inventione* 1.51, 2.4, 2.59; *Rhet. ad Herennium* 3.6; Quint., *Inst. Orat.* 3.4.

13 Aristotle distinguished between *epainos* (ἔπαινος) and *enkōmion* (ἐγκώμιον), the latter being a praise of deeds, not a person (*Rhet.* I.9, 1367B). In the later Greek rhetorical theorists, the relation between these two terms is changed. According to Hermogenes, an *enkōmion* is a longer form of praise, composed of a number of *epainoi* (Hermogenes, *Prog.* 7, *RG* 2.11); Aphthonios adds that *enkōmion* refers to people, while *epainos* to gods (Aphthonios, *Prog.* 8, *RG* 2.35). On the relation between the two terms, see Awianowicz 2004b. A different opinion can be found in Pernot (1993: 481–482), who considers *psogos* as a subgenre of *enkōmion*.

14 The affinity of blame and praise had not been formed on the ground of rhetoric only, but, as shown by Nagy (1976: 194), it can be seen in the poetry of Greeks and other Indo-European peoples as well.

15 Later on, Quintilian, while retaining Aristotle's tripartite division, would notice the hidden persuasive character of epideictic speeches (Albaladejo 2003: 54).

16 Arist., *Rhet.* I.3, 1358B.

17 *Rhet. ad Alex.* 35, 1440B.

18 Rountree (2001) notes that Aristotle's division was an abstract one and did not reflect the rhetorical practice of his time, when it had been difficult to find a "pure" example of *psogos*, while blame appeared in the compositions rather categorized as deliberative speeches, of which the best known are Demosthenes' *Philippics*. The usage of oratories of "blame" in deliberative and judicial rhetoric was already noticed by classical theorists of rhetoric (*Rhet. ad Herennium* 3.15; Quint., *Inst. Orat.* 3.7, cf. Powell 2007: 4 ff).

Characteristically, nearly all of the rhetorical theorists had regarded praise as a "primary" genre in comparison with the oratory of blame. For instance, Theon (in all probability, the first century AD[19]) states only that "blame" should be written in a way opposite to "praise," i.e., to consider the same circumstances but look for reasons therein to castigate a given person.[20] In his *progymnasmata* (preliminary exercises in epideictic oratories[21]), Aphthonios, a Late Antique author (identified sometimes with a disciple of the famous Antiochene rhetorician Libanius[22]), provides a succinct example of *psogos*, referring to Philip of Macedon.[23] Four, even more terse, instances of the "didactic" *psogoi* are preserved in Libanius' own writings.[24] These examples concern some figures from the very distant past (Achilles, Hector, Philip of Macedon, and the Athenian politician Aischines), and even though Libanius resorts to invective in his speeches relating to the contemporary time as well,[25] it is difficult to find among them a "pure" case, a model speech. As a matter of fact, even those model "didactic" *psogoi* depart from the recommended pattern.[26] It is an instructive observation, urging us to be cautious in making any clear-cut distinctions – even among epideictic orations, it is difficult to encounter a "pure" oratory of blame constructed according to a model scheme. It encourages us all the more to seek elements of "blame" in orations of other types.

As a matter of fact, those later rhetorical theorists had employed classifications more subtle than that of Aristotle. Besides *psogos*, they also mentioned another genre of oration, characterized by verbal attacks. They called it *koinos topos* (κοινός τόπος, "common place"). As much as *enkomia* and *psogoi* were to be praises and blames of specific figures, *koinoi topoi* aimed to praise or castigate the "abstract" deeds. In fact, those authors would not agree

[19] Kennedy 1983: 57.

[20] Theon, *Prog.* 8 (*RG* 2.112). The tradition of embracing "blame" as the opposite of "praise" originates from as early as the *Rhetoric for Alexander* 35, 1441B. Cf. Flower 2013: 49–50.

[21] *Progymnasmata* were preliminary rhetorical exercises preceding composition of proper speeches (Awianowicz 2004a: 31); in their structure, they were simpler than the regular speeches (Bolonyai 2000: 29).

[22] This hypothesis is supported by Kennedy 1983: 59–60; whereas Cribiore (2007: 59–60) considers the question to be impossible to resolve.

[23] Aphthonios, *Prog.* 9 (*RG* 2.40–42). Long (1996: 78) notes that even this oratory does not follow the *topoi* pattern, as copied by Aphthonios, typical of *psogos* (prologue – genealogy – upbringing – deeds – comparison – epilogue). It is now questioned whether such a pattern had been used indeed in formulating actual "invectives" (Powell 2007: 17–18).

[24] Lib. *Prog.* 9.1–4.

[25] *Or.* 37 on former friend Polikles; *Or.* 38 on his personal adversary Silvanus; cf. Long 1996: 79–81; on invectives in further speeches of Libanius, see Long 1996: 84–90. Cf. also Pernot 1993: 484, Flower 2013: 53–54.

[26] Flower 2013: 50–51.

on the nature of this genre of oration. According to Theon, oratories of this type are to condemn deeds, not people, and do not demand that a concrete example of them be pointed out.[27] Hermogenes (a rhetor living in Mark Aurelius' reign[28]) provides an example which is a denunciation of a specific perpetrator of a sacrilege, clearly within a judicial-type oratory.[29] In turn, according to Aphthonios, *psogos* condemns a specific individual person, while *koinos topos* a phenomenon, e.g., *psogos* – a definite tyrant, *koinos topos* – tyranny as a phenomenon.[30] For the objective of the present study, this distinction is of no major significance. In fact, we do not argue that the authors of documents in Late Antiquity had used *psogoi* or *koinoi topoi* therein, but that they employed certain stylistic measures suitable for such orations. And the applied means were similar: both oratories of "blame" and "common places" are characterized as genres noted for their usage of amplification (*auksēsis*, αὔξησις, "augmentation" – in this case, of negative traits).[31]

Nonetheless, the *psogoi* are not the only classical compositions where certain instances of offensive, aggressive orations can be found. In the literature of ancient Greece, the art of language aggression had established its place long before the rhetorical theorists put forward their theory of "blame." First statements of this nature can be found in the *Iliad*.[32] Here, as in the classical Greek tragedy later on, they are part of the discourse held by quasi-historical figures.[33] But there was soon to appear a genre definitely linked with language aggression, and this aggression manifested itself in statements directed against contemporary individuals – namely, iambic poetry.[34] As it was found, the element of derision, insult, also prevailing in the old-Attic comedy had drawn its inspiration exactly from that poetry.[35] Aristophanes' scathing satire had touched on the life of the contemporary *polis* and as such was to have an impact on the language of the Athenian orators.[36] Over time, however, the theme of the genre was to change. In Latin literature, verbal attacks first appeared within the realm of comedy. Yet their target is different than in the case of the old-Attic comedy.

27 Theon, *Prog.* 7 (*RG* 2.106).

28 Kennedy 1983: 58.

29 Hermogenes, *Prog.* 6 (*RG* 2.9–11).

30 Kennedy 1983: 62–63.

31 Aphthonios, *Prog.* 7 (*RG* 2.32).

32 Koster 1980: 41–50.

33 Koster 1980: 54, 68–69.

34 Nagy 1976; Koster 1980: 55–62.

35 The roots of comedy in iambic poetry is demonstrated in Nagy 1976: 194 ff.; Rosen 1988; Neumann 1998: 552; Zanetto 2001.

36 For the relationship between invective in comedy and rhetoric, cf. Rowe 1966. In turn, Davies 1985 points to similarities between the invective of Attic orators and that found in Alkaios' works.

They are no longer concerned with public affairs, focusing instead on the private sphere – as Opelt notes, it is precisely from Plautus or Terentius that we draw most of the examples, in Latin, of "abusive words" referring to that area of life.[37] Interestingly, Latin comedy had also exerted some significant influence on the forming of the language of invective in Cicero.[38]

As I have already noted, the art of constructing verbal offences had not been monopolized – contrary to rhetorical theorists – by epideictic rhetoric. The rhetoric which had flourished in the democratic Athens would gladly resort to invective against adversaries, both in judicial and political orations.[39] The situation would be similar in the Roman world. The period of heated political controversies towards the close of the Republic was conducive to the development of verbal aggression.[40] It would appear in the speeches delivered by adherents of all the political parties, yet it was Cicero who would elaborate this craft to masterly levels. Some of his works are of a character similar to "pure" *psogoi*, e.g., *In Pisonem* or the II *Philippic*, but its elements can be found in almost all of his orations.[41] Although predominantly present in political rhetoric, invective may also appear in judicial orations, yet in the latter it is subjected to the requirement of presenting the proof of the actuality of crimes (in political orations, not all of the charges being made had to be convincing for the audience).[42] Cicero's orations, which were rife with invective, were a treasure-trove from which the Late Antique rhetoricians could draw; in particular, the *Catilinian Orations* had been the subject of intense school study at that time.[43]

When we look upon individual instances of "language aggression" in Antiquity, it is hard to resist the feeling that they had come from a long line of tradition. Let us consider, for example, the case of the *Historia arcana* by Procopius of Caesarea. Averil Cameron sees this work as innovative, an introduction

---

[37] Opelt 1965a: 19; cf. also Miniconi 1958.

[38] Kubiak 1989: 244–245; Hughes 1998; Sussman 1998: 115; Harries B. 2007. Whereas Adamik (1977–1978: 95, 99) highlights the pioneering nature of the invective found in Latin folk poetry in relation to the invective proper, present in speeches and historiography.

[39] Koster 1980: 76–90; Kamińska-Szmaj 2007: 47; Muñoz Llamosas 2008.

[40] On the appearance of the invective in the Roman public discourse from the second century BC, see Adamik 1977–1978: 95–96.

[41] Wirszubski 1961; Dunkle 1967; Korpanty 1979: 206–210; Koster 1980: 210–281; Achard 1981: 186–355; Wood 1986; Kubiak 1989; Taldone 1993; Palmieri 1996; Hughes 1998; Sussman 1998; Craig 2004; Gildenhard 2006; Berno 2007; Gildenhard 2007; Harries B. 2007; Powell 2007; Seager 2007; Uría 2007.

[42] Craig 2004: 213.

[43] Hagendahl 1983: 79. On the influence of Cicero's invective on the rhetoric of the Church Fathers, see Wood 1986; Adkin 1992.

of invective into the genre of historical biography writing.[44] Jacqueline Long, in turn, convincingly argues that it is only a peak phase in the development of the elements of verbal aggression, which had long since permeated into various genres of historiography.[45]

The period of Late Antiquity is not just a continuation of old-time patterns in the domain of language aggression. Let us remember the fact that it was exactly at that time when the very term *invectiva* appeared. There are, in my view, two reasons of great significance why this particular epoch had become a period of growth for the art of verbal offence. On the one hand, it was the golden age of the classical panegyric. And oratories of "praise" are, as we may remember, the genre closest to those of "blame." It is not surprising that they are both intertwined in the panegyric of Late Antiquity. The invective aimed against the opponents of the person being praised turns out to be an important element of the laudation itself.[46] In certain compositions, the proportions are even opposite. This is the case, in particular, of those Claudian's works which possess a special character of anti-panegyric in verse: *In Rufinum*, *In Eutropium*, and *De bello Gildonico*. These compositions condemning the opponents of *magister militum* Stilicho are usually characterized as "invectives."[47]

Another principal source of aggressive statements in the Late Antique literature is religious polemics. The invective that had accompanied philosophical disputes in the Greco-Roman world[48] is only a modest forerunner of that which appears in the polemics between Christians and pagans, or in various conflicts within the Christian world. The cause is not just the depth of the conflicts. The Scriptures contain innumerable examples of language aggression. Indeed, even though the Gospels forbid insulting the fellow man with words,[49] it should

44 Koster 1980: 96, n. 336; Cameron 1985: 58–60.

45 Long 1996: 99. The impact of invective on Roman historiography is traced by Adamik 1977–1978: 96–97, 99; cf. also Dunkle 1971, on the depiction of the tyrant in Roman historiography.

46 Lassandro 1981; Rees 1998: 89–90, 98–99.

47 Levy 1958; Cameron 1970: 83–84, 255 ff. (with caveats); Koster 1980: 298–351; Long 1996; Ware 2004; Seager 2007: 41–43; Garambois-Vasquez 2007 – the latter author postulates that the *De bello Gildonico* should be considered along with *In Rufinum* and *In Eutropium*. Let us recall, however, that we are not confronted with the *psogos* pattern here (the genre of speech that these authors call "invective"), but only with the application of its elements in a historical epic (with respect to *In Rufinum*, it is demonstrated by Levy 1946 and, more sceptically, Barr 1979: 184–188).

48 Cf., e.g., Owen 1983; let us note here that Koster (1980: 30–31) denies the existence of invective in philosophical polemics with the obstinacy worthy of a better cause.

49 *Matthew* 5.22: "Again, anyone who says to his brother, *raka* [Hebrew: "despicable person"], is answerable to the Sanhedrin. But anyone who says 'godless' (or 'fool', μωρέ), will be

be, nonetheless, treated primarily as indicative of the deeper intent accompanying the statement being spoken, as Jesus himself did not evade strong, reprimanding expressions towards his opponents.[50] Herein lie the deepest causes for the Church Fathers' ambivalent attitudes to the ancient legacy of invective. On the one hand, they condemned insulting adversaries, also in poetry, as a sin,[51] but on the other, in their polemical works, they employed, developed, and enriched classical patterns.[52] Already since at least Tatian the Assyrian in the East and Tertullian in the West, one could speak of the growth of the "Christian" art of language aggression,[53] directed in particular against the collective enemy, i.e., heretics and pagans. In the fourth century, the most notable achievements in this field would be those of Jerome, who translated many offensive expressions present in the Bible into Latin[54] (on the other hand, Jerome had remained, more so than other Church Fathers, influenced by Cicero's orations[55]). Other writers drawing on the tradition of classical invective are Gregory of Nazianzus – in his poetry and speeches,[56] and John Chrysostom – in his homiletics.[57] As soon as the doctrinal controversies had entered the political arena, the Christian authors also began to make use of verbal attacks aimed against some emperors; Constantius II was to become their best known target.[58] In fact, this emperor was seen as a villain character not only by the adherents of the Nicene *Credo*, but also by Libanius or Julian the Apostate.[59] Likewise, in the writings of Hellenic authors directed against

---

in danger of the fire of hell."

50 E.g., *Matthew* 12.34, 23.33: "brood of vipers" (γεννήματα ἐχιδνῶν) referring to the Pharisees; *Luke* 13.32: "fox" (ἀλώπηξ) to Herod; cf. Longosz 1971: 537.

51 Agosti 2001: 226.

52 Longosz 1971: 530–534.

53 Longosz 1971: 534–535; Opelt 1980: 4–68.

54 Wissemann 1992.

55 Abbott 1979: 194; Adkin 1992.

56 Wilken 1983: 115–116; Agosti 2001: 230–233.

57 Wilken 1983: 116–123.

58 Longosz 1971: 535–536; Opelt 1972; Opelt 1973; Humphries 1998, Flower 2013. In his overview of the tradition of the Christian invective against the emperors, the latter author concludes that the clear instance can be found only in *De Mortibus Persecutorum* by Lactantius. In the earlier Christian literature, the figures of the persecutors are treated in fairly reserved terms, despite the long-standing tradition of the original and unique invective aimed at the enemies of the true faith, as represented especially in the Apocalyptic literature (Flower 2013: 62–68). Interestingly, the Christian political invective appears to rearrange the ancient classical repertoire of values, for the absence of which the ruler was criticized rather than to modify this list in conformity with the Old Testament patterns (Flower 2013: 66, 99).

59 Lib., *Or.* 18 (on Constantius), Amm. Marc. 21.10.7.

Christians there are certain aggressive statements, e.g., aimed against monks.[60] Particularly ingenious instances of invective would be elaborated by the proponents of late Platonism, drawing on, for example, the myth of the struggle between Zeus and the Titans.[61]

The concepts of invective and the language of invective

Even a superficial survey of the phenomenon of "invective" in classical literature makes us ponder on the meaning of the term. Does it offer anything more than just an illusion of being precise? Does not it seem to narrow down the broad concept of "language aggression" to its definite instances in literary works, at the same time remaining imprecise enough to be unsuitable for denoting any given example of that "aggression" in literature? The most consistent approach towards formulating a strict definition was that adopted by Severin Koster, the author of the most important study attempting to encompass the whole of the phenomenon of "invective" in classical literature. At the starting point of his research, he defines "invective" as "Schmährede oder Schmähschrift" ("offensive speech or writing"), he even identifies it with *psogos* and *vituperatio*,[62] but, on the other hand, he remains aware of the fact that "condemnatory speeches" may only constitute fragments of a certain whole, which would not lend themselves to be defined as *psogoi*. For that reason, these expressions do not appear in the final definition: "Die Invektive ist eine strukturelle literarische Form, deren Ziel es ist, mit allen geeigneten Mitteln eine namentlich genannte Person öffentlich vor dem Hintergrund der jeweils geltenden Werte und Normen als Persönlichkeit herabzustellen" ("The invective is a structured literary form whose goal is to publicly denounce, by means of all the measures available, a person identified by name, as a personality against the background of the values and norms obligatory in a given situation").[63] The "invective" thus defined turns out to be an "inter-generic" phenomenon, appearing within diverse literary compositions and assuming, in each particular case, the form appropriate for them.

[60] E.g., Lib., *Or.* 2.32, *Or.* 30.8, passages collected by Agosti 2001: 243, n. 127.

[61] Dzielska 2004: 483–485. On the political and historiosophical dimensions of the criticism of the Christian state by the late Platonic philosophers, see Saffrey 1992.

[62] Koster 1980: 1–2.

[63] Koster 1980: 39. Supplements added to this definition in the conclusion part of the book (Koster 1980: 354) are irrelevant from the point of view of our stated goals.

Most probably, this capriciousness of the subject of his study led the German scholar to feel the need to refer to some more general (and not fully defined) notion, pointing more to the features of invective that were common to various literary genres, to the "idea" independent of the structure, rather than to the structure itself, which was different for various genres. He designates this abstraction, in reference to Aristotle, as *iambikē idea* (the name is due to the fact that the primary literary form whose aim was to stigmatize the opponent's flaws was the iambic poem; it is from there that the orators' *psogos* draws its inspiration).[64] One should remember that even though the term itself is of ancient origin, the content imparted by Koster is actually a new one; it is also difficult to say that modern scholars are in full agreement with him as to the content of the notion of *iambikē idea*.[65]

The idea in question may be "embodied" in a literary composition or a fragment thereof. One could ask how large the said fragment ought to be. Koster leaves no doubt: the "least" instance of *iambikē idea* is, in his view, a single offensive word – *Schimpfwort*.[66] These "offensive words" had become a little bit earlier the object of research study for another German scholar, Ilona Opelt. According to the definition she had formulated, *Schimpfwort* is "nominale prädikativische Feindeeinrede oder Feindebezeichnung normbezogen-negativen Inhalts, die im beleidigender Absicht geschieht und in der sich zugleich die Erregung des Schimpfenden lost" ("a predicative statement to or about an enemy, of a negative content as regards norms, with an intent to insult, in which at the same time the speaker's outrage is released").[67] Opelt deliberately formulates her definition in a way allowing it to encompass spontaneous utterances of colloquial speech. It is thus much closer to the current usage of the word "invective." On the other hand, in narrowing down the scope of her interest to individual words and phrases, the German scholar consciously ignores more complicated rhetorical figures, used in order to build or reinforce the negative image of a person.

None of the above concepts corresponds with the subject of my study in entirety. It would be naive to seek forms or tasks of the *psogoi*, epideictic oratories of blame, in Imperial documents. Koster would be likely inclined to notice the *iambikē idea* in them, as on several occasions he makes reference to some edicts of Republican officials, which assume the "invective" character.[68]

64 Koster 1980: 38. Taking the term from Aristotle, he refers to Arist., *Poetica* 5, 1449B.

65 Agosti (2001: 219–220) assumes a wider definition of the *iambikē idea*, embracing not only statements that can be characterized as invective, but also those merely obscene and offensive.

66 Koster 1980: 41.

67 Opelt 1965a: 18.

68 Koster 1980: 138–139 on such contemporary characteristics referring to some edicts of Antonius (*Inter alia*, Cic., *Phil.* 3.15) and Bibulus (Cic., *Att.* 2.20.6, 2.21.4).

Yet some of the additional conditions for "invective" set forth by this author (the criticism must refer to persons identified by name and their personal flaws) are so restrictive that they would immediately exclude a vast majority of Imperial laws. The same conditions refer, indirectly, to *iambikē idea* as well. In turn, Opelt's "offensive word" is only one of the means of expression used to denounce a person (even if most commonly applied). In order to distinguish the subject of my study from the phenomena designated by Koster and Opelt, I have not termed it simply as "invectives" but "the language of invective," thereby embracing all the means of expression serving to formulate the invective, which are rooted in the classical tradition of creating this type of deprecating statements.

Essential features of analyzed statements

The narrowing down of the concept of "invective" only to certain insulting, abusive expressions is problematic. If the least instance thereof is an "offensive word,"[69] there is no point in seeking a structure that would be valid for each "invective." Indeed, even though Koster attempts to find some criteria, asking who the speaker of the invective selects as his target, which characteristics he sets out to condemn, what kind of goal he intends to achieve,[70] it is difficult to consider the effects of his endeavours as satisfactory. He argues that the target of a verbal attack must be a specific person, and at the same time he notes that the ancient authors had allowed a *psogos* directed against a collective entity, a city or people.[71] In a vague way, he differentiates between the invective aimed exclusively at "the private sphere" and the criticism *ad rem*.[72] Finally, he is content with a declaration that the author has no intention to discredit, in his work, the person being

69 As Koster's statement (Koster 1980: 41) is understood by Neumann 1998: 550.

70 Neumann (1998: 549) also says clearly that the term *invectiva* points to the purpose of a speech, not a definite literary genre.

71 Koster 1980: 155. Let us add here that the Late Antique theorist of rhetoric treated Isocrates' speech *Against the Sophists* as an example of *psogos* (Nicolaus, *Prog.* 9, *RG* 3.482).

72 The German scholar arbitrarily makes the difference between polemics and invective. While the former relates to "the thing itself," the *iambikē idea* can be found only where the criticism reaches *ekso tou pragmatos* – thus he precludes the existence of invective in philosophical polemics and judicial orations (Koster 1980: 30–31, 76, 96, n. 336). Nevertheless, in politically oriented speeches, he is ready to judge, without much hesitation, the charge of "treason" as an invective (Koster 1980: 90), even though, in this case, it would be difficult to find any argument more pertinent to "the thing itself."

criticized (and, for example, induce the audience to change their conduct in a given matter), so as to preclude the presence of any "invective" here. This latter criterion appears to lead to an outright absurdity: Koster makes an *a priori* exclusion from the scope of his interest of, for instance, Cicero's *Catilinian Orations*, as he finds them to be *suasiones*, deliberative orations.[73] The incongruity of such a position is all too clear; the same phrases and rhetorical figures, targeting the same sphere of behaviour of the person being condemned, and the identically formulated statement ceases to be an invective, as soon as some purpose allegedly different than a denouncement of an opponent is indicated (albeit the said denouncement is in plain view). In fact, not all of the classical theorists would be willing to agree with Koster as to whether denunciation of an adversary is the proper objective of *psogoi* as such, e.g., Quintilian emphasizes the distinctly educating purpose of oratories of "praise" and "blame" (*laudationes* and *vituperationes*).[74]

It seems that Koster's most significant postulate is the one that refers to the very object of vituperation. According to the German scholar, one may speak of an invective only when a given expression is directed against "a person identified by name," who is to be thereby "publicly discredited."[75] He contrasts the invective proper with satire. In the former case, it is about discrediting a specific person, while in the latter – of a given fault, which is only conveniently represented by that person ("an example" – *exemplum*).[76]

This distinction is only apparently quite clear. The object of an aggressive pronouncement may also be represented by a specific collective group, for example, Athenians,[77] or Imperial officials.[78] Yet even then the criticism may be directed not at a given fault but against a concrete group of people. Similarly, in the case of the criticism concerning the "ideal types," e.g., "the tyrant" or "the heretic,"

---

[73] Koster 1980: 113; he also terms *II Philippic* as *suasio*, as its goal is to lead Antonius to change his ways (Koster 1980: 129)! A similar opinion on the *Catilinian Orations* (but not so on *II Philippic*) is held by Powell 2007: 2; this author also denies the appearance of invective in the *Verrinae* (Powell 2007: 9). I would be inclined to accept Seager's position according to which the invective is not a specific literary genre, which is why its elements can also be identified in orations such as the *Verrinae*, which do not lend themselves to be characterized as "invectives" (Seager 2007: 25).

[74] Quint., *Inst. Orat.* 2.4.20.

[75] Koster 1980: 39.

[76] Koster 1980: 23–30.

[77] Isocrates, *Peri eirenes*, cf. Michelini 1998. The Late Antique rhetorical theorist Aphthonios holds that the laudation can refer to both an individual citizen of Athens and the Athenians in general (Aphthonios 8, *RG* 2.36); considering the affinity between the genres, his comment must also hold true for oratories of "blame."

[78] Cf. Chapter IX: 248–251.

it seems that one is confronted with the condemnation of the fault-bearers, not just the faults they come to represent. In the texts to be analyzed, condemnatory statements will be directly related to certain acts, yet indirectly they also strike against those who commit those acts. There can be no doubt, on account of the object considered, that the classical rhetoric theorists would characterize the statements in question as characteristic of *koinoi topoi* rather than *psogoi*; for this reason, the use of the term "invective" in reference to them may appear as problematic. It is still beyond doubt that the both types of blame statements were formulated with the aid of the same measures,[79] so for this reason the usage of the term "language of invective" should not raise any objections.

It also seems that the aggressive statements to be analyzed possess further characteristics which Koster attributed to invective. One of such features, which is comprised in Koster's definition in an unexplicated but (as the author himself points out) necessary way, is descriptiveness. The goal of invective is to discredit, and thus to persuade the public of the wickedness of the person being discredited. Consequently, the invective carries some information in it.[80] It should be strictly distinguished from a curse, a malediction, whose function is to express the wish that something bad happen to a given person. The curse replaces the deed (and if understood in terms of magic, it is the deed itself). It usually concerns the person already previously discredited. At least in literary works, it presupposes the reader's previous knowledge of the nefariousness of the person being reviled.[81]

Finally, an extremely important element in Koster's definition is the reference to the generally accepted system of "values and norms" – discrediting "against the background" of that system. There will be no invective, then, involved in the case of expressing a purely personal disgust with a particular person, without its roots being firmly placed in the commonly valid normative system. It is obvious in that the invective is to bring about a general condemnation of someone; it thus has to appeal to the universally accepted norms. It is here that some important indirect aims of the invective come

[79] Cf. Chapter III: 63–65.

[80] This remark is also important with regard to all abusive language in general: "its constituent is a certain negative judgement concerning the recipient (the person being reviled), even though sometimes it may only come down to an emotionally charged epithet or an insult uttered" (Grzegorczykowa 1991: 194).

[81] Koster 1980: 36–37. In such case, one should consider as completely misplaced those of Zuccotti's statements which suggest that the Imperial laws addressed against religious dissenters are a sort of exorcism meant to banish, on the strength of the words, the demonically inspired heretics or pagans beyond the frontiers of the Roman world. On this interpretation, the "language of invective" present in the Imperial laws would be perceived as a kind of anathema.

into view. In its appealing to the norms, the invective at the same time propagates, and even formulates, them. One can imagine an invective in which denouncing the opponent is a secondary objective, while the primary one is the persuasive, educating function: i.e., enforcing some definite norms and values as generally valid.[82] On the other hand, the invective shows the author as directly the defender and indirectly a representative of those values and norms. And again, one could imagine a situation where the invective's primary goal is self-presentation, looking for acceptance among the audience. Speakers of the invective present themselves as defenders of the norms, but also as representatives thereof.[83] We shall see that the both functions are among the fundamental ones in the Late Antique Imperial letters and, generally, in the Roman Empire's legislative tradition, beginning from the Principate.

Opelt's definition, as well, contains an element that is of some value for the present study. It is a seemingly obvious indication that each "offensive word" contains a declaration of hostility and serves, at least formally, to release the invective speaker's emotion. As a result, it also carries the information on the author and his relation to the person being the object of the invective. This person is defined as an "enemy."[84] Of course, such a generally conceived "hostility" does not decide what shape the "struggle" between the invective speaker and the targeted person is about to assume. In each case, however, the invective forms a dualistic reality,[85] in which the author of the statement can be found, as a rule, on the "good" side, while the person being condemned – on that of "evil." This is exactly the latter property of invective that permits us to seek "enemies" thereby and categorize them.

The two latter features (looking for acceptance among audiences and building a hostile relation towards the addressee) are closely linked with each other. As Irena Kamińska-Szmaj points out in simpler terms, one of the messages conveyed by the invective is that "the SENDER negatively evaluates the ADDRESSEE, because he wants the good for the RECIPIENT and does

---

82 I do not agree with Preisert (2004: 114), who claims that "if the deeds are condemned with the intent to indicate a certain system of values, then such an action cannot be considered as intentionally hostile." It can be considered, however, whether it is not a case that each verbal insult (also in a straightforward person-to-person relation) needs to take place already on a common level of some shared values and if, in the absence of such level, the person being insulted can feel offended at all. Cf. Conley 2010: 98.

83 It was already noted by Aristotle in his *Rhetoric* I.9, 1366A. Another rhetorical theorist Quintilian had noted that for an invective to be efficient, it must address the audience sharing the same values (Quint., *Inst. Orat.* III.7.23–25; cf. Albaladejo 2003: 54).

84 This function of invective is also mentioned by Nagy 1976: 197–198.

85 Opelt 1965a: 19; cf. also Kamińska-Szmaj 2007: 42.

it in the latter's interest"[86] (according to the author, SENDER is the author of the statement, ADDRESSEE – the person affected by the invective, RECIPIENT – the audience to whom the statement is directed[87]).

To sum up, it could be said that an aggressive statement carries some definite information with it (as a denouncing description), discredits by contrasting the person being condemned with the generally accepted values and norms, and, finally, constructs the binary opposition "defender – enemy," in which the condemning person automatically takes the side of the audience and the commonly held values.

The aggressive statement thus defined perhaps does not fulfil all the criteria that one would expect of an invective – first of all, it does not have to offend a specific person in each case. Yet once again, it should be noted that all the attempts to formulate, as if technically, a more strict definition of "invective" are efforts undertaken in modern scholarship, while the Latin term *inveho* points to a verbal attack not necessarily directed against a specific individual.[88] Consequently, there is none more appropriate term than "invective" that can be found also for those aggressive utterances which directly condemn actions or attitudes. For the purpose of this study, therefore, I have decided to call such aggressive statements "invectives." Likewise, particular individual "offensive words" will be termed as "invective" as well, irrespective of whether in a given case their function is to insult a specific person or only to express condemnation of concrete acts and conduct.

---

86 Kamińska-Szmaj 2007: 60.

87 Kamińska-Szmaj 2007: 59.

88 Powell 2007: 2.

Chapter II: The position of the "language of invective" in the ideological message of the Imperial documents

Imperial documents of Late Antiquity

In his still topical study on the diplomatics of Late Antiquity, Peter Classen makes the following classification of Imperial documents in the period in question: constitutions, rescripts, *codicilli* and more broadly – all the documents connected with office appointments, permits allowing the use of the Public Post, letters.[1] Of all these types of documents, only constitutions and certain forms of rescripts (namely, pragmatics) are represented in the documents within the scope of this study. In consequence, these particular types will be of more interest for the purpose of this study.

Constitutions. An overwhelming majority of the Late Antique documents modern scholars have got at their disposal are those connected with legislation process. It is to them (and never to rescripts or Imperial letters) that the Latin term *leges generales* is applied; also, some scholars believe that the term *leges* itself should be used exclusively in reference to them.[2] In their opinion, the application of the word *lex* to the said documents is a conscious innovation

1 Classen 1955: 15–50. This particular division should be of course distinguished from the divisions into genres of constitutions and rescripts, which will be discussed further on in this chapter.

2 Kussmaul 1981: 51 ff. On the basis of an analysis of the laws containing general regulations, and of the rescript form closest to them, pragmatics, in the body of the Post-Theodosian Novels and council acts. Also recently, Liebs has argued for Constantine's deliberate adoption, in 312, of the name *leges* with regard to the Republican *leges rogatae* (Liebs 2006: 99–100). Nonetheless, Sirks 2007: 92 is sceptical about this statement.

introduced by the Emperor Constantine. Until then, the word – which referred to the *leges rogatae* of the Republic and early Principate, had rather been avoided.[3] It was assumed that the Emperor was more concerned with maintaining and improving the existing time-honoured state of affairs than changing it; also in the sphere of legislation, each novelty met with an effort to construe it as the more adequate or corresponding with the spirit of *humanitas* interpretation of the old *lex*. Constantine represents himself as restorer of the Empire, deliberately using the term *leges* with reference to those documents which establish the new general rules of the law in force in the Empire (until then, this Latin term tended to be avoided, even though it was not the case with its Greek equivalent – *nomos*).[4] Each one of the new *leges* could constitute a conscious correction of the state of law until then; there are numerous references therein to the old laws which are either confirmed or repealed. The term *constitutio* is, technically speaking, an equivalent of the word *lex*, but it does not possess the same rank on the rhetorical level. That is why one may often encounter a situation where a new act of law uses the term *lex* to refer to itself, while the designation *constitutio* is reserved for the earlier laws which it refers to.[5] Thus, on the level of rhetoric as well, there appears a superiority of the newly promulgated law over the previous one. We shall see that this superiority will be given prominence in the rhetoric of invective as well.[6]

It seems to be justified to use the names "acts" or "constitutions" in reference to those of the relevant sources where one may assume the presence of the intention to establish a general regulation, valid in the legislative system of the Later Roman Empire,[7] while the general name appropriate in reference

---

3 In the Roman Republic, the laws (*leges*) were initially established by the *comitia centuriata* in response to an official's *rogatio*, whereas beginning from the *lex Hortensia*, which had empowered the Plebeian Assemblies with legislative powers, more and more frequently by the *concilia plebis* upon the motion of a popular tribune. The prerogative of submitting constitutions for Plebeian Assemblies' judgement was taken over by August along with the *potestas tribunicia*. His successors had simply resigned the formality of submitting drafts of new constitutions to the Assembly and only promulgated the *leges* they had drafted. Yet this practice was discontinued as early as in the first century AD, when it was evidently recognized that everything which needed to be settled in this field had been already settled.

4 Kussmaul 1981: 97; Liebs 1992: 12.

5 Kussmaul 1981: 76.

6 By applying the term *audacia* to denote, in particular, the cases of violations of the newly issued law, rather than of the one in force until then, cf. Chapter VI: 155.

7 It would be problematic, nevertheless, to use the term "laws." It should be noted that Millar clearly refuses to refer to the *leges* of Late Antiquity as "laws," agreeing (at most) to put the English word in inverted commas. In his opinion, only the general rules contained in the *leges* would be laws in the fullest sense of this word, whereas he considers the *leges* to be only letters to officials or the Senate (Millar 2006: 7, 71).

to all the Imperial documents, distinguishing them from contemporary documents of other types is *praeceptum*.[8]

The Imperial constitutions of this period can be divided in terms of who they are addressed to (the division into edicts, rescripts, decrees, and mandates, which was held to be valid in the time of the Principate,[9] had already become outdated by Late Antiquity). There are definitely fewer Imperial speeches (*orationes*), addressed to the Senate,[10] and edicts addressed directly to the people.[11] The prevailing form is that of a letter directed to an official, whose duty it is to transfer the emperor's decision to the governing bodies under his authority, and ordinarily simply to take care of publication.[12] In the case of the letters addressed to officials, one must keep in mind the double character of the texts in question: they constitute a general regulation, yet simultaneously are letters[13] formulated in correspondence with the guidelines of rhetoric characteristic of this genre.[14]

On the basis of one of the extant acts, scholars have managed to recreate the process of formulating a constitution.[15] Similar to the documents

---

8 Classen 1955: 51–52.

9 Wenger 1953: 425 ff.; Giaro 2009: 62.

10 These orations are a successive incarnation of the old *senatus consulta*; in Late Antiquity, the emperor's role had increased so much that the very fact of the emperor's speech before the Senate had presupposed the approval thereof (Liebs 1992: 15). *Orationes* to the Senate were not published in the form of edicts of the officials. The constitution *C.Th.* 6.4.22 (373), discussed in more detail in Chapter IV: 83–89, is an example of *oratio*.

11 Imperial edicts of Late Antiquity cannot be treated as documents of a rank higher than those *leges* which have the form of a letter to an official. Alongside the edicts directed to the Roman people as a whole, we also have other, addressed to the people of one of the capital cities (Rome or Constantinople) or provinces (there are two extant edicts addressed to the inhabitants of Africa). The most famous edict of Late Antiquity is likely the one directed to the people of Constantinople *C.Th.* 16.1.2 (380). Imperial edicts ought to be distinguished, of course, from the ones in which officials published the laws as ordered by the emperor. In that case, the persons figured as issuing the edicts are not emperors but collegial bodies of prefects (*ACO* I.1.3 para. 112, pp. 69–70, *ACO* I.1.4, para. 139, p. 67).

12 Orations to the Senate and edicts are mentioned as the sources of *lex generalis* in Valentinian III's constitution *C.J.* 1.14.3 (426); further on, the act provides for conditions for other texts to become *lex generalis*.

13 This statement is further elaborated by Fergus Millar in his book. He argues that the Imperial constitutions should be recognized as the emperor's letters to officials or the Senate, serving as a medium of internal communication between the emperor and other governing bodies (Millar 2006: 7, 71), providing answers to inquiries (*suggestiones*) of individual officials, solving current, often also individual, problems, additionally mentioning threats against disobedient or negligent officials (Millar 2006: 7, 35).

14 A close affinity between Imperial letters and orations is noted by Classen 1955: 58–59.

15 Honoré (1998), in his attributing the authorship of the contents of also ordinary Imperial letters to quaestors, extends by default the process described below over that type of Imperial documents as well.

of lower rank, the Imperial laws had not been created spontaneously in most cases, but in response to a query or request of those concerned. In the case of *leges generales*, it was usually an official who prepared a proposition of the text of a constitution, the so-called *suggestio*. After discussing the issue at *consistorium*, the *suggestio* passed on to one of the four Imperial ministers (in the fourth century, they were known as *consistoriani*[16]), namely the Imperial quaestor (ordinarily, yet not very precisely, called *quaestor sacri palatii*).[17] It was the quaestor's duty to draft the text of a constitution. This official did not possess a bureau of his own, which is why he would have to resort to the bureaux (*scrinia*) serving another minister, *magister officiorum*.[18] It remains a matter of dispute if the quaestor had indeed been the figure behind each Imperial constitution, or whether in some cases his role was taken over by, for example, the *magister scriniorum*, the official directly in charge of the Imperial bureaux.[19] The already prepared text

---

[16] Apart from the quaestor, other permanent members of the *consistorium* were: *magister officiorum*, *comes sacrarum largitionum*, and *comes rerum privatarum* – cf. Delmaire 1995: 31, 75–95, 119–122; 134–145; Feissel 2007: 118–122. On the change in the meaning of the term *consistoriani* in 399 – cf. Olszaniec 2007: 25–26.

[17] The function of the Imperial quaestor (the recorded name *quaestor sacrii palatii* is only one of the many in the sources that refer to this office, as pointed out by Harries 1988: 154) can be roughly defined as an Imperial secretary responsible for drafting documents to be signed by the emperor himself, i.e., letters and, particularly, constitutions (Harries 1988: 163); over time, the quaestor was also entrusted with other functions (Delmaire 1995: 61 ff.). The role of quaestors in drawing up constitutions was not established at once; the first quaestor known by name, whose involvement in preparation of acts is mentioned in sources, was Eupraxius, in the years 367–370 holding this office in Valentinian I's *consistorium* (Honoré 1998: 11 ff.). The office itself was created earlier: the first quaestors known by name appeared in 354 as representatives of Constantius II, acting on behalf of his orders in state affairs of topmost importance (De Bonfils 1981: 41–68; Olszaniec 2007: 271 ff.). On the increasing role of the quaestor in the fourth century, see also Vera 1986.

[18] According to the *Notitia Dignitatum* (ed. Seeck), 12.6. In turn, *Nov. Just.* 35 (535) mentions that the quaestor had been provided, "since a long time," with 12 aides from the *scrinium memoriae*, and 7 each from the *scrinia libellorum* and *epistularum*. Cf. Voß 1982: 29–30.

[19] Similar conclusions may be drawn on the basis of the role that *magister scriniorum* Benivolus was to play during Valentinian II's reign, when he had refused to draft the text of the law favourable to the believers of the "Arian" confession from Ariminium (Ruf., *HE* XI.16, Sozom., *HE* VII.13); still, Harries (1988: 162–163) interprets this event to the effect that Benivolus had refused to prepare a copy of the constitution that was already written down by the quaestor and signed by the Emperor. Honoré, who seems to ascribe, generally speaking, the sole responsibility for the texts of the constitutions to the Imperial quaestors, allows nonetheless that the Emperor Theodosius I, particularly involved in the legislation process, may have personally influenced the formulation of its text (Honoré 1998: 34 ff.).

of the constitution was passed back to the *consistorium*, and after their final approval it was read out to the emperor and signed by him.[20]

The characteristic feature of the Imperial constitutions in the relevant period is the fact that they were formulated only in Latin (for both the Western and Eastern parts of the Empire). As Fergus Millar has pointed out, there was a clear division maintained in the East: Latin was the language of discourse inside the political power apparatus (not only between the emperor and his officials, but also among the officials themselves), while Greek served the purpose of communication between the authority and the subjects.[21] It is worth recalling then that the documents under consideration are primarily the expressions of that first discourse, not direct pronouncements addressed to the subjects. They should be distinguished, nevertheless, from those Imperial letters that do not contain the above-mentioned general regulations.[22]

Rescripts. Imperial *leges* are different from rescripts, decisions that were accepted as imperial at least formally, issued in individual cases and usually in response to private persons' requests, submitted either directly or through proper officials. In agreement with the principle stated in the third century by Ulpian: *Quod principi placuit, legis habet vigorem* (*D.* 1.4.1), they should constitute a source of law as well. In Late Antiquity, nonetheless, this is not the case. In the fourth and fifth centuries, the legislators ardently oppose the practice of using rescripts by individuals for the purpose of evading duties and obligations resulting from the enforced general rules.[23] The constitution preserved in the Theodosian Code as *C.Th.* 1.2.2 (315) pronounces: *Contra ius rescripta non valeant, quocumque modo fuerint impetrata.* The extant *interpretatio* of this principle (which can be possibly dated to the turn of the fifth and sixth centuries) leaves no room for doubt: *Quaecumque contra leges*

---

20 The procedure is recreated on the basis of the law that modifies it, i.e., *C.J.* 1.14.8 (446), which stipulated that drafts be read out not only before the *consistorium*, but subsequently also before the Senate. Cf. Voß 1982: 25–28; Honoré 1986: 136–137.

21 Millar 2006: 20–23, 84–97, 138–139.

22 As based on the terminology appearing in such Imperial letters, they can be divided into *sacrae iussiones* (also called *sacrae littere* or *sacrae*) and common *epistulae*. This division is not entirely accurate. The emperor uses the former term when the letters contain a definite order, whereas the other term is applied to avoid the impression that the recipient is ordered to do something (Kussmaul 1981: 43–44).

23 Honoré 1998: 210. This struggle is not perceived in older studies, e.g., P. Classen states that until 426 there had been no significant attempt to introduce a clear division between Imperial documents containing *leges generales* and all the rest (Classen 1955: 50), whereas he sees the constitutions limiting the importance of rescripts as proof of the difficulty in distinguishing, in actual fact, between these two types of documents (Classen 1955: 32).

fuerint a principibus obtenta, non valeant. As a result, the general principles, contained in the old and new *leges generales*, are always to have the priority over the Imperial decisions in lower-ranking documents.[24] Another constitution (*C.Th.* 1.2.11, 398), ruling that rescripts cannot be used as precedents in matters other than those to which they had directly referred, attempts to eliminate a very hazardous practice, still being applied in the fourth century.[25] A particularly perilous practice was the extorting of rescripts with decisions that were individually favourable but contrary to the valid *leges generales*, a practice which was extremely difficult to control. For that reason, the laws had to determine precisely in what cases some possible tax reliefs, acts of clemency, and the like, are to be held as valid or not.[26]

In reality, not all the rescripts reached the emperor's hands and not all of them were personally signed by him. In theory, all of them should have been drawn up with at least the Imperial quaestor's knowledge; any practice to the contrary is condemned, but we do not know if anything was done in order to prevent it.[27] Not all the rescripts were identical in terms of their actual significance. A special group were the so-called pragmatics, a type of rescripts created in the early fifth century, which had subsequently evolved over time into the so-called pragmatic sanctions. Pragmatics had not concerned, at least

---

24 The controversy in academic circles if the *C.Th.* 1.2.2 was Constantine's innovation or the confirmation of the hitherto existing regulations, is therefore of fundamental importance in order to understand the nature of the legislation of this ruler. Following the generally held opinion on the role of the rescripts as sources of law in the previous period, Kussmaul considers this law to be an expression of the Constantine revolution. In turn, Turpin (1985: 349–350) argues that as a matter of fact even previously rescripts had been only valid when they were in conformity with the general regulations; to prove it, he refers to Claudius II's rescript *C.J.* 1.23.2 of the year 270. Generally speaking, the author supports the statement that even though rescripts had been used secondarily for confirming general laws, they were never meant to serve in formulating thereof (Turpin 1991). There are also scholars who deny the letter of Constantine's order and believe that also in the fourth century rescripts had constituted a source of law (Wenger 1953: 43; Simon 1977: 13–14 concurs, in part, with this opinion).

25 But Humfress (2007: 124) notes that the constitution concerns only one kind of rescripts (those addressed to officials) and did not eliminate, in fact, the jurists' practice of referring to private rescripts.

26 For instance, *Novella* 19 of Valentinian III decides that the Imperial *adnotationes* with acts of clemency for the guilty of homicide are only valid in the case of involuntary manslaughter. Other acts provide, for example, that an exception to a given rule can only be established through a pragmatic or *adnotatio*, but not a "common" rescript. On measures against illegal usage and obtaining of *adnotationes*, see Mathisen 2004: 28–32; more on rejecting orders contrary to *leges generales*, present in all sorts of low-ranking documents, see Honoré 1998: 160–161.

27 Kussmaul 1981: 39, cf. *Nov. Theod.* 17.2.

initially,[28] private citizens' matters, but public affairs (*ta pragmata*), in particular any issues connected with the functioning of corporate bodies (including the Church). As opposed to common rescripts, which could be understood only in conjunction with requests submitted by supplicants, a pragmatic did not require such a request to be appended.[29] The type of rescripts directed to officials, not private persons, was called *rescripta ad consultationem emissa*.[30] Common rescripts addressed to private individuals (*rescripta simplicia*) were also clearly distinguished from *adnotationes*, in whose formulation the emperor's role was more significant.[31] Their contents were ordinarily concerned with confirming personal privileges or acts of clemency for perpetrators.

Among the preserved normative sources of Late Antiquity, rescripts and *adnotationes* are very scarce.[32] Only among the *Novellae* of Valentinian III and council acts there is a greater group of pragmatics. As one can see, an overwhelming majority of the texts to be examined are Imperial constitutions, and among them – those which represent the type of a letter addressed to an official. Let us now consider in what kind of circumstances the language of invective could appear in this type of documents.

---

28 The practice begins to change in Zeno's reign (the Emperor attempts to combat the existing state of affairs with the constitution *C.J.* 1.23.7, 477), and the issue of pragmatics for individual persons will be approved by Justinian (Kussmaul 1981: 94).

29 As clearly reflected in *comes* Marcellinus' response, during the 411 colloquium at Carthage, to an allegation made by one of the bishops, who had apparently mistaken an Imperial pragmatic for a common rescript, cf. Kussmaul 1981: 89.

30 They contained resolutions in individual cases and could not be applied apart from the case for which they had been issued (*C.Th.* 1.2.11, cf. Liebs 1992: 17). Simon (1977: 6–7) states that the Theodosian Code also included *rescripta ad consultationem emissa*, which only acquired the character of *lex generalis* as part of the Code (similar, in all probability, to the rescripts incorporated in the Code of Justinian, according to the constitutions *Haec* § 2 and *Summa* § 3, cf. Van der Wal 1980: 17). Humfress seems to treat *Const. Sirm.* 1 as precisely a rescript to an official (Humfress 2007: 158–161). Let us add Matthews believes that the Theodosian Code had also comprised at least one "common" rescript, namely *C.Th.* 8.15.1 (Matthews 2000: 16, note 14).

31 It is generally assumed that the characteristic feature of an *adnotatio* was the emperor's personal signature. Thus, it acquired a rank higher than "common" rescripts. However, Turpin (1988: 291, 306–307) argues that in fact the difference between the *adnotatio* and rescripts was that responses to the former had been indeed formulated in the emperor's presence, whereas to regular rescripts – only by officials on the emperor's behalf. For a discussion on the nature of *adnotatio*, see Mathisen 2004: 24.

32 Simon 1977: 5 ff.; Liebs 1986: 486; Liebs 1992: 18.

Criticism of the post-classical law in terms of language

A combination of the legislative language, especially as regards acts of law providing for penal sanctions, and the language of invective seems nowadays not only artificial but also particularly glaring. Squashing opponents not only with court verdicts but also with accompanying or preceding messages was the characteristic goal of invective in the language employed by the twentieth-century rulers of totalitarian regimes in addressing their own subjects.[33]

One must refrain from drawing simplistic comparisons. For instance, when one reads the constitution *C.Th.* 9.40.17 (399), issued after the ousting of Eutropius, the until-then influential grand chamberlain of the Sacred Bedchamber at Constantinople, it is difficult to resist the impression that its primary goal is to trample on the defeated opponent. And yet, the language of condemnation is here only a part of a broader phenomenon, i.e., the presence of ideological messages in the law, which had incidentally happened to assume such a revolting shape at this particular point in the document.[34] It is worth mentioning here Richard Honig's comment on the contrast between the essentially nihilistic ideology underpinning the twentieth-century dictatorships and the strong presence of values in the language of the Late Antique law.[35] One could also add that while in the reality of totalitarian states the message expressed through invectives was one-sided,[36] the Late Antique constitutions were, on principle, responses to *suggestiones* of officials, and rescripts to requests (*preces*) of supplicants, also in their ideological message and rhetorical phrasing.[37]

Still, even with the pertinent knowledge at one's disposal, it is hard to resist the feeling of inadequacy. In the mid-nineteenth century, the German scholar Franz von Holtzendorff, commented on the above-mentioned act in a jocular

---

[33] Grzegorczykowa 1991: 193; Preisert 2004: 113. Whereas Kamińska-Szmaj (2007: 60), using the already mentioned triple division SENDER – ADDRESSEE – RECIPIENT, offers the following characteristics of particular aims of invective in the political communication of the communist Polish People's Republic: "The SENDER wants the RECIPIENT to know that the SENDER has the right to insult and punish the ADDRESSEE"; "The SENDER wants the RECIPIENT to know that if he behaves like the ADDRESSEE, he will be insulted and punished as well." It would be difficult to render the functioning of invective in the Later Roman penal law as well in any simpler terms!

[34] Cf. the analysis of this constitution in Chapter IV: 94–98.

[35] Honig 1960: 8.

[36] Kamińska-Szmaj 2007: 14, 30.

[37] The effect of the encomium rhetoric on the petitions of Late Antiquity is analyzed in Fournet 2004; as should be assumed, his observations would also hold true for the encomium's mirror image, i.e., *psogos*.

way: "Individual laws (…) resemble the Chinese music full of resounding noises, which flatters itself that it can force the enemy, whom it is afraid to fight, to flee by the mere noise."[38] This deprecating opinion comes from someone who was not only a representative of the nineteenth-century intellectual European culture but also a Romanist. According to his belief, the overblown rhetoric had spoilt the purity of law, which should not contain any messages other than the dry content stating what steps must be taken in a given situation.

The later scholars of Roman law, less prone to formulating such vivid opinions, had been fairly unanimous in denouncing this particular aspect of the Late Antique legislation. One sign of its decadent nature was to be, among others things, the language it used; the compilers of the Late Antique laws and commentaries, without proper legal education, resigned the clarity of the technical terms worked out in the course of the previous period, instead resorting to accidental words, descriptions, ambiguous notions, while the technical terms themselves were often used incorrectly, in their conventional meanings. The majority of Romanists have been of the opinion that the rich language of the law of the post-classical period constitutes "the abstruse flood of words" ("der krause Wortschwall"), as it was called in a German-language textbook from the 60s.[39]

None the less, this was not a generally accepted opinion. As early as 1913, Eugène Vernay put forward his defence of the language of the "post-classical" law.[40] He pointed out that our opinion exalting the classical language of the Roman legislation over the one which had allegedly superseded it in Late Antiquity, may be a misunderstanding reflective more of the state of the preserved sources than reality. As a matter of fact, for the pre-Constantine period, the extant sources are primarily the rescripts drawn up by the bureau *a libellis*, which was headed by educated jurists, both in the pre-Constantine era and the period beginning from the reign of that Emperor. On the other hand, we have almost no rescripts from the Christian Roman Empire; the devaluation of the significance of this form as a source of Imperial legislation would cause that the authors of the Theodosian Code cited only the excerpts from the *leges generales*. These higher-ranking documents, in turn, had been prepared by the bureau *ab epistulis*, both before and after Constantine's reign. Very few surviving pre-Constantine documents produced by that bureau were

---

38 Holtzendorff 1859: 134: "Einzelne Gesetze (…) gleichen der geräuschvollen chinesischen Musik, die sich schmeichelt den Feind, den man sich zu bekämpfen scheut, durch bloßen Lärm in die Flucht zu schlagen."

39 Schulz 1961: 415; the author also mentions "wild rhetoric" ("wilde Rhetorik"). The criticism of the "post-classical" law with reference to its language is extensively surveyed in Voß 1982: 4–5, 8, more briefly in Turpin 1985: 351.

40 Vernay 1913.

written in a style similar to that characteristic of the Late Antique laws. Thus, the period of Constantine's reign would not have ushered in any new style, would not have replaced educated jurists with rhetors, but simply had given precedence to a type of legislation that was richer in rhetorical forms than the more modest style of rescripts.

Moreover, the Diocletian-era rescripts did not have to possess, originally, the modest form in which we know them as they are transmitted in the Code of Justinian. In their work, the compilers of the Code had used the late-third-century collections: *Codex Gregorianus* and *Codex Hermogenianus*. The compilers of these Codes had most likely taken out from the original texts and re-used some individual phrases that were significant for the relevant law. It would have been an interference in the text much greater than in the case of the Theodosian Code, and this is also what could possibly explain different states of the laws' preservation in the two periods.[41]

Such explanations can be considered as an attempt to "justify," rather than "rehabilitate," the style of the Late Antique legislation. A more daring approach was proposed by Richard Honig, who in the didactic qualities of the language of the post-classical law saw a deliberate agenda originated by Constantine the Great. In his view, the moralistic rhetoric of the laws aimed to forge stronger bonds between the subjects and the Empire; he contrasted it with the tendency to impose sheer coercion on them, which made scholars define the Later Roman state as "Zwangsstaat" – "coercive state."[42] It is worth noting that since when Honig's work had been published, the theory of the Late Antique "coercive state" has undergone a considerable devaluation;[43] quite recently, Marie-Theres Fögen has even argued that the phenomenon of "Zwangsstaat" exists primarily on the level of the rhetoric of the Late Antique laws.[44]

It is certainly a misunderstanding to perceive the compilers of the texts of Late Antique laws as incompetent and lacking in legal acumen. The prosopographical research on the very few known secretaries of the Imperial bureaux indicate that also in the post-classical period they would possess, as a rule, the proper legal education.[45] Likewise, they could have recourse to the assistance of their subordinates, i.e., jurists. This latter note can also be applied to Imperial quaestors, who were primary officials responsible for the texts

41 Volterra 1959.

42 Honig 1960: 4–5. A similar view had already been tentatively presented before by Classen 1955: 61 ff.

43 Rilinger 1985; Sirks 1993a.

44 Fögen 1993: 149–150.

45 Voß 1982: 30–33 (here, contrary to the popular opinion that is unsubstantiated by any thorough study, cf. Voß 1982: 23).

of the Late Antique *leges*, also possibly assisted by their bureau staff.[46] As a matter of fact, quaestors were required to be educated in law as well.[47] If Tony Honoré argues that some officials holding this office are sensitive to the law terminology, while others give precedence to the rules of rhetoric,[48] it cannot be explained by the inadequacy of the latter group. They were most evidently concerned with meeting a more important demand (in their own view): to avoid a situation when the precision of the legal language takes priority over another, equally important, goal of the document being prepared.[49]

Three *genera dicendi* vs. the language of post-classical law

The theorists of Latin rhetoric: the author of *Rhetorica ad Herennium*, Cicero, Quintilian, Cassiodorus, recognized three styles of the *genera dicendi* ("manners of expression"). The *summum genus* was marked by grandiloquence, ornateness, floridity, and its primary task was to "move" the listener. At the opposite end, there was the *genus humile*, which was the closest to colloquial speech – unembellished, calm, but not monotonous. The intermediate type was the *genus medium*, which had drawn from the previous two styles. The orator employing this style should make moderate use of the stylistic measures characteristic of the *summum genus* and evade the most "vulgar" vocabulary; their speech should be light and easy to the listener's ear.[50] Each of these styles was appropriate for given definite circumstances.

The language of the classical jurisprudence, so favourably treated by lawyers – concise, full of strictly defined "technical" terms elaborated on its foundations – was a genre of the *genus humile*. Apparently, rhetoric theorists should recommend using it in the forensic discourse in all circumstances, but it was just the opposite. Quintilian recommended that the *genus humile* be used only for matters of lesser importance (*res minores*), whereas the issues of greater importance (*res maiores*) ought to be expressed in a style more ornate, yet with strict caution on the clarity with which the matter is being communicated (*perspicuitas*). We deal with the *res maiores* when we aspire

46 Voß 1982: 30.

47 Voß 1982: 37–39.

48 Honoré 1998: 41–45, 84–90, 164–167.

49 Voß 1982: 11.

50 Voß 1982: 52–53.

to elicit some definite emotions among our audience.[51] The situation may be easy to understand in the case of a lawyer's appearance before the court, but, as we shall see, Imperial constitutions were also intended to arouse certain specific emotions.

Cassiodorus, Theodoric the Amal's quaestor,[52] and therefore a practitioner sharing his deliberations, claims that the *summum genus* should be used when addressing monarchs, the *genus mediocre* – officials, while the *genus humile* – common people.[53] Hence, the Late Antique constitutions, which were, as a general rule, letters directed to officials, should be also written in the *genus mediocre*.[54] In reality, the actual practice was very much different from Cassiodorus' precision. Those constitution passages where the emperor solemnly referred to the addressee, as well as *praefationes* containing ideological messages, were usually written in the *summum genus*, while the fragments containing Imperial dispositions – in the *genus mediocre*.[55]

Abandoning the *genus humile* in the legislator's language entailed certain consequences. It was exactly in this particular style that "technical terminology" was allowed to be used. The *genus mediocre*, and even more so the *summum*, required that technical terms be replaced by means of metaphor, description,[56] also recommending that one notion should be, if necessary, rendered with various synonyms.[57] Research on the education possessed by Late Antique Roman graduates of law schools has shown that they were well prepared for applying the rules of rhetoric in practice. They were taught to replace legal terms by descriptions and *vice versa*: to discern strictly defined technical terms in descriptions. They employed their skills in practice, as compilers of laws and commentators.[58] It does not mean they were poorly trained lawyers; it meant that they also possessed other (e.g., rhetorical) abilities, and they could combine them at the right moment (or so they believed) with their knowledge of the law, or even give precedence to them over that knowledge.

---

[51] Quint. *Inst. Orat.* 5.14.33; cf. also Quint. *Inst. Orat.* 2.4.33ff., with references to *laus* and *vituperatio legum*.

[52] In the years 407–411, after completion of his quaestor's tenure, as *magister officiorum* and prefect pretorio, Cassiodorus also executed quaestor's duties, on account of his particular predisposition (Classen 1955: 73–74).

[53] Cass., *Variae*, Praef. 17. It should be stressed that it was Cicero who had already differentiated his style depending on whether the oration was addressed to the Senate or to the people, cf. Adamik 1995: 9.

[54] Voß 1982: 29.

[55] Voß 1982: 57.

[56] Voß 1982: 43.

[57] Voß 1982: 62–64.

[58] Voß 1982: 47–51.

According to their view, in using circumlocutions instead of technical terms,[59] they retained clarity and directness of the text. Nevertheless, modern readers of the Late Antique *leges* may have different opinions on the issue.

Let us ask once again why the *genus humile* was found to have been a style unworthy of *leges*. Following Cassiodorus' trace, one must notice that all types of the Late Antique *leges generales*, except for edicts, were addressed not to the people, but to officials of senatorial rank or the Senate as a whole. In turn, following the clues in Quintilian, one could try to discern the wish to move the recipient as expressed in the texts of the laws. It indicates that the enactment of law was not the sole purpose of those texts.

Education- and propaganda-related functions of the law in Antiquity

Cassiodorus, who had been entrusted, as I have already noted, with the quaestor's duties at Theodoric the Amal's court is a particularly interesting witness of his time. His comments on the role of the emperor's use of rhetoric refer to his own duties. This is how he compares them with the tasks of the orator delivering his speech before the court: "For if the orator's task is to give his speech in a more solemn and ornate way, in order to move the minds of the judges, how much more eloquent should be he who can admonish the people with the emperor's words, so that they may appreciate what is right, hold in contempt what is perverse, praise the good to no end, accuse the wicked vigorously" (*Nam si oratoris est proprium graviter et ornate dicere, ut possit animos iudicum commovere, quanto facundior debet esse, qui ore principis populos noscitur ammonere, ut recta diligant, perversa contemnant, bonos sine fine laudent, pessimos vehementer accusent* – Cass., *Variae* 6.5.3). Cassiodorus outlines the ideal in which the art of rhetoric fulfils the educational role in relation to the people, in which the power of persuasion present in the text of the Imperial laws is sufficient to make sure that the threats expressed in the same laws do not have to be applied in practice. However idealistic such a position may sound compared to what we know about how the subjects of Theodoric

[59] Voß (1982: 61–62) cites an example where the legislator considers it as appropriate to explain the use of a proper term defining a certain action: *...qui eos excidunt aut diminuunt aut, ut proprio verbo utar cupiditas, adrodunt...* (*C.Th.* 12.7.2) – and even the right term – *rodere* is replaced here by an equivalent one *adrodere*, in order to form a full hexameter.

or those of the Roman emperors had actually approached the law,[60] this was not a sort of isolated idealism. In the very texts of the Imperial constitutions, one may encounter the view that resorting to penal sanctions is the result of a defeat, the final measure against those who do not heed the words of persuasion. This is how Diocletian justified his edict on maximum prices,[61] and Theodosius II – his novel against religious dissenters.[62]

The idea of utilizing the texts of enacted laws as a tool in educating the subjects had shaped the rhetoric of the Late Antique legislation in a particular way. And yet, it was not anything new in the Greco-Roman world. It was already Plato who postulated, in opposition to the contemporary political reality of Athens in this aspect, that the law should not only enforce correct conduct by the force of arbitrary decisions, but also fulfil an educational role, explaining why a given conduct is considered wrong and reprehensible. This postulate, formulated in Plato's *Nomoi*, a relatively late work,[63] remains in tune with Socrates' ethical intellectualism: someone who can be persuaded as to what is right and what is wrong, will not need any more external restrictions on his behaviour. That is why Plato treated the persuasive function of law as more important than positive solutions established in laws.

The right place for such educational instruction, according to Plato, is the preface to a constitution (Greek: *prooimion*, Latin: *praefatio*).[64] The postulate of including such "educational" *prooimia* was only slightly implemented in legislations of the Greek *poleis*,[65] and laws of the Roman Republic had lacked *praefationes*, either.[66] Yet with the advent of the Empire, the persuasive function of law takes on a great significance. At first glance, it is surprising indeed that the less the rulers had to take into account limitations in their legislative authority, the more ardent were they in their belief in explaining the motives for their legislative actions to the subjects.

There is a great paradox behind this phenomenon. The persuasion, present in a document promulgated by the political authority, is a manifestation of propaganda as well. A presentation of the values that are worthy of being emulated and the anti-values to be avoided is, indirectly, an act of self-presentation

---

60 Voß 1982: 78.

61 Diocl., *Ed. de pret.*, pr. 6–8. More recent views and the literature concerning the edict are collected in Brandt 2004.

62 *Nov. Theod.* 3.6–14.

63 Plato, *Nomoi* 723a. Cf. Benner 1975: 1–4; Ries 1983: 106–111.

64 Plato, *Nomoi* 730b. Plato himself had perhaps composed such *prooimia* for Dionysius the Younger of Syracuse (*Ep.* 3, 316A, cf. Classen 1955: 67).

65 Ries 1983: 117–118.

66 But it is worth taking note of the effect of the literary style of the Hellenistic rulers' letters on those addressed by the Roman Republican officials to the Greek cities, cf. Benner 1975: 12–13.

of the authority. Thereby, it declares which values it holds in respect and is based on, and where it can see potential threats.[67] Such a declaration may also be perceived as an expression of solidarity with the citizens: the authority understands their hopes and fears. When it uses harsh words to reprimand dishonest officials, at the same time it communicates the message that it is not to blame for any abuses; what is more, it takes care of common people and is on their side in the face of abuses. The authority thus makes known its noble motives, which induce the authority holder to enact a given legislation. The more it becomes autocratic, the more it seems to require such a propaganda-based legitimization.[68]

The educational function is also intertwined with the propaganda role in the acts enacted by Roman emperors. They are a medium through which the emperors communicate to officials and subjects their solicitude for well-being, justice, *humanitas*,[69] and other superior values. They are part of the discourse carried on between the ruler, on the one side, and subjects and officials, on the other, who send their own requests and inquiries to the emperor, formulated in the same language of the Imperial propaganda. As a matter of fact, the affinity between the both messages is so close that the emperor's reply in the form of a rescript cannot be considered apart from the citizen's request, and the response in the form of a constitution is based on the text of a *suggestio* of a solution to a given problem as contained in the official's inquiry.

In the extant laws of the Principate period, the appropriate place for such educational and propaganda contents[70] is the *praefatio* of a constitution. This preface, in which the emperor's motives for enacting the constitution are stated, is separated quite clearly from that part of the law where the positive legal provision is given by means of a "disposition formula," for example, with the words *ideo (...) iubemus*.[71] This other, and principal, part of the law will

---

[67] Cf. Harries 1999a: 58.

[68] Ries (1983: 215–216) explains this phenomenon with the fact that the legislative power of the Republican institutions was something obvious and well-entrenched, whereas the authority of the *princeps* required proper justification – focusing, in particular, on the conformity of the enacted laws with the ideal of justice. The phenomenon is also noticed in Classen 1955: 60–66.

[69] Both in the sense used in legal discourse (*aequitas*, i.e., equity, conformity with the natural concept of justice) and in the wider popular meaning, which in Late Antiquity should be associated with *philanthropia* rather than *paideia* (cf. Honig 1960: 29).

[70] Benner (1975: 14) links the Imperial propaganda present in the Principate–era edicts with the appeal to Imperial *auctoritas*.

[71] Cf. Kussmaul 1981: 53–54, 58–61, 65. This formula corresponds to the *promulgatio* of medieval documents. I have definitely curtailed here the proposition of recognizing the consecutive elements of a medieval document in the texts of Late Antiquity, as it was put forward

be tentatively called "disposition" here, yet one should be aware of the fact that the term extends the modern meaning of the word "disposition" into words of sanction as well;[72] it does not correspond to the Late Antique sense of the word, either.[73] The boundary between the *praefatio* (similarly, understood more broadly than the medieval *arenga*, as it had also contained an exposition of circumstances surrounding the enactment of a given constitution) and thus conceived "disposition" does not become blurred in constitutions of Late Antiquity, either. It is not respected, nonetheless, in the sense that ideological contents, strongly judgemental words and phrases, also trickle over en masse into the disposition proper.[74] It can be said that the entire text of a constitution, not just its preliminary part, begins to perform the ideological function.[75]

It is a definitely fortunate circumstance for the scholars concerned with the study of this subject. The original *praefationes* have only survived in relatively few contemporary constitutions (and they are not identical with those fragments indicated as *praefatio* by the editors of the Late Antique normative

in Fridh 1956: 9–10 (*arenga, promulgatio, narratio, dispositio, sanctio, corroboratio*), especially as in the documents I have examined the *narratio* had merged with *arenga* into one, while the *promulgatio* would only follow afterwards.

72 The part of a constitution where the emperor states his will is designated as "juristic-dispositional" by Ries (1983: 184, 187); Voß 1982: 57 and Honoré 1998: 154 use the term "disposition part". As can be seen, the most distinguished experts in the relevant sources can be referred to. Nevertheless, we should take into account that apart from the disposition proper, it also frequently contained sanctions (Dölger, Karayannopoulos 1968: 49), while it was preceded by a hypothesis. A significant feature of the Late Antique constitutions was the separation of this disposition part from the *praefatio* (containing, in the broad sense, not only the *arenga* but also the *narratio*) by means of the so-called disposition formula (cf. above). Unfortunately, most scholars involved in the study of this subject avoid naming the constitution's part that ensues after this formula, which is why I am inclined to use the simplistic term "disposition" in this work, as it was exactly Imperial dispositions that constituted, as a general rule, the dominant contents in this particular fragment. Let us also note that Schmidt-Hofner has proposed a different meaning of the term: Imperial decisions issued on the emperor's own initiative are called "directives," reserving "disposition" to refer to new legal solutions introduced in response to an official *suggestio*, whereas, in the author's opinion, the repeating of the existing solutions is only an "instruction" (Schmidt-Hofner 2008a: 33–34).

73 As denoting the provisions contained in a testament or the testament itself (Berger 1953: 438).

74 For the first time, this phenomenon can be found in Severus Alexander's act on *aurum coronarium* (text in Schubart 1941: 44–59), cf. Classen 1955: 60–61.

75 These conclusions are based on the approach proposed by G. Ries, who describes how the idea put forward by Plato was reflected in the successive periods of the Greek and Roman legislations. In the light of this author's studies, R. Honig's assumptions turn out to be wrong, since he considered the emergence, in Late Antiquity, of the idea of educating through laws as *novum*, a specific response of the emperors to the challenges posed by the crisis of the third century and other threats of the period (Honig 1960: 4).

sources[76]). The compilers of the *C.Th.* and *C.J.* followed clear instructions to remove from the text anything that is not essential for expressing legal provisions themselves, before incorporating the text in the Code. The constitution *Haec*, which had served as an instruction for the formulation of the Code of Justinian, refers explicitly, in this context, to *praefationes*. But the question was not that simple in the case of ideological contents present in the text of the disposition itself. Quite often, there was no point in excising individual judgemental epithets, in an effort to substitute some more neutral words for others. In consequence, the scholar involved in examination of the ideological aspect of normative sources is now confronted with the body of extensive (though quite difficult to construe) material, composed of individual words and phrases rather than full sentences and longer statements.

The position of the language of invective in the ideological message of the Late Antique constitutions

As it is indicated in Cassiodorus' sentence at the beginning of the previous subchapter, condemning wrong deeds and their perpetrators is almost as important a goal of the Imperial propaganda as demonstrating what is right and praising good deeds. Almost, because, after all, they are placed at the second position. The world of "anti-values" is treated autonomously in this endeavour, yet this is not to ignore the fact that in relation to the world of the extolled values it is naturally derivative, or at least of secondary importance.

In order to understand what, and why, was condemned by the rhetoric of the Imperial constitutions, we must be aware of the values which that rhetoric had served. The Emperor Majorian's novel pronounces: "..., We must consider in what ways Our State may be preserved and may make progress by arms, by laws, and by wholehearted reverence for religion." (*nostra res publica et armis et legibus et integra religionis reverentia conservetur atque proficiat*).[77] The duty of the emperor, as the protector of the civil community, is summed up then in the solicitude for external security, legal order, and reverence to the true religion. The easiest task is the first one: defence against outside threats. But it would not have much of a value on its own, if the Roman state

[76] Van der Wal 1980: 21.

[77] *Nov. Maio.* 6.2–3 (458).

were not governed by laws.[78] For the Roman community, the laws do more than just ensure the concordance with the innate human sense of justice (*aequitas*). The emperor is solicitous about the welfare of the subjects, relieves the burdens that become unbearable, defends the weak against abuses committed by the powerful, the citizens against officials, the disadvantaged against those who in their cruelty and greed would not be inclined to accommodate the needs of the former.[79] Finally, the most important values are those connected with taking proper care of religion. The emperor ensures that it is implemented by taking care of the Church, with particular attention focused on respecting episcopal decisions as regards orthodoxy. In this way, he assures that the state receives God's protection and blessing.[80]

As such values are regarded as positive, it is to be expected that the enemies of the Roman state will be stigmatized where we encounter threats from the outside, injustice, oppression of the citizens by officials and powerful elites, and, finally, also those who refuse to accept the orthodox Christian faith.[81] Towards all the enemies, the emperor demonstrates his sternness – in his words as well. He condemns everything that is in opposition to what is right and all those who stand in opposition to what is right. The "brutality" of the language of the Imperial acts is the dark side of the same propaganda that makes the emperor point to his own *clementia*.[82]

The legislator makes use of the tools from the arsenal of rhetoric in order to stigmatize these adversaries; they are means of expression characteristic

78 *Nov. Theod.* 16.1–3 (439): *Ita prodest gentes barbaras nostri numini imperio mancipari, ita nostrae victoriae videbuntur fructuosae, si pacis commoda legum regulis conponantur.*

79 Honig demonstrates that the same actions may result from *humanitas* understood as both *philanthropia* (Honig 1960: 72–80) and *aequitas* (Honig 1960: 80–84). Essentially, then, appealing to the *humanitas* points to both aspects.

80 *Nov. Theod.* 3.1–4: *Inter ceteras sollicitudines, quas amor publicus pervigili cogitatione nobis indixit, praecipuam imperatoriae maiestatis curam esse perspicimus verae religionis indaginem; cuius si cultum tenere potuerimus, iter prosperitatis humanis aperimus inceptis.* The role of the rhetoric of constitutions in constructing the world of values in Late Antiquity is generally discussed in Harries 1999a: 58.

81 In practice, it signifies of course: considered to be orthodox by the part of the Church supported by the emperor.

82 It is not always well comprehended. Honig (1960: 27) accuses the Imperial constitutions of perversion when they promise to win over criminals with clemency, whereas Fögen (1993: passim) stresses the brutality of the language of the Late Antique constitutions. Yet, as a matter of fact, these are two sides of the same medal. The emperor may show his *clementia*, recognizing the humanity even in an offender, while at other times he would take the side of a person wronged by a criminal or of the good that was violated, and express his indignation by proceeding to the harshest epithets against the culprit. These two attitudes are in fact so close to each other that the emperor quite often refers to his own *clementia* while administering the most severe penalties.

of the language of invective. Let us stress here the distinction between target and tool. In my view, the rhetoric is not identical with the former. The misunderstanding may have been due to the fact that some of the authors who have contributed much to the study of this subject, such as Fridh, Honig, or Voß, are inclined to employ a peculiar metonymy, applying the name "rhetoric" to what the rhetoric had been actually only a vehicle of expression for, i.e., the ideological message present in the Imperial constitutions. Contrary to these authors' intentions, one could assert (perversely refusing to comprehend that metonymy) that the "rhetoric" is the only essential goal of the aforementioned texts, that is the particular words, phrases, rhetorical figures had been placed in the texts in question with the sole purpose to adorn them, not to communicate anything.[83] As a result, one should determine with all due emphasis that the rhetorical means of expression and the ideological message using those measures are two different things. Both the message and the disposition itself were formulated in accordance with the requirements of the art of rhetoric. This does not deprive the both parts (or aspects) of the text of the character of a message (communication). Of course, in describing the emperor's good will or the ugliness of a crime, the author of a given act had a much greater opportunity to display his rhetorical skills than at the times when he attempted to enliven the dry message of a disposition. According to the requirements he was supposed to meet, he ought to do so by using the *summum genus* in the *praefatio*, while for the disposition the lower *genera* were considered as more appropriate. Yet it does not mean that the use of rhetorical figures should be construed as a signal "what I am saying now is of no importance at all." In my opinion, it is just the opposite. It was exactly that message, which was particularly intended to drive through to the consciousness of the audience, was emphasized by use of the figures typical of the language of invective.[84]

One must also acknowledge that the message in question is characterized by the above-mentioned peculiar "collective" authorship just as the constitution as a whole. Although the Imperial quaestor's role in preparing the text and selecting specific phrases could have been decisive, the responsibility for the contents therein rests with all of the participants in the legislative process: the author of the *suggestio*, members of the *consistorium* and the emperor himself. If one does not treat the invectives contained in the text of a given constitution as a purely rhetorical manoeuvre, designed to embellish the text,

83 On a more general tendency to interpret the rhetoric of blame in Late-Antique texts as "mere abuse," see Flower 2013: 55.

84 As Preisert points out, strong emotions, which accompany verbal aggression, enhance the process of remembering (Preisert 2004: 27).

but consider it as an expression of the essential ideological message, one must also attribute this "collective" authorship to them. It is beyond doubt that the language of invective belongs to the high literary style, which is characteristic of Imperial constitutions, and which the quaestor was entrusted to take care of. Nevertheless, I am convinced that it was a vehicle for conveying significant ideological contents, which had to be approved by the quaestor as well as all the other co-compilers of the constitution. Otherwise, one would arrive, just as Tony Honoré did, at the verge of absurdity, in arguing that the pagan quaestor could have, under the Christian emperor's rule, effected the enactment of the laws openly disregarding the religion and the Church to which the emperor adhered.[85]

[85] This obvious incongruity with regard to the research which attempts to determine the religious views of the quaestor based on the constitution style was pointed out to the British scholar by Fögen (cf. Fögen 1998: 9).

Chapter III: The possibility of researching the "language of invective" in the Imperial documents of Late Antiquity

Methods used to formulate the "language of invective" – amplification

It was already Aristotle who had recognized that the rhetorical figure of thought known as amplification (*auksēsis,* αὔξησις) is in natural harmony with epideictic speech; this view was also shared by later theorists of rhetoric.[1] Amplification serves to augment or diminish the object being referred to in a statement, so as to make it, as much as possible, worthy of praise or censure. The theory of amplification, elaborated by such eminent authors as Cicero and Quintilian,[2] does not have apparently much to say about the straightforward "offensive words" that are of relevance in the present study. This is on account of the fact that in the case of our sources the proper way to express an invective will be mostly the use of a single, negative and condemnatory term, not a whole structure. It is worth noting that in literary texts, as well, emotionally charged

1 Aristot., *Rhet.* I.9, 1368A. I shall also use the term "amplification" to refer to augmentation of negative values, even though the philosopher also finds the term to express the opposite of amplification, i.e., diminishing – "depreciation" (Aristot., *Rhet.* II.26, 1403A). Amplification is also extensively mentioned in *Rhet. Ad Alex.* 3, 1426A–B. Aristides, *Techne rhetorike, Peri psogou* (*RG* 2.506) mentions amplification as one of the four means to formulate *psogos* (next to ridicule, comparison to negative figures, and insult). In Late Antiquity, Aphthonios treated amplification as a feature distinguishing four genres of oration: of praise, blame, *koinos topos* (which, according to this author, is in fact an oratory of blame directed against a specific type rather than a single individual) and *synkrysis* (comparison between two individuals). Bolonyai 2000: 32.

2 Lausberg 1960: 220–227.

words are the fundamental elements out of which more complex forms of invective are constructed. Likewise, in academic practice, the studies of classical language of aggression are focused on simple "offensive words." This is the case of scholars such as Opelt, who begins with assuming that *Schimpfwörter* will be the target of her research, but also Koster[3] and numerous other authors whose works are referred to in the notes throughout this present book.[4]

However, the *Schimpfwort* does not remain unnoticed in the theory of amplification. As a matter of fact, the basis on which various kinds of amplification may be built is to find some emotionally marked synonym for a given deed or quality. In the case of oratories of blame, it is of course a synonym characterized by a negative content, i.e., exactly what we call an "offensive word," *Schimpfwort*.[5] This section of the work is defined as a preliminary phase in the construction of an argument of magnification (*incrementum*). In its complete form, an *incrementum* enumerates such negative terms in the increasing order, e.g., *facinus est vincire civem Romanum, scelus verberare, prope parricidium necare; quid dicam in crucem tollere?* ("it is a crime to imprison a Roman citizen, a felony to have him flagellated, to kill [him] is akin to parricide; how should I call the crucifixion?" – Cic., *In Verr.* II.5.170).[6] Still, even the a thors of speeches would not have usually gone beyond the creating of a basic form of *incrementum*, i.e., the finding of a single synonym. For this reason, in their case as well, the most suitable way to examine the content of a given invective is to juxtapose individual terms expressing blame.

Apart from the preparatory *incrementum*, another type of amplification can be distinguished, prominently represented in Imperial documents. It is a concentration (*congeries*) of synonymous words and similar grammatical forms creating the effect of a reinforced condemnation. This effect is not based here on individual elements,

---

3 Cf. the material collected by this author, Koster 1980: 358–364.

4 Badian 1975; Bruggiser 2002; Cañizar Palacios 2006; Dauge 1981: 424–440; Dunkle 1967; Dunkle 1971; Escribano 1997; Fögen 1993; Grodzynski 1974; Grout-Gerletti 1998; Hellegouarc'h 1963: 186–201, 525–542; Honig 1960: 145–186; Janssen 1975; Janssen 1979; Kahlos 2007b; Kubiak 1989; Lazzarini 1982; Martin 2004; Miniconi 1958; Muñoz Llamosas 2008; Müller 1913; Murphy 1997; Sachot 1991; Salzman 1987; Stachura 2007a; Sussman 1998; Taldone 1993; Thome 1992; Thome 1993; Weische 1966: 11–65; Wirszubski 1961; Wissemann 1992; Wood 1986; Zuccotti 1992.

5 Kamińska-Szmaj (2007: 63–65) divides words of this type into evaluative primarily (negative judgement forms part of the word definition) and connotatively (their negative judgement is shaped secondarily). In the case of the invectives being subject to analysis here, the former will comprise such as *hostis, scelus*, whereas the latter (those whose meaning [one of the meanings] had secondarily acquired a negative judgemental character) – e.g., *barbarus, audacia, furor, contagium, superstitio*.

6 Lausberg 1960: 221–222.

but on a seemingly chaotic accumulation of such elements, resembling a passionate statement.[7] Among examples of *congeries*, one could mention accumulations of successive rhetorical questions, negations, but also pleonasms that can be very often found in the texts of constitutions, as far as they refer to describing, in various ways, qualities or actions subjected to negative judgement.

As can be seen, any analysis of invective must be focused, in the first place and for each classical text, on individual negatively marked words. In the case of Imperial documents, this postulation is all the more relevant as those texts, unlike literary ones, would not have left in general very much room to elaborate on more embellished rhetorical formulas. Still, when it comes to the Late Antique constitutions, one is compelled to take into consideration yet one more factor: the actual state of the texts' preservation.

The texts of the fourth- and fifth-century constitutions have usually not survived in complete form to our time, as they had been much curtailed during the compilation phase of the *C.Th.* and *C.J.* According to the working assumptions followed by the committees in charge of the Codes, the sections of the texts subject to abridgement were to be those not indispensable for expressing the sanction itself, demonstrating the motives that would have guided the emperor in enacting the law, and consequently the ideological message in question. Fortunately, the Late Antique legislation would not strictly follow the rule that the *praefatio* is the only appropriate part where such a message could be possibly promulgated. This is the reason why some traces of the said message, expressed, among other things, in the language of invective, can still be found in the constitutions of the *C.Th.* and *C.J.* Nevertheless, in order to explore the problem, one is compelled to fish for individual words and phrases in the texts of the Imperial dispositions. All the more so, it is necessary to concentrate on what is available, i.e., individual words marked by negative emotions.

Relevant documents: the actual state of preservation

An overwhelming majority of the material analyzed in this work comes from the **Theodosian Code**. On March 26, 426, the Emperor Theodosius II, reigning in the Eastern part of the Roman Empire, issued the constitution (*C.Th.* 1.1.5) that was to establish a committee of Imperial officials and set up rules according

7 Lausberg 1960: 224. Examples of such "accumulations" in modern-day invective are shown in Kamińska-Szmaj 2007: 67. Zuccotti (1992: 134) calls such concentrations "obsessive repetition," yet also noticing its amplificatory character (Zuccotti 1992: 143).

to which the committee was to compile a Code out of the constitutions promulgated since as early as Constantine's reign. This enormous task proved to have been too far-reaching; in consequence, on December 20, 435, it was corrected by a new constitution (*C.Th.* 1.1.6), which also modified the composition of the committee. Ultimately, the Code was made public in the East by means of the constitution now known as *Nov. Theod.* 1, on February 15, 438, with effect from January 1, 439. In the West, the solemn Reading of the Code took place at the Roman Senate's session of December 25, 438 (there has survived a proceedings protocol from that session known as the *Gesta Senatus Romani de Theodosiano Publicando*).[8]

The time-frame presented above points to the history of the making of the Theodosian compilation, encompassing the laws dated from June 1, 311 (*C.Th.* 13.10.2) until March 16, 437 (*C.Th.* 6.23.4). In less than a century later, the Theodosian Code had become one of the principal sources in the creation of the new compilation – the Code of Justinian. After the work had been completed, all the copies of the Theodosian Code were destroyed by the Emperor Justinian's order. Fortunately for us, the Code continued to remain in force beyond the frontiers of the Roman Empire as the law of the Roman population living in the states established by the Germanic rulers.[9] It should be noted that the *interpretationes*, often found under the texts of constitutions, had been created exactly in those particular legal and political realities of the barbaro-Roman states.[10]

The Theodosian Code contains a little over 2,500 constitutions, divided into sixteen books, and these in turn are divided into chapters dealing with specific issues. Each chapter has a chronological arrangement, and it is possible to notice the compilers' efforts to recreate the dates of the constitutions on the basis of the abbreviations in the original text (their work is often emended by modern scholars, especially for the reigns of Constantine and his sons[11]). This sequencing according to dates was of particular significance. In his instruction

---

8 On the creation of the Code, cf. Wenger 1953: 536–543; Fusco 1974; Archi 1976; Gaudemet 1976; Honoré 1986; Sirks 1986; Matthews 1993; Sirks 1993b; Sargenti 1995; Honoré 1998: 123–153; Wipszycka 1999: 595–601; Matthews 2000: 55–84; Schlinkert 2002; Sirks 2007.

9 The Code was recreated primarily on the basis of manuscripts from the territory of the Merovingian state (both the manuscripts of the Code itself and the *Breviarium* of Alaric II, king of the Visigoths, cf. Wood 1993: 164–166). The Code's complicated manuscript tradition is presented by Mommsen in *Prologomena* to the Code edition, and summarized by Matthews 2000: 85–90; Sirks 2007: 163–172.

10 Wenger 1953: 557; Sirks 2007: 215–226.

11 The dates of the constitutions amended in Mommsen's edition were subsequently corrected by Seeck (Seeck 1919, strongly criticized – cf. Mommsen 1900; Voß 1989; Sirks 2007: 111); more corrections were introduced in the 1952 edition of the English translation of the Code

(*C.Th.* 1.1.5), Theodosius II ordered the incorporation in the Code also of the laws that were no longer valid;[12] their repeal was to be decided by the text of a more recent legal provision contained in a given chapter.

It was the commission's task not only to seek out the Imperial *leges* and assigning them among the chapters of the Code, but also shortening each text to the words of disposition only. The instruction *C.Th.* 1.1.5 reads as follows: "the very words themselves of the constitutions, in so far as they pertain to the essential matter, shall be preserved, but those words which were added not from the very necessity of sanctioning the law shall be omitted" (*constitutionum ipsa etiam verba, quae ad rem pertinent reserventur, praetermissis illis, quae sanciendae rei non ex ipsa necessitate adiuncta sunt*). More briefly, but just as clearly, it is formulated in the instruction *C.Th.* 1.1.6: "the words which do not pertain to the force of the sanction shall be removed from each constitution, and the law alone shall be left" (*circumcisis ex quaque constitutione ad vim sanctionis non pertinentibus solum ius relinquatur*).

The constitution of 429 says nothing about any possibility to emend the texts. It is only the subsequent instruction dated 435 that provides the compilers with an authority (*potestas*) not only to remove superfluous words (*demendi supervacanea*), but also to add necessary (*adiciendi necessaria*), replace ambiguous (*demutandi ambigua*), emend inappropriate ones (*emendandi incongrua*). There is an ongoing debate in academic circles if that change resulted in a break in the codification work, only to resume it anew,[13] or merely proceeding to another stage of the works, a necessary complement to the instruction prior to the passing from the query phase to the writing of the Code itself.[14] In any case, the emendations permitted by the instruction were not intended to alter the contents of any provisions of the Imperial laws as found in the archives, but only to achieve a clearer exposition thereof.

It is much easier to survey the scope of corrections introduced in the original texts by referring to the constitutions of the Code of Justinian, which are liable to be compared with the complete texts of the laws in the Post-Theodosian Novels.[15] Nonetheless, the laws of the Theodosian Code, used to be compared

---

(Pharr 1952), and finally, not to mention some emendations in particular dates in specific studies, in Honoré 1998.

12 It is fairly generally assumed that the compilers of the Theodosian Code had such a permission; it has been opposed lately by Sirks 2007: 149–154; even though he makes an exception for the sixteenth book of this Code.

13 Mommsen, *Prologomena* IX, Wenger 1953: 536; Jones 1986: 475; Van der Wal 1980: 8 ff.; Sirks 1986: 271. Yet the author is now inclined to argue that the programme of the *C.Th.* 1.1.6 had never been implemented (Sirks 2007: 63).

14 Archi 1976: 33–37; Honoré 1998: 125–126; Matthews 2000: 60–71.

15 Wenger 1953: 648; Van der Wal 1980: 22.

in this respect as well, particularly with the Sirmondian Constitutions.[16] Such comparisons allow us to form an opinion about the extent of the compilers' interference in the original text. Primarily, omission would be applied to those fairly considerable fragments located beyond the disposition: the titles of the emperor and the official (recipient of the document), prefaces (*praefationes*) explaining motives and circumstances surrounding the publication of a given law, the ensuing disposition formula (*sancimus*, *decernimus*, but also simply *promulgamus*, *volumus*[17]), and finally the directive to publish the law addressed to the official. Subsequently, constitutions could have been divided, according to subject-matter, into particular chapters; this would pose an enormous challenge, as occasionally some specific provision, which was intended to form a distinct constitution within the Code, would have been introduced by means of a subordinate clause, e.g., *ablativus absolutus*, in the original. In such case, it was necessary to resort to some stylistic efforts turning the subordinate clause into the principal one. Ambiguous, fuzzy, or metaphorical expressions were sometimes elaborated in order to explain them better; they were rarely substituted using a simpler phrase.[18] As a general rule, efforts were made to retain the original words (*ipsa verba*) of the primary text, with only necessary changes in grammatical form of individual words or a conjunction added. The cases where certain words of the Code constitutions are significantly different from the known original may be explained by the fact that the compilers had already laboured on the text being a variation of the one that we have.[19]

The question of changes in the original texts of the constitutions is of a fundamental significance for the purpose of our study. The thing that the compilers were to preserve from the primary text of the constitutions were the words of the Imperial disposition, forming the *lex generalis*. The ideological message, possibly contained in the *lex*, was not part of the "law as such." Ordinarily, it formed fairly clearly distinguished contents of *praefationes*, which could be easily omitted.[20] Fortunately, the relevant contents had largely found their way into the text of the disposition, morphing into a cohesive whole. It was often almost impossible here to tell the ideological content from "the law itself," if it were to be done at the expense of grammatical correctness or intelligibility of the text. The postulation of the "clarity" of the text does not

---

16 Fridh 1956: 21–24; Matthews 2000: 127–160, 254–279.

17 Kussmaul 1981: 53.

18 Van der Wal 1980: 22.

19 Thus, Matthews 2000: 147 while comparing *Const. Sirm.* 4 with *C.Th.* 16.8.5 and *C.Th.* 16.9.1.

20 In the case of the Code of Justinian, the constitution *Haec* had clearly pointed to the *praefationes* as the parts of the constitution to be removed.

mean, either, that *C.Th.* 1.6.6 had ordered that the style of rhetoric be changed into the *genus humile*.[21] Although the compilers attempted to clear the text of overly sophisticated phrases, much of the original rhetoric has survived so that it is now possible to carry on with serious research into that rhetoric. With this assumption, Tony Honoré had commenced his strenuous work, comparing styles of the successive constitutions from the reigns of the emperors of the Theodosian dynasty. The objective was to find out who were the authors behind the texts in question, consecutively serving as Imperial quaestors. Irrespective of how we assess the methods used by Honoré, it cannot be denied that he discovers a certain amount of stylistic phenomena, regularly occurring over a brief period of time,[22] and thus pointing to one author of the constitution. It is an indirect proof that the primary text was changed to such a small extent by the compilers that one can still discern the characteristics of its style.

On the other hand, it is worth keeping in mind Nicolaas Van der Wal's warning: if we do not possess the original text, we cannot be absolutely certain that a given word had not been added by the compilers.[23] As far as this study is concerned, it is not very likely that they may have added a particular ideologically charged term to the text. At the most, one may speak of taking it out of the original context.

Another collection of constitutions of pivotal importance in the present study are the so-called **Post-Theodosian Novels** (*Novellae*).[24] It is a collection of fully preserved constitutions and pragmatics,[25] published already after completion of the work on the Theodosian Code, either coming from the emperors of the Western part of the Empire or sent to the West by their Constantinopolitan colleagues (years 438–468). Meyer's 1905 edition combines three collections of novels into one *corpus*; the collections are different with respect to groups of preserved texts, but corresponding as to the sequence in which the texts are arranged.[26]

The origin of the collection goes back to the autumn of 447, when, ten years after presenting Valentinian III with a copy of the Code, Theodosius II decided

---

21 Voß 1982: 73.

22 Honoré 1998: passim.

23 Van der Wal 1980: 26.

24 Using the term *novellae* to refer to these constitutions is attested in contemporary sources, cf. Meyer 1905: XII.

25 Kussmaul 1981. See above.

26 The most complete one, preserved in the Vatican manuscripts, contains all the novels of the Emperors Theodosius II, Valentinian III, and most of Majorian's; the second one was appended to the *Breviarium* of Alaric, the third one is dependant on the other two collections, cf. Meyer 1905: XIII–XXIV.

to send to the West all[27] *leges generales* published over that ten-year period. Apart from the laws, there is a pragmatics here attesting the Emperor's authorship of the constitution (*Nov. Theod.* 2). Later on, five novels of the Emperor Marcian were sent over from the East (there are definitely many more constitutions of that Emperor preserved in the Code of Justinian). The remaining Novels come from the Emperors of the West: Valentinian III, Majorian, Severus, and Anthemius (however, a fragment of Anthemius' third Novel is a citation from a constitution issued by the contemporaneous Emperor of the East, Leo). As can be seen, the collection contains laws from the Western part of the Empire as well as laws of the Eastern emperors, approved in the West. According to Boudwijn Sirks, it is not so much an attempt at the Empire's legal unification as extending a peculiar legislative protectorate over the West.[28]

Each emperor's novels are principally arranged in chronological order, but those of Theodosius II and Valentinian III are grouped into rubrics. If such a rubric comprises several constitutions, its placement depends on the date of the first one.[29] Moreover, Theodosius II's Novels are headed by the constitution *Nov. Theod.* 1 (February 15, 438, whereas *Nov. Theod.* 3 was issued on January 31, 438), promulgating the Theodosian Code, while the second one is occupied by the aforementioned pragmatics of 447, which is at the same time a letter to Valentinian III with the request for approving the transmitted constitutions.[30]

In total, the collection contains 35 constitutions of Theodosius II, divided into 26 rubrics, 46 constitutions of Valentinian III (36 rubrics), 9 of Majorian (and 3, of which only the titles have survived), 5 of Marcian, 2 of Severus, and 3 of Anthemius.

For a variety of reasons, these texts are of particular value for students of the Late Antique law. Firstly, one encounters here not only the *leges*, but also some indisputable pragmatics, and even two documents the legislator classifies as something in between, referring to them as *leges pragmaticae*.[31] Secondly, they are complete texts, containing both *praefationes* and the formulas ordering publication of the former. Thirdly, the subject-matter of the Post-Theodosian Novels is not restricted to one type of issues, covering

---

27 Sirks 2007: 233–234. In the Code of Justinian, there are fragments of Theodosius II's laws from that period, which cannot be assigned to the texts of his Novels; the author offers the following explanation: the compilers of the Novels collection either had not found those texts or had not seen any *leges generales* in them.

28 Sirks 2007: 236–237.

29 E.g., *Nov. Theod.* 6 (438), *Nov. Theod.* 7.1 (439), *Nov. Theod.* 7.2 (09.440), *Nov. Theod.* 7.3 (12.440), *Nov. Theod.* 7.4 (441), *Nov. Theod.* 8 (439).

30 Sirks 2007: 230–231.

31 *Nov. Marc.* 2 (450) and *Nov. Marc.* 3 (451), cf. Kussmaul 1981: 33–34, 64–65.

a broad spectrum of problems besetting the Imperial authority in the course of this watershed period. Particularly emphatic are the contents of Valentinian III's successive novels, which attempt to find some remedy for the increasing turmoil caused by the Vandal invasion of Africa.[32] And, finally, the laws found in this collection had served as material for the authors of the Code of Justinian; comparing the texts of the former with the respective constitutions of the Code allows one to evaluate how far they may have proceeded in transforming the original text of the law.

For the sake of this analysis, the second point is of particular significance. Unlike the constitutions preserved in the Codes, the Post-Theodosian Novels provide the texts of *praefationes*, the parts of constitutions inherently serving to represent motives behind the issue of a given law, in principle written in the *summum genus*. Therefore, one could expect here a more fertile ground for the art of rhetoric, including the formulating of the language of invective.

A much more modest collection of constitutions is the **Sirmondian Collection**, named after its discoverer, robber, and publisher: a Jesuit scholar named Jacques Sirmond.[33] The date of the origins of this collection (placed between the beginning of the fifth and the sixth century) is controversial.[34] The collection is undoubtedly of ecclesiastical origin,[35] as all of the texts are concerned with issues within the sphere of interest of the Church: matters related to clergy, religious dissidents, Easter amnesties. The scholars turned their particular attention to the question of *episcopalis audientia*, which is the subject of *Const. Sirm.* 1 (333),[36] as well as of *Const. Sirm.* 17 and 18. The latter two come from the Theodosian Code and had served as a basis for recreating the chapter

---

32 *Nov. Valent.* 9 (440); *Nov. Valent.* 1.2 (440/441); *Nov. Valent.* 2.3 (443); *Nov. Valent.* 12 (443); *Nov. Valent.* 6.3 (444); *Nov. Valent.* 13 (445); *Nov. Valent.* 34 (451); *Nov. Valent.* 35 (452).

33 In 1631, Jacques Sirmond published 21 constitutions as a complement to an edition of the Theodosian Code. 18 of them had come from a manuscript borrowed from the chapter-house library of the Lyons Cathedral and never returned there. In 1764, after the Jesuit college had been dissolved, its library was partitioned among various private collectors. Via the Netherlands and Britain, the manuscript in question had finally reached Berlin, where Th. Mommsen used it to complement his edition of the Theodosian Code. 16 constitutions from the manuscript are featured here as an enclosure, the remaining two had turned out to be identical with the texts of the laws already present in the Code. For a history of the collection, see Matthews 2000: 121–122.

34 Sirks 2007: 253.

35 For a thorough discussion of the time and place of the origin of the collection, cf. Vessey 1993.

36 This constitution brought some cause for suspicions that the entire collection was in fact a forgery meant to help to expand the scope of competence of episcopal courts (the statement refuted by Huck 2003). It is much more likely that one phrase had been added here to the original text (Sirks 2007: 243–246).

De episcopali definitione (*C.Th.* 1.27).[37] The previously mentioned 16 constitutions do not come, in all certainty, from the Code. They are, for the most part, complete texts, containing *praefationes* and publication formulas. For many of their fragments, parallel texts can be found in the Theodosian Code. Thus, the Sirmondian Constitutions give us a valuable insight into the work of their authors[38] – just as the Post-Theodosian Novels do for the Code of Justinian.

The research method and its limitations

The actual condition of the Late Antique laws' preservation limits our possibilities of examining the ideological message contained therein. Only in a relatively small group of the constitutions can this particular content be now read and recreated in its complete form. In the constitutions which have been preserved as part of the Theodosian Code, it is not only considerably abridged, but also preserved in a random manner – as it was the Code compilers' deliberate intention to reject it. In consequence, the scholar analyzing this subject-matter may follow two courses of action: limit their interest to the fully preserved constitutions, possibly also adding some selected examples from the Theodosian Code or take into consideration the whole of the material at our disposal.

There is no doubt that only in the completely preserved constitutions is it possible to discern the relevant ideological message, as there is no risk of error resulting from the incompleteness of the text. One can notice in which part of a given constitution (*praefatio*, disposition, epilogue) specific terms characterized by a negative content can be found; there is also an incomparably greater chance to interpret their context properly. Reading and interpreting each constitution separately is recommended on the strength of the fact that every one of them was a separate source, a distinct document in itself. Combining them into chapters and books according to their subject-matter is artificial, just as the making of a comprehensive *corpus* out of normative texts may be considered as such, too.

Such research may be, of course, also undertaken in the case of more extensive texts of the Theodosian Code, yet the risk of an error would be much greater. Simultaneously, we must not forget that they are not original texts, as they had been transformed during the work on the Code. It would be simplistic, then, to date them back to the year of publication of the original.

---

37 Sirks 2007: 247.

38 For such an analysis, cf. Matthews 2000: 127–160.

In fact, we do not possess the original texts, as they are rather as if of double authorship. Theodosius II was well aware of the fact; he believed that even though the constitutions in the Code came from various emperors of the past, he was ultimately responsible for the text of each one of them as part of the Code.[39]

The totally opposite view is represented by the research which takes into account, as its source basis, a complete body of normative texts from a given period. An example of this approach may be Richard Honig's study, already mentioned in the introduction, selecting into groups and analyzing all the statements found in the Theodosian Code and Post-Theodosian Novels concerning *humanitas*. This sort of research is the most suitable one in searching for meanings of particular terms. Their occurrences in individual texts may be accidental, but a collection of their appearances throughout the *corpus* of those texts delineates the semantic field of a specific term. Furthermore, with such abridged texts as these, embracing the semantic field of a given word allows us to draw more conclusions than the sum of its individual occurrences. A phrase found in one constitution makes it possible to account for incomprehensible places in other texts, which themselves in turn may enable its interpretation.

The massive volume of the source also facilitates, in the case of the more frequently appearing terms, a quasi-statistical treatment of research results. It is possible to note which meanings are characteristic of a given term, and which are only present in single instances. But let us remember that such quasi-statistical observations are only admissible with homogenous sources. This is no doubt the case of the Theodosian Code. The material therein is curtailed, indeed, but it is curtailed according to uniform rules, which had concerned all the extant acts in equal measure.[40] Although the material of the first books is not preserved completely, the instructions for the codification committees do not contain any injunction to omit or, on the contrary, meticulously seek out any constitutions with definite subject-matter. It allows one to consider the Code – a collection of more than 2,500 extant texts – as a statistical attempt, albeit imperfect, targeting on the legislation of the period which it covers. Still, linking the Code with collections created in accordance with other principles, e.g., the Post-Theodosian Novels, appears to be inadmissible, as it would distort the uniformity of the collection under examination. In the case of the corpus composed of all the normative texts of the period in question, it is possible to determine the semantic field

---

[39] *Nov. Theod.* 1, cf. Sirks 2007: 76.

[40] It is none the less noticed, in the case of Book 16 of the Code (religious issues), that there is a greater esteem given to the texts of the laws which had already become no longer valid, cf. Honoré 1998: 146.

for a given term, but any pertinent observations of a statistical nature should be approached with much caution.

This method assumes that the body of the texts being examined constitutes a certain complete whole. It is not an obvious feature in the case of the constitutions that are known to have come from different authors (recently, Laurence Guichard has noted how very different is the negatively marked vocabulary employed in the documents concerning religious issues by the emperors of the second Flavian dynasty as compared with the one used by Valentinian I). Nonetheless, one could possibly refer to the common place of origin of all the relevant documents, namely the central bureaux of the Roman Empire. As a result, all the texts of the Imperial constitutions can be treated as a homogenous complex of sources.[41] We could also ask what exactly makes normative texts different from other texts of the period, such as epistles or narrative works. Why would a specific term acquire some characteristic sense in such texts? The response is clear for a normative statement, but is it also the case with an ideological one? In my opinion, the latter should also be recognized as specific for Imperial constitutions. They were indeed the proper means for the emperor to address his subjects, especially officials,[42] while the other sources of the period had not performed a similar role. Even if the language of those other sources proved to be similar to the language of the laws, its function would have been definitely different.

Finally, let us note that the method proves to be of value only if we take into consideration all of the appearances of a term in a given body of texts. Isolating single instances can serve illustration purposes only, which cannot form the basis of any solid analytical research. Unfortunately, some modern studies reduce their method to illustrating their theses in this way, which can hardly yield any more information than a mere fact that, e.g., heretics may be named using this or that particular term.[43]

In this study, I must refer to both of these methods. Chapter IV, in which I intend to show the place occupied by the language of invective in the particular individual texts, shall present each constitution separately, as a distinct document. It is clear I shall not be able to represent in this way all of the manifestations of that language in the material in question, yet I do hope I can

---

41 Voß 1982: 13.

42 Honig 1960: 25–27; Harries 1999a: 56–58, 97–98, 214; Millar 2006: 7, 35.

43 This charge may be raised, in some measure, with regard to the studies by Hunt 1993; Maceratini 1994: 51–53; Coyle 2004 – even though they do undertake to explain the epithets referring to heretics, they do not examine their sense throughout the body of the texts of the Theodosian Code. An extreme example is the book by Zeddies 2003; the author has used the relevant phrases as mottoes for her chapters, yet she does not analyze them at all.

demonstrate, on the basis of a selected group of constitutions, where in the texts, both complete and those abridged during the codification, elements of the language of invective can be found and what kind of role they play in those texts.

The following chapters are comprised of analyses of particular terms, which can be considered as nothing short of *Schimpfwörter*, "offensive words" marked by a negative emotional content. They are not only "minimum" but also elementary manifestations of the language of invective; a majority of the more complex amplification figures are based on suitable combinations of words characterized by their emotional content. In consequence, compiling a dictionary of offensive terms used by a specific author should always be regarded as the basis for any study of invective. This postulation is all the more urgent if the author had avoided more complex forms of invective. Moreover, in the case of the Codes, one is confronted with the situation in which such more complicated forms were to be omitted, as a rule, and what has been left of them are precisely their elements: words marked by a negative content. On their basis, I have undertaken to compile a specific "dictionary of negatively marked words" present in the documents of the relevant period; drawing their semantic fields, I also proceed to explain their origin in the tradition of classical invective (for the most characteristic terms).

Arranging terms with negative meanings in order is a major problem in itself. Let us mention here examples of such eminent authors as Ilona Opelt and Michel Wisseman.[44] Their typologies are based on the context in which a given "offensive word" (*Schimpfwort*) appears: against whom or what it is directed. This method of arranging the material has an unquestionable advantage: if one knows the context, one is sure that the "abusive word" has been indeed uttered, at a given place, with an intent to insult. Thus, it is known who was affected, and why, by that particular word. But, as it seems, the system has its drawbacks. It makes it difficult to discern if the same offensive word, in various cases, has got the same or different meanings. What is most important, this method of arranging the material does not show the way it has been collected, only the end result of the job. If the purpose of the work is to identify groups of stigmatized "enemies," as it is in this case, a method like this would even go on to limit our research possibilities. For instance, instead of looking for the meaning of the term *hostis*, one would assume in advance what sort of "enemies" one is concerned with and only look to check if they are indeed called *hostes* or not. It is by all means the right method but only for an exposition of the previously analyzed material, and that is why I intend to use it in the final

44 Opelt 1965a; Wissemann 1992.

part, in the chapter summing up the results of the work, where I construct a typology of "enemies of the Empire."

But is it possible to arrange the relevant material in a more fitting way? A demand to put it in a properly arranged order seems to be obvious. Any arrangement of "offensive words" in alphabetical or grammatical order would lead us into a chaotic situation in which both the reader and the author would be bound to get confused. One should make an attempt, then, to seek out divisions made by predominant meanings of individual terms. This is why I have chosen to set the material in order according to meaning: Chapter V is devoted to words explicitly indicating at the hostile relation between the legislator and a castigated individual; Chapter VI to the attitude of that individual, which determines his actions; Chapter VII is focused on the action itself, i.e., crimes which he commits. In turn, Chapter VIII deals with terms describing errors, in particular of religious nature, which do not fall within the limits of the above classification.

Chapters IX and X are not simple recapitulations of the previous ones, but constitute a presentation of a different, synthetic, approach to the material subjected to our study. A classification of the relevant material into groups, this time according to whom a given invective refers to, makes it possible to formulate some additional conclusions, yet referring not to the language of invective as such, but to how it would have functioned with regard to definite groups of "enemies," condemned in the light of the Imperial legislation. The nature of these two chapters differs from that of the chapters of the analytical part – as much as the latter are supposed, in particular, to serve as an aid in interpreting a specific Late Antique document, I consider the third part to be a contribution to the studies on the world-vision typical of the documents addressed to Imperial officials as well as the representation of particular groups recognized as "enemies" of the Later Roman order.

Part II: Analysis

Chapter IV: Composition of invective in documents of Late Antiquity – examples

As I have already explained in the previous chapter, the analytical work on the language of invective in the Late Antique documents may follow one of two courses: studies of particular texts or attempts to delineate semantic fields of individual terms. At the same time, both of these methods of research complement one another: writing a commentary on the text of a constitution, one must be constantly aware of the meanings of individual terms, while in searching for the meaning, one cannot depart from the contexts of particular constitutions, from a concrete and unique structure which the language of invective created in each one of them. The sequence in which to present results of this research shall remain a somewhat problematic question; nevertheless, I believe that it will be easier for the reader to refer to detailed discussions of terms further on, while analyzing the relevant Imperial constitutions, than wade through these discussions without having any general idea of the appearance of the texts under examination and the way in which the language of invective worked in them.

It is obvious that any complete representation of the research I have conducted would require presenting, in this chapter, commentary on the texts of all the documents in which I have found at least one element of the language of invective in question, yet such an effort would have been daunting and not very productive. The composition of invective in particular constitutions is indeed unique in its details, yet in the general outline (i.e., the place and function of "abusive words" in the text) it tends to repeat itself in a definitely monotonous manner. As I believe, it will be more useful to select several examples allowing me to present this composition in the acts preserved both in the form abridged for the codification purposes and in the primary form of the Novels.

I have selected ten constitutions. The choice is not a random one. As it is shown in Chapter X of this work, even though about 29% of the constitutions of the Theodosian Code contain at least one objectively "insulting" word, only 3% of these constitutions contain five or more such words.

In the Novels, which are completely preserved and first of all much more extensive texts, the percentages are 76% and 24%, respectively; whereas only the constitutions comprising greater numbers of negative expressions can create forms of invective elaborate enough to make it possible to analyze whole structures. As a result, I can demonstrate how numerous elements of the language of invective could interact with one another, make up the whole of the statement. These cases also show where exactly within the act "concentrations" of such elements have taken place. Finally, they allow us to find out how much of the material had been irretrievably lost due to the reduction of the codified constitutions to the form of bare dispositions.

Out of the 76 constitutions of the Theodosian Code and 24 Novels that contain some more complex forms of invective, I have chosen 8 constitutions of the Code and 2 Novels for illustration purposes. I have tried, at the same time, to make this selection reflect the most characteristic features which I had encountered during my research: repetitions and other cases of accumulation, enumerations of crimes and heresies, metaphors constructed of allusion, inserting admonitions for officials into the principal text, building links between *furor* and *audacia*. To a lesser extent, the choice was made with respect to subject-matter of statements and diversity of abusive terms used. Still, in consequence, I have also shown the three most characteristic groups of "enemies": religious dissidents, dishonest officials, certain categories of offenders (the latter one, perhaps in the least degree, but by means of the specific text of the Easter amnesty). The constitution *C.Th.* 9.40.17, of Eutropius, the deposed *praepositus sacri cubiculi*, may be a more distinct example – compared with other texts – of dealing with an internal enemy. The two Novels presented at the end are perhaps not among the longest ones and the most abundant in words charged with negative content (the place of prominence belongs here to *Nov. Theod.* 3 against non-Catholics and *Nov. Valent.* 23 against those who transgress the inviolability of graves), but it is exactly their relative terseness that gives them an advantage. It enables one to demonstrate the original structure of the constitution more clearly and put forward a legitimate hypothesis as to which fragments thereof may have been omitted by the compilers of the Theodosian Code, and thus which particular invectives might have been lost in the codification process.

In the present chapter, I shall focus on analyzing the rhetorical content of the texts, giving only so much attention to their historical context and the contents of the disposition as necessary for our principal goal. In doing so, I will frequently refer to observations on the meanings of particular terms, which are elaborated in full only in the further chapters of the book. At this point, I must also ask the reader to excuse this unavoidable inconvenience arising from providing first a number of text-rich illustrative examples and only then detailed analyses of specific words contained therein.

C.Th. 1.16.7

Idem. A.*[1] *ad provinciales
Cessent *iam nunc* ***rapaces*** *officialium manus,* ***cessent****, inquam: nam nisi moniti* ***cessaverint****, gladiis praecidentur.* ***Non*** *sit venale iudicis velum,* ***non*** *ingressus redempti,* ***non*** *infame licitationibus secretarium,* ***non*** *visio ipsa praesidis cum pretio. Aeque aures iudicantis pauperrimis ac divitibus reserentur. Absit ab inducendo eius qui officii princeps dicitur* ***depraedatio****; nullas litigatoribus adiutores eorundem officii principum concussiones adhibeant; centurionum aliorumque officialium parva magnaque poscentium intolerandi* ***inpetus oblidantur*** *eorumque, qui iurgantibus acta restituunt, inexpleta* ***aviditas temperetur****. Semper invigilet industria praesidalis, ne quicquam a praedictis generibus hominum de litigatore sumatur. Qui si de civilibus causis quidquam putaverint esse poscendum, aderit armata censura, quae* ***nefariorum*** *capita cervicesque detruncet, data copia universis qui concussi fuerint, ut praesidum instruant notionem. Qui si dissimulaverint, super eodem conquerendi vocem omnibus aperimus apud comites provinciarum, aut apud praefectos praetorio, si magis fuerint in vicino, ut his referentibus edocti super talibus* ***latrociniis*** *supplicia proferamus.*

Dat. Kal Novemb. Constant(ino)p(oli) Basso et Ablavio Conss.[2]

The same Augustus to the Provincials
The rapacious hands of the apparitors shall immediately cease, they shall cease, I say; for if after due warning they do not cease, they shall be cut off by the sword. The chaber curtain of the judge shall not be venal; entrance shall not be gained by purchase, the private council chamber shall not be infamous on account of the bids. The appearance of the governor shall not be at a price; the ears of the judge shall be open equally to the poorest as well as to the rich. There shall be no despoiling on the occasion of escorting persons inside by the one who is called chief of the office staff. The assistants of the aforesaid chiefs of the office staff shall employ no exortion on litigants; the intolerable onslaught of the centurions and other apparitors who demand small and great sums shall be crushed; and the unsated greed of those

---

1 Constantine the Great.
2 November 1, 331.

who deliver the records of litigants shall be restrained. Always shall the diligence of the governor guard lest anything be taken from a litigant by the aforesaid classes of men. If they should suppose that anything ought to be demanded by them from those involved in civil cases, armed punishment will be at hand, which will cut off the heads and necks of the scoundrels. Opportunity shall be granted to all persons who have suffered exortion to provide for an investigation by the governers. If they should dissemble, we hereby open to all persons the right to express complaints about such conduct before the counts of the provinces or before the praetorian prefects, if they are closer at hand, so that We may be informed by their references to Us and may provide punishment for such brigandage.
Given on the kalends of November at Constantinople in the year of the consulship of Bassus at Ablabius.

(transl. Pharr 1952: 28)

Constantine's edict[3] concerns the curtailing of extortions perpetrated by the personnel of the *officium* (the office of provincial governor),[4] who had incurred payments from parties for allowing the latter to appear before the governor's court.[5] The offence was to be punished with an extremely severe penalty: decapitation and dismemberment;[6] in the case when, despite being notified of the complaint, the provincial governor failed to commence investigation, the aggrieved party is given an option to appeal to the higher instance with their complaint.

The language of invective, as present in the constitution, has two purposes here: accusing such officials and also showing the Emperor's revulsion at this punishable practice. The latter effect had been achieved through the use of anaphoric repetitions – beginning three successive sentences with *cesso*, and subsequently four sentences with *ne*. As Honig has noted, this is one

3 The address phrase *ad provinciales* indicates that the act is an edict.

4 The fundamental work on how this office had functioned is Palme 1999. In this case, one is concerned with the act in which the staff of the *officium*, along with the *princeps*, i.e., the head of that office, are directly criticized (Palme 1999: 108), whereas the governor himself is not.

5 Since the regular pay received by officials (*annona*) was not sufficient for covering maintenance costs, the practice of incurring payments for official services had developed (*sportulae*). As a matter of fact, Constantine had not abolished all the similar payments with this particular act, but only aimed to curtail any related abuses (cf. Karayannopoulos 1958: 176; Palme 1999: 113, contrary to Stein 1922: 19–21). More extensively on *sportulae*, cf. Stein 1922: 20–23; Karayannopoulos 1958: 168–177; Noethlichs 1981: 196–198; Jones 1986: 496–498; Schmidt-Hofner 2008a: 40–49.

6 On how this latter penalty was actually disseminated in the fourth century, see MacMullen 1986: 158–159.

of the Code's most striking cases of *deinosis* (expression of rejection).[7] The Emperor's revulsion is corroborated not only by the severity of the punishment, but also by the language stylized to resemble a passionate speech. It contains such verbs as *oblidare* – to quell, *temperare* – to subdue. Several times, the Emperor urges governors to exercise their caution and severity, and in the last sentence he presents himself as the one who shall administer dispensation of penalties should they neglect to do so.

The legislator endeavours to be consistent in referring to the practice carried on by such officials as robbery (*latrocinium*), which is also matched by the aforementioned harshness of the punishment. This particular method of building up an *incrementum* here is further attested by subsequent terms associated with robbery: *rapaces*, *depraedatio*, *latrocinium*, but also referring to officials' demands of payments with the term *impetus* (attack, raid), taken from the military parlance. They are also labelled as *nefarii*, which points, as we shall see, to a stronger condemnation of the crime attributed to them. The fault they are guided with is, of course, *aviditas* – greed; multiple suggestions to this effect can also be found in the second sentence, where the essence of their practice, i.e., demanding payments for allowing aggrieved parties in front of the provincial governor's court, is condemned four times.

C.Th. 6.4.22

[Idem AAA.]*[8] *ad Senatum

Ante X annos cuiuslibet editionis prae[to]rem nominari et intra quinque menses designatum iussimus commoneri, ut aut editurus praestet adsensum aut, si praeferet contrariam voluntatem, futuri examinis iudicium non moretur.

1. *Nam intra septem menses adcelerandae cognitionis terminus constitutus dilationis licentiam imperio fundatae definitionis excludit. Nec enim allegationibus cuiusquam ulla poterit esse reparatio per ignaviam, si silentii* ***pigrioris*** *definitum tempus fuerit evolutum, si posthabita taciturnitate serae voluerit merita defensionis ostendere.*
2. *Decem vero auri libras ab universo officio per singulas nominationes iubemus inferri, si designatus praetor intra quinque menses nulla fuerit admonitione conventus: ita ut cum praefecto urbi electi ex ordine candid[a]to cum allegationes suas praetor nominatus exp[o]nit, suscipiant officium, audirique singulis cupim[us] patienter, et, si*

---

7 Honig 1960: 48.

8 Valentinian I, Valens, and Gratian.

admittenda sunt quae dicuntur, ar[bi]trio iustitiae vindicari, sin vero inanis probatur a[dser]tio, ***inprobas*** *voces severioris sententiae auctor[ita]te conpesci. Disceptandi ergo moderatio cuncta co[n]ponat;* ***cesset*** *potentia ac similiter ambitionis patro[ci]-nium* ***repellatur****; nullum inique temporibus nostris [a] quoquam vel opprimi patimur vel defendi.*

3. *Quo[d si] quisquam iudicum haec praecepta transcenderi[t] vel* ***novae praesumptio-nis insania****, quae sunt san[c]tionibus consecrata,* ***violarit****, ut* ***hostis publicus*** *at[que]* ***expugnator utilitatis inventae*** *contra senat[us] consulta* ***inportuni furoris temeritate*** *congredi[etur], et arbitrio nostro et vestro iudicio notam perpe[trait] criminis sortietur; similis culpae insimulatione* ***[plect]endis****, qui cum eodem residentes propriae no[bilita] tis obliti adulantis gratiae* ***turpissimam*** *praet[exe]rint* ***vilitatem****. Nec sane fas erit huiuscemodi reis veniam relaxari, qui per patrocinia iudicum distrahentes et senatus* ***temptaverint infamare*** *collegium et* ***sub auctione vendiderint*** *ius Romanum.*
4. *Nominatores autem praetorum iudices esse non patimur, qui, dum arbitrium suum cupiunt adprobari,* ***insolentius*** *aliquid, quam moderatio patitur, sui contemplatione decernunt.*
5. *Si quem vero ex nominatis praetoribus pro huius auctoritate gravior condemnatio sauciaverit, ab editionis eum placet onere submoveri, duabus, videlicet existentibus causis, quod vel erogationi idoneus [es]se non valeat vel suscipere* ***qui culpam meruit non [d]ebeat dignitatem****. Cavendum est autem, ne sub hac per[m]issione concessa etiam illis, qui levi fuerint emen[d]atione correcti, huiusce patrocinii gratia deferatur, [c]um his utique tantum debeat provideri, quos gravissimi dispendii mole fatigatos subitum pondus obpressit. Quod si probabilis fuerit et iusta conquestio, relevatae necessitatis gratiam consequatur.*

Dat. V Id. [I]un. Val(entini)ano et Valente IIII AA. Conss.[9]

The same Augustuses to the Senate

We command that praetors shall be nominated ten years before they are to provide for any exhibition of games and that within five months the praetors designate shall be admonished that they must either give their consent to undertake the exhibition, or if they manifest a contrary desire, they shall not delay the trial of the future suit.

1. For the estabilished limit of seven months for the hastening of the trial excludes the license of a delay of the decision based on authority. For no person shall be able to renew his claims if through idle and indolent silence he should allow the estabilished period of time to elapse, and if afterward he should repent his silence and wish to demonstrate the merits of a defense that is too late.
2. We command that ten pounds of gold shall be paid by the entire office staff in the case of each nomination if the praetor designate should not be notified

[9] June 9, 373.

by any warning within five months. The matter shall be so conducted that men selected from the Senatorial order, along with the prefect of the City, shall undertake this duty when the praetor elect sets forth his allegations. It is our will that each man shall be patiently heard, and if his claims must be allowed, it is Our will that he shall be vindicated by a just decision; but if his defense if proved to be unfounded, it is our will that his shameless claims shall be repressed by the authority of a very severe sentence. Therefore, the regulations of the trial judge shall settle everything. The influence of powerful persons shall cease, and likewise protection of corrupt sollicitation shall be repelled. We allow no person to be unjaustly opressed or defended by anyone in Our times.

3. If any judge shall overstep these commands or by the madness of an unprecedented presumption should violate that which has been consecrated by Our sanctions, he shall be regarded as a public enemy and as a ravager of that which has been devised for the general good. Thus if he should act counter to the decrees of the Senate, by Our decision and by your judgment he shall receive the brand of the crime that he has perpetrated. Those Senators who sit on the case with the aforesaid prefect of the City shall be involved in the accusation of a similar offense, if they should forget their own nobility and cloak the most disgraeful baseness of their sycophantic favoritism. Nor indeed shall it be righteous for pardon to be granted to such guilty persons who, through the protection of the judges, become vendors and thus attempt to disgrace the body of the Senate and sell Roman law at auction.
4. Moreover, We do not allow the nominators of praetors to be their judges, for while such nominators strive to have their judgment as nominators approved, in consideration of themselves they make their decisions more arrogantly than a moderate judgment allows.
5. If indeed any of the nominated praetors should be injured by a crushing condemnation in accordance with the authority of this law, it is Our pleasure that he shall be exempted from the burden of the exhibition of games. There are, of course, two reasons for such exemption, both because he would not be wealthy enough to undertake the expense and because he ought not to receive this dignity after he has deserved this censure. Moreover, provision must be made lest under the pretext of this concession, the favor of such protection may be granted also to those nominees who have been punished with a light fine, since the aforementioned alleviation shall be provided, of course, only for those who had already been exhausted by the mass of very heavy expense when they were overwhelmed by the sudden burden of the fine. But if the complaint of any person should be justifable and lawful, he shall obtain the favor of relief from this necessity.

Given on the fifth day before the ides of June in the year of the consulship of Valentinian Augustus and the fourth consulship of Valens Augustus.

(transl. Pharr 1952: 125)

The constitution is one of the Code's few *orationes* to the Senate, which is why it could be reasonably expected that it would have been written with the use of the elevated style (*summum genus*).[10] It concerns the City praetor's duty to organize games for the public, which was his principal task in Late Antiquity.[11] In its fundamental content, it orders the exhorting and possible prosecuting of a *praetor* attempting to evade this obligation. In the resolution that concludes the text, a certain hesitation may be noticed: if the *praetor*, who is punished with a fine, fails to provide sufficient arguments for relieving him of this duty, he is released from it, nonetheless, if the burden of both the fine and the costs of games organization turns out to be excessive. The whole comes across as a text that was still considered while being written, with successive sentences added as the course of thought went on. In any case, it is worth noticing that in the exposition of the main subject there are few invectives, such as in charging the praetor with negligence for being tardy in stating his claims and in interpreting (which is objectively favourable to the guilty) that the one who has deserved to be punished does not deserve to hold the *praetor's dignitas*.

Many elements of the language of invective are present in a digression concerned with describing the function of the *ad hoc* tribunal, composed of the prefect of the City and some selected senators, entrusted with passing judgement on the legitimacy of the praetor's claims related to releasing him from the duty. Already in the second sentence, there is some doubt expressed as to whether the tribunal will be just in its decisions. "We allow no person

[10] For instance, referring to the Senate as *ordo candidatus* may be a sign of such refinement of style. On the title, cf. Schlinkert 1996: 70.

[11] In Late Antiquity, the City praetor (*praetor urbanus*) had almost lost all his previous judicial authority – he was only authorized to resolve questions connected with custody and personal liberty. Practically, the office offered no privileges, it was not a necessary intermediate step in obtaining positions of higher rank, whereas it entailed some burdensome duties: participating in costs of building projects at the capital and organizing public games. This particular duty (*cura ludorum*) had its origin in the reign of August, under Constantine it had already become so cumbersome that the senators balked at assuming the praetor's office. Thus it began to be treated as *munus*, not as *honor*. Marcian's and Valentinian III's act of 450 (*C.J.* 12.2.1; *C.J.* 1.39.2) even perceives the office as the holder's misfortune and stresses that it should not be assumed under duress. In case of the praetor's death, costs of games organization were to be covered by his daughter (*C.Th.* 6.4.17). The holding of this office was subject to some exemptions: appointments to the praetorian prefect and consul, as well as senators nominated from families other than the senatorial families of the City of Rome. The office was then transferred to Constantinople, where under Justinian it was replaced by the rank of *praefectus populo*, entrusted with police functions (Koch 1954: 1602–1604). On the position of praetorship in a senatorial career, *in extenso* in Chastagnol 1992: 267–276. On the importance attached by the Late Antique emperors to the praetor's duties related to organization of games, see Dagron 1974: 150–152; Kuhoff 1983: 20; Jones 1986: 537 ff.; Schmidt-Hofner 2008a: 330–336.

to be unjustly oppressed or defended by anyone in Our times," the Emperor writes. In the following sentence, he begins to express his indignation upon considering possible offences of the judge (most likely, he means the prefect of the City presiding over this court; *iudex* is an imperial official, while the senators also present as part of the same tribunal are mentioned in the next sentence). The abuses in question are connected with transgressing or violating the letter of the law (and it is precisely this law that may be concerned here; even though the *senatus consulta* are actually being mentioned, it is *oratio ad senatum*, as accepted by the Senate, which had corresponded in the Later Roman Empire to the former *senatus consulta*[12]). The motive for this sort of office abuse would be, as indicated in the further sentences, patronage (*patrocinium*), possibly in connection with bribery practices (*sub auctione vendiderint ius Romanum*).

Motives for the actions of the judge are castigated twice with the following three-word expressions: *novae praesumptionis insania* and *inportuni furoris temeritas*. Let us note that the content of the two phrases is similar. *Praesumptio* (in this case) signifies insolent presumption, *temeritas* – reckless bravery. In the Code's language of invective, both of these terms are strongly linked with the notion of *audacia*. Further on, *furor* and *insania* make reference to a peculiar notion of "madness," similar to *audacia*, which had originated in the language of political invective of the late Roman Republic. *Novus* and *importunus* both mean, in this case, "unusual," yet with a negative tone, while *importunus* – also "inconsiderate to others." As can be seen, there are two sequences of the mutually reinforced negative terms here; the presence of both within one and the same sentence forms an amplification figure of "accumulation" (*congeries*).

The judge guilty of the offence is defined in very harsh terms: as an *expugnator* of that which has been established for the benefit of the public good, and as *hostis publicus*. Already the nomen agentis *expugnator* is tinted with a negative connotation. As for *hostis publicus*, it is the only case in the constitutions when this particular appellation was used with reference to an official abusing his authority, not someone depicted as a rebel against the Imperial rule. It appears that we deal with a metaphor here, as it is indicated by the word *ut*, and also by the fact that ultimately the official is only to be branded with a crime label (the term *nota* is a synonym of infamy[13]); there is no mention of capital punishment, property confiscation, or proceedings proper for offenders guilty of *maiestas*. Comparing with a serious crime should be also regarded as a form of amplification.[14]

---

12 Liebs 1992: 15.

13 Cf. Heumann, Seckel 1914: 372; Wolf 2009: 60–61.

14 *Incrementum* rather than *comparatio*, as the latter would require recognizing the stigmatized offence as worse (cf. Lausberg 1960: 222–223), not only comparing it with a definite evil.

A number of invectives are also meted out against the senators guilty of complicity in the offence. *Nobilitas* of their lineage is contrasted with *turpissima vilitas* of their conduct, consisting in some vague wish to ingratiate themselves with either the unjust prefect or patrons of the accused *praetor*. With their conduct, they "shake up" and "betray" the Roman legal order, and also bring disgrace to the senatorial rank. In actual fact, as Dirk Schlinkert points out, this particular constitution displays a negative image, the opposite of what the senatorial class should be.[15]

The latter invective refers to a hypothetical case when the senator who had nominated a given *praetor* became a member of the tribunal. He would be potentially biased in his judgements, prone to "act in a way more insolent (*insolentius*) than good measure permits." The situation posing such a threat is recognized as unacceptable.

It is interesting to note that the constitution could certainly have done well without this stream of invective suddenly released by the legislator. All the directives pertaining to *meritum*, i.e., deciding on the *praetor*'s case, are written in the language that is balanced, though not neutral. One could mention, for instance, the allegation of negligence addressed against the *praetor* failing to submit his claims in due time or the decision relieving the *praetor* of his obligation to organize public games, as "the one who deserves to be punished, should not hold offices." But the hardest words in the text are those of the digression: the Emperor appoints judges of the tribunal, and then proceeds as if absorbed in his anger at the random thought of that court turning out to be corrupt or transgressing the provisions of this act. There are following evident reasons for the Emperor's indignation: disgrace to the Emperor's reign (*tempora nostra*), violations of both Imperial sanctions and *senatus consulta*, disgrace to the Senate caused by the conduct of its individual members, putting up the *ius Romanum* "for auction." The transgression of these fundamental values clearly justifies the harsh language of invective, but one could ask why the Emperor would have suddenly come up with the idea that the tribunal passing judgement on the case might prove to be venal. There is no doubt there may have arisen some suspicions of solidarity or illicit patronage among the members of the senatorial circles, which is in fact fairly directly indicated. Should one deal with such a constitution having been issued in the West, one could point to the tensions between the administration of the Emperor Valentinian I and the Senate (even though one agreed that the scale of those tensions tended to be considerably exaggerated by historians[16]). Still, while I would concur with Sebastian Schmidt-Hofner's view

---

15 Schlinkert 1996: 77, note 62.

16 For a critical evaluation of this fairly common academic view, cf. Lenski 2002: 220–223; Prostko-Prostyński 2008: 15–27. It is worth noting, following the latter author, that Ammianus Marcelli-

that the speech was addressed to the Senate of Constantinople,[17] It should be mentioned that the figure serving as the prefect of the City at that time, i.e., Clearchus, was among the Emperor Valens' most trusted officials.[18] It is thus not the figure of the official that may possibly explain the tough words directed at the judge.

Nevertheless, resorting to a historical fact seems to be unjustified in this particular case; the context of the constitution appears to be a more general one. As Jill Harries notes, one is confronted here with the Emperor's need to stress the strict control exercised over his officials, who are thus subjected to exaggerated criticism.[19] The need was revealed, as in this constitution, in the unexpected and apparently unnecessary critical remarks addressing the officials, who were purely hypothetically accused of negligence in performance of their duties and at the same time described in exceptionally harsh terms. This hypothetical corruption did not have to reflect the actual reality, as the primary goal was the Emperor's preventive demonstration of his authority that would not allow administration officials to get out of control.

C.Th. 9.16.5

Idem A.*[20] *ad populum. Post alia
Multi magicis artibus ***ausi*** *elementa* ***turbare*** *vitas insontium* ***labefactare*** *non dubitant et manibus accitis* ***audent*** *ventilare, ut quisque suos conficiat* ***malis*** *artibus inimicos. Hos, quoniam* ***naturae peregrini*** *sunt,* ***feralis pestis*** *absumat.*

Dat. Prid. Non. Decemb. Med[iolano] Constantio A VIIII et Iuliano Caes. II Conss.[21]

nus is silent about the City prefect's role in the then ongoing trials directed against, among others, members of the Roman senatorial aristocracy (Prostko-Prostyński 2008: 22) – if, as a result, the role of this official was indeed a lesser one, one could speculate on the Emperor's lack of confidence in a specific person: although the prefect's stance in April of 373 (Principius 1) is not known indeed (*PLRE* 1: 726), his successor, Fl. Eupraxius, while serving as quaestor, had opposed the cruelty of the Emperor Valentinian I (Amm. Marc. 27.6.14; 28.1.25, cf. *PLRE* 1: 299–300).

17 Until recently, the prevailing view among scholars had been that it was impossible to determine if the Senate in question was that of Rome or Constantinople; still, Schmidt-Hofner (2008b: 522) argues in favour of the latter option.

18 *PLRE* 1: 212.

19 Harries 1999b: 97.

20 Constantius II.

21 December 4, 356; redated 357 according to Constantius II's itinerary, cf. Pharr 1952: 238, note 23.

The same Augustus to the People

(After other matters.) Many persons who dare to disturb the elements by magic arts do not hesitate to jeopardize the lives of innocent persons and dare to torment them by summoning the spirits of the dead, so that everyone may destroy his enemies by evil arts. A deadly curse shall annihilate such persons, since they are foreign to nature.

Given on the day before the nones of December at Milan in the year of the ninth consulship of Constantius Augustus and the second consulship of Julian Ceasar.

(transl. Pharr 1952: 237–238)

The edict[22] of Constantius II against magic practices had been issued at the time of increasing suppression of sorcery and soothsaying during his reign. The concise text featured in the Theodosian Code was only a part of a larger constitution which had also comprised some other questions, as attested by the added phrase "post alia." The constitution appears as a classic example of the strictly legal text of the sanction being overwhelmed by rhetorical and ideological aspects. While the critical judgement applied to magic practices is relatively easy to discern in the text above, the penalty instituted for magicians is veiled behind a vague metaphor.

The principal difficulty in interpreting this metaphor is the ambiguity of the adjective *feralis*. It may be derived from *fera* ("wild beast") or *feralia* ("funeral"). Pharr's English translation suggests following the latter sense, rendering *feralis pestis* quite freely as "deadly curse." A translation closer to the original ("deadly plague") is assumed and at the same time ridiculed by Olivia Robinson, as it is rather not a conventional method of punishing offenders.[23] The phrase in question is interpreted differently by Fögen. The German scholar correctly notes that *feralis pestis* is in direct reference to *naturae peregrini*. Yet *natura*, in her opinion, does not stand here for the natural order but the human one (that is to say, implicitly, *natura humana*). The magicians stand in opposition to the human order, and for this reason their death should be "bestial" as well, i.e., according to Fögen, the punishment of being torn by wild animals.[24] Let us note here that Fögen's interpretation does not eliminate the element of metaphor. It only makes the metaphor more comprehensible.

[22] Due to the address *ad populum*.

[23] Robinson 2000: 773.

[24] Fögen 1993: 46–47.

This interesting interpretation, which takes up the explanation already proposed by Gothofredus in the sixteenth century,[25] seems to be in contrast with the idea evident in the background of the constitution. The magicians are defined here as those who dare (the notion of *audacia*) to disturb the elements, thus interfering with the cosmic order. Their practice, which is here explicitly condemned, consists in summoning spirits of the dead in order to harm the living. This harmful activity is defined by means of the verb *labefactare*, to which *pestis* may be a direct reference; both of them harbour a disaster arising in response to *contagium*. It appears that the entire description points here to a definitely fundamental disturbance of the natural order and a taint caused by the summoning of spirits of the dead. In my opinion, the interpretation of *feralis* as an adjective denoting funeral rites seems to be more appropriate, especially as it is also present elsewhere in the Code, where it refers to penalties.[26] In this case, it would just point to death penalty for those who play with death in such a terrifying manner.

C.Th. 9.38.6

***Imppp. Gr*[*ati*]*anus, Val*[*entini*]*anus et Theod*[*osius*] *AAA. ad Antidum V. C.* Vic[ari]um**
Paschalis laetitiae dies ne illa quidem gemere sinit ingenia, quae flagitia fecerunt; pateat insuetis horridus carcer aliquando luminibus. Alienum autem censemus ab indulgentia, qui ***nefariam*** *criminum conscientiam in maiestatem* ***superbe*** *animaverit, qui parricidali* ***furore*** *raptus sanguine proprio manum* ***tinxit****, qui cuiusque praeterea hominis* ***caede maculatus est****, qui genialis tori ac lectuli fuit* ***invasor*** *alieni, qui verecundiae virginalis raptor extitit, qui venerandum cognati sanguinis vinculum* ***profano caecus violavit*** *incestu, vel qui* ***noxiis*** *quaesita graminibus et* ***diris*** *inmurmurata secretis mentis et corporis venena conposuit, aut qui sacri oris* ***imitator*** *et divinorum vultuum* ***adpetitor*** *venerabiles formas sacrilegio eruditus inpressit. His ergo tali quoque sub absolutione damnatis indultum nostrae serenitatis eo praecepti fine concludimus, ut remissionem veniae crimina nisi semel commissa non habeant, ne in eos liberalitatis augustae referatur humanitas, qui inpunitatem veteris admissi* ***non emendationi potius quam consuetudini*** *deputarunt.*

Recitata XII Kal. Aug. Rom[*ae*] *Syagrio et Eucherio Conss.*[27]

---

[25] Fögen 1993: 47, note 63.

[26] See below.

[27] July 21, 381.

Emperors Gratian, Valentinian, and Theodosius Augustuses to the Most Noble Antidius, Vicar

The day of Easter joy permits not even those persons that have commited crimes to be afraid. The terrible prison shall at that time be open to the unaccustomed light. We decree, however, that any person shall be excluded from this grant of pardon who in his haughtiness has been incited against the Imperial Majesty by the nefarious consciousness of his own crimes; or who, seized by a parricidal madness, has stained his hands with the blood of his own kin; or who is defiled, moreover, by the killing of any man; or who has invaded the marriage bed or couch of another; or who has been a ravisher of virginal modesty; or who, in his blindness, has violated the revered bond of cognite blood by unholy incest; or who has compounded poisons for mind and body, poisons sought from noxious herbs and murmured over with incantations in dread secrecy; or the skilled worker, who, by copying the sacred imperial features and thus assailing the divine countenance, has sacrilegiously coined their venerable images. Furthermore, for those persons also who are condemned for crimes subject to such absolution We restrict the indulgence of Our Serenity by this limit of Our regulation, namely, that only those crimes shall receive the remission of pardon, which have been commited only once, in order that the kindness of Our august generosity may not be extended again to those persons who have used their impunity for an old crime, not for the purpose of reformation, but for the purpose of habitual criminality.
Read on the twelfth day before the kalends of August at Rome in the year of the consulship of Syagrius and Eucherius.

(transl. Pharr 1952: 253–254)

The Easter amnesty, which is typical for the late Imperial period,[28] comprises two different contents: an order to pardon offenders and a list of those who are excluded from the amnesty. It ordinarily includes perpetrators of the most serious crimes, the list of which is not finally determined.[29] The crimes which are usually featured under this category are: high treason (*maiestas*), sorcery and poisoning (*maleficium et veneficium*), murder (*homicidium*),

[28] *C.Th.* 9.38.3; 9.38.4; 9.38.6; 9.38.7; 9.38.8; *Const. Sirm.* 7; 8. Cf. Waldstein 1964: 188–195; Robinson 2001: 119–121; Di Berardino 2003: 133.

[29] In spite of the name *quinque crimina* (*C.Th.* 9.38.2, *Const. Sirm.* 7), the list is not a fixed one. It is even controversial what exactly the said “five crimes” refer to. Di Berardino (2003: 137–149) mentions the following: treason, violation of a grave, sorcery and poisoning, adultery, abduction of a woman; it is similarly interpreted by Robinson 2001: 118, but Waldstein (1964: 185, note 33) follows D. 48.20.3 Ulpian 33 *ad ed.* and offers the following list: treason, riots (*seditio*), killing of a close relative (*parricidium*), poisoning, and murder. In turn, the amnesty *C.Th.* 9.38.1 (likewise, *C.Th.* 11.36.7) mentions only the three most serious crimes: murder, adultery, sorcery and poisoning.

adultery (*adulterium*),[30] abduction of a woman (*raptus*),[31] counterfeit of coins (*adulteratio nummorum*),[32] violation of a grave (*violatio sepulchri*).[33] In this particular case, "violation of a grave" is not mentioned; apart from "murder" (*homicidium*), the crime of *parricidium*, i.e., the killing of a close relative, is condemned;[34] moreover, "incest" is added as a separate crime. In addition, which is specific to this amnesty, repeat offenders guilty of committing minor offences are also excluded.

The rhetoric of the amnesty constitution serves a two-sided purpose. On the one hand, it justifies the very order of amnesty, ordinarily pointing to contradiction between the joy of Easter and the sufferings of those who are imprisoned. On the other, it has to explain that certain categories of offenders are excluded from the benefit of the amnesty. It is exactly where the language of invective can find a fertile ground to thrive, as it is necessary to demonstrate the whole wickedness of the criminal deed with all due emphasis, which does not make it possible to pardon the offender for his guilt even at such a festive occasion. It is all the more difficult as the Emperor had just validated the amnesty by mentioning the necessity to rejoice on the day of Easter. Yet, in this case, it must be shown that the joy of a certain category of condemned criminals would be in contradiction with this great joy. In consequence, amnesty laws are rare examples of elaborate invective used to stigmatize typical, serious crimes. Apparently, only at this particular occasion it was deemed as necessary to justify the wickedness of monetary counterfeit or murder. In addition, due to the structure of the constitution, the invective, which forms part of the verdict justification, has become an element of the disposition that would be extremely difficult to find a substitute for, as in all the cases in question the description of the villainy of a given crime turns out to be an extension of its name. For that reason, several instances of such invective can be found in the Codes.

In the constitution cited above, the invective is focused on the most grievous offences. Acting against the *maiestas* of the Imperial authority is described with epithets such as *superbus* ("haughty") and *nefarius* ("wicked" – an amplification of the notion of a crime). The crimes involving bloodshed are depicted with expressions related to "contagion" (*contagium*): *sanguine proprio manum tinxit*; *hominis caede maculatus est*; furthermore, *parricidium* (patricide – stands for

---

30 *C.Th.* 9.38.3; 9.38.4; 9.38.7; *Const. Sirm.* 8. In *Const. Sirm.* 8, astrology is also added to sorcery and poisoning.

31 *C.Th.* 9.38.3; 9.38.4; 9.38.7.

32 *C.Th.* 9.38.7; *Const. Sirm.* 8.

33 *C.Th.* 9.38.3; 9.38.7; *Const. Sirm.* 8.

34 On the meaning of *parricidium* in Roman law, cf. Jońca 2008: 76 ff.

the killing of a close relative) is defined as "madness" (*furor*). In turn, *adulterium* is represented as an "incursion" (*invasio*) on another person's woman.

A similar logic is applied to charging an incestuous person with the *profanatio* of a sanctity (which is here, of course, bonds of kinship blood) and with a crime of violence – *violatio*. The adjective *caecus* does not mean that someone guilty of incest was unaware of his own deed, but he committed the act "blinded" to the evil, which again points to the state of *furor*, i.e., *mente caecitas* (*Nov. Theod.* 3). A counterfeiter is depicted as someone transgressing against the countenance (*adpetitor*) of the emperor. *Invasor, imitator, adpetitor* – providing a number of *nomina agentis* is another method of toughening the language. Finally, the practices of sorcerers-poisoners are described as gathering "noxious" (*noxii*) herbs and chanting malign (*dires*) incantations – references are being made here to ancient ideas related to evil and the underworld.

Compared with the stern statements mentioned above, the invective aimed against repeat offenders appears to be even lenient; it is also of quite an ironic character: instead of taking the chance of the Emperor's good grace to rehabilitate themselves, they use it to make a life of crime their custom. Let us note that here as well the invective was practically irremovable, as it was used to describe the thing itself, i.e., it referred to the practice of reoffending in descriptive terms. It confirms the aforementioned rule that in the case of the amnesty constitution, it was the composition of the statement that had enforced the preservation of the invective as part of the text transferred into the Code.

C.Th. 9.40.17

Idem AA.*[35] *Aureliano P[raefecto] P[retori]o

Omnes res Eutropi, qui quondam praepositus sacri cubiculi fuit, aerarii nostri calculis adiunximus, erepto splendore eius et consulatu a ***taetra inluvie*** *et a commemoratione nominis eius et* ***caenosis sordibus*** *vindicato, ut eiusdem universis actibus antiquatis omnia mutescant tempora nec eius enumeratione* ***saeculi nostri labes*** *appareat nec ingemiscant aut qui sua virtute ac vulneribus Romanos fines propagant vel qui eosdem servandi iuris aequitate custodiunt, quod divinum praemium consulatus* ***lutulentum prodigium contagione foedavit****. Patriciatus etiam dignitate atque omnibus inferioribus spoliatum se esse cognoscat, quas* ***morum polluit scaevitate****. Omnes statuas, omnia simulacra, tam ex aere quam ex marmore seu ex fucis quam ex quacumque materia*

[35] Arcadius and Honorius.

quae apta est effigendis, ab omnibus civitatibus oppidis locisque privatis ac publicis praecipimus aboleri, ne tamquam ***nota nostri saeculi obtutus polluat intuentum****. Adhibitis itaque fidis custodibus ad Cyprum insulam perducatur, in qua tua sublimitas relegatum esse cognoscat, ut ibidem pervigili cura vallatus nequeat* ***suarum cogitationum rabie*** *cuncta* ***miscere****.*

Dat. XVI Kal. Feb. Constantinop[oli] Theodoro V.C. Cons.[36]

The same Augustuses to Aurelianus, Praetorian Prefect
All the property of Eutropius, who was once grand chamberlain, We have annexed to the account of Our treasury; he shall be stripped of his splendor, and his consulship shall be vindicated from the foul stain and from the memory of his name and from his low meanness. All his acts shall be annuled, that all ages may be mute about him, that a blot may not appear on Our age through the recital of his deeds, and that neither those men who by their courage and their wounds extend the Roman boundaries nor those who guard these territories by preserving the equity of the law may lament the fact that this vile monster defiled the divine gift of the consulship by his contagion. He shall know that he has been despoiled also of the dignity of the patriciate and of all the lesser dignities which he has polluted by the perversity of his morals. All his statues, all his images, in bronze as well as in marble, in pigments, or in whatever material is suitable for portraiture, We order to be destroyed in all cities and towns, both in private and public places, in order that the stigma of our age, so to speak, may not pollute the sight of those who look at such images. And so, in the custody of faithful guards, he shall be conducted to the island of Cyprus, to which Your Sublimity shall know that he has been relegated, there surrounded by vigilant guards, he shall not be able to throw all things into confusion by the madness of his own designs.
Given on the sixteenth day before the kalends of February at Constantinople, in the year of the consulship of the Most Noble Theodorus.

(transl. Pharr 1952: 257–258)

The constitution was issued after the deposition of Eutropius, grand chamberlain of the Sacred Bedchamber (*praepositus sacri cubliculi*), who had been practically in charge of Constantinople's politics for several years. The circumstances of his downfall are not the subject of this study; suffice it here to mention that soon after he had been stripped of his property and office, and exiled to Cyprus, he was finally sentenced to death. This particular constitution, nonetheless, records the situation still prior to that verdict.[37] It was

36 August 17, 399; the date of issue was shifted from January to August due to the period of Eutychians' prefecture – cf. Pharr 1952: 258, note 29.

37 Demandt 1989a: 158; Dewar 1990; Scholten 1995: 223–226; Schlinkert 1996: 266–270.

inserted by the compilers of the Code in the chapter entitled "On Penalties"; as a result, it treats the reprisals against Eutropius as an example of the verdict punishing the offender.

The reprisals in question are described clearly as: confiscation of property, divesting of consulship, patrician rank, as well as of all other honours, destruction of the former chamberlain's statues and images, and, finally, sending him off under guard to Cyprus. If this constitution had aroused some criticism on account of its language, it was not because that language was unclear. The reprisals are accompanied here with an equally harsh verbal attack unleashed on the former chamberlain, and it is this particular attack that used to be the object of criticism.[38]

The rhetoric of the constitution, levelled against the chamberlain, is not only harsh but also very specific. In no other constitution of the period, perhaps except for Valentinian III's constitution against "The Violators of Tombs" (*Nov. Valent.* 23) is the notion of *contagium* so diversely elaborated. One by one, successive expressions obviously amplify the relevant content, and here once again the case in point is an "accumulation" (*congeries*). Eutropius was to defile his consulship with *taetra inluvies* ("foul stain"), *caenosis sordibus* ("low meanness"); this consulship is described as *labes nostri saeculi* ("a blot [or perhaps "a calamity"] on Our age"), while he is himself labelled as *lutulentum prodigium* ("vile monster"), who had "defiled ... by his contagion" (*contagione foedavit*) the Emperor's gift of consulship. Eutropius had also "polluted" (*polluit*) his other dignities with *morum scaevitate* ("perversity of his morals" [or better "of his habits"]). The statues of the chamberlain are "the stigma of Our age" (*nota nostri saeculi*) that "so to speak, may not pollute the sight of those who look at such images" (*tamquam obtutus intuentum polluit*). The apprehension that Eutropius might "throw all things into confusion" (*cuncta miscere*) in his exile also fits in with the rhetoric of "pollution" – it refers, of course, to turmoil in the affairs of the state, as "confusion" is indeed the very essence of *contagium* as well.

Let us find out what this *contagium* might be in this case. Eutropius does not perform magic practices or desecrate graves, which would bring in some real *contagium* into the world; on the face of it, it is also difficult to speak of any sexual impurity. The accused chamberlain is also far from any breach of orthodoxy, also associated with the notion of "contagion." It may be argued that the formulation of this charge was strongly influenced by the aversion that the contemporaries would have felt towards eunuchs.[39] Nonetheless, it does not obviate the need to explain why this revulsion had taken on such a form. Let us take a closer look,

[38] See Chapter II: 50–51.

[39] Scholten 1995: 186–191.

then, what (according to the text of this constitution) becomes "polluted" and how it is done. The Emperor points out twice that the very holding of the consul's office by Eutropius constitutes "a calamity" and "a stigma" (*labes*, *nota*) of "our age" (*saeculum nostrum*). There is no doubt that the Emperor is also guided by the solicitude for the good name of his reign. But the honour of the consular office comes to the fore. The company of Eutropius was to be the reason for complaints by those who had been justly honoured with that highest distinction: persons who owed it to their valour and the wounds suffered in the name of patriotic sacrifice, or the solicitude for the justice being done. Obviously, Eutropius cannot be credited with the former or, apparently, the latter merits as well. It is evident, then, that the Emperor's rhetoric is meant to contrast, on the one hand, the unworthy figure of the chamberlain and his perverse demeanour in execution of his office and, on the other, the highest dignity that a Roman may hold. It is exactly the presence of Eutropius on the consuls list that turns out to be this metaphorical "pollution," variously mentioned in the text. It can be only nullified through a total obliteration of the memory of this unfortunate consulship, including destruction of any statues and other images of the consul.[40] One of the sentences also mentions his patrician rank and some other minor titles that had been disgraced as well.[41]

In order to understand the sense of the *contagium* caused by the incriminated eunuch's consulship, let us have a look at the invective used by Claudian against Eutropius. The monstrosity ascribed to the chamberlain is the fact of his reaching for the consul's rank; the eunuch's accession to this office is seen as something worse than if a woman served as consul.[42] Such an event may be understood as an impermissible combination of the two things considered as opposite: the place reserved for the best and most deserving of men is occupied by someone inferior to a woman.

The invective in this particular text also serves the purpose of stressing how much value is attached to consulship and other offices. This is the reason why Eutropius is reviled in such terms. In the final sentence, the Emperor warns that without proper custody, even deprived of his dignities and exiled, Eutropius might still be able to interfere with state affairs. At the same time,

40 For more on this provision, see Rollin 1979: 169.

41 Granting the consulship to Eutropius had already incited a great deal of uproar before. In the West, he was not recognized at all. Scholars perceive this event as the last drop which had overfilled the influential eunuch's cup of guilt (Schlinkert 1996: 268 with references to the earlier literature). Claudian highlights the fact of the eunuch's fall exactly upon the moment of his greatest elevation, cf. Dewar 1990: 583.

42 Claud., *In Eut.* I.320–321, cf. Cameron 1970: 126; Garambois-Vasquez 2007: 219. Cf. also Long 1996: 121–134.

an extremely harsh term is used – *rabies*; it refers, of course, to an extreme case of madness (*furor*), even though found very seldom across literature, and in the text of the Code only once, this accusation takes on such a drastic form, which goes so far as to associate *furor* with an animal disease, i.e., rabies.

Let us notice that there are also some other invectives appearing just once in the same material. Although *contagium*, *polluere*, *foedare*, *sordes* are regularly used in metaphorical expressions related to the notion of "pollution," the terms such as *lutulentus*, *taetrus*, *inluvies* are employed exclusively in the text cited above. This attests to a considerable originality of the language of this constitution, which cannot be explained by the originality of the writing style used by the quaestor.[43] It can be explained by the fact that this is the unique preserved example of a specific person being castigated in the Code. This type of content was more characteristic of *praefationes*, but here it turned out to be so much embedded within the text of the disposition that it proved impossible to be separated. The injunction to divest Eutropius of his consulship would have had to be substantially changed, had it been stripped of its justification elements. This is an exceptional case. By analogy, it may be assumed that in the two constitutions on resolving certain issues in the Western Empire, after the usurper Eugenius' downfall, where some individual words also suggest the notion of *contagium* connected with the offices held under the "tyrant's" reign,[44] this metaphor could have been a prevailing one in its now lost *praefationes*.

C.Th. 12.1.85

> ***Idem AAA.***[45] ***Eutropio P[raefecto] P[retori]o***
> *Omnes iudices provinciarumque rectores a* ***consuetudine temerariae usurpationis*** *abstineant sciantque neminem omnino principalium aut decurionum sub qualibet culpae aut erroris offensa plumbatarum cruciatibus esse subdendum. Quod si quis*

---

43 According to Honoré (1998: 81–92), the then-current quaestor, incidentally a long-standing associate of Eutropius, was primarily a well-educated jurist; in the laws from the period of the hypothetical quaestorship of the latter man, Honoré finds much evidence for his "juristic" thinking, whereas there is no proof of the style's rhetorical refinement.

44 *C.Th.* 15.14.11: *...qui tyrannici tempore militavit vel etiam qualibet administratione donatus est aut honoraria dignitate perfunctus vel quicumque in aliquo honore diversis locis aut exactionibus praefuerunt, notam infamiae sustineant, aut deformi vocabulo polluantur*; *C.Th.* 15.14.12: *His, quos tyrannici temporis labes specie dignitatis infecerat, inustae maculae omnem abolemus infamiam.*

45 Gratian, Valentinian, and Theodosius.

forte iudicum in hanc ***pertinaciam inliciti furoris*** *eruperit, quod* ***audeat*** *principalem ac decurionem et suae, si sic dici oportet, curiae senatorem plumbatarum ictibus subduere, XX librarum auri inlatione multatus et perpetua infamia inustus ne speciali quidem rescribto notam eluere mereatur; et officia quinquaginta librarum auri multam fisco nostro cogetur inferre, quoniam, ut* ***pertinaciae*** *iudicis resistat, liberam eidem contradicendi permittimus facultatem.*

Dat. XII Kal. Aug. Heracleae Eucherio et Syagrio Conss.[46]

The same Augustuses to Eutropius, Praetorian Praefect

All judges and governors of provinces shall refrain from the custom of lawless usurpation, and they shall know that no chief decurion and no decurion at all shall be subjected to the tortures of lashes with lead tips, under any accusation of crime or wrongdoing whatsoever. But if perchance any judge should burst forth into such obstinate and illicit fury that he dares to subject the blows of lashes tipped with lead a chief decurion or a decurion and a senator of his own municipal council, if it may be so called, such judge shall be fined by the payment of twenty pounds of gold, and he shall be branded with perpetual infamy, so that not even by a special imperial rescript shall he obtain permission to remove this blot. His office staff also shall be compelled to pay Our fisc a fine of fifty pounds of gold, since We grant to the aforesaid office staff full opportunity to oppose the judge, so that they may withstand his pertinacity.

Given on the twelfth day before the kalends of August at Heraclea in the year of the consulship of Eucherius and Syagrius.

(Pharr 1952: 355)

The constitution prohibits Imperial officials from subjecting decurions to a certain form of torture,[47] i.e., carrying out a whipping by means of a whip fitted with leaden attachments (*plumbata*).[48] This procedure is called *consuetudo temerariae usurpationis*, while in the following sentence *pertinacia inliciti furoris. Consuetudo* suggests that the practice in question was unlawful, yet widespread;[49] *pertinacia* points to the obstinacy of those judges who would continue to apply it in contravention of the explicit prohibition. The illegal nature of the practice is indicated by the noun *usurpatio* in the first phrase, and the adjective *illicitus* in the other one. But the strongest terms are

---

46 July 21, 381.

47 Decurions, as well as senators, could not be subjected to torture and corporal punishment (except for torture during interrogations in trials on cases of *maiestas* and sorcery practices). For the decurions' privileged position, see Garnsey 1970: 242–245.

48 Cf. Kołodko 2006: 139–142.

49 Honig 1960: 137–144.

mutually related: *temeritas* (here, expressed by the adjective *temerarius*) and *furor*. Once again, then, this is an instance of the terms *furor* and *audacia* appearing in the text together (emphasized by the verb *audeo*). An official guilty of this abuse of authority is punished with severity: infamy (that is, depriving of his official *dignitas*) and a fine of 20 pounds of gold; in addition, a fine of 50 pounds of gold is levied on his *officium*. It is because, in this case, the members of the *officium* have got the possibility, but also the duty, to oppose the obduracy (*pertinacia*) of their superior.[50]

C.Th. 16.5.6

Idem AAA.[51] ***Eutropio P[raefecto] P[retori]o***

Nullus haereticis mysteriorum locus, nulla ad exercendam ***animi obstinatioris dementiam*** *pateat occasio. Sciant omnes etiam si quid speciali quolibet rescripto* ***per fraudem elicito*** *ab* ***huiusmodi hominum genere*** *impetratum est, non valere.*

1. *Arceantur cunctorum haereticorum ab* ***inlicitis congregationibus turbae****. Unius et summi dei nomen ubique celebretur; Nicaenae fidei dudum a maioribus traditae et divinae religionis testimonio atque adsertione firmatae observantia semper mansura teneatur;* ***Fotinianae labis contaminatio, Arriani sacrilegii venenum, Eunomianae perfidiae crimen*** *et* ***nefanda monstruosis nominibus auctorum prodigia sectarum*** *ab ipso etiam* ***aboleantur*** *auditu.*
2. *Is autem Nicaenae adsertor fidei, catholicae religionis verus cultor accipendus est, qui omnipotentem deum et Christum filium dei uno nomine confitetur, deum de deo, lumen ex lumine: qui spiritum sanctum, quem ex summo rerum parente speramus et accipimus, negando non* ***violat****: apud quem intemeratae fidei sensu viget incorruptae trinitatis indivisa substantia, quae Graeci adsertione verbi οὐσία recte credentibus dicitur. Haec profecto nobis magis probata, haec veneranda sunt.*
3. *Qui vero isdem non inserviunt, desinant* ***adfectatis dolis alienum verae religionis nomen*** *adsumere et* ***suis apertis criminibus*** *denotentur. Ab omnium submoti ecclesiarum limine penitus* ***arceantur****, cum omnes haereticos* ***inlicitas*** *agere intra oppida congregationes* ***vetemus*** *ac, si quid* ***eruptio factiosa temptaverit****, ab ipsis etiam*

---

[50] Such a double punishment for the judge and his *officium* is a peculiar phenomenon, present in some of the laws of the period since Constantine's reign (Noethlichs 1981: 223–225; Rosen 1990). Its origin and the idea behind it is clarified, in the fullest, by Rosen, who notes, that we do not know of any instance of applying this penalty in practice (1990: 287) and its subsequent disappearance over the fifth and sixth centuries attests to its inefficiency (Rosen 1990: 291–292).

[51] Gratian, Valentinian II, and Theodosius I.

urbium moenibus ***exterminato furore propelli*** *iubeamus, ut cunctis orthodoxis episcopis, qui Nicaenam fidem tenent, catholicae ecclesiae toto orbe reddantur.*

Dat. IIII id. Ian. Const(antino)p(o)li Eucherio et Syagrio Conss.[52]

The same Augustuses to Eutropius, Praetorian Praefect

No place for celebrating their mysteries, no opporunity for exercising the madness of their excessively obstinate minds shall be available to the heretics. All men shall know also that even if some concession has been impetrated by that kind of men through any special rescript whatever, if it has been fraudulently elicited, it shall not be valid.

1. Crowds shall be kept away from the unlawful congregations of all the heretics. The name of the One and Supreme God shall be celebrated everywhere; the observance, destined to remain forever, of the Nicene faith, as transmitted long ago by Our ancestors and confirmed by the declaration and testimony of divine religion, shall be maintained. The contamination of Photinian pestilence, the poison of Arrian sacrilege, the crime of Eunomian perfidy, and the sectarian monstrosities, abominable because of the ill-omened names of their authors, shall be abolished even from the hearing of men.
2. On the other hand, that man shall be accepted as a defender of the Nicene faith and as a true adherent of the Catholic religion who confess that Almighty God and Christ the Son of God are One in name, God of God, Light of Light, who does not violate by the denial the Holy Spirit which we hope for and receive from the Supreme Author of things; that man who esteems, with the perception of inviolate faith, the undivided substance of the incorrupt Trinity, that substance which those of the orthodox faith call, employing a Greek word, *ousia*. The latter beliefs are surely more acceptable to Us and must be venerated.
3. Those persons, however, who are not devoted to the aforesaid doctrines shall cease to assume, with studied deceit, the alien name of true religion, and they shall be branded upon the disclosure of their crimes. They shall be removed and completely barred from the threshhold of all churches, since We forbid all heretics to hold unlawful assemblies within the towns. If factions should attempt to do anything, We order that their madness shall be banished and that they shall be driven away from the very walls of the cities, in order that the Catholic churches throughout the whole world may be restored to all orthodox bishops who hold the Nicene faith.

Given on the fourth day before the ides of January at Constantinople in the year of the consulship of Eucherius and Syagrius.

(transl. Pharr 1952: 451)

[52] January 10, 381.

This is one of the most significant constitutions in the history of anti-heretical struggles, promulgated by Theodosius I shortly before the commencement of the Council of Constantinople.[53] The constitution points to the true faith, by citing the content of the *Credo*, not (as practicised until then) the names of the orthodox bishops. It also makes specific what sort of repression should be applied against those Christians who do not profess the aforementioned faith, that is, heretics. It is, first of all, the ban on any gatherings (religious services) in the cities; the guilty of the breach of this prohibition (most probably, referring to all community members) may be banished outside the city walls. It is quite possible that the text of the constitution may have been influenced by the bishop Gregory of Nazianzus or Meletius of Antioch.[54]

The invective used in the constitution is directed against heretics; on the one hand, it is meant to reinforce the tone of the prohibition, while, on the other, it also underscores the Emperor's involvement in favour of the Nicene faith, i.e., against heresy. It is already in the first sentence that the obduracy of heretics is explicitly denounced. In the following one, they are scornfully called *huiusmodi hominum genus*;[55] it is suggested that if there exists any rescript in their favour, it had been obtained by deceit. On this occasion, the Emperor is also afforded the opportunity to apply, in practice, the maxim *contra ius resripta non valeant*.[56] Next, the word *turba* appears in the text; it may carry a contemptuous tone ("rabble"), denoting all heretics that are to be prevented from taking part in public meetings.

The Emperor shows his strongest outrage in the sentence which has otherwise a very practical purpose: to indicate the castigated heresies by name. It mentions Photinians,[57] Arians,[58] and Eunomians.[59] Of these three groups, the first is called *labis contaminatio* – thus, by reference to the pat-

---

53 Ritter 1965: 35.

54 Di Mauro Todini 1990: 152–153.

55 The scorn is indicated by the pronoun *huiusmodi*, as well as the use of a descriptive expression.

56 See above.

57 The followers of the teachings of bishop Photinus of Sirmium, who had combined Sabelian (denying the real distinctness of Divine Persons) and Adoptionist views (Jesus Christ ultimately elevated to Son of God); initially, they were only tolerated by the adherents of the Nicene Creed in the West, whereas in the East already regarded as heretics for a long time. Cf. Simonetti 1975: 203–206; Kelly 1988: 184 (these are also fundamental studies on the theological controversies of the fourth century).

58 The followers of the thesis that the Son of God is only "similar" (*homoios*) to the Father, not "consubstantial" (*homoousios*). Until as late as 378, they had been a group supported by the authorities of the Eastern part of the Empire. A fundamental book on the history of this ecclessiastical faction: Brennecke 1988.

59 The followers of the thesis that the Son of God is "dissimilar" (*anomoios*) to the Father; already persecuted as heretics in Valens' reign. Principal studies: Kopecek 1979, Vaggione 2000.

tern of the guilt of *contagium* and the plague it caused. In turn, the Arians are *sacrilegii venenum*. The usage of the word "venom" is an invective very rarely used in the Imperial constitutions; here, it may be attributed to the influence of the bishops (the Christian writers used to compare heretics to venomous snakes).[60] On the other hand, the term *sacrilegium* points to the actuality of the offence against faith. A similar meaning will be also carried by the *perfidiae crimen* – "crime of perfidiousness."

The Emperor does not mention these three heresies only; in a peculiar way, he also adds the phrase "and all others," in reference to the previous three parallel formulas. These heresies are charged with "monstrous wickedness"; once again, the adjective *nefandus* points to a crime (this time with an inherent religious overtone), while *prodigium* – to a dehumanizing monstrosity. Another similar invective is levelled at the names of the founders of these unnamed sects which should be never even heard of anymore. The phrase "perverse names of the founders" reaches back to the previously mentioned heresies named after Photinus, Arius, and Eunomius.

The theological content of this constitution is very interesting. The name of the Macedonian heresy is not mentioned, the closest to the followers of *homoousios*, but differing from the latter in, among others, the lack of faith in the Holy Spirit's being equal with the Father and the Son. Yet their heresy is mentioned, though not explicitly: only those are orthodox who do not "violate" (*violat*) the Third Person of the Trinity by denying it. Supposedly, such an enigmatic statement is deliberate; the Macedonians' false teachings, rejecting the recognition of the Holy Spirit's equality with the Father and the Son, were thus condemned, but they were nevertheless given a chance to rejoin the Church.[61]

In the further sentences, the Emperor returns to the invective against heretics. The thought that they lay traps to lure people, by assuming the name which is alien to the true religion, is vague,[62] yet the conclusion is clear: from now on, they are to be stigmatized with the names of their offences, i.e., the names of heresies. A superfluous repetition that it is forbidden (*veto*) to hold illicit (*inlicitae*) gatherings can be considered as an elementary figure of accumulation (*congeries*). Another "accumulation" can also be discerned in the presence of a multitude of the words calling for "rejecting" heresies: *aboleor, arceor, exterminare, propellere.*

---

60 See Chapter VI: 173–174.

61 Cf. King 1961: 43. Let us note that among the participants at the Council of Constantinople there had been initially present a group of 36 "Macedonian" bishops (Socr., *HE* V.8.5).

62 Cf. Pharr 1952: 451.

The invective also reaches its peak in the following conditional clause: *si quid eruptio factiosa temptaverit*. There is a clear reference here to the language of the political criticism of the Republican period: calling the heresy descriptively *eruptio factiosa*,[63] or an allusion to *audacia* through the verb *temptare*.[64] The response is just as tough: to exterminate *furor*, "madness" of heretics, the expression which is stronger than *dementia* at the constitution's beginning.

C.Th. 16.5.24

Idem AAA.*[65] *Rufino P[raefecto] P[retori]o
Haereticorum ***dementia*** *nec ulterius* ***conetur*** *perpetrare quae reppererit nec inlicita habere concilia, nusquam* ***profana*** *praecepta vel docere vel discere:* ***ne antistes eorundem audeant fidem insinuare, quam non habent, et ministros creare, quod non sunt****, ne per coniventiam iudicantum omniumque, quibus per constitutiones paternas super hoc cura mandata est, eiusmodi* ***audacia*** *neglegatur et crescat.*
Dat. VII Id. Iul. Const[antino]p[oli] Arcad[io] III et Honorio II AA. Conss.[66]

The same Augustuses to Rufinus, Praetorian Prefect
The madness of heretics shall not attempt further to perpetrate the criminality which they have devised nor to hold unlawful councils. Nowhere shall they attempt to teach or learn their profane doctrine; their bishops shall not dare to teach a faith which they do not have and to create ministers who are not ministers. Such audacity shall not be neglected nor increase through the connivance of judges or of any person to whom the care of this matter was entrusted through the constitutions of Our father. Given on the seventh day before the ides of July at Constantinople in the year of the third consulship of Arcadius Augustus and the second consulship of Honorius Augustus.
(transl. Pharr 1952: 454)

The constitution deals with a religious issue, namely the prohibitions on gatherings and consecrating priests by heretics. The subject of the first sentence is *dementia haereticorum*, "madness of heretics" (*furor* and *dementia* are synonyms in this case). In this particular sentence, the "madness of heretics" stands for heretical communities, which the consecutive prohibition refers to. It appears

63 Hellegouarc'h 1963: 100–109.
64 Cf. Chapter VI: 153–154.
65 Theodosius I, Arcadius, and Honorius.
66 July 9, 394.

jointly with an allegation of *audacia*, already implicit in the verb *conor*. Heretical communities are forbidden to hold gatherings to teach their views, as one may infer from the previous words, and ordain priests. The principles of their teachings are defined as *profanae* – blasphemous, or at least profane. At the same time, there is a certain paradox formulated here: heretical bishops do not have the faith, yet they attempt to teach it; they are not clergymen, yet they attempt to ordain priests. All this activity is called *audacia*, but in a very interesting context. Notably, dissemination of heresy and violations of paternal contitutions[67] are possible because officials (judges) and some other unidentified persons (most probably decurions) responsible for the enforcement of "paternal" constitutions against heretics turn a blind eye to the threat.[68] It can be seen that the "increasing" impudence of the heretics, i.e., transgressing against the established laws, is the direct result of the failure of those who were entrusted with law enforcement duties. As a result, the criticism aimed at heretics is accompanied here by the background criticism of the apparatus of state authority – which is guilty of negligence, not abuse of power.

Nov. Theod. 15.2

> ***Idem AA.***[69] ***Zoilo P[raefecto] P[retori]o***
>
> *Non esset huius promulgandae necessitas sanctionis, si* ***inproborum temeritas*** *aut metu legum aut pudoris imperio frenaretur. Sed quoniam utrumque despexit* ***audacia,*** *nostrarum statim debet provideri remediis sanctionum, ne ultra* ***serpat*** *iniuria.*
>
> 1. *Quantum igitur magnitudinis tuae suggestio patefecit, Valerianus Emisenae civitatis curialis, iuris publici legumque* ***grassator,*** *ob hoc sibi inlustris cingulum honoris inmerito per subreptionem adsumpsit, ut illius subnixus infulis dignitatis contumeliosum sui posset amplificare propositum. Magna enim stipatus* ***barbarorum caterva*** *secretarium provinciae moderatoris* ***inrupit,*** *priorem sibi locum* ***ausus est*** *vindicare, dexter adsedit ei, cui iura commisimus, cui fata provincialium duximus*

67 The constitution was issued in Constantinople at the time of Theodosius I's absence. For this reason, it was probably to his constitution that Arcadius, residing at the capital, had referred. Perhaps, the constitution's tough words directed at officials are a response to a certain mitigation of the anti-heretical policy, which may have ensued after Theodosius' departure to the West (Noethlichs 1971: 159).

68 The Emperor Arcadius may have referred, at this point, to his father's laws, despite the fact that the latter was still alive; or, perhaps, this may be a general reference to the laws of the earlier emperors.

69 Theodosius II and Valentinian III.

esse credenda, ita ut omnes eius fugaret officium, ***vasta omnia ac sola relinqueret****. Qui* ***non magis opibus dives quam sceleribus plenus****, aliis quoque curialibus domi suae susceptis, ut publica ratio fraudaretur, servile praesidium exactoribus contra publicam obposuit disciplinam, quo magnum dispendium nostrae serenitatis aerarium per eius pateretur* ***vesaniam****. In quem oportuerat acerbioribus legum aculeis vindicari, nisi nos mansuetudo, quae adsolet, temperaret et ad suam consuetudinem lenitatemque redigeret. Quapropter eum et cingulo et dignitate simul inlustri privari hac generali sanctione decernimus et curiae redditum per se aut substitutam personam, si ita v[iro] c[larissimo] moderatori et curialibus visum fuerit, suarum periculo facultatum omnibus curiae fungi muneribus, iudicariis ad similitudinem ceterorum sententiis pariturum.*

2. *Verum quia principale remedium generale esse oportet, ceteros quoque civitatum omnium curiales ab inlustri dignitate cum cingulo seu citra cingulum volumus in posterum prohiberi nec sibi infulas huius honoris adpetere.*
3. *Quod si* ***temere*** *post hanc nostri numinis sanctionem huiusmodi honorem subreptione quadam impetrare potuerint, sciant infructuosum sibi hoc fore nec ullum inter eos atque alios curiales, qui talem non meruerint dignitatem, esse discrimen; illos autem, qui vacantem iam vel honorariam dignitatem adepti sunt, per substitutas personas omnium suarum periculo fortunarum muneribus curiae absque ullo patrocinio respondere, Zoile p[arens] k[arissime] a[tque] a[mantissime].*
4. *Inlustris igitur auctoritas tua hanc nostri numinis legem publicis commoditatibus profuturam edictis sollemniter ubique propositis ad omnium notitiam faciat pervenire.*

Dat. XIII kal. Aug. Constantinopoli Theod[osio] *A. XVIII Cons.*[70]

The same Augustes to Zoilus, Praetorian Prefect

There would be no necessity for promulgating this sanction if the rash lawlessness of wicked men were restrained either by fear of the laws or by the authority of shame. But since audacity despises both of these restraints, wise provision must be made immediately by the remedies of Our sanctions, in order that such outrage may not thus stealthy proceed any further.

1. Therefore, in so far as the report of Your Magnitude has revealed, Valerianus, a decurion of the municipality of Emesa, a transgressor of the public law and the statutes, assumed for himself unjustly and surreptiously the cincture of office of an Illustrious honor, in order that he might rely on the insignia of such high rank and might be able to fulfill his insolent design. For accompanied by a great horde of barbarians, he rushed into the private council chamber of the governor of the province, he dared to vindicate the prior place for himself, he seated himself on the right of the man to whom We have commited the laws, to Whom

[70] July 20, 444.

we considered that the fate of the provincials should be entrusted, and thus when he had put to flight all the office staff of the governor, he left everything devastated and deserted. He was not richer in resources than he was full of crimes, and he also received other decurions at his home, in order that the public accounts might be defrauded. He placed a garrison of slaves in opposition to the tax collectors, contrary to the public discipline, and thereby the treasury of Our Serenity suffered a great loss through his madness. Vegenance should have been taken on him by the more severe stings of the laws, if Our customary clemency had not restrained Us and restored Us to Our customary mildness. Wherefore, We decree by this general sanction that he shall be deprived both of his cincture of office and at the same time of his Illustrious rank, that he shall be restored to the municipal council and at the risk of his own resources he shall perform all the compulsory public services of the municipal council himself, or through a substituted person, if it should thus seem best to the Most Noble governor and to the decurions. He shall obey judical sentences in the same manner as all the others.

2. But because an imperial remedy must be a general one, it is Our will that all the other decurions also of all municipalities shall be debarred in the future from the rank of Illustrious, with the cincture of office or without the cincture of office, nor shall they strive for the insignia of this honor for themselves.
3. But if after the issuance of this sanction of Our Imperial Divinity, they should be able rashly and surreptiously to impetrate such an honor, they shall know that it will be fruitless to them and that there is no distinction between them and other decurions who have not obtained such rank. Those decurions, moreover, who have already obtained an empty, or honorary, dignity shall be responsible through substituted persons for the compulsory public services of the municipal council, at the risk of all their fortunes, without any patronage, O Zoilus, dearest and most beloved Father.
4. Therefore Your Illustrious Authority by duly posting edicts everywhere shall cause to come to the knowledge of all this law of Our Divinity which shall profit the public welfare.

Given on the thirteenth day before the kalends of August at Constantinople in the year of eighteenth consulship of Theodosius Augustus.

(Pharr 1952: 500–501)

The above Novel of Theodosius II is one of the very few constitutions of the period giving us an idea of the circumstances in which laws were promulgated in the Later Roman Empire. It was caused by a certain individual case. A decurion of the city of Emesa, Valerian,[71] committed a series of transgressions

[71] Unknown in other sources, cf. *PLRE* 2: 1141–1142.

in his efforts to reach the goal of getting rid of some cumbersome duties connected with his status. He made unlawful claims to the senatorial rank through illegal appropriation of the Imperial office *insignia*; used a group of barbarian brigands to intimidate a provincial governor; acted in complicity with other decurions; also, he ordered slaves, acting as guardians, to chase away the Imperial tax-collectors.[72] The Emperor had been notified of it all in a *suggestio* filed by his Praetorian Prefect. It could be expected that the most severe sanctions would have been applied to punish the offender, but the Emperor, acting on his "usual" clemency, only orders the culprit to return to the *curia* and his duties there, either in person or through a deputy, even though the choice is not up to the guilty but to the provincial governor and fellow-decurions. The Emperor also orders him to relinquish his unlawfully held insignia of the office and submit to the governor's decisions along with other decurions – all of this under threat of property confiscation.[73] It is notable that even this individual injunction is called "general sanction," as if we were already at this moment dealing with a generally binding law. As a matter of fact, in the further part of the constitution this particular ordinance becomes a regulation obligatory for all decurions who would endeavour to obtain the senatorial dignity by deceitful means. Even those who would lawfully assume a vacant or honorary office are obliged, under threat of property forfeiture, to put up their deputies at the *curia*, who would perform all of their previous curial duties.[74]

The constitution's structure is very clearly arranged. It is commenced with some sentences that validate the issue of a new constitution: it would not have been necessary, if everybody had been prevented by their own shame of breaking the law or at least by the threats of the previously existing constitutions. The legislator proceeds then to relating the circumstances of the specific case (as presented in the official's *suggestio*) for which the constitution is being issued. The deeds

---

72 Jones (1986: 752) identifies those barbarians and slaves as the same, claiming that Valerian had made use of his armed slaves of barbarian origin.

73 This clemency, incommensurate with the actual guilt, is noteworthy. The Emperor seems to distance himself from the description of Valerian's deeds, known from the Prefect's *suggestio*. Perhaps, he does not want to alienate either side of the conflict, especially as the decurion with some connections among "barbarians" (Arabs) might have possibly held a prominent position in the frontier city of Emesa. I would like to acknowledge Prof. J. Komorowska for her suggestion indicative of this possibility.

74 Decurions obtaining the senatorial rank (and thus entering the Senate of Rome or Constantinople) automatically ceased to be citizens of their cities and, as a result, were also relieved of any duties related to the citizenship. Consequently, the emperors made attempts to enforce legal measures restricting such a path of social advancement (Jones 1986: 536, 743–744). In any case, their efforts could not hinder the existence of this phenomenon (Jones 1986: 547 ff., 752–754).

in question are so drastic that only appealing to the Emperor's clemency can justify a relatively moderate decision, without any penal sanctions. Subsequently, the legislator presents this decision in order to turn it into a rule applicable to any similar cases. It is notable that this part is concluded with a phrase ordering that any patronage (*patrocinium*) be rejected; it is quite evident here that implementation of the Imperial orders had met with some resistance from high-ranking dignitaries. Eventually, after formally referring to the Prefect Zoilos with the address *parens karissime et amantissime*, there follows an injunction to publish the law in the form of edicts, which is called "epilogue" by modern scholars.[75]

It can be seen that the disposition proper is only a section of the whole text, beginning with the words *civitatum omnium curiales*, and ending with *ullo patrocinio respondere*. It corresponds with the fragments of the acts which can be found in the *C.Th.* and *C.J.* It is noteworthy indeed, as almost all of the words marked by negative contents that occur in the constitution are accumulated beyond it, i.e., in the *praefatio*. It gives us an idea of how little of the invective appearing in the original texts of the constitutions can be presently found and identified in the Codes.

Even the initial sentences, which constitute a general outline of the situation, are very stern and contain the harshest expressions in the entire text. Allegations of *audacia*, referring to those who disregard the Imperial laws, are formulated twice. The word *serpo* (appearing as *hapax* in the texts of the constitutions) conjures up a metaphor of evil spreading out like a nest of vipers. The invective becomes less "accumulated" as the text proceeds on to the actual description of specific facts: Valerian's deeds speak for themselves. But even at this point, there appears another accusation of *audacia* (in reference to his usurped place at the provincial governor's right hand), as well as that of *vesania* (madness), that is, resorting to violence against tax-collectors. The whole account of his wrongful actions recalls a crime of *latrocinium* (a metaphor of "devastation" caused to the provincial governor's office), and the rebellious decurion is actually called *grassator*, which is the proper term to refer to robbery, yet this sort of brigandage pertains to the public law and constitutions.

Compared with the vivid language of the *praefatio*'s opening sentences, the style of the disposition part seems almost ascetic. The idea of *audacia* is recalled here again, through the adverb *temere*; the accusation of obtaining the senatorial rank through *subreptio* ("insidiously") is mentioned once again as well. It would be impossible to infer how much drastic a case of infringement,

---

75 Van der Wal 1980: 16–17, 21 – the modern publishers have not been consistent, as the term "epilogue" is sometimes used to refer to the order of publication only, while in other cases it may also refer to the accompanying part of what I call "disposition" in this study.

and in what language described, formed the basis for the issue of this sanction. Yet the sanction itself appears to be disproportionately lenient in comparison with the faults. Apparently, the Emperor had not so much intervened because of Valerian's criminal offences as found in them a fairly evident pretext to issue an order applicable to any, including those less flagrant, cases of violations of the law by those decurions who would attempt to depart from their status and its related obligations through an "upward" climb to advance into the ranks of the senatorial estate.

Nov. Valent. 18

DD. NN. Impp. Theod[osius] et Valent[inianus] AA. Albino II P[reafecto] P[retori]o

Superstitio *paganis quoque* ***damnata*** *temporibus,* ***inimica publicae disciplinae et hostis fidei Christianae****, ad excidium sui clementiam nostram non inmerito provocavit. Manicheos loquimur, quos* ***execrabiles*** *et* ***toto orbe pellendos*** *omnium retro principum statuta iudicarunt. Nec dissimulationem crimina nuper detecta patiuntur. Quae enim et* ***quam dictu audituque obscena*** *in iudicio beatissimi papae Leonis coram senatu amplissimo manifestissima ipsorum confessione patefacta sunt? adeo ut eorum quoque qui diceretur episcopus et voce propria proderet et omnia* ***scelerum*** *suorum secreta perscriberet. Quod notitiam nostram latere non potuit, quibus tutum non est neglegere tam* ***detestandam divinitatis iniuriam*** *et inpunitum relinquere* ***scelus****, quo non solum corpora deceptorum, sed etiam animae* ***inexpiabiliter polluuntur****.*

1. *Unde, Albine p[arens] k[arissime] a[tque] a[mantissime], inlustris et praecelsa magnificentia tua hac nos in aeternum victura lege statuisse cognoscat, quam in omnium provinciarum faciet notitiam edictis propositis pervenire, ut ubicumque terrarum quisquis Manichaeorum fuerit deprehensus poenas, quas in sacrilegos iura sanxerunt, auctoritate publicae severitatis excipiat.*
2. *Sitque publicum crimen et omni volenti sine accusationis periculo* ***tales*** *arguere sit facultas.*
3. *Nec cuiquam licitum tutumque sit aut celare* ***tales*** *aut* ***talibus*** *conivere, cum omnia de his a nobis confirmata sint retro principum constituta, ut noverint universi hac edictali lege proposita Manichaeos dignitate militiae et urbium habitatione privandos, ne quis innocens* ***talium*** *conversatione aut societate capiatur. Successiones nec capiant nec relinquant, sed fisci nostri viribus adgregentur. Nec his quod palam interdicimus ulla fraude quaeratur. Iniuriarum careant actione, contractus liberos omnino non habeant.*

4. *Primates uniuscuiusque militiae vel officii mox exigenda per apparitionem vestram X librarum auri multa percellat, si quem hac* ***superstitione pollutum*** *siverint militare. Neque enim aliquid nimium in eos videtur posse decerni, quorum* ***incesta perversitas*** *religionis* ***nomine lupanaribus quoque ignota vel pudenda*** *committit.*
Dat. XIII Kal. Iul. Romae D. N. Valent(iniano) A. VI et Nomo VC. Conss.[76]

Our Lords the Emperors Theodosius and Valentinian Augustes to Albinus, Praetorian Prefect for the second time

That superstition which was condemned also in pagan times, which is hostile to the public discipline and an enemy to the Christian faith, has not undeservedly provoked Our Clemency to its own destruction. We are speaking of the Manicheans, whom the statutes of all the former Emperors have adjudged execrable and worthy of expulsion from the whole world. Their crimes which have been recently detected do not permit Us to disregard them. For what things that are obscene to tell and to hear have been revealed by their very manifest confession in the court of the most blessed Pope Leo, in the presence of the most august Senate! Thus even the man also who has said to be their bishop both betrayed with his own voice and wrote out all the secrets of their crimes. This matter could not escape Our notice, since it is not safe for Us to disregard so detestable an outrage to the Divinity of God and to leave unpunished a crime whereby not only the bodies of deluded persons, but also their souls, are inexpiably polluted.

1. Whence, O Albinus, dearest and most beloved Father, Your Illustrious and Excellent Magnificence shall know that We have decreed by this law, which shall live forever and which you shall cause to come to the knowledge of all the provinces by posting edicts, that if any of the Manicheans should be apprehended anywhere in the world, he shall receive, by the authority of the public service, the penalties which the laws have sanctioned against persons guilty of sacrilege.
2. This heresy shall be a public crime, and every person who wishes shall have the right to accuse such persons without the risk attendant upon an accusation.
3. It shall not be licit and safe for any person either to conceal such persons or to connive at them, since all the constitutions of the former Emperors in regard to such heretics have been confirmed by Us, so that all men shall know that by this edictal law that has been published the Manicheans shall be deprived of the dignity of the imperial service and of the right of residence in the cities, in order that no innocent person may be ensnared by the intercourse and association of such persons. They shall neither take nor leave inheritances, but such inheritances shall be added to the resources of Our fisc. They shall not seek by any fraud that

---

76 June 19, 445.

which We publicly forbid them. They shall forfeit the right of action for outrages against them; they shall have no freedom of contract at all.

4. The primates of every branch of the imperial service and of every office staff shall be punished with a fine of ten pounds of gold, which shall be exacted by your apparitors, if they should permit any person polluted by this superstition to perform imperial service. For it does not appear that anything too severe can be decreed against those persons whose unchaste perversity, in name of religion, commits crimes that are unknown and shameful even to brothels.

Given on the thirteenth day before the kalends of July at Rome in the year of the sixth consulship of Our Lord Valentinian Augustus and the consulship of the Most Noble Nomus.

(transl. Pharr 1952: 531)

Valentinian III's constitution is one of the two instances of the laws against non-Catholics, which can be found in the collection of the Post-Theodosian Novels. Unlike Theodosius' Third Novel, concerning Jews and Samaritans, as well as pagans and heretics, this one appears to be extremely narrow in its specified goal, as it only targets the Manichaean religion.[77] At least since the reign of Valentinian I, the Manichaeans had been the most rigorously persecuted "heresy"; there can be found a number of constitutions specifically directed against them.[78] A particularly prominent idea which can be clearly seen there is that of excluding the followers of this "heresy" from the Roman civic community: by depriving them of the right to draw up last wills and testaments, inherit property, and enter into contractual obligations.[79] The constitution of Valentinian III is another one in this string of the previous constitutions; it is also the most radical in the sanctions it decrees, prohibiting the Manichaeans from holding any offices in the Imperial administration, dwelling within the cities, and even undertaking *actio iniuriarum*.

The constitution is not very typical in its structure. At the beginning, as may be expected, there is a *praefatio*, giving a justification of the sanctions being issued. The legislator passes here from a general view of the Manichaean hostility towards the state and the religion, and of the tradition of anti-Manichaean struggle, to the detail which is the direct cause of his indignation, i.e., the Manichaean "crimes" disclosed before the tribunal of the Bishop of Rome,

77 As a matter of fact, Manichaeans were a splinter group with their origins in the Persian religion under a considerable Gnostic influence, yet in the territories of the Roman Empire they represented their teachings as Christian. For that reason, they were mostly treated as a Christian heresy. On the history of Manichaeism, see Lieu 1985.

78 *C.Th.* 16.5.3; 16.5.7; 16.5.9; 16.5.18; 16.5.35.

79 Stachura 2007b. On the anti-Manichaean legislation, see also Kaden 1953; Beskow 1988; Dębiński 1992; Gibel 2006; Myszor 2007.

in the presence of the senators. Next, he reverts to the more general idea of the danger he would be exposed to if he left such “crimes” unpunished and also reveals the detrimental effect Manichaeism inflicts on bodies and souls. It is the direct justification of the promulgation of this constitution, after which we would expect words of the disposition to follow. But what actually ensues is the legislator’s address to the responsible official and an order to publish the law in the form of edicts, i.e., the content which would normally appear in the ending of the text and could be called an “epilogue.” It is only further on that the sanction against Manichaeans appears, from some more general provisions (all the Manichaeans are to be held liable to the penalty for *sacrilegium*, accusing them shall not be subject to the threat of penal sanctions, all the hitherto valid provisions against them are to be renewed) up to the listing of everything that results out of their exclusion from the Roman civic community. As part of the sentence, there is an element of the sanction’s being justified by the wish to separate the Manichaeans from “the innocent,” otherwise at risk of submitting to their influence. The disposition part is closed with a penal provision directed against officials in charge who are not ardent enough to make sure that one of the provisions listed above is fulfilled, that is, they allow Manichaeans as subordinated officials. But the constitution does not end at this point. Once again, the last sentence belongs to the justification, and for this reason it is formally a part of the *praefatio*. The disposition part itself (in this case, primarily composed of sanctions) is located between the words: *ubicumque terrarum quisquis Manicheorum* and *si quem hac superstitione pollutum siverint militare*.

Let us notice that even though it does possess some elements of the invective language, this part contains a much lower amount of them than the justification. In particular, the rhetoric of exclusion may be traced here,[80] but it is difficult to separate from the matter itself, that is, the provisions against Manichaeans. This rhetoric includes an order to punish the Manichaeans “in whichever land, whoever one of them should be found,” as well as a declared intent to deprive them of any opportunity of contact with the innocent. Yet all of the penal provisions, aimed at the Manichaeans or individuals even only “overlooking” their presence, can be interpreted in the same spirit. Besides, several instances of referring to the Manichaeans as *tales* (here serving as a derogatory pronoun) can also be considered as expressions of invective. The final words of the disposition part also mention the stain of the Manichaean *superstitio*; both of these terms, *superstitio* and *polluo*, had already appeared beforehand among the words of the *praefatio*.

[80] Hunt 1993: 156.

The justification itself contains several elements of interest. The opening phrase is: *superstitio paganis quoque damnata temporibus*. At first glance, this reference to Diocletian's anti-Manichaean legislation may be seen as somewhat strange. Why are pagan times to be held as an example in the initial words of a constitution which is supposed to attest to the Christian character of the state? It may be explained by analogy to the justification of the church asylum constitution (preserved in the acts of the Council of Ephesus), which also cites the ancient temple asylum as a model to be followed.[81] The idea behind this justification is: we cannot be any worse than our pagan forefathers. Since even they had considered persecution of the Manichaean *superstitio* as their duty, it ought to be all the more fulfilled by the Christian emperor. In the text, the Emperor refers twice to the laws of the earlier Roman rulers, which he retains as still valid, although actually he does not restore Diocletian's law providing for death penalty for Manichaeans.[82]

Another phrase puts an emphasis on the Manichaeans' hostility towards both public order and the Christian religion. There is a substitution here, most likely a deliberate one,[83] of terms: *hostilitas*, which is ordinarily used to refer to hostility towards the state, here pertains to the Christian religion, whereas *inimicitia* indicating personal enmity, or towards the Church, God, or religion, is associated here with public order.

In the Emperor's words, the old laws had described the Manichaeans as damnable (*execrabiles*) and liable to be banished from the whole world (*toto orbe pellendos*). In the second charge, we encounter the above-mentioned idea of banishing the Manichaeans from the community, here at the highest possible level of generality: after all, the order to banish them from the whole world is much more radical and far-reaching than even banishment beyond the city walls. Of course, it should be interpreted as part of the *praefatio*, and thus not as a sanction but rather as an ideal to which the sanction only strives to achieve. One should also take a closer look at the points where the Manichaeans are depicted as "damnable." If in the case of the terms *execrabilis* and *detestandus* the legislator's utmost disgust is indeed clearly expressed, the phrase *superstitio paganis damnata temporibus* may signify not that it was "accursed" at the time, but simply regarded as an offence.[84]

The criminal nature of the Manichaean religion is repeatedly stressed both in the justification and as part of the successive sanctions directed against

81 Dreher 2006: 157 ff.

82 *Coll.* 15.3 (= *FIRA* 2: 580–581).

83 See Chapter V: 120.

84 See Chapter VII: 206–208, for adjectives ending with *-bilis*. On the meaning of the verb *damno*, see Liebs 1968: 216–226, 252; Stachura 2004: 254–255.

the adherents of that religion. The necessity to punish this offence is emphasized by means of multiple rhetorical measures. First, a rhetorical question is asked: Was it not openly confessed, in the presence of the Pope and senators? Subsequently, it is twice called *scelus*, which is a synonymous and emotionally intense term, usually applied in Latin to amplify the notion of a "serious crime." Finally, its essence is clearly indicated: it is an "insult to Divinity" (the term *iniuria*, appropriate for private law, is used here in its metaphorical sense), belonging to those crimes which cannot be erased (*inexpiabilis*). The idea of contamination by crime is highlighted through a reference to the notion of *pollutio*, characteristic for descriptions of crimes of both religious and sexual nature.

This comparison between these two types of crimes is, apparently, the most interesting and untypical feature of the act in question. There is already an allusion in defining the secrets of the Manichaean religion as too *obscenae* to speak of or hear about them; all the more, any open disclosure of them must be deemed as indecent. Most clearly, the relationship is evident in the last sentence of the constitution. The Manichaean religion is here first compared with incest, as *incesta perversitas*. Then, a peculiar case of amplification through *comparatio* is formulated,[85] which is unique for the entire analyzed material. A house of prostitution is mentioned here as an *exemplum minus*, because what Manichaeans practise under the guise of religion is not known even there, and even there it would be shameful. At the end of the text, this strong accent is a masterpiece of conclusion; it is as if the Emperor became momentarily ashamed of his own severity, and felt that in order to defend his directives, he had to provide the strongest argument in favour of the claim that no sanction can be harsh enough for the Manichaeans.

---

85 Lausberg 1960: 222–223.

Chapter V: Terms indicating the nature of the opposition to Roman or ecclesiastical communities

One of the fundamental assumptions for the present analysis is the axiom that expressing an invective always sets up the addressee as an "enemy" of the author of the statement. It is fitting then that one should examine, first of all, the terms pointing to the "hostility"/"enmity" itself, derived from *hostis* and *inimicus*, respectively. It should be taken into consideration in which cases these terms indicate hostility towards the Roman community or, alternatively, describe relations between individual persons. The hostility towards the Roman community may also be pointed out by some terms used to designate individuals held to be in opposition thereto: *barbarus* (barbarian), *tyrannus* (tyrant), *latro* (robber), but also *haereticus* (heretic). Of course, these terms charged with negative contents will mostly appear as specific names, in which case only some other elements of the communication may point to its condemnatory character. On the other hand, one can speak of an invective when the terms in question are used to refer metaphorically to a Roman citizen who is not a member of any of those groups, e.g., when a cruel owner of a slave is called *barbarus*.

Hostis, inimicus, adversarius

Of all the terms which confront an individual or a group with the Roman community, the one that should be definitely considered in the first place is that of an "enemy." When it is used to refer directly to an adversary, it may be understood as an element of the language of invective, as it points directly to the hostile relation on the speaker's part or towards him. Yet there is a different situation when the speaker only communicates relations between some third parties. It should be considered whether the kind of "hostility" thus confronted can be identified on the basis of the term used to express it, or only from the context.

The English meaning of the term "enemy" seems to represent equally the "public" and "private" enmity, and also, e.g., in Polish, where there exist two different terms, "wróg" and "nieprzyjaciel"; nevertheless, in practice, both are used as synonyms.[1] It is more complicated in Latin. At least theoretically denoting a "public enemy", the term *hostis* should be clearly distinguished from the one referring to a "private" one, *inimicus*. As it is explicitly indicated by Cicero, *hostis* stands for an enemy of a community, while *inimicus* – refers to one's personal enemy.[2] Following the relevant entry in the *Thesaurus Linguae Latinae*, it is worth adding that, in its earliest sense, the term *hostis* indicates a "stranger," rather than an "enemy";[3] this component of "strangeness" is not present in the case of *inimicus*, coined as a negation of the word *amicus* ("friend"). But, in practice, the Latin authors would not adhere to such a differentiation very strictly. Both of these terms tended to be used as synonyms (in both of the above-mentioned meanings). It is not to say, of course, that the principal shades of meaning were not predominant, yet it is possible to observe a considerable laxity in the way the two terms were distinguished (it also applies to the Later Roman literature).[4]

There is an entirely different situation in examining the Later Roman normative sources (whose authors were otherwise not very careful in applying the assumed terminology consistently). It is striking to note the almost consistent adherence to the principal meanings of the both terms.

The term ***hostis***,[5] as opposed to *inimicus*, is used, consequently, in the constitutions directed against "enemies" of the Roman state. Basically, it is ascribed to two types of enemies: external (it is then near-synonymous with the term

---

1 Skorupka 1988: 166.

2 For the distinction between *inimicus meus* and *hostis communis* – cf. Cic., *Or. De domo sua*, 101. For further examples of the distinction, cf. Bettini, Borghini 1983: 311 – *hostis* pertains to relations beyond the Roman community and is contrasted with *socius*, *inimicus* – within that community, the terms opposite to *amicus*.

3 *ThLL* 6.3: 3056.

4 In Cicero, the term is *inimicus rei publicae* (*Philip.* 5.4), Ambrose of Milan used *communis inimicus* as equivalent with *hostis* (*De fuga saeculi* 7.41), whereas *hostis meus* also in Ambrose (*Ep.* 72.15), Augustine of Hippo in reference to the Devil (*Enarr. in Psalmos*, Ps. 41.10). Further numerous examples in *ThLL* 6.3: 3061–3064, *ThLL* 7.1: 1625–1626.

5 Enumerations of the term's appearance in particular designated meanings are provided, for reasons of clarity, at the end of the respective entry, not in footnotes.

barbarus) and domestic, defined several times as *hostis publicus*. It is the former usage that definitely prevails in terms of quantity.[6]

With regard to "external enemies," this term is often used in an abstract way, designating any enemy from outside the Empire.[7] In other cases, one can discern specific "enemies" beyond the texts, thanks to the knowledge of their historical context.[8] Also, in that case, one should remember that when those constitutions had been incorporated in the Theodosian Code, they became "enemies" in general. Indeed, it was the Code compilers' goal to record a general rule, and thus to lift the constitution out of its narrow historical context.

The designation *hostis* is ascribed not only to strictly "external" barbarians, but also to Alaric's troops whose core was made up of the rebel Gothic *foederati*.[9] As a result, they were also treated as a factor "alien" and "external," from the Empire's perspective.

The other group are "internal" (domestic) enemies. In the presently discussed normative texts, the phrase *hostis publicus* is used four times, all in reference to specific persons. Defined as such are the ill-fated usurpers from African provinces: Gildo (*C.Th.* 7.8.7; 400) and Heraclianus (*C.Th.* 9.40.21; 413), as well as Stilicho (*C.Th.* 7.16.1; 408), also considered as a "public enemy." The fourth case may be interpreted (*C.Th.* 10.8.4) depending on the dating of the constitution, as the said *hostis publicus* may be either the defeated Emperor Constantine II (if the constitution had been issued in 346 by his brother Constans, with whom he had been previously in conflict) or the usurper Magnentius (if it had been issued by Constantius II in 353).[10] It is notable that the laws were promulgated after the aforementioned *hostes publici* had been vanquished, and they concerned the questions such as how their followers should be treated[11] or the invalidity of the decrees those two "tyrants" had issued.[12]

---

6 Contrary to what is written by Cañizar Palacios 2006: 146.

7 *Nov. Theod.* 24, *Nov. Maio.* 1. In this latter constitution, the emperor writes of liberating the Roman world *ab externo hoste et ab domestica clade* ("from external enemy and domestic disaster"). It can be seen that the term *hostis* is used, first of all, in reference to external, not domestic, enemies.

8 Such as Goths (*C.Th.* 1.32.5; 5.6.2; 7.13.16; 11.28.12; *Nov. Valent.* 32), Alemanni (*C.Th.* 5.7.1), Suebi (*C.Th.* 11.31.7 – cf. Pharr 1952: 333, note 22), Vandals (*Nov. Valent.* 2.3; 6.3; 9; 12; 13; 34; 35). The fact that all of the instances of *hostis* are references to Germanic peoples, and not, for example, to Persians, who also appear in *Nov. Theod.* 5.3 as external enemies, is apparently only a coincidence.

9 *C.Th.* 5.6.2; 11.28.12; *Nov. Valent.* 32.

10 The year 353 corrected to 346 by Pharr 1952: 272. Cf. Cañizar Palacios 2006: 140–141, note 24.

11 *C.Th.* 7.8.7; 9.40.21; 10.8.4.

12 *C.Th.* 7.16.1.

Twice, the status of *hostis publicus* is ascribed to individuals who had committed specific acts. According to *C.Th.* 6.4.22 (373), a venal judge is defined as *hostis publicus*; while *C.Th.* 9.45.5 (432) speaks of a fugitive slave who, "in his madness," had raised his weapon to defend himself at the place of asylum. Let us note that in the latter case the term *hostilitas* is linked with the notion of *furor* (discussed more extensively further on).

To these two groups of *hostes*, let us also add a few examples of metaphorical application of the term, referring to the idea of an "external enemy."[13]

In addition, there are three instances of the usage of the term *hostis*, which cannot be considered within the aforementioned pattern. For once, it can be found in an accusation of hostility towards the Christian religion (*hostis fidei Christianae*). It is used as part of a more complex phrase, defining the Manichaean teachings as *inimica publicae disciplinae et hostis fidei Christianae.*[14] It is apparently a confusion in terms: in all of the other known cases, it is *hostilitas* that is supposed to be directed against the Roman community, whereas against the Christian faith and the Church, as we shall soon find out – *inimicitia*. In this particular case, the relevant terms may have been reshuffled: enemies of the Roman order and *inimici* of the Christian faith become "*inimici* of the Roman order and enemies of the Christian faith." Perhaps, it was intended to stress that the hostility towards the Christian faith is something much worse than the one against the Roman state? In any event, this is the only case here where heretics (here: Manichaeans) are indicated as opposing the Roman state, not just the Church. Most likely, it may be in connection with the fact that the first part of the sentence (and at the same time, the opening words of the constitution) mentions persecutions of this particular *superstitio* already undertaken previously by the pagan emperors (*superstitio paganis quoque damnata temporibus*), who obviously could not have been concerned for the Christian religion.

In two specific statements, the term is used in reference to individuals practising sorcery and to those perpetrating sepulchral violations. The former are depicted as "*hostes* of the public good"[15] (but also, similarly, as "*inimici* of mankind"[16]). Tomb robbers are described as "*hostes* of the light itself."[17]

---

13 *Nov. Valent.* 1.3 condemns fiscal officials, practising corrupt solicitation, for treating citizens "like enemies"; *Nov. Valent.* 17 – deals with the bishop who had "encircled the enclosures of the walls by a siege, in the manner of an enemy," intending to impose his illegitimately ordained bishops on them.

14 *Nov. Valent.* 18 (445).

15 *C.Th.* 9.16.11: *hostis communis salutis.*

16 *C.Th.* 9.16.6: *inimici humani generis.*

17 *Nov. Valent.* 23: *hostis lucis ipsius.*

Thus, sorcerers would be enemies of all people, whereas those guilty of grave violations – of the nature itself. As it appears, in the latter case, the accusation being made is the one of *contagium*, i.e., bringing out ashes of the dead into the light of day.[18] Likewise, sorcerers are charged with disturbing the balance of the very elements of nature,[19] yet such a clear and early contrast drawn between them and the entire Roman community[20] is connected with the fairly common condemnation of magic practices, not only among Christians. Sorcerers were the most obvious "common enemy" that the emperors of the Later Roman Empire could have possibly pointed out to their subjects.[21]

hostis, hostilis, hostilitas

A. external enemy: *C.Th.* 1.32.5.3; 5.6.2.4; 5.7.1.[2]; 7.13.16.1; 8.11.3.3; 11.18.1.5; 11.18.1.3[2]; 11.28.12.2, 11.31.7.3; *Nov. Theod.* 24.65; *Nov. Valent.* 2.3.6; 6.3.14; 9.4; 9.12; 9.14; 9.17; 12.13; 13.63; 13.65; 32.44; 34.6; 34.15; 34.24; 35.72; *Nov. Majo.* 1.15; *Nov. Marc.* 2.3.

B. domestic enemy (*hostis publicus*): *C.Th.* 6.4.22.17 (metaphorically); 7.8.7.1; 7.16.1.1; 9.40.21.1; 10.8.4.2; moreover, *C.Th.* 9.45.5.15: treating a slave (who reached for his weapon when taking refuge at asylum) as *hostis*.

C. enemy of the public good (in reference to magic): *C.Th.* 9.16.11.3.

D. enemy of the light itself (in reference to grave desecrations): *Nov. Valent.* 23.26.

E. enemy of the Christian faith: *Nov. Valent.* 18.2.

F. description of the situation of a person who had lost his case in a personal liberty trial: *C.Th.* 4.8.5.5[2].

G. a metaphor referring to treating fellow-citizens as enemies: *Nov. Valent.* 1.3.28; 17.16 (*hostilis*).

In the material under consideration, there are basically three possible ways to understand the term ***inimicus***. In the first and principal sense of this word in Latin, it denotes one's personal enemy. Still, unlike the neutral (in the Code's language) term *adversarius*, it is usually the party which is subjected to negative evaluation, and against which the legislator defends the citizen.[22]

---

18 Cf. Chapter VI: 199–200.

19 *C.Th.* 9.16.5.

20 Analogous, and expressed in less harsh words, exclusions of Manichaeans and apostates are only dated back to the years 381 (*C.Th.* 16.5.7) and 383 (*C.Th.* 16.7.1).

21 Fögen 1993: 250–251.

22 The sole exception is the situation when a person who had already confessed his guilt under torture is forbidden to accuse his personal enemies, presumably with the intent to "share the last moment with them," i.e., also causing their condemnation to death (*C.Th.* 9.1.19). Yet the Emperor does not resolve the question if the person thus accused would be actually guilty or not, which is why we cannot speak of any positive evaluation of the party defined as *inimicus*.

Another meaning in which *inimicitia* appears in the Later Roman constitutions is the enmity towards the Church, religion, and God. As the text of *Const. Avell.* 39 points out, it is one and the same "enmity," interpreted transitively: he who is an "adversary" of the Church, is at the same time an "adversary" of God.[23] The use, in this case, of the term *inimicus*, not *hostis*, is so regular that there can be no question of any coincidence. This is certainly a deliberate application to the "enmity towards religion" of the same term which describes "enmity" of one person towards the other, on a personal level. It is not the only clue hinting at such an idea on the legislator's part. In several cases, offences against religion and God are described with a term from the field of private law, i.e., *iniuria*.[24] In Roman law, *iniuria* was a technical term used to designate a *delictum* in private law, referring to an offence against a person.[25] In Late Antiquity, more and more provisions appeared in defence of particularly notable figures harmed in such a manner, ordering the punishing of offenders according to public law.[26] I am convinced that in calling an insult to religion *iniuria* (which is a term completely out of place here) the following analogy was formulated: the legislator stood up in defence of the "religion," Church, and God, in exactly the same way he would have defended a particularly worthy private person.[27] In consequence, their enemies should be referred to as *inimici*, not *hostes*. Even though they were enemies of the Church, they were not yet enemies of the Roman state.

The third sense of *inimicus* is an explicit insult with reference to magicians and tax (fiscal) informers; they are defined (each of these groups once) as *inimici humani generis* ("*inimici* of mankind").

There are indeed some cases when *inimicitia* clearly designates the hostility towards the Roman state or order. One of them has been already discussed above: in Valentinian's Novel 18 *hostis* and *inimicus* are simply interchangable.

---

[23] *Coll. Avell.* 39.1 (386): *si quis esset inimicus, quam adversus ecclesias dei, hoc est adversus deum ipsum,*

[24] *C.Th.* 16.5.15: *mysteriorum simulationem ad iniuriam verae religionis aptare*; *C.Th.* 16.10.12: *plena religionis iniuria*; *C.Th.* 16.6.6: *in iniuriam sacrae legis*; *Nov. Theod.* 3: *ad supernae maiestatis iniuriam*; *Nov. Valent.* 18: *tutum non est neglegere tam detestandam divinitatis iniuriam*. *C.Th.* 16.5.40 provides that what is committed contrary to religion, occurs to the outrage of "everything" (*quod in religionem divinam conmittitur, in omnium fertur iniuriam*), whereas *C.Th.* 16.5.65 speaks of the *iniuria* done to the nature itself: *quoniam nihil his omnibus relinquendum loci est, in quo ipsis etiam elementis fiat iniuria.*

[25] Steinwenter 1916: 1555. Besides this strict meaning of *iniuria*, there had been also a more comprehensive one, encompassing any acts contrary to the law (cf. Ulpian's statement, *D.* 47.10.1.pr).

[26] Hagemann 1998: 159–182.

[27] For more on the subject, see Stachura 2004: 233–235.

For the remaining three instances, the case in point is a short-cut – "enmity" concerns two subjects, one of which is the state, whilst the other one can be absolutely correctly referred to as an *inimicus*:

C.Th. 10.11.1 (317): *fisci et mulieris pariter inimicus* (an *inimicus* of both the woman and the *fiscus*; he concealed the testament which provided for the bequeathed goods to be divided between the widow and the *fiscus*),

C.Th. 11.12.1 (340): *publicus ac noster inimicus* (Constantine II as a personal *inimicus* of the Emperor and a public enemy),

Nov. Theod. 3 (438): *supernae maiestati et Romanis legibus inimici* (Jews and Samaritans as the *inimici* of God and Roman laws).

In each case, one could speak (at most) of the state of *inimicitia* being "extended" over the Roman community.

inimicus, inimicitia

A. personal enmity: *C.Th.* 2.19.2.13^2; 2.19.2.14^2; 9.1.19.14; 9.16.5.3; 9.16.11.8; 9.34.6.3; 9.34.10.2; 9.38.9.7 (*inimicus iudex* about Rufinus – an unfair judge whose enmity continued to cause some specific persons to suffer due to his verdicts); 9.44.1.7; *Const. Sirm.* 15.5.

A1. also towards the state: *C.Th.* 10.11.1.8 (*fisci et mulieris pariter inimicus*); 11.12.1.1 (*publicus ac noster inimicus*).

B. enmity towards Church, religion, God: *C.Th.* 16.5.42.2 (*catholicae sectae inimici*); 16.5.51.2 (*sanctae legis i.*); 16.5.56.2 (*sacrosanctae legis*); 16.5.62.2 (*catholicis*); 16.5.63.2 (*catholicae legis*); 16.5.64.2 (*catholicis*); *Const. Sirm.* 6.22^2 (*catholicis*).

B1. also towards the state: *Nov. Theod.* 3.22 (*supernae maiestati et Romanis legibus inimici*); *Nov. Valent.* 18.2: *(superstitio) inimica publicae disciplinae et hostis fidei Christianae* (here the meanings of *inimicus* and *hostis* are interchanged).

C. *inimicus humani generis*: *C.Th.* 9.16.6.3 (on magic practices); 10.10.10.1 (on *delatores*).

Alongside the term *inimicus*, there is another word used to refer to someone's opponent, i.e., ***adversarius***. In the documents in question, this particular term appears, basically, as a neutral one; it denotes the opposite party in a lawsuit or the prosecuting party. Of course, the thus-conceived *adversarius* is simultaneously an *inimicus* of the private person concerned; also, he may act in a highly reprehensible manner.[28] Only once, the phrase *adversarii catholicae fidei* turns up in the text.[29] This example also attests that the term may be used

[28] E.g., *C.Th.* 11.36.7: *adversarii calliditas testes subtrahat, qui veritatem audacia vel acrimonia superet* ("the cunning adversary withdraws witnesses and overcomes the truth by audacity and vehemence").

[29] *C.Th.* 16.6.4.

as a synonym of *inimicus*. Only in the *interpretatio* to the *C.Th.* 5.7.1, there also appears its usage which is synonymous with *hostis*.[30]

adversarius

A. personal adversary: *C.Th.* 1.16.1.3; 1.22.2.7; 2.14.1.1²; 4.8.5.12; 4.8.5.7²; 4.22.2.2; 9.2.6.7; 11.30.67.4; 11.31.3.3; 11.31.5.2; 11.31.5.4; 11.31.5.6; 11.31.6.2; 11.31.9.9; 11.36.7.10; *Nov. Theod.* 7.1.34; 7.4.5; *Nov. Valent.* 35.11;. 35.22; 35.83; *Nov. Marc.* 1.9; 1.14; 1.23; 1.25; 1.31; 1.34; 1.40; 1.46; 1.51.

B. adversary of the Christian faith: *C.Th.* 16.6.4.1.

Barbarus, barbaricus

Following the terms that may directly indicate the hostile attitude towards the Roman community, I should like to mention those which refer to individuals or groups outside its limits or in opposition to it. It may be assumed that since the Roman community is perceived as a positive value, the names of all persons and groups which remain contrary to it will, for this very reason, be charged with some negative content. It is evident both in making them more specific by means of negative epithets and through metaphorical use of such terms in relation to other stigmatized groups. Nonetheless, it is necessary to consider the character of the invective for each individual name separately.

The group on the outside of the Roman community is, of course, referred to as "barbarians" (*barbari*). The idea pertains to external enemies (*hostes*) of the Empire and in the language of the constitutions is, as we shall see, clear of that ambivalent attitude which can be traced in the approach of certain Roman authors towards the people unaffected by the Roman *humanitas*.

The term *barbarus* is derived from Greek. The notion of "barbarians" (*barbaros*, βάρβαρος) was formed within the sphere of Greek culture to describe the peoples different from Greeks in respect of their language or customs.[31] In the Archaic period, the term "barbarians" was not yet associated with a strongly negative judgement, which only appeared in the era following the Persian wars (i.e., the fifth century BC).[32] It was only in the aftermath of the instilling of negative connotations into the term *barbaros* that there

[30] *Quicumque necessitate captivitatis ducti sunt et non sua voluntate, sed hostili depraedatione ad adversarios transierunt...*

[31] The Romans integrated it into their perceptions of foreign peoples after an interim period when they were still able to accept being called *barbaroi* by the Greeks (Speyer, Opelt 1967: 259).

[32] Speyer, Opelt 1967: 254–255.

would arise the possibility to use it as an invective, also in reference to a Greek.[33] Interestingly, it was only then that the idealization of the barbarian's image would come into view.

This ambivalence can be already observed in the Greek literature of the fourth century BC and since then in all the periods of Antiquity.[34] Both negative and positive opinions had usually referred to the "absence of culture," with all its beneficial, but also harmful, effects.[35] The Romans are certainly the case in point here; some occasional admiration of the "barbarian," which can be found in Roman literature, is in fact the admiration of the purely Roman *virtutes* ("virtues") that had not succumbed to any decadent influence of civilization.[36] This idealizing approach to certain "barbarian" features does not have anything to do with the openness to what is different, which can be seen, for instance, in Herodotus. It was the same in Late Antiquity. Even Salvian of Marseilles remained essentially within a sphere of values that was classical yet modified in the Christian spirit: "when we should beware, since we possess all *vitia* (vices) of barbarians, why cannot we have their *virtutes*?"[37] Salvian of Marseilles, whose *De gubernatione Dei* is almost contemporaneous with the Theodosian Code, is not the only Late Antique author whose work contains an ambiguous attitude to the barbarians.[38]

In the Late Antique constitutions, no positive associations with the words *barbarus* or *barbaricus* can be found. There is not any elaboration of conceptions related to these terms, either. The "barbarian" is primarily an invader from the outside; this trend, which can be seen in the literature of the period,[39] is a rule in the normative sources.[40] Some individual cases that mention slaves

---

33 Speyer, Opelt 1967: 257.

34 Speyer, Opelt 1967: 255 ff.

35 Speyer, Opelt 1967: 251.

36 Ohnacker 2003: 42.

37 Salvian, *De gubernatione Dei* 4.14.65. On the idea expressed by Salvian of Marseilles, cf. Ohnacker 2003: 100–108.

38 For instance, Sozomen's positive depiction of one of the Goths, conquerors of Rome (*HE* 9.10), as part of a more general tendency among the Christian authors to represent this event in "mild" terms. Nonetheless, "good barbarians" can also be found in the work of Zosimus, a pagan historian, even though those were barbarians "converted" into the Greco-Roman culture (Fravitta, Generidus, cf. Zos., *Historia Nova*, 5.20.1, 5.46.2–5).

39 The association of "barbarity" with cruelty and violence is so strong that in the literature of the period there can be found a view that a "civilized," peaceful barbarian actually ceases to be a barbarian (Mathisen 2006: 33). It is then quite natural to stop referring to him as such.

40 Rugullis states that a barbarian "assimilated" into the Roman community as a soldier (*foederatus*) will never be called "barbarian" in normative sources, as he had already obtained a different legal status (*Rechtsstellung* – cf. Rugullis 1992: 49–50).

of barbarian origin refer, as a matter of fact, to captives taken prisoner in wartime.[41] The depiction of the *barbari* in the Imperial constitutions is at the same time of a very rudimentary character in terms of its employed means of expression. The only perceived feature of barbarians turns out to be *feritas*, meaning their animal-like, uncivilized cruelty, actually mentioned fairly infrequently.[42] This contrasts with a more ingenious criticism of "tyrants," whose presence in the Code is even more marginal (and thus offering relatively few opportunities for such criticism). The both cases of metaphorical usage of the terms in question make references to the kind of cruelty or some broader inhumanity that is characteristic of barbarians, in depictions of such crimes as killing a slave under torture and robbing a tomb.

There is no doubt that according to the law a "barbarian" is someone alien, outside the Roman world;[43] at the same time, a rebel *foederatus* is not any different from a foreigner coming from beyond the boundaries of the Empire.[44] *Barbarus* and *hostis* are sometimes treated as synonyms;[45] Sven Rugullis has even postulated that in the Late Antique law they are synonymous in all

---

[41] "Barbarian" slaves appear in the constitutions *C.Th.* 3.4.1 and *C.Th.* 13.4.4, and in the former one they are contrasted with *provincialibus servis,* i.e., slaves from the provinces. Rugullis (1992: 97, 99) argues that the question here is of the distinction between the slaves on the basis of *ius civile* and those on *ius gentium* – the latter ones are exclusively those who had been taken prisoner during wars with external enemies. Moreover, *Nov. Theod.* mentions a Roman bureau known as *scrinium barbarorum*, dealing, among other things, with delegation issues and matters concerning some soldiers of barbarian origin (cf. Rugullis 1992: 95, where the *varia lectio* – *barbaricorum* is rejected).

[42] Cf. Chapter VI: 175–176. *Feritas* is the primary characteristic in descriptions of barbarians in literary sources, yet it is not the only one – cf. the listing of charges against barbarians, Dauge 1981: 437 (*feritas* – 35.5% of the cases); Speyer, Opelt 1967: 263–264; for various observations on *feritas* in Ammianus Marcellinus – see Ohnacker 2003: 78, note 250, in Claudian, see Danvoye 2007: 136. *Feritas* may be understood as a consequence of barbarians' animal-like conduct, *bios thēriodēs* (Speyer, Opelt 1967: 251, 258) or as the most drastic manifestation of barbarians' inability to control their passions (Ohnacker 2003: 54), which should also lead to accusations of *furor*. Nevertheless, even though this is a typical charge that could be seen in the literary sources of the period (e.g., Amm. Marc. 16.12.31), it cannot be found in any normative sources.

[43] In the constitutions *C.J.* 6.1.3; *C.J.* 4.41.1, *C.J.* 4.41.2 and *C.J.* 4.63.2, the term *barbaricum* can be found, in *C.J.* 4.41.2 distinguished from the *Romanum solum*, Roman soil. Cf. Rugullis 1992: 93 in his polemical discussion with Lemosse 1967: 8, who held the opinion that there had been no strict demarcation between the Roman and barbarian territories.

[44] A rebel *foederatus* became a *barbarus*, but following a treaty with the Romans he rejoined the category of *foederati* (Rugullis 1992: 87–88).

[45] In *C.Th.* 5.6.2 (409), there is a reference to *barbarorum praeda* (barbarians' spoils), and afterwards to those who had been displaced from their abode by the enemy (*hostis*). In other documents, the terms *hostis* or *barbarus* can be found, but it is impossible to find here any difference in the semantic fields of these terms.

cases.[46] Barbarians' ordinary activity are incursions into the Roman territories (*incursus*, etc) and all the ensuing devastations (*vastatio* etc, whereas *depraedatio* appears to be more typical of deviations and abuses in actions of the state apparatus).[47] Responding to the damage they cause or the threat they pose forms the first group of circumstances in which they are mentioned. Frequently, the legislator is urged here to issue this constitution by concrete, identifiable events,[48] yet at least once the term "barbarians" is used *in abstracto*, as a danger that the Emperor must ward off (*Nov. Theod.* 16).

Another question refers to acts of treason committed by Roman citizens in favour of barbarians. These may comprise a wide range of forms: from inciting barbarians to "riots,"[49] through joining their ranks and taking part in plunders, up to "disclosing" to them secrets of ship-building and such acts of "treason" as marrying a barbarian woman. Even if the latter provision was limited in its subject and duration of validity,[50] it clearly demonstrates the idea of a total separation between the communities of the Roman Empire and barbarians.

barbarus, barbaricus

A. enemy (in principle, treated as external): *C.Th.* 3.14.1.2 (prohibition of marriage); 5.6.2.2; 5.7.1.[8]; *C.Th.* 5.7.2.[2] = *Const. Sirm.* 16.7; 5.7.2.6 (here: purchase of captives from barbarians) = *Const. Sirm.* 16.17; *C.Th.* 7.1.1.1; 7.12.1.1²; 7.13.20.1²; 7.16.2.9; 9.14.3.2; 9.40.24.2; 9.42.22.3; 10.10.25.1; 15.14.R; 15.14.14.1; *Nov. Theod.* 4.9; 15.2.7; 16.2, *Nov. Valent.* 1.2.7; 13.47; 13.58; 34.21; 34.22.

---

46 Rugullis 1992: 46–51 in his polemic with Vismara 1947: 445, 448.

47 Cf. Chapter VII: 210–211.

48 Cf. attempts to re-create historical context of the laws on barbarians – Rugullis 1992: 53–89.

49 Stilicho was charged with inciting disturbances among barbarians (*C.Th.* 9.42.22). This typical accusation of using barbarians for nefarious causes was previously made by Claudian against Stilicho's enemies (Garambois-Vasquez 2007: 223–225).

50 Demandt (1989b: 77) demonstrates that the law concerns only foreign barbarians, not the ones who are inhabitants of the Empire. In turn, Rugullis (1992: 68) states that in fact *C.Th.* 3.14.1 had initially been one with *C.J.* 4.41.1 and concerned exclusively (Rugullis 1992: 71–72) a particular situation in Africa during the conflict with Firmus, usurper and leader of the Moors – the purpose was to discourage the Roman population from any contact, as regards both trade and intermarriage, with the Moors fighting on the usurper's side. The law was so tough since, as a matter of fact, it was supposed to erect a frontier where in the minds of the inhabitants of the province it already began to disappear (even among the Roman soldiers, Firmus had enjoyed some support). In Rugullis' opinion, the provision was already defunct at the time of the compilation of the Theodosian Code, preserved only because invalid regulations had been incorporated in the Code; as no longer valid, it was not included in the Code of Justinian. A similar view can be found in Sivan 1996: 140–144. The author notes that according to the constitution it was not so much the proscribed marriages themselves as the resulting suspect or criminal acts that were subject to death penalty (*susceptum vel noxium*).

A1. trading with barbarians: *C.Th.* 7.16.3.3; *Nov. Valent.* 33.R; 33.23.

B. slaves and *coloni* of barbarian origin: *C.Th.* 3.4.1.4; 5.6.3.1 (here referring to the Scires, their native tribe); 13.4.4.5.

B1. *Scrinium barbarorum* or *barbaricorum*: *Nov. Theod.* 21.20.

C. comparisons: *C.Th.* 9.12.1.10 (punishment inflicted on a slave); *Nov. Valent.* 23.17 (grave robbery).

Tyrannus

The Greek-based term *tyrannus* has two shades of meaning. On the one hand, it denotes a sole ruler who had assumed his power by coming into conflict with the accepted laws or customs; on the other, a sole ruler whose power was in contravention of the laws or customs.[51] These two meanings merge with and reinforce each other: bad governance may give rise to the legitimacy of the rule being questioned, while the illegitimacy of the usurped power often results in the unrighteousness of his rule.[52] In consequence, there may actually arise the problem of how to discern which of these two "aspects" of tyranny is being referred to.

Scholars concerned with the study of Late Antiquity have to face this difficulty as well. Allegations of "tyranny"[53] are often caused by numerous usurpations of the period as well as conflicts arising among the rulers in the time of the disintegration of the tetrarchy system. Illegitimacy of power is not, and cannot, be always in the foreground. Writings of panegyrical nature, where the theme of fighting against a tyrant is normally a *leitmotiv*, are focused on the iniquity of the tyrant's actions (who should be finally defeated, for the benefit of all humanity, by the positive protagonist of the panegyrical work).[54] The Christian authors complement this image by adding the stereotype of a tyrant-persecutor.[55] In the background, there is always the image

51 It has been a matter of controversy when the terms *tyrannus* and *usurpator* had actually merged, in the works of the fourth-century, or perhaps earlier, authors (cf. Escribano 1997: 87).

52 Wardman 1984: 222–223; Neri 1997: 73 ff. For Late Antiquity, one is confronted with an additional, "Christian" component, i.e., portraying the "tyrant" as a persecutor (cf. Barnes 1996: 58–60; the pagan tyrant as a model for the Christian image of a persecutor, cf. Opelt 1967: 252–253, 257).

53 As Barnes points out (1996: 56), the term *tyrannus*, used "technically" to designate usurpation, does not lose its negative shade at the same time.

54 Lassandro 1981, Lassandro 2000: 37–41 on Latin panegyrics.

55 Opelt 1967, Opelt 1980: 87 ff., 185 ff., 227, 233.

of an impulsive tyrant, unable to control his passions, which is traditional for the Roman historiography and rhetoric,[56] and stemming from Plato's *Republic*.[57]

With one exception, the constitutions speak of "tyrants" already deposed,[58] yet the additional reason is the subject in question: the constitutions simply refer to the problems left by the "tyrants" after their removal, not the situation while they were still in power. The above-mentioned exception is very specific. It is about having control – in the Eastern part of the Empire ruled by Theodosius II – over envoys from the West, who may have actually arrived (as the allusion to tyranny allows us to think) not on behalf of the legitimate Emperor Honorius but of the usurper Attalos.[59] Even here, then, the question is not what direct actions are taken against the tyrant. An overwhelming majority of the laws are concerned with invalidating (less frequently confirming) decisions taken under the "tyrant's" reign (constitutions, rescripts, verdicts, office appointments). The issue of interest is the legitimacy of the tyrant's rule, and (more broadly) the problem of hiatus in the continuum of the legal authority caused by the *tempus tyrannicum*,[60] whereas the "tyrant" figure is in the background.

All the more noteworthy is the fact that in spite of this background presence, the "tyrant" is depicted by numerous and diverse negative epithets. That criticism is in part justified by the purpose of the constitutions. The tyrant's injustice is indeed a good justification for repealing his decisions taken in person or, generally, under his reign. Thus the tyrant turns out to be *iniquissimus* (the most iniquitous – the opposite of the ideal of *aequitas*), spreads injustice (*iniuria*,[61] in particular 15.14.7.2: *iniuriam, non iura reddenda*), his actions are motivated by his envy of the justice of the *saeculum nostrum* (*Const. Sirm.* 6: *privilegia ecclesiarum... quae seculo nostro tyrannus inviderat*). But the tyrant is also described in terms of the language of political condemnation traditional in the Roman rhetoric: tyranny is *audacia*, *praesumptio*, while the tyrant is "mad" and

---

56 Dunkle 1967; Dunkle 1971; Erskine 1991. Claudian's inclusion of the usurper Gildo within the same negative stereotype, cf. Scheithauer 2004: 312, 314; Ware 2004: 100.

57 Plato, *Resp.* 572C–592B.

58 *C.Th.* 7.16.2 (410). Also the constitutions concerning the African usurper Heraclianus, *C.Th.* 9.40.21 and *C.Th.* 15.14.13, were issued on August 3, 413, soon after his downfall and probable execution (Oost 1966: 240). Cañizar Palacios' contrary opinion seems to be a misunderstanding; he is also wrong in his dating to the time of Attalos' usurpation of the constitutions *C.Th.* 9.38.11 (redated by Pharr from 410 to 413) and *C.Th.* 9.38.12 (dates uncertain: August 6, 410 or 415–421, cf. Pharr 1952: 255; the text itself of this particular constitution attests that the tyrant in question was already deposed). Cf. Cañizar Palacios 2006: 140.

59 *C.Th.* 7.16.2.

60 Escribano 1997: 115–116.

61 Here, in its broader sense, cf. note 354.

"cunning" (negative mental features), and also *infandissimus*. Finally, tyranny is compared with natural disasters: *incendium* (fire) and *labes* (calamity[62]).

tyrannicus, tyrannus, tyrannis
A. opposition to the tyrant: *C.Th.* 7.16.2.9.
B1. repealing of legal decisions from the tyrant's reign: *C.Th.* 5.8.R; 5.8.1.[2]; 9.38.2.2; 9.38.11.3; 15.14.R; 15.14.1.1; 15.14.2.1; 15.14.3.1; 15.14.4.1; 15.14.5.2; 15.14.6.2; 15.14.7.2; 15.14.8.1; 15.14.10.1; 15.14.11.4; 15.14.11.7; 15.14.12.1; 16.2.47.2; *Const. Sirm.* 6.4.
B1a. confirmation of legal decisions from the tyrant's reign: *C.Th.* 7.18.9.5^2; 9.38.11.3; *C.Th.* 15.14.9.2.
B2. other references to the tyrant's reign: *C.Th.* 8.4.1.2; 9.38.11.2; 9.38.12.1.
II. other associated invectives: *audacia* (*C.Th.* 15.14.6.2); *praesumptio* (*C.Th.* 15.14.6.2, *C.Th.* 9.38.11.2); *furor* (*C.Th.* 7.16.2.9); *vafra mens* (*C.Th.* 15.14.7.2); *incendia* (*C.Th.* 9.38.11.3); *labes* (*C.Th.* 15.14.12.1); *infandissimus* (*C.Th.* 15.14.7.2); *iniquissimus* (*C.Th.* 8.4.1.2).

Praedo, latro, rebellis, desertor

Other domestic enemies are robbers (*latrones, praedones*). Roman jurisprudence distinguished them from *hostes*, because, in spite of similar activities, they were not at war with the Roman state.[63] At the same time, *latrones* were different from *hostes* both external and, which is less obvious, domestic.[64]

[62] Natural disasters, such as plague, as well as military defeats, cf. *ThLL* 7.2: 768–769.

[63] *D.* 49.15.24 (Ulpianus, liber primus institutionum): *Hostes sunt, quibus bellum publice populus Romanus decrevit vel ipsi populo Romano: caeteri latrunculi vel praedones apellantur* (there is a difference further on: a captive taken in a declared war becomes a slave, while a captive taken by brigands does not); *D.* 50.16.118 (Pomponius libro secundo ad Quintum Mucium): *Hostes hi sunt, qui nobis aut quibus nos publice bellum decrevimus: ceteri latrones aut praedones sunt. D.* 48.19.11.2 (Marcianus, libro secundo de publicis iudiciis) mentions *factiones*, formed by *latrones*. The term *praedo*, which on the basis of those statements should be considered as synonymous with *latro*, is mentioned several times in the Theodosian Code, but not even once in reference to an actual *latrocinium*. Pfaff (1925: 979) defines *latrocinium* as a particularly harshly punishable case of robbery (*rapina*), as it is assumed that a homicide is not the aim here, but the means to achieve the actual goal, that is, robbery. Nonetheless, since Sulla's time, *latrocinium* had been prosecuted according to the *Lex Cornelia de sicariis et veneficis*.

[64] The fundamental difference between a *latro* and a tyrant was the wearing of the purple by the latter (cf. Escribano 1997: 90–91). Pomponius (*D.* 50.16.118.pr.) and Ulpian (*D.* 49.15.24.pr.) defines the difference by the state of *bellum publicum*, which *latrones* do not cause (cf. Grünberger 2004: 16).

Calling real "enemies" *latrones* or *praedones* should be seen as an expression of degradation.[65] In fact, this phenomenon can be often found in the sources, primarily in reference to usurpers,[66] but also to foreign invaders.[67]

The term *praedo* is used in such a derogatory sense in the Theodosian Code. Referring to Stilicho as *praedo publicus* should be treated on par with being called *hostis publicus*; also, the resistance of frontier garrison troops to *praedones* is in fact the opposition against an external enemy. Moreover, the term *praedo* is used metaphorically to refer to a man who takes someone's property by force while the dispute is still pending,[68] and *praedor* in reference to bribes extorted by officials from unfortunate prisoners. It can be seen that all the instances of this term in the Code are essentially metaphorical.

Latrones are a different case altogether. In the Late Antique constitutions, mentions of *latrocinium* are relatively rare, yet there can be no doubt that it is recognized as one of the gravest offences.[69] The constitution orders decurions to send off such criminals immediately to proper courts for trial, instead of keeping them in custody.[70] Another constitution allows interrogating Isaurian *latrones* under torture also at Easter season, as extracting vital information they may possess is in the interest of safety of many people (*multorum salus et incolumitas*).[71] Everybody has the right to resort to armed response towards *latrones publici* (and deserters, as we shall see further on in this chapter).[72]

---

65 It was already very clear in Cicero that the term *archipirata* was more derogatory than *tyrannus* (Dunkle 1971: 13–14). In this way, on the strength of the charge of *latrocinium*, the tyrant is pictured as an enemy of the entire humanity, not only of the Roman *res publica* (cf. Lassandro 1981: 240). For an example in the literature of Late Antiquity, see Claud., *De Bello Gildonico* 15.161. In his cross-sectional typological study on the topic Grünberger 2004: 3 argues that the metopharical meanings of the term were dominating.

66 MacMullen 1963b (the Principate), Wardman 1984: 224–225; Lassandro 1981: 241, 248 (Latin panegyrics), Grünberger 2004: 72-89.

67 MacMullen 1966: 255.

68 See Chapter VIII: 213.

69 MacMullen (1966: 256) notes that in the constitutions of the Theodosian Code *latrones* were the same as *abactores* (cattle and horse rustlers). If this conclusion is drawn from his interpretation of *C.Th.* 9.30, it is certainly an exaggerated interpretation. The constitutions *C.Th.* 9.30.1 and *C.Th.* 9.30.2 impose the penalty sanctioned for *abactores* on those who are not allowed to keep horses; *C.Th.* 9.30.2 and *C.Th.* 9.30.3 justify such orders with the potential risk of horses being used – in the former case, by robbers (*latrones*), in the latter, by real cattle rustlers (*abactores*). Even if the two constitutions make reference to the same group, the legislator is clearly focused on two aspects of its activity: in *C.Th.* 9.30.2 – robbery (*latrocinium*), *C.Th.* 9.30.3 – cattle rustling.

70 *C.Th.* 9.2.5.

71 *C.Th.* 9.35.7.

72 *C.Th.* 7.18.14; 9.14.2.

Latrones is the term used with reference to those who act against *pax publica* (public peace),[73] against *quies communis* (common tranquillity);[74] once, their activity is described as *insania*.[75] In the first of these cases, the word *latro* is replaced by *rebellis*, which is treated as a synonym in the Theodosian Code.

The affinity between *latrones* and *desertores* is not accidental. Notably, deserters were principal groups of people joining *latrones* and vice versa, their main source of subsistence being robbery.[76] It should not come as a surprise then that fugitive soldiers were often compared with *latrones* and *rebelles*. These terms are not used as invective, but simply state that deserters are *latrones* and, as a result, they must be treated accordingly.[77] Still, the statement is not obvious, e.g., *C.Th.* 7.18.11 requires that deserters should be treated as *latrones* only when they reach for their weapons while trying to resist being captured. A veteran living off *latrocinium* is, of course, a robber – *latro* (considered as unworthy of being called a veteran).[78] Considered as *rebelles* are also those who give refuge to deserters[79] or give their children to be raised by shepherds (regarded as at least potential *latrones*[80]).

There is a different situation when the term *latrocinium* is used metaphorically, with a clear intention of castigating a certain action. Once, the avarice of officials taking illegal payments for office duties is described as *latrocinium*; as I have shown in the previous chapter, the constitution consistently elaborates on this particular metaphor.[81] Twice, individuals who dare to disregard decisions of Imperial officials are called *rebelles*.[82] Finally, there is also one reference in the context of the owner's right to punish his disobedient slaves.[83]

Since, as already noted, *latrones* are placed close to deserters, it is worth asking if the designation *desertores* is used as an invective as well. In actual fact, the term is used primarily in reference to those who desert their duties

---

[73] *C.Th.* 11.36.31.

[74] *C.Th.* 7.18.4.

[75] *C.Th.* 1.29.4.

[76] MacMullen 1966: 267; Giuffrè 1981: 216.

[77] This view is defended by Giuffrè 1981: 215, contrary to De Dominicis 1964: 128, who was even inclined to assume there was an interpolation in *C.Th.* 7.18.7.

[78] *C.Th.* 7.20.7. Fugitive soldiers were, of course, the main group joining ranks of *latrones* (cf. MacMullen 1966: 267).

[79] *C.Th.* 7.13.21. On the practice of providing protection for deserters and brigands by landowners or their tenants, see Krause 1987: 218–223.

[80] *C.Th.* 9.31.1.

[81] *C.Th.* 1.16.7.

[82] *Nov. Valent.* 23.44; *Nov. Majo.* 2.72.

[83] *C.Th.* 10.10.33.3.

at municipal *curiae*.[84] In the case of this particular *nomen agentis*, it would be difficult to speak clearly of a metaphor (as everybody who "abandons office" deserves this definition), but some negative overtone may have been implied in the very fact of the term having been a *nomen agentis*. Nevertheless, it does not appear to be very strong, as there are basically no terms reinforcing possible condemnation contained in this designation.

praedo
A1. external enemies: *Nov. Valent.* 9.4.
A2. domestic enemies: *C.Th.* 9.42.22.1 (*praedo publicus*).
B. officials who accept bribes from prisoners: *C.Th.* 9.3.6.5 (*praedor*).
C. who takes over disputed property by force: *C.Th.* 4.18.1.2; 4.18.1.8.

latro, latrocinium, rebellis
A. literal usage: *C.Th.* 1.29.8.2 (*latro*); 4.20.1.3[2] (*latrocinium*); 7.18.7.2 (*latro*); 7.18.14.3 (*latro*); 7.18.15.2 (*latrocinium*); 7.19.1.14 (*latro*); 7.20.7.2 (*latrocinium*); 9.2.5.3 (*latrocinium*); 9.29.R (*latro*); 9.29.2.2 (*latro*); 9.29.2.6 (*latro*); 9.30.2.1 (*latro*); 9.35.7.2 (*latro*); 9.35.7.4 (*latro*); 9.42.24.2 (*latro*); 11.36.31.5 (*rebellis*).
B. treating "the same as": *C.Th.* 7.13.21.3 (*rebellis*); 7.18.11.7 (*rebellis*); 9.14.2.7 (*latro*); 9.31.1.4 (*latro*).
C. metaphorical usage: *C.Th.* 1.16.7.12[2] (*latrocinium*); 10.10.33.3 (*rebellis*); *Nov. Valent.* 23.44 (*rebellis*); *Nov. Majo.* 2.72 (*rebellis*).

desertio, desertor
A. literal uses: *CTh.* 7.18.R; 7.18.1.2; 7.18.1.5; 7.18.3.1; 7.18.4.1; 7.18.4.5; 7.18.4.1[2]; 7.18.5.1; 7.18.5.4; 7.18.6.1; 7.18.6.4; 7.18.7.1; 7.18.8.1; 7.18.8.11; 7.18.9.2; 7.18.9.7; 7.18.9.5[2]; 7.18.10.3; 7.18.11.1; 7.18.11.3; 7.18.11.10; 7.18.11.11; 7.18.12.1; 7.18.13.1; 7.18.13.2; 7.18.14.1; 7.18.14.3; 7.18.17.2; *Nov. Valent.* 6.R; 6.1.14.
B. metaphorical uses: *C.Th.* 6.27.15.3[2]; 6.30.16.8 (on decurions); 6.30.17.4 (ditto); 8.7.16.2[2] (ditto); 12.1.29.1 (ditto); 12.1.84.5 (ditto); 16.6.6.12.

---

84 As based on the terms characteristic of this offence (*fugere, derelinquere, elabi, perfugere, transfugere*), Crogiez-Pétrequin, Jaillette (2009): 232–235 specify the following four groups seen as *desertores*: fugitive soldiers, *officiales* (one controversial case at *C.Th.* 12.15.1), members of trade associations, and decurions.

Haereticus

The frontiers of the Later Roman community ran not only along the Rhine and the Danube, but also along the lines within the Roman Empire, namely the boundaries between the religious communities. In 380, the Emperor Theodosius I stated his will that all the peoples of the Empire confess the same religion as Bishop Damasus of Rome and Bishop Peter of Alexandria.[85] Scholarly circles had long recognized the pivotal significance of this act; since then, at least theoretically, Roman citizenship was to have been regarded as strictly connected with the adherence to the community of the Catholic Church. Modern interpretations tend to be more balanced. Malcolm Errington notes that the above-mentioned words are not part of the Imperial disposition, but only an expression of the will within the extant fragment of the constitution's *praefatio*.[86] On the other hand, Maria Pia Baccari indicates that not all religious dissidents were considered to be outside the Roman community, according to the constitutions. The ones "on the outside" were heretics and apostates, but not pagans and Jews.[87] It was only Justinian's extended interpretation of Theodosius' constitution and of the term "heretic" itself that had banished them beyond the margin of that community.[88]

The term *haereticus* was too direct in its reference to a specific offence[89] to be treated metaphorically. It is of course insulting in itself (as all the honest heretics consider themselves to be orthodox), but let us note that the legislator did not have any less derogatory word describing the matter in question.

Similarly, in traditional Christian discourse, it was an insult if some specific name of a heresy was used. The anti-heretical literature championed the view of contrasting heretical communities, which were named after their founders' own names, with orthodox Christians (always and only named after Christ).[90] Of course, also those who had adhered to the Church supported by the emperor were given names derived from some alleged founder or a heretical doctrine, as it was clearly confirmed by Augustine.[91] Those who were named

85 *C.Th.* 16.1.2.

86 Errington 1997: 412–416. Let us pass over the dispute between Di Mauro Todini 1990: 117–141, who considers the edict to have been a territorially limited directive and J. Gaudemet 1997, who stands for general extent of the promulgated law.

87 Baccari 1996: 263–300.

88 Baccari 1991: 267–268, for definitions of heresy, see Berger 1955: 360 ff.

89 Stachura 2004: 228–229, 264.

90 Cf. Humfress 2007: 222. The very fact of labelling the theological adversaries with proper names may be considered, therefore, as a form of stigmatization (Lyman 1993).

91 Aug., *Contra Julianum Opus Imperfectum* 1.75 – called "Athanasians" or "Homoousians" by Arians, "Tradutionists" by Pelagians, "Macharians" by Donatists, "Pharisees" by Manichaeans.

after their alleged founder protested: show me some proof of my heresy, then you will have a right to do so.[92]

In many anti-heretical laws, there appear such "proper" names of various heresies – not individually, but enumerated one by one. It was Constantine who had already written in his letter addressed to heretics (preserved in Greek in the *Vita Constantini*): "Let it be known to you by this constitution, all you Novatians, Valentinians, Marcionites, Paulicians, and the so-called Phrygians."[93] The constitution of 381, already discussed in Chapter IV, mentions only three names of heresies as part of the ingeniously formulated invective,[94] yet two years later there will be as many as nine, enumerated one by one.[95] Theodosius II's constitution *C.Th.* 16.5.65 of the year 428 gives a record number of twenty-three names mentioned.[96]

Such a meticulous listing of heresy names may have simply served the purpose of defining the enemy in explicit and unambiguous terms. It does appear much more often than definitions of "heresies" based on other criteria, such as the content of orthodox teachings or indications of bishops (the communion with them as the condition for orthodoxy).[97] It enabled the judges to find out if they were actually confronted with a heresy or not in each particular case.[98] That is why it was so important to mention names of heretical sects, including those they could have been used as "disguise."[99]

This phenomenon also had some propaganda-related significance; by listing names of heresies, the Emperor subscribed to the tradition of anti-heretical struggle, which was shaped by successive heresiological works.[100]

---

92 For a remonstrance against the name of "Luciferians," cf. *Coll. Avell.* 2.86.

93 Euseb., *Vita Const.* III.64.

94 *C.Th.* 16.5.6, see Chapter IV: 100–104.

95 *C.Th.* 16.5.11.

96 *C.Th.* 16.5.65.

97 Stachura 2000b: 66–68.

98 How risky it was to rely only on the distinction orthodoxy – heresy is exemplified by Humfress in the Donatists' intrigue as described by Augustine; presenting themselves as "orthodox" at court, the Donatists recovered a church building from "schismatics" who had departed from their own sect (Humfress 2007: 265–266).

99 Let us note the surprising content of the constitutions *C.Th.* 16.5.7 (AD 381) and *C.Th.* 16.5.9 (AD 383), directed in particular against the Manichaeans concealed as *Encratitae, Apotactitae, Hydroparastatae,* and *Saccofori.* Possibly, the point was to prevent the Manichaean practice of assuming the names long used by Encratic Christian sects, cf. Humfress 2007: 247–248; on the other hand, the provision had also afforded an opportunity to persecute Encratic Christians as Manichaeans (Barone-Adesi 1986: 140 f.).

100 I have elaborated here on the view expressed in Humfress 2007: 237 on the Emperor's joining the theological discourse. Heresiologies are works enumerating names of various heresies and describing the "false doctrines" hidden behind them. The origins of such

Nevertheless, it would be difficult to resist the impression that in addition to these two practical goals the legislator had achieved a peculiar rhetorical effect based on amplification. The point is to accumulate multiple synonymous/near-synonymous names (as one notion of "heresy" is broken down into individual pieces), i.e., the figure of *congeries*, which is essentially centred on reinforcing condemnation through creating an impression of "obsessive" reiteration of the same content.[101]

A peculiar type of anti-heretical invective is the practice of "calling" one heresy by means of the name of some other "false teaching." This phenomenon is typical of religious controversies in Late Antiquity, when the opponent taking part in a dispute is "stigmatized" with the name of a third party (which is condemned by the two), e.g., Manichaeans and Christians had both called one another "pagan."[102] In the Imperial documents, there are three instances of such "name-calling" as applied to heresy. For the first time, when Constantine the Great calls Arius' followers "Porphyrians" (named after Porphyry, Hellenic philosopher, who was an ardent opponent of Christianity). The point of Constantine's letter in question was to ensure that Arius' books should be destroyed just the same as Porphyry's anti-Christian writings, and those who possessed them – suppressed alike.[103] Theodosius II's constitution makes conscious reference to this Constantine's order, as it announces that the followers of Nestorius should be similarly, from then on, called Simonians (after the first, according to the heresiological tradition, heretic, i.e., Simon Magus). The reference also concerns methods of suppression, notably obligatory hand-over and burning of Nestorius' writings.[104] For the third time, the tradition of "name-calling" in legislation was employed by the Emperor Marcian, who labelled Eutyches' adherents as Apollinarians.[105] This particular designation is a better conceived one, as the followers of the concept of the Two Natures of Christ had long accused their opponents of secretly professing the heresy of Apollinaris of Laodicea.[106] It is clearly stated that the extension of the name also signifies that Eutychians should be subjected to suppression that had

works may be dated back to the second century (Hegesippus, Irenaeus); in the fourth century, the most extensive heresiological works were written by Epiphanius of Salamis, whereas in the fifth century, he was followed by Filastrius of Brescia, Theodoret of Cyrrhus, and Augustine of Hippo.

101 This "obsessiveness" was noticed by Zuccotti 1992: 134.

102 Kahlos 2007a: 74–75.

103 Socr., *HE* I.9.30–31.

104 *C.Th.* 16.5.66.4–5.

105 *C.J.* 1.5.8.19–20.

106 Strictly speaking, it was contrived to equate the teachings of Mani, Apollinaris, Eutyches, and Timothy Ailuros, leader of the anti-Chalcedonians, cf. Grillmeier 1991/2004, 2/1:

previously affected the Apollinarians (already since the reign of Theodosius I[107]). It can be seen that in all the three cases the "name-calling" applied to heresies serves definite practical purposes, namely to justify suppressing it in "the same way" as som thing that had already been subject to suppression for a long time. As a result, this is not without some effect on the sanctions. It would be also impossible to overlook to overlook the element of invective: new heresies are designated with the names of old movements, already long condemned by the Christian world, including those who are thus labelled. There were obvious insults involved in calling a follower of Arius "Porphyrian," a Nestorian – "Simonian," or an opponent of the decisions of Chalcedon – "Apollinarian." Let us add that an equally unfair insult would be calling a moderate opponent of Chalcedon "Eutychian," but this is a different question, associated with simplifications used in various Chalcedon-related theological debates.[108]

haereticus
C.Th. 16.1.2.9; 16.1.3.13; 16.2.1.1; 16.2.7.2; 16.2.34.5; 16.5.R; 16.5.1.2; 16.5.4.2; 16.5.6.1; 16.5.6.4; 16.5.6.11^2; 16.5.10.2; 16.5.20.1; 16.5.21.1; 16.5.22.1; 16.5.24.1; 16.5.25.2; 16.5.26.1; 16.5.28.1; 16.5.28.4; 16.5.29.2; 16.5.30.2; 16.5.30.7; 16.5.39.1; 16.5.41.3; 16.5.44.1; 16.5.46.2; 16.5.47.1^2; 16.5.51.2; 16.5.52.1^2; 16.5.54.1; 16.5.58.4; 16.5.58.5; 16.5.59.3; 16.5.60.1; 16.5.62.2; 16.5.64.1; 16.5.65.1; 16.5.65.3^2; 16.5.65.21^2; 16.5.65.23^2; 16.6.6.3; 16.6.6.18; 16.8.19.5; 16.8.26.3; 16.10.13.5; 16.10.13.9; 16.10.24.2; *Const. Sirm.* 6.21^2; 12.1; 12.6^2; 14.12^2; *Nov. Theod.* 3.R; 3.11; 3.82.

haeresis (in the sense: heresy)
C.Th. 16.5.5.3; 16.5.11.2; 16.5.14.2; 16.5.19.3; 16.5.54.6^2; 16.5.56.1; 16.5.63.1; 16.6.4.3; 16.6.4.7.

schismaticus
C.Th. 16.5.1.3; 16.5.62.2; 16.5.64.2; *Const. Sirm.* 6.21^2.

schisma
C.Th. 16.5.62.5; 16.5.63.2; 16.6.4.3; 16.6.4.7.

220. On the Christology of Apollinaris of Laodicea, see Kelly 1988: 217–221; Grillmeier 1990/2004, 1: 480–494, 673–679.

107 *C.Th.* 16.5.12 (383).

108 As a matter of fact, it was already Timothy Ailuros, leader of the Miaphysite movement after Chalcedon, who had considered Eutychians (adherents of the radical wing of Miaphysitism) as heretics (Grillmeier 2004, 2/4: 17–23). On the positions held by opponents of the Council of Chalcedon, see Kelly 1988: 246–255; Grillmeier 2004, 2/1: 292–294.

Apollinariana, Apollinariani, Apollinarii
C.Th. 16.5.12.2; 16.5.13.2; 16.5.14.1; 16.5.33.1; 16.5.65.11

Apotactita
C.Th. 16.5.7.10^{2}; 16.5.11.3

Arrianus
C.Th. 16.5.6.8; 16.5.8.1; 16.5.11.2; 16.5.12.2; 16.5.13.1; 16.5.16.1; 16.5.59.2; 16.5.60.2; 16.5.65.10; 16.5.66.3;

Audianus
C.Th. 16.5.65.19

Borborianus, Borborita
C.Th. 16.5.65.18; *Nov. Theod.* 3.83.

Caelestianum
Const. Sirm. 6.14^{2}

Caelicola
C.Th. 16.5.43.5; 16.8.R; 16.8.19.1; *Const. Sirm.* 12.16

Donatista
C.Th. 16.5.37.1; 16.5.37.4; 16.5.38.1; 16.5.40.2; 16.5.41.3; 16.5.43.1; 16.5.43.8; 16.5.44.1; 16.5.46.1; 16.5.52.3; 16.5.54.1; 16.5.54.3^{2}; 16.5.55.3; 16.5.65.19; 16.6.4.4; 16.6.5.2; *Const. Sirm.* 12.9; 12.12; 12.19; 12.6^{2}; 14.11^{2}.

Encratita
C.Th. 16.5.7.10^{2}; 16.5.9.7; 16.5.11.3.

Enthusiasta
C.Th. 16.5.65.18.

Euchita
C.Th. 16.5.65.18.

Eunomianus
C.Th. 16.5.6.8; 16.5.8.1; 16.5.11.2; 16.5.12.2; 16.5.13.1; 16.5.17.2; 16.5.23.1; 16.5.25.1^{2}; 16.5.27.2; 16.5.31.1; 16.5.32.1; 16.5.32.2; 16.5.34.1; 16.5.36.1; 16.5.49.1; 16.5.58.1; 16.5.58.9; 16.5.58.12; 16.5.58.13; 16.5.58.3^{2}; 16.5.58.3^{2}; 16.5.58.4^{2};

16.5.58.4^{2}; 16.5.58.4^{2}; 16.5.58.12^{2}; 16.5.58.14^{2}; 16.5.59.3; 16.5.60.2; 16.5.61.2; 16.5.65.16; 16.6.7.1; 16.6.7.4; *Nov. Theod.* 3.82.

Fotiniana, Fotiniani, Fotini
C.Th. 16.5.6.7; 16.5.65.20; *Nov. Theod.* 3.83.

Fryga, Montanista, Montenses
C.Th. 16.5.34.2; 16.5.40.3; 16.5.40.14^{2}; 16.5.43.1; 16.5.48.1; 16.5.57.1; 16.5.57.12; 16.5.59.1; 16.5.65.17; 16.5.65.17; 16.6.5.2, *Const. Sirm.* 12.12; *Nov. Theod.* 3.82; 3.83.

Hydroparastatae
C.Th. 16.5.7.10^{2}; 16.5.9.8; 16.5.11.3; 16.5.65.19; *Nov. Theod.* 3.83.

Macedoniana, Macedoniani
C.Th. 16.5.11.2; 16.5.12.2; 16.5.13.1; 16.5.59.3; 16.5.60.2; 16.5.65.10.

Manichaeus, Manichaea, Manichaei
C.Th. 16.5.3.2; 16.5.7.1; 16.5.7.1; 16.5.7.3^{2}; 16.5.9.1; 16.5.11.3; 16.5.18.1; 16.5.35.1; 16.5.38.1; 16.5.40.3; 16.5.40.13^{2}; 16.5.41.3; 16.5.43.2; 16.5.59.1; 16.5.62.1; 16.5.64.1; 16.5.65.22; 16.5.65.24; 16.7.3.4; 16.7.3.8^{2}; 16.10.24.1; *Const. Sirm.* 6.21^{2}; 12.12; 12.6^{2}; *Nov. Theod.* 3.81;
Nov. Valent. 18.R; 18.3; 18.14; 18.19.

Marcellianus
C.Th. 16.5.65.20.

Marcianista
C.Th. 16.5.65.17.

Messalianus
C.Th. 16.5.65.18.

Novatianus
C.Th. 16.5.2.1; 16.5.59.3; 16.5.65.14; 16.6.6.12; 16.6.6.14.

Ofitae
Nov. Theod. 3.83.

Pauliani
C.Th. 16.5.65.20.

Pelagianus
Const. Sirm. 6.14².

Pepyzitae
C.Th. 16.5.59.2; 16.10.24.2.

Pneumatomachi
C.Th. 16.5.11.2.

Porfyriani
C.Th. 16.5.66.4.

Priscillianista
C.Th. 16.5.40.3; 16.5.40.14²; 16.5.43.2; 16.5.48.1; 16.5.59.2; 16.5.65.17; *Const. Sirm.* 12.13; *Nov. Theod.* 3.83.

Protopaschitae, Sabbatiani
C.Th. 16.5.59.3; 16.5.65.14; 16.6.6.13.

Simoniani
C.Th. 16.5.66.5

Tascodrogitae, Ascodrogi
C.Th. 16.5.10.1; 16.5.65.20; *Nov. Theod.* 3.83.

Valentiniani
C.Th. 16.5.65.16.

Paganus

Unlike heretics, followers of traditional ancient religions are not excluded from the Roman civic community by the fourth- and fifth-century Imperial legislation. An exception to this rule would be only those who renounced the Christian faith, i.e., apostates (*apostatae*).[109] But as there were many constitutions dealing with restrictions and prohibitions imposed on traditional religions, there had

[109] Baccari 1996: 220–221, 226–232.

to appear a term referring to their believers. In fact, there are even two names, *gentilis* and *paganus*, applied to them in the Imperial documents.

The former one appears to be neutral. As we have seen before, it was occasionally used by the legislator instead of *barbarus*, although it did not convey its negative tone. Nevertheless, it must be noted that the use of *gentilis* as "pagan" can be clearly distinguished from its usage in the sense "barbarian."[110]

Paganus is perceived as a word synonymous with *gentilis*, even though it comes from beyond the discourse proper for Imperial documents (as one of the constitutions pronounces: *gentiles, quos vulgo paganos apellant*[111]). It is the evidence that along with the Latin translations of the Bible this new meaning of the word *gentilis* gained its own position in the language spoken by the elites, whereas *paganus* continued to be seen as something "vulgar," and thus perhaps also insulting. Let us also add that the religious meaning of the word *paganus* is new, only beginning to be commonly used in the Christian writings in the fourth century.[112] It is noteworthy that in its first attested usage in the Theodosian Code the term *paganus* is simply a synonym of "citizen";[113] when it appears again, it refers to individuals of a "pagan spirit," that is, those who oppose privileges of the Church.[114] At the beginning of Theodosius I's reign, the word *paganus* is used to describe the state of apostasy;[115] in 392, *superstitio* of pagans receives a more specific term *gentilicia*.[116] Further, already more frequent, examples of *paganus* and *gentilis* can be found after that date. It is quite interesting as there were numerous constitutions against pagan offerings prior to that date, in which any mention of "pagans" was evidently avoided. Apparently, only with the prohibition of all sacrifices enacted by the *C.Th.* 16.10.12 (392) pagans as such began to be stigmatized; beforehand, efforts were made to create the impression that only the act itself, i.e., making an offering, is proscribed.

It must be clearly noted that also during the fifth-century pagan sacrifices, designated with terms such as *sacrificium*, *ritus*, or *superstitio*, continue to remain the subject of the legislator's interest.[117] It is also the proper target of invective in the "anti-pagan" constitutions. It would be wrong to define

---

110 Also in the constitution *C.Th.* 3.14.1 (Chapter *de nubtiis gentilium*); cf. Bianchini 1988: 225 ff.; Frezza 1989: 65 ff.

111 *Const. Sirm.* 14.14².

112 Opelt 1965b: 14–16; Kahlos 2007a: 24; Jürgasch 2016.

113 *C.Th.* 7.21.2 (AD 353).

114 *paganorum animi* (*C.Th.* 16.2.18, AD 370).

115 *C.Th.* 16.7.1 (AD 381): *qui ex Christianis pagani facti sunt*; *C.Th.* 16.7.2 (AD 383): *Christianis ac fidelibus, qui ad paganis ritus cultusque migrarunt*.

116 *C.Th.* 16.10.12.

117 Kahlos 2007a: 16. This latter term is also often used in reference to the practice of making offerings to gods, e.g., in the constitutions *C.Th.* 16.7.6; 16.10.16; 16.10.20; cf. Stachura 2008: 182, note 18.

a pagan as someone who performs such cult practices.[118] A constitution sets out to defend those pagans who do "nothing against the laws,"[119] e.g., those who do not make offerings. Let us note that in the constitutions, incorrectly called "anti-pagan," there are no enumerations of cults related to various gods and names of religious communities, analogous to lists of heresies. Still, there are listed types of offerings,[120] as well as names of collegial groups of pagan priests.[121]

apostata
C.Th. 16.7.R, 16.7.7.2.

paganus, paganitas
C.Th. 2.8.22.[2]; 7.21.2.1; 15.5.5.11; 16.2.18.1²; 16.5.46.3; 16.7.1.2; 16.7.2.1; 16.8.26.2; 16.10.R; 16.10.13.5; 16.10.19.2²; 16.10.20.1; 16.10.21.1; 16.10.22.1; 16.10.23.1; 16.10.24.6; 16.10.25.2; *Const. Sirm.* 6.24²; 12.25; 14.14²; *Nov. Theod.* 3.R; 3.11; 3.62; 3.71; 3.76; *Nov. Valent.* 18.2.

gentilicius, gentilis (in the sense: pagan, a pagan)
C.Th. 16.5.43.2; 16.5.46.3; 16.5.63.2; 16.10.12.16; 16.10.20.19; 16.10.21.2; *Const. Sirm.* 12.2; 12.9; 12.13; 12.7²; 14.14²; *Nov. Theod.* 3.62.

Maleficus

As noted before, individuals practising magic and soothsaying are regarded to act not just against the Roman community, but even in defiance of the entire humanity.[122] They are the last group to be discussed in this subsection.

As in the case of various heresies, the legislator lists in succession, and several times, names of diverse groups involved in forbidden divination and fortune-telling practices, e.g., in *C.Th.* 9.16.4 (357), the following terms are mentioned: *haruspex, mathematicus, hariolus, vatus, Chaldeus, magus, maleficus*. These groups are considered to have possessed their own peculiar "teachings," comparable with those of heretics.[123]

---

118 One could only attempt to form such a definition by analogy to some definitions of "apostate" found in the constitutions, cf. Stachura 2008: 181.

119 *C.Th.* 16.10.24: ...*nihilque temptantibus turbulentum legibusque contrarium*.

120 *C.Th.* 16.10.12.

121 *C.Th.* 16.10.20.

122 *C.Th.* 9.16.6: *inimici humani generis*; *C.Th.* 9.16.11: *hostis communis salutis*.

123 *C.Th.* 9.16.4 uses the term *confessiones*; *C.Th.* 16.5.34 compares heretical books with the ones used by magicians; *C.Th.* 9.16.12 orders *mathematici* (the soothsayers practising astrology and

Among these various names, there is one which is the object of a certain unique invective; the above-mentioned constitution gives the following definition of sorcerers: *ceteri, quos maleficos ob facinorum magnitudinem vulgus apellant* – "generally called *malefici* (literally: "evildoers") due to a magnitude of their crimes." Both magic and soothsaying are then depicted by means of further invectives,[124] with a notable example of *divinandi curiositas* in reference to the wish of getting to know the future.[125] As Fögen notes, this is the only case in the normative texts when *curiositas* takes on a pejorative shade of meaning.[126]

augur
C.Th. 9.16.4.2; 9.16.6.6.

hariolus
C.Th. 9.16.4.2; 9.16.6.6.

haruspex
C.Th. 9.16.1.1; 9.16.1.4; 9.16.2.1; 9.16.4.1; 9.16.6.6; 16.10.1.3.

magus
C.Th. 9.16.4.2; 9.16.6.3; 9.16.6.5; *Const. Sirm.* 8.26.

maleficus
C.Th. 1.16.6.8; 9.16.R; 9.16.4.3; 9.16.6.5; 9.16.11.6; 9.38.3.4; 9.38.8.10; 11.36.1.4; 11.36.7.3.

mathematicus
C.Th. 9.16.R; 9.16.4.1; 9.16.6.6; 9.16.8.1; 9.16.12.1; 16.5.62.2; *Const. Sirm.* 6.21[2].

vates
C.Th. 9.16.4.2.

---

numerology) to burn their books of errors in the presence of a bishop, renounce their own error (*error* – the word characteristic for descriptions of heresies), and accept the Christian faith.

124 C.Th. 9.16.1: referring to haruspicy as *superstitio*; C.Th. 9.16.3: black magic called *scientia punienda et severissimis ... legibus vindicanda*; C.Th. 9.16.5: *malae artes*, while magicians are *naturae peregrini*; C.Th. 9.16.6: *magicis contaminibus adsuaeti*; C.Th. 9.16.11: *maleficiorum labe polluti*; C.Th. 9.16.8 and C.Th. 9.16.12: referring to the craft of *mathematici* as *error*.

125 C.Th. 9.16.4: *Sileat omnibus perpetuo divinandi curiositas.*

126 Fögen 1993: 288.

Chapter VI: Terms indicating the perpetrator's attitude

In the present chapter, I shall be concerned with a group of terms denoting not so much a deed itself as the perpetrator's attitude, determining or accompanying his actions. This attitude reveals his wickedness, at the same time explaining why he had undertaken that action, and indicates his opposition to the order of accepted moral values. As we shall see, traditional vices tend to play a less important role here; instead, a more prominent part is given to some attitudes traditionally denounced in the Roman world, and difficult to render without any ambiguity, such as *audacia* (specifically conceived "audacity") and *furor* (specifically conceived "madness"). For these two terms, which may seem quite "exotic" from the perspective of our modern way of thinking, it was necessary, in my opinion, to provide a brief outline of their history. An important role can also be assigned to some other negative attitudes, contrasted with the ideals such as *humanitas*, *fides*, and *pietas*. Of course, for all of these terms, one could place an emphasis on the act itself, not on the perpetrator, and argue that, e.g., what is condemned as *audacia* is not a person's attitude but the very nature of the act. Nonetheless, I have decided to explain these terms in a separate chapter, on the assumption that the perpetrator's specific vice is indicated here by means of condemning the act, while, e.g., an accusation of *scelus* does not involve such unambiguous assumptions as to its motivation.

Avaritia, cupiditas, desidia, invidia

"It is an impropriety to leave a virtue without praise, just as it is (to leave) a vice without castigation," says Aphthonios at the beginning of his exemplary *psogos* against Philip.[1] Even though the proper target of this oration are

[1] Οὔτε τὴν ἀρετὴν ἐπαίνων χωρὶς οὔτε τὴν κακίαν ἔξω ψόγου προσήκει καταλιπεῖν (Aphthonios, Prog., 9, RG 2: 40). Rendering κακία in this text as „vice" seems to be justified

Philip's actions, it is through them that the vices of the person being castigated are expressed. Thus, for instance, there were traditionally four vices attributed to tyrants: *vis*, *libido*, *superbia*, and *crudelitas*.[2] Over the course of time, these features passed on to criticised Roman officials[3] and emperors.[4] Barbarians are characterized by the inability to control their impulses, resulting primarily in cruelty.[5] Dishonest officials' typical vice is, in turn, their *avaritia*. It is an urge that leads both Cicero's Verres[6] and Claudian's Rufinus[7] to crime.

Yet verbal aggression in the Late Antique constitutions is not concentrated on vices. As a matter of fact, when they are mentioned, it serves to characterize the attitude guiding the perpetrator at the moment of the performance of the castigated act.

The most frequent accusation that can be found in our texts is avarice (*avaritia*, *aviditas*, *cupiditas*, *libido*). And here as well, this vice seems to affect officials in a particularly great extent. In the Theodosian Code and Novels, reprehensible greed can be attributed just as often to Imperial officials as to citizens guilty of various offences.[8] "Avarice" thus becomes a significant motive for the emperors' criticism of the state administration apparatus. As may be expected, it is often ascribed to dishonest tax-collectors,[9] yet it seldom affects venal judges.[10] Generally speaking, it is apparently mostly typical of low-ranking officials and functionaries of various *officia*,[11] as if there were some more serious charges reserved for judges. In the case of citizens not in public service, the avarice may lead them, for instance, to unjustified litigation in court[12]

---

by contrasting it with „virtue" (ἀρετή), although further on Philip is only directly accused of „barbarian lack of self-control" (βαρβαρικὴ ἀκρασία).

2 Dunkle 1967: 151, 159–170.

3 Dunkle 1967: 161 ff.

4 Dunkle 1971: 17.

5 Ohnacker 2003: 54.

6 Of all Cicero's adversaries, Verres is the one most often accused of *avaritia*. 48 mentions of this word can be found in the *Verrinae*, out of a total number of 118 in all of Cicero's works (*CLCLT-6*).

7 James 1998: 167, 171.

8 21 and 20 mentions in the Code and 13 and 15 in the Novels, respectively.

9 *C.Th.* 7.4.35.3; 7.4.35.4; 11.8.1.5; *Nov. Valent.* 1.3.17; *Nov. Valent.* 1.3.51; *Nov. Valent.* 7.1.8; *Nov. Valent.* 7.1.16; *Nov. Valent.* 7.1.21; *Nov. Valent.* 7.2.2; *Nov. Valent.* 7.2.14; *Nov. Valent.* 7.2.23; *Nov. Majo.* 2.49.

10 *C.Th.* 9.27.6.4; very generally in *C.Th.* 1.5.9.4; *C.Th.* 12.1.61.3; also, *Nov. Theod.* 24.10; *Nov. Theod.* 24.52 on *duces*.

11 *C.Th.* 1.16.3.5; 1.16.7.6[2]; 1.32.2.6; 6.27.3.12; 6.30.17.6; 7.1.7.4; 7.4.32.5; 8.1.16.6; 8.10.2.8; 11.4.1.6; *Nov. Majo.* 2.32; 2.49 and on other lower-ranking officials: *C.Th.* 4.13.3.4; 6.29.5.2; 8.5.7.2; on decurions: *C.Th.* 7.7.2.2.

12 *Nov. Theod.* 4.27 (2×); *Nov. Marc.* 1.67.

and submitting unjust petitions;[13] when there are references made to illegal appropriation, it is usually concerning public property.[14]

A much less frequently mentioned vice is lust or covetousness (*libido, cupiditas, luxuria*), occurring in a variety of contexts: sexual offences,[15] illicit marital relations,[16] other reprehensible deeds motivated by lust,[17] but also simply as a trait characteristic of human nature in general.[18]

avaritia, avarus

A. avarice of public officials: *C.Th.* 1.16.3.5; 1.32.2.6; 4.13.3.4; 6.29.5.2; 6.30.17.6; 8.1.16.6; 8.5.7.2; 8.10.2.8; 11.4.1.6; *Nov. Valent.* 1.3.17; 7.1.8; 7.2.2; 28.14.

B. avarice of private individuals: *C.Th.* 1.29.5.6; 3.18.2.10; 5.8.1.3²; *Const. Sirm.* 16.12; *Nov. Theod.* 4.27; Nov. Marc. 1.67; 3.2 (non-performance of duties connected with the person's own property).

aviditas, avidus

A. greed of public officials: *C.Th.* 1.5.9.4; 1.16.7.6²; 7.4.32.5; *Nov. Theod.* 24.52; *Nov. Valent.* 7.1.16; 7.2.14; *Nov. Majo.* 2.32.

B. greed of private individuals: *C.Th.* 10.10.11.2; 15.1.25.4; 15.2.2.2; 15.2.6.8; *Nov. Theod.* 23.24; *Nov. Majo.* 6.102.

luxuria (in the sense: covetousness): *Nov. Majo.* 9.18.

cupiditas, cupidus

A. cupidity (greed) of public officials: *C.Th.* 6.27.3.12; 7.1.7.4; 7.4.35.3; 9.27.6.4; 11.8.1.5; *Nov. Valent.* 1.3.51; 7.1.21; 7.2.23; *Nov. Majo.* 2.49.

B. cupidity (greed) of private individuals: *C.Th.* 5.14.33.[5]; 7.15.1.1²; 9.17.3.1; 9.38.7.3 (ambiguous, permissible rendering: covetousness); 10.10.29.1²; 10.19.2.1; 12.1.69.2; 12.1.161.10; 12.7.2.2; 15.2.6.8; *Const. Sirm.* 1.8²; *Nov. Theod.* 4.27; 10.1.3; 19.5; *Nov. Valent.* 8.1.5; 12.34; 21.2.11; 25.17; *Nov. Majo.* 6.94; 6.107.

C. covetousness: *C.Th.* 3.16.1.2; 4.12.6.2; *Nov. Majo.* 6.14; 6.17; 6.48.

D. in positive and neutral meanings (wishing, craving): *C.Th.* 6.24.3.4; 12.1.177.2; 14.3.4.3; 14.9.1.2.

---

13 *C.Th.* 10.10.11.2; 10.10.29.1².

14 *C.Th.* 5.14.33.5; 7.15.1.1²; 15.1.25.4; 15.2.2.2; 15.2.6.8 (2×); moreover, *C.Th.* 9.17.3.1 accuses grave robbers of *cupiditas*, while *C.Th.* 3.18.2.10 attributes *avaritia* to dishonest tutors.

15 *C.Th.* 9.16.3.3 (a vaguely stated goal of black magic practices); *Nov. Maio.* 6.48 (abduction); *Nov. Maio.* 9.18 (adultery); *Nov. Maio.* 9.19 (ditto).

16 *C.Th.* 12.1.6.8.

17 *C.Th.* 2.1.3.4; 3.16.1.2; 4.12.6.2 (2×).

18 *C.Th.* 9.43.1.11; *Nov. Majo.* 6.14; 6.17.

libido
A. lawlessness of public officials (associated with avarice): *C.Th.* 7.4.35.4; 7.7.2.2; 8.5.47.3; 12.1.61.3; *Nov. Theod.* 24.10.
B. lawlessness of private individuals (associated with avarice): *C.Th.* 1.16.6.10; 10.10.25.3; 11.16.3.3; *Nov. Theod.* 5.2.5.
C. covetousness: *C.Th.* 2.1.3.4; 4.12.6.[2]; 9.16.3.3; 9.43.1.11; 12.1.6.8; *Nov. Majo.* 9.19.

Sloth, or sluggishness, is a vice which is relatively rare in the Late Antique constitutions, depicted mostly with terms such as *desidia* and *segnitia*.[19] It is interesting to note, nonetheless, that they tend to appear, almost exclusively, in reference to Imperial officials, in particular *iudices*. Moreover, they are usually linked with such censurable attitudes as *neglegentia* (negligence)[20] and *coniventia* (connivance).[21]

segnitia, segnis, segniter, segnities, desidia, desidiosus
A. attitude of officials:
A1. *Iudices*: *C.Th.* 1.5.9.3 (*desidia*); 1.10.7.7 (*desidia*); 1.11.1.9 (*desidia*); 1.15.17.4 (*desidia*); 2.6.2.3 (*desidia*); 6.4.13.17 (*segniter*); 8.8.5.5 (*desidia*); 9.1.7.3 (*segniter*); 9.1.18.1 (*desidia*); 10.1.16.12 (*segnitia*); 15.1.2.3 (*desidia*); *Const. Sirm.* 12.10 (*desidia*); *Nov. Theod.* 3.84 (*desidia*).
A2. members of *officium*: *C.Th.* 1.9.3.3 (*segnis*); 6.4.13.22 (*segnities*); 8.1.9.3 (*segnitia*); *Nov. Theod.* 24.62 (*desidia* – of soldiers).
A3: attitude of evasion of duties by officials in Imperial service: *C.Th.* 7.12.2.7 (*desidia*); 7.18.16.1[2] (*desidiosus*); *Nov. Valent.* 7.3.3 (*desidia*); 7.3.3 (*segnis*).
B. attitude of municipal councils: *Nov. Valent.* 7.2.12 (*segnities*); *Nov. Valent.* 7.2.5 (*desidia*).
C. attitude of private individuals: *C.Th.* 11.31.5.8 (*desidia*).
D. other: *C.Th.* 8.12.6.2 (*segniter*).

Another vice responsible for motivations leading many people to certain actions is *invidia*. It may be rendered as "envy" or "hatred," and gives rise to so diverse actions that any attempt to categorize them is pointless. At the same time, it does not have to appear as a hard accusation. Even the emperors concede that they may be motivated by *invidia*. For instance, Valentinian III retracted his hasty decision, which, as he would openly state himself, was

---

19 Also, *iners* in *C.Th.* 8.7.10.2 and *C.Th.* 14.18.1.4. *Piger* in *C.Th.* 6.4.22.6, 12.1.84.4, *pigresco* in *C.Th.* 8.2.5.2 – rather closer to "slow."

20 *C.Th.* 2.6.2.3.

21 *C.Th.* 1.11.1.9; *Const. Sirm.* 12.10.

taken as a result of his own *invidia*. Conversely, the *invidia* towards the benefits of *nostrum saeculum* may be a motivation for the tyrant's withdrawal of some privileges,[22] whilst the *invidia* towards the dead may lead to depriving them of the last rites (*munus extremum*), as the legislator descriptively refers to the crime of sepulchral desecration.[23] As can be seen, the charges of *invidia* may be interpreted, depending on the actual circumstances, as either relatively mild or very serious.

invidia

A. in the sense *odium*: *C.Th.* 1.15.10.6; 6.35.14.6; 7.18.9.4^2; 8.5.23.9; 8.8.5.6; 9.40.21.5; 10.10.16.4; 11.1.27.3; 11.30.61.5; 14.3.16.3; 15.14.14.3; 16.5.9.12; *Nov. Valent.* 23.50.

B. envy, hatred:

B1. towards the emperor: *C.Th.* 10.26.1.4.

B1a. towards *nostrum saeculum* on the usurper's part: *C.Th.* 16.2.47.2 = *Const. Sirm.* 6.4 (*invideo*).

B2. towards official capacity: *C.Th.* 1.10.4.7; 1.31.1.2^2 (*invideo*); *Nov. Valent.* 22.4.

B3a. of the prosecution: *C.Th.* 9.1.12.6 (*invidiosus*); 9.16.10.2; 10.10.2.3.

B3b. of the plaintiff in a civil lawsuit: *C.Th.* 2.26.4.4; 10.12.2.4^2; *Nov. Marc.* 1.67.

B3c. of the judge: *Nov. Marc.* 1.54.

B4. towards citizens, in other cases: *C.Th.* 9.44.1.3; 9.44.1.7; 15.14.14.2 (*invidiose*); 16.2.32.3; *Nov. Theod.* 22.2.28 (*invideo*); 22.2.37; *Nov. Valent.* 1.3.9 (*invidus*); 5.6.

B5. towards the dead: *Nov. Valent.* 23.17 (*invideo*).

B6. of the emperor (he has no *invidia*): *C.Th.* 15.7.3.2 (*invideo*); *Nov. Theod.* 1.28; *Nov. Valent.* 8.2.8 (the emperor was first motivated by his rash anger, but now retracts his decision).

B7. the fate seen as envious: *C.Th.* 13.5.13.5 (*invideo*).

B8. as a motivation for assuming the forbidden title of chiliarch: *C.Th.* 16.10.20.2^2.

Audacia

The most frequent negative judgemental words that can be found in the Late Antique normative texts are those connected with accusations of *audacia*. It also has a very elaborate set of connotations derived from the tradition of using this term as part of the language of invective.

---

[22] *C.Th.* 16.2.47.2 = *Const. Sirm.* 6.4.

[23] *Nov. Valent.* 23.17.

It is actually a negative term of a long-standing tradition and with a broad, and quite elusive, semantic range. It turns out to be flexible enough to encompass a wide spectrum of reprehensible phenomena, in both political and private areas, and this is exactly what makes it so appealing as a vehicle to express invective. Simultaneously, it entails a number of specific negative perceptions and associations; without such contents, it would be practically useless for the direct purpose of invective, i.e., discrediting a person to which a given characteristic is assigned.

This term has a long and complicated history. For the Greeks of the Classical period *thrasytēs* and *tolma* (θρασύτης and τόλμα, whose later counterpart is the Latin term *audacia*[24]) did not have any clearly identified emotional content. In Thucidydes' historiography, *tolma* refers to a sort of undaunted boldness that may be both a fault and a merit.[25] In fact, there is a similar situation in Plato's *Laches* – unlike real valour (*andreia*), "audacity" (both *thrasytēs* and *tolma* being used) is an excessive and untimely kind of courage, but not necessarily in a bad cause.[26]

At the same time, both referring to a political opponent as a *thrasys* and accusing him of *tolma* is already a perfectly clear invective. The charge was undoubtedly right in reference to Cleon, as it is attested by Aristophanes.[27] This invective would be employed by Isocrates, Aeschines, and, in particular, Demosthenes.[28] The terms *thrasytes* and *tolma* became tremendously popular in the discourse of political philosophy. It was already in one of Plato's most famous descriptions that the demagogue turned into a tyrant was characterized as *drimytatos* ("the most impulsive").[29] In the Hellenistic period, this "impulsiveness" would become a typical feature of popular leaders and reform-oriented rulers accused of tyrannical inclinations.[30] This political significance is exactly what would have the strongest effect on the Latin evolution of the term *audacia*.

In the archaic Latin, the term *audacia* could possess positive or neutral overtones in reference to war or politics. This observation can be drawn

---

24 Weische 1966: 32. Cf. *ThLL* 2: 1240.

25 It is a merit in, e.g., Pericles' oration, Thuc. 2.65.5. Cf. Weische 1966: 67–68.

26 Plato, *Laches* 197B.

27 Aristophanes, *Eq.* 303; more examples concerning Cleon – cf. Wirszubski 1961: 22, note 68.

28 Examples of *thrasys* and *thrasytēs* are collected in Wirszubski 1961: 11, note 4, 22, note 68; for examples of *tolma* and other derived forms, see Weische 1966: 32–33. Let us note that in the *Iliad* there already appears a protagonist's name coined from that negative feature, i.e., Tersites (*Iliad* II.212–270).

29 Plato, *Respublica* 564D.

30 Weische 1966: 23, for an example from Polibius 4.81.2–3, with a mention of the term *tolma*.

on the basis of some archaizing fragments in Sallustius,[31] but also in Caesar's writings[32] and the *Aeneid*[33] *audacia* may even take on some positive shade of meaning. In the Late Antique literature as well, *audax* appears as a clearly positive designation, e.g., in Ammianus' depiction of Julian.[34] Generally speaking, *audax* may have a positive sense ("bold") in military contexts, when referring to a soldier or a commander.

On the other hand, in Latin comedy, beginning from as early as Plautus' works, in references to private life, the term assumes a definitely negative overtone, associated with *malus* ("bad").[35] It appears that Cicero, who deliberately made use of various comparisons from Greek comedy in his political rhetoric, also consciously combined comedic and political meanings of *audacia*.[36] But the main source utilized by Cicero and the *optimates* was the image of the *populares* leaders as "bad" (*kakoi*), aspiring to reform. Their postulation of a redistribution of property had been a particular cause for offence.[37]

In the first century BC, the negative way of perceiving *audacia* was typical for only one party involved in political controversies of the period, i.e., the *optimates*. It was brilliantly depicted by Sallustius in his *Catiline's Conspiracy*: the term *audacia* assumes here a clearly negative shade of meaning, contrary to *virtus* and *fortitudo*, only in Cato the Younger's speech,[38] whereas the approach of the historian himself, as displayed in the narration, is much more ambivalent.[39] Although there are very few examples of polemical statements on the *populares*' part, yet they allow one to note that the term *audax* was relatively seldom applied with reference to their opponents, instead preferring to describe them as "haughty" (*superbi*).[40] Conversely, the enemies of the *optimates* and Cicero are normally depicted as being *audaces*, and this charge is in turn linked with accusations of "madness" and their apparently instinctual inclination to incite riots, *seditiones*. Those who had used this term as an in-

31 E.g., Sallust., *In Catil.* 9.3. Weische 1966: 66; Bruggiser 2002: 269–270, 287.

32 E.g., Caes., *De bello civ.* 3.26.1, cf. Bruggiser 2002: 284–285, with all the mentions listed.

33 Lazzarini 1982 – on a passage in Verg., *Aen.* 10.284, cf. also *ThLL* 2: 1245.

34 Amm. Marc. 21.10.1.

35 Opelt 1965a: 55, 62, 81, 95, 96.

36 Sussman 1998 demonstrates how Cicero makes use of the comical stereotype of an "audacious harlot" (*meretrix audax*), first to project it into an incident from Antonius' private life, then turn that incident into a proof of *audacia* as his adversary's general characteristic.

37 Weische 1966: 16–22.

38 Bruggiser 2002: 275.

39 Bruggiser 2002: 287.

40 Wirszubski 1961: 19–20; Weische 1966: 54–55. The only case of *audacissimi* being used in reference to those who consider themselves as *optimi* is a citation from C. Memmius in Sallust., *Iug.* 31.16.

vective deliberately contrasted the *audaces* with *boni cives*, "good citizens," i.e., themselves, and perceived their opponents' activity as subversive, aimed against the political order of the Republic.[41] *Audax* is the one "who in the *res publica* has dared to do what no good man would ever have done" (*is qui in re publica ausus est ea quae nemo auderet bonus*),[42] that is to say, none of the politicians deserving their esteem. In consequence, *audacia* will always be an act directed against the established order. The essence of "audacity" is not in the courage or impulsiveness, with which a given deed is done, but in that a "good citizen" would never dare to undertake such an attempt aimed at the public good.[43] The stress is thus laid not upon the boldness of the act, but on its essential wickedness. *Audacia* is attributable only to the "unrighteous," *improbi*;[44] whereas, as Cicero suggests, the impulsiveness (even when deserving reprimand) of a "good citizen" cannot be called *audacia*, but only, at most, *temeritas*.[45]

Incidentally, let us note that this particular distinction between the two terms would not prove to be enduring. For instance, in Late Antiquity, Marius Victorinus made a totally opposite claim that *audacia* was possible in a good cause, while *temeritas* was always bad.[46] It would be also incorrect to assume that the negative sense of *audacia* only appeared in political rhetoric. In his judicial orations, Cicero frequently describes individuals accused of various offences as *audaces* (or even *audacissimi*), without any apparent political context.[47]

In the transformed political reality of Late Antiquity, accusations of *audacia* are directed against tyrants – depicted as villainous characters in panegyrics. Their conduct is described as irrational flinging between fear and audacity.[48] On the other hand, the Latin Fathers of the Church, beginning from Tertullian, use this term in reference to heretics.[49] Still, as we shall see, the negative meaning of *audacia* in normative texts cannot be reduced only to such cases.

---

41 Wirszubski 1961: 13–14; Śnieżewski 2003: 184–186.

42 Wirszubski 1961: 15, in a paraphrase of Velleius Paterculus II.24.5.

43 In *De officiis* I.63, Cicero defines the difference between *fortitudo* and *audacia* in that the former strives for *utilitas communi*, whereas the latter – one's own *cupiditas*.

44 Wirszubski (1961: 12, note 4) notes that the connection between *improbi* and *audaces* in Cicero has its counterpart in the connection between *thrasys* and *poneros* in Demosthenes.

45 Cic., *Ad Att.* 10.1.4: *Aut nos temeritatem bonorum sequamur aut audaciam improborum insectemur. Utrumque periculosum est.* As a general rule, the *optimates'* political rhetoric treated the two terms as synonymous (Weische 1966: 28–30).

46 Marius Victorinus, *Explanationes in Ciceronis Rhetoricam* 1.3: *audax potest interdum et pro bono accipi, temerarius non nisi malus.*

47 E.g., Cic., *In Verrem* I.7: *audacissimus et amentissimus.* Cf. Wirszubski 1961: 15–16.

48 *Paneg. Lat.* 2.43.1.

49 Tert., *De praescr. haer.* 15.

In the constitutions under consideration, the notion is expressed in the form of the abstract nouns *audacia* and *ausus*, as well as the verb *audeo*; there are also single instances of the adverb *audaciter*, adjective *audax*, and participle *ausus*. As a term close in meaning, there also appears *temeritas* (as well as the verb *temero*, adjective *temerarius*, and *nomen agentis* – *temerator*). No differences in the intensity of condemnation can be identified in the applications of these various forms (which could be expected as based on Cicero's opinion) – *audacia* and *temeritas* seem to be equal in their intensity.[50] Conversely, they often both reinforce one another as part of the rhetorical figure of *congeries* (accumulation); as a matter of fact, it is one of the most frequent cases of this sort of amplification in the Late Antique normative texts.[51]

As part of "accumulation" figures, the notion of *audacia* is often reinforced with forms of the verb *praesumo* and other derivative forms (*praesumptio*, *praesumptor*). In the language of the Late Antique documents, there are indeed various neutral meanings of this verb ("take," "undertake," "give priority to," "have priority," as well as "presume" in the technical sense), yet the clearly negative meaning tends to prevail, and it may be rendered as "presume to do something" (that reprehensible action is not so much connected with "presuming", interpreting the content of a law on one's own, as simply acting without any legal basis or even contrary to a prescription).[52] The thing which is indicated here is one's making impudent claims, inherently associated with the attitude of *audacia*. Likewise, the verbs that denote "attempting" (*tempto*, *conor*) take on the amplificatory effect ("whoever would attempt ...")

---

50 It should be noted that Pharr's English translation does not recognize the terms as synonymous, rendering *temeritas* as "lawlessness."

51 One is confronted here with either two ways of referring to the same action: ...absente senatus defensore nihil se **praesumat** vel curiales vel iudices ordinare, ne quid contra commodum coetus amplissimi iustitiae ratione despecta **temerariae usurpationis** decernat **audacia** ... (*C.Th.* 1.28.3); or the subordinate clause explaining what the condemned action is about: ...quos in **tantum furorem** provexit **audacia**, ut quod iurgaturi apud examinis fidem sperare non possent, ante eventum iudicialis arbitrii inlicita **praesumptione temerarent** (*C.Th.* 4.22.3), or simply two terms in describing the same action: ne inpune ullus **temeritas** contra statutum nostrum possit **audere** (*C.Th.* 6.18.1). It is, unfortunately, impossible to point to any rule in how this rhetorical figure was used for some specific type of *audacia*. As a result, they cannot be used for the purpose of formulating "systematization" of the Empire's enemies, and for measuring the "force" of condemnation. Still, they can show that the very charge of *audacia*, so often "amplified," is a fairly readily employed element of the invective rhetoric in the Late Antique legislation.

52 Heuman, Seckel 1914: 454 – *sich anmaßen*. Examples: *C.Th.* 8.5.54.5 – officials make use of the *cursus publicus* in violation of the prescription; *C.Th.* 16.5.8.3 – heretics build their churches in contravention of the prescription.

in the context of *audacia*. At the same time, the verb *tempto*, similarly to *audacia*, very often directly points to attempting to transgress against a given law.

Only over a dozen times mentioned, there is also another word, which may be treated in certain cases as a synonym of *audacia* – ***insolentia*** (*insolens*, *insolenter*). Only once (*C.Th.* 7.13.7.6) does the term refer to excess; in all other cases, it concerns audacity. Close relations with *audacia* are particularly evident in *C.Th.* 1.29.7 (usurping the authority of a higher office; being associated with *temeritas*) and *C.Th.* 10.20.6.5 (failure to comply with prohibitions, punished more severely than prior to the constitution's promulgation). Individual mentions of other terms possibly indicative of "audacity" (*procacitas*, *protervitas*, *petulans*) do not allow us to venture any generalization.[53]

Even the listing of grammatical forms (verbs and verbal forms tend to prevail) indicates that directly the action is being castigated, and only indirectly the perpetrator. It is definitely more rarely than in the literature cited above that the adjective *audax* (or *temerarius*), characteristic of the perpetrator, appears. The deed itself is condemned directly, even though there is no doubt that this is indirectly a negative evaluation of the offender as well. The word "invective," in its extended meaning I have chosen to apply, can be used here without much hesitation. The situation is very clear: accusations of *audacia* do not entail any legal consequences; their sole function is to express condemnation for the "audacity" of a given deed and its perpetrator.

Describing a specific action as "audacious" is therefore an evaluative judgement. It does not always have to concern the subject-matter of the act alone, but also its circumstances, and, above all, against whom or what it is directed. *Audacia* may be wrong either on account of the goal which the *audax* intends to achieve or because of the value which should be respected, yet the *audax* refuses to do so or even transgresses against it.

In the first case, one would have to deal with criminal offences. This charge cannot be found very often, though. *Audacia* is sometimes used in reference to abduction (*raptus*), whereas the only case when the legislator speaks of the *audacia* of murderers actually refers to their abuse of Imperial rescripts. Furthermore, accusations of *audacia* can be found where there is *crimen vis*, i.e., acts of unlawful use of violence. The further two, very serious, offences, whose descriptions include charges of *audacia*, are magic and sepulchral violation. Both of them involve infringement of the order at the highest (cosmic) level,[54] and consequently the lack of regard for a very profound value. As for the crime of *maiestas*, the most serious violation of the order of authority,

[53] But let us notice the connection between *procax* and *vesania* at *C.Th.* 11.36.14.7.

[54] Cf. Chapter IX: 252–254.

it is not, in itself, depicted as *audacia*. Yet the term is sometimes used with reference to usurpers ("tyrants"), robbers (*latrones*), and deserters, who are seen at the same level as *latrones*. To sum up, the legislator calls offences "audacious" when their most significant feature is violence or when, in addition, they infringe on some higher value.

In an overwhelming majority of the cases, the term *audacia*, as present in the analyzed texts, indicates an "impudent" violation of some specific value. The Imperial law – a specific, recently issued constitution – is what usually constitutes this value. It is notable that the emperor's references to concrete, previously issued laws are relatively rare. Very often, still, *audacia* turns out to be a violation of the law which has just been made public. The formula "if he dared to" is made more specific here in the following way: "and who, after this law is published, would still dare to … ." The act already recognized as unjust acquires an additional negative value after the publication of a given constitution, and that value is marked by reference to *audacia*. It is an overt disregard of the newly promulgated Imperial law: castigated (and punished) should be he "who in his *audacia* would consider this order to be insignificant (*parvus*)."[55] Such a ruling may, but does not have to, be accompanied by imposition (or toughening) of the penalty for those who would dare to commit a given crime after the constitution is already promulgated.[56]

One could speak of a similar *audacia* when an individual aware of the illegality of their actions endeavours to reach their goals by means of legal proceedings: either in court or trying to obtain a special Imperial rescript in their favour. This latter possibility, characteristic of the reality of the Later Roman Empire, encounters strong resistance – in one of the constitutions, the Emperor provides for penalties against "bureau clerks or others" who would agree to draw up texts of such illegal petitions.[57]

Where the term *audacia* points to the "impudence" in relation to the status of the law already in force, it usually refers to disregarding Imperial prohibitions, or sometimes the related penalties. In such cases, rendering the term as "audacity" seems to be justified indeed. There are definitely fewer cases of disregarding Imperial laws "in general," which are always in connection with some specific provisions being contravened in a given situation.

Considering dozens of instances of *audacia* and *temeritas* in regard to deliberate violations of the dignity of the Imperial law (which make up a great majority of the collected material), one could ask if there is any point in further

[55] *C.Th.* 12.1.9.3–4: *Quod si pro sua audacia parvi aliquis hanc fecerit iussionem…*

[56] E.g., *C.Th.* 8.5.57.

[57] *Nov. Theod.* 5.3.19.

searching. Is it not that each act described in such terms is referred to in this way just because it represents the infringement of a specific constitution? In many cases, it is indeed difficult to identify if the legislator calls a specific act *audacia* on account of the fact that it constitutes the violation of the dignity of the state office or Christian religion or because it is simply a breach of the law. Nonetheless, in my opinion, when the existing text does not permit one to make a clear connection between some accusation of *audacia* and the fact that a certain provision of the law may have been violated, it is worth asking what other value may have been involved here.

An analytical survey of the relevant cases makes it possible to identify a wide spectrum of such "values." But it cannot be said that "all possible" values have thus been found. First of all, it is notable that nearly all of the deeds defined as *audacia* are aimed against the state or religion. There is only one area of relations between common citizens in which the term *audacia* may be legitimately used, namely between a slave and his owner as well as an emancipated slave and his patron. In both of these cases, there is an instance of *audacia* when a slave or a freedman appears in court to accuse his owner or patron, and both of the cases are treated on par. Such a practice is, of course, forbidden and punishable by duly severe penalties. The state acts here, so to speak, as a guardian of the respect that slaves (or freedmen) owe to their owners (patrons).

Much more often would the state act in defence of the authority of its offices and the Senate. The dignity of the office may be violated by disregarding the official's instructions and decisions, encroaching on his competence by another official, as well as encroaching on the competence of the Senate. From this situation, where the ruler extends, in a way, his protection over the administration office and the Senate, one should distinguish some comparatively rare cases in which the "audacity" is manifested in acting against the *sacrum* of Imperial authority; they may rather be compared with the previously described *audacia* of opposing the law promulgated by the Emperor.

The Emperor protects both officials and the privileges; it is an "audacity" if private persons or state officials act against them. In most cases, references are made to the privileges of decurions, but among other groups mentioned in the context are also former palace officials and members of the *navicularii* corps.

Roman citizens may also run the risk of being accused of *audacia* in other circumstances: when they usurp assuming an official position they are not allowed to hold. They may be barred from holding that office due to their lower social status (e.g., decurions are forbidden, as a rule, to assume Imperial offices that would relieve them of their duties at the *curia*) or on account of the administrative regulations of a given office (e.g., those serving as *agens in rebus* cannot run for another term at this office after their tenure has expired). In these two cases, "impudence" consists in attempting to reach up higher than it is possibly permitted, and such an attempt is perceived as aiming to take what rightfully belongs to the state. A similar qualification should be applied, I believe, to many other cases in which *audacia* is used with regard to acts of misappropriation of state or municipal property for private purposes.

The last case worth considering here is the term "audacity" used in reference to acting against the orthodox Christian faith (which is subject to the Emperor's protection). Even allowing for a great number of texts concerning religious issues, it is striking to note how many instances of *audacia* can be found in this field. Most frequently, it is used with reference to heretical activity and pagan offerings. In such cases, however, it could be often not certain if the insult in question actually concerns religion or Imperial law (the latter proscribing heretical and pagan practices). Moreover, *audacia* is applied to acting against bishops, other clergymen, and, finally, the institution of the Church, which is quite often caused by other bishops, responsible for creating "turmoil" in the Church.

It is interesting that several times some actions directed against the Jews are described as *audacia* (in one instance, against a Jewish patriarch). It is difficult to determine if this is indeed in defence of the dignity of the Jewish communities, in a similar (albeit much less committed) way to the defence of the Church, or if all these cases may be limited to the situation when the Imperial law is challenged by unlawful and illegal activities.

audacia, audeo, audax, ausus, temeritas, temero, temerarius, temerator, praesumo, praesumptio, praesumptor

A. The term is used in direct reference to the breach of a constitution:

A1. the breach of this particular constitution:

A1a. indication to contravening the law "from now on": *C.Th.* 6.29.12.5 (*audeo*); 7.4.30.6 (*audeo*); 8.2.3.4 (*audeo*); 8.4.30.11 (*audeo*); 8.5.54.5 (*praesumo*); 8.5.54.5 (*temeritas*); 8.5.57.3 (*temeritas*); 9.38.9.4 (*audeo*); 11.7.10.3 (*audeo*); 12.1.182.2 (*audeo*); 12.1.188.6 (*audeo*); 16.5.51.4 = 16.5.56.1[2] (*temeritas*); 16.8.1.4 (*audeo*).

A1b. other cases with direct indications to a given constitution: *C.Th.* 4.22.2.6 (*audeo*); 4.22.2.6 (*temeritas*); 6.29.5.6 (*audeo*); 6.35.13.8 (*temerarius*); 7.4.32.4[2] (*audacia*); 7.4.32.4[2] (*temero*); 7.4.36.4[2] (*temerator*); 8.5.30.4 (*audeo*); 8.8.1.3 (*audeo*); 12.1.9.3 (*audacia*); 12.6.32.10[2] (*ausus*); 12.6.32.11[2] (*audeo*); 12.6.32.15[2] (*temeritas*); 14.16.3.8 (*audeo*); 16.4.2.3 (*ausus*); 16.4.2.1[2] (*audeo*); *Nov. Theod.* 10.1.37 (*temero*); 20.24 (*temerator*); *Nov. Valent.* 27.52 (*praesumo*).

A1c. indirect indication to a given constitution: *C.Th.* 6.18.1.6 (*audeo*); 7.8.5.1[2] (*temeritas*); 8.1.16.7 (*temero*); 8.5.66.6 (*temerarius*); 8.8.2.3 (*praesumptio*); 8.8.2.4 (*temero*);

8.8.4.6 (*temero*); 10.19.9.6 (*audacia*); 11.14.2.4 (*temero*); 11.30.11.7 (*audeo*); 12.1.176.8 (*audeo*); 16.5.8.3 (*praesumo*); *Nov. Theod.* 5.1.25 (*temerarius*); 18.19 (*temeritas*); 24.23 (*audeo*); 24.53 (*audeo*); *Nov. Valent.* 6.1.2 (*temeritas*).

A2. the breach of some other specific law: *C.Th.* 6.18.1.5 (*temeritas*); 6.27.11.3 (*audeo*); 6.29.9.[2] (*praesumo*); 10.26.1.10 (*audeo*); 16.8.10.4 (*audeo*); 16.10.2.3 (*audeo*); *Const. Sirm.* 6.3^{2} (*audeo*); 6.3^{2} (*praesumptio*).

A3. the breach of constitutions in general: *C.Th.* 6.4.22.16 (*praesumptio*); 6.4.22.18 (*temeritas*); 8.5.62.4 (*temero*); 10.1.5.10 (*temero*); 10.20.13.5 (*temero*); 11.22.5.6 (*temero*); 11.30.59.2 (*audeo*); *Const. Sirm.* 3.2^{2} (*temeritas*; cf. also E7a); 11.4^{2} (*praesumptio*); 11.4^{2} (*temerarius*); 16.18^{2} (*temeritas*; cf. also E7a); *Nov. Theod.* 5.2.12 (*temerator*); 8.3 (*temerator*); 21.16 (*temerator*); *Nov. Valent.* 36.41 (*praesumptio*).

A4. charges aimed at the disregard:

A4a. of a prohibition: *C.Th.* 1.6.11.15 (*temeritas*); 6.35.10.5 (*temero*); 7.4.36.4^{2} (*temerator*); 7.10.1.9 (*praesumo*); 7.10.1.9 (*temeritas*); 7.12.1.5 (*audeo*); 7.13.21.3 (*temerator*); 8.4.29.3 (*praesumo*); 8.5.61.2 (*temeritas*); 8.7.20.5 (*praesumo*); 8.7.23.7 (*temerarius*); 9.17.6.5 (*audeo*); 9.23.2.1^{2} (*audeo*); 10.10.15.4 (*audeo*); 12.1.80.6 (*temerarius*; see also F3); 13.5.16.3 (*audeo*); 13.5.16.4 (*ausus*); 16.5.24.7 (*audacia*); 16.5.26.2 (*audeo*); 16.5.26.4 (*audeo*); 16.5.29.3 (*audeo*); 16.5.38.4 (*audeo*); 16.5.45.5 (*audeo*); 16.5.56.2^{2} (*temero*); 16.5.57.4 (*audeo*); 16.5.58.10 (*audeo*); 16.5.65.5 (*temeritas*); 16.5.66.2^{2} (*audeo*); 16.8.9.4 (*praesumo*); 16.10.13.5 (*audeo*); 16.10.24.7 (*audeo*); *Nov. Theod.* 3.45 (*ausus*); *Nov. Valent.* 8.1.16 (*ausus*); 27.52 (*audacia*).

A4b. of penalties: *C.Th.* 16.8.19.10 (*audeo*); *Nov. Theod.* 3.69 (*audacia*).

A5. unlawful attempt to obtain something: *C.Th.* 2.23.1.5 (*audeo*); 2.23.1.10 (*audeo*); 3.13.3.4 (*audeo*); 5.15.21.3 (*temeritas*); 10.10.15.3 (*audeo*); 11.1.30.2 (*audeo*); 11.16.16.5 (*audeo*); 11.36.13.2 (*audeo*); 11.36.26.5 (*audeo*); 13.1.20.6 (*audeo*); 14.19.1.3 (*audeo*); 15.14.6.2 (*audeo*); *Nov. Theod.* 4.30 (*audax*); 5.1.25 (*temerarius*); 5.3.19 (*audeo*); 17.2.20 (*audeo*); *Nov. Theod.* 17.2.27 (*temeritas*); *Nov. Valent.* 27.51 (*temeritas*); 27.51 (*temero*).

A6. other unauthorized actions: *C.Th.* 4.4.5.5^{2} (*audeo*, registering alleged oral testaments); 12.8.1.2 (*praesumo*, smelting of gold); 16.5.12.5 (*praesumo*, organizing heretical gatherings); *Nov. Valent.* 17.10 (*praesumo*, unlawful action of a bishop).

II. Cases which cannot be explained by direct reference to item A as well as ambiguous cases:

B. misappropriation (or illegal misuse) of public property:

B1. Imperial postal service: (*cursus publicus*): 8.5.6.2 (*praesumo*); 8.5.12.2 (*praesumptio*); 8.5.15.2 (*audacia*); 8.5.15.3 (*audeo*); 8.5.22.11 (*praesumo*); 8.5.55.1 (*praesumo*); 8.5.59.2 (*praesumo*); 8.5.61.1 (*praesumptio*); 8.5.62.2 (*praesumo*); 8.5.63.2 (*praesumptio*); 8.5.65.2 (*praesumptio*); *Nov. Majo.* 7.76 (*praesumo*).

B2. a boat: *C.Th.* 10.20.12.2 (*audeo*); 13.8.1.2 (*audeo*).

B3. (theft of) public water: *C.Th.* 15.2.4.2 (*audacia*); 15.2.8.2 (*praesumo*); 15.2.8.4 (*audeo*); 14.15.4.2 (*audeo*).
B4. (theft of) public grain: *C.Th.* 11.2.2.2 (*praesumptio*); 11.14.3.2 (*temerator*); 11.14.3.3 (*audeo*); 14.3.16.2 (*praesumo*); 14.15.3.6 (*audeo*); 14.15.4.5² (*audeo*); 14.17.5.8² (*temeritas*); 14.17.6.3 (*temeritas*); 15.1.12.4 (*audeo*).
B5. unlawful construction or demolition of public structures, adorning private houses with ornaments from public buildings, etc: *C.Th.* 15.1.14.1 (*praesumptio*); 15.1.25.6 (*praesumptio*); 15.1.25.6 (*temero*); 15.1.27.8 (*audacia*); 15.1.28.2 (*audaciter*); 15.1.37.1 (*temeritas*); 15.1.37.3² (*audeo*); *Nov. Majo.* 4.8 (*praesumo*); 4.15 (*temero*).
B6. demanding undue benefits: *C.Th.* 6.30.7.5 (*praesumo*); 7.7.4.4 (*praesumo*); 15.1.33.4 (*praesumo*).
B7. an attempt to appropriate public debts by decurions: *C.Th.* 11.28.10.1² (*temero*).
C. type of offence:
C1. magic: *C.Th.* 9.16.5.1 (*audeo*); 9.16.5.2 (*audeo*).
C2. sepulchral violation: *C.Th.* 9.17.2.8 (*audeo*); 9.17.5.1 (*audacia*); *Nov. Valent.* 23.6 (*ausus*); 23.8 (*praesumptio*); 23.29 (*temeritas*); 23.31 (*praesumptio*).
C3. abduction of a woman (*raptus*): *C.Th.* 9.24.1.12 (*audacia*); 9.24.2.4 (*audacia*); 9.24.3.1² (*audacia*); 9.25.2.1² (*audeo*).
C4. while condemning those who robbed the *navicularii*, and described as *raptores* in *C.Th.* 13.5.29.5 (*audacia*).
C5. taking disputed property by force: *C.Th.* 2.29.2.3² (*temeritas*); 4.22.2.6 (*temeritas*; see also E3a); 4.22.3.6 (*audacia*; ditto); 4.22.3.9 (*audacia*; ditto); 4.22.3.1² (*praesumptio*; ditto); 4.22.3.1² (*temero*; ditto); *Nov. Valent.* 8.1.2 (*temeritas*); 8.1.3 (*praesumptio*); 8.1.16 (*ausus*); 8.1.33 (*temeritas*).
C6. *crimen vis*, in general: *C.Th.* 10.1.15.4 (*temeritas*).
C7. offences, in general: *Const. Sirm.* 7.5² (*audeo*).
D. the attitude of:
D1. false accusers: *C.Th.* 9.5.1.5 (*temeritas*); 9.39.2.2 (*praesumo*); 10.10.4.2 (*audacia*); 10.15.1.3 (*audeo*; see also D5); 11.36.7.11 (*audacia*).
D2. a tyrant: *C.Th.* 9.38.11.2 (*praesumptio*); 15.14.6.2 (*audacia*); 15.14.6.3 (*praesumptio*); 16.2.47.5 = *Const. Sirm.* 6.6² (*praesumptor*; see also E7i).
D3. *latrones*: *C.Th.* 7.19.1.17 (*temeritas*).
D4. deserters: *C.Th.* 7.13.10.4 (*audeo*); 7.18.11.7 (*temeritas*); 7.18.14.2 (*audeo*).
D5. officials committing abuses (other than at item B): *C.Th.* 1.12.6.4 (*temeritas*); 1.34.3.2 (*audeo*); 6.29.4.3² (*audeo*); 8.7.7.4 (*audeo*); 8.10.4.3 (*temeritas*); 9.41.1.9 (*praesumo*); 10.4.1.10 (*audeo*); 10.15.1.3 (*audeo*; see also D1); 11.16.11.4 (*temeritas*); 11.16.11.7 (*temeritas*); 11.30.30.8 (*audeo*); *Nov. Valent.* 1.3.48 (*audeo*); 7.1.4 (*praesumptio*); 7.1.32 (*ausus*).
E. violation of dignity:
E1. violation of the emperor's dignity: *C.Th.* 10.1.15.4 (*temeritas*); 11.16.17.3 (*temero*, levying extraordinary taxes on Imperial lands); 11.30.34.1 (*audeo*, violation

of the palace space); 16.4.4.3 (*audeo*); *Nov. Valent.* 16.2 (*ausus*; insulting the emperor's predecessors and relatives by refusing to acknowledge *solidi* bearing their images[58]); 16.2 (*temerarius*); 17.24 (*ausus*); 19.2 (*audacia*, abuse of Imperial rescripts by perpetrators of a homicide).

E2. violation of the dignity of the Senate: *C.Th.* 1.28.3.3 (*praesumo*); 1.28.3.4 (*temerarius*); 1.28.3.5 (*audacia*).

E3. violation of the dignity of an office:

E3a. disregarding the competence of an official (his verdict): *C.Th.* 1.14.1.9 (*audax*, failing to fulfil duties); 4.22.3.6 (*audacia*; see also C5); 4.22.3.9 (*audacia*; ditto); 4.22.3.1^{2} (*praesumptio*; ditto); 4.22.3.1^{2} (*temero*; ditto); 9.40.16.19 (*audacia*); 11.22.4.2 (*temeritas*); 12.1.173.4^{2} (*audeo*); *Nov. Theod.* 7.2.11 (*audacia*); *Nov. Valent.* 7.3.2 (*temerarius*); 7.3.4 (*audeo*); *Nov. Majo.* 9.7 (*temero*).

E3b. imposing services on an official: *C.Th.* 6.10.1.6 (*temerarius*); 6.35.4.1^{2} (*temeritas*).

E3c. appropriating the competence of another office (primarily in tax-related issues): *C.Th.* 1.5.13.5 (*audeo*); 1.6.11.2 (*praesumo*); 8.8.7.5 (*praesumo*); 11.7.17.4 (*audeo*); 12.10.1.2^{2} (*praesumo*); 14.15.6.4 (*praesumo*); 15.1.41.6^{2} (*praesumo*).

E4. the breach of *publica disciplina*: 9.33.R (*audeo*).

E5. acting against the *populus*: *C.Th.* 1.29.7.4 (*temeritas*).

E6. violation of the time of a religious holiday by collecting taxes on that day: *C.Th.* 8.11.2.3 (*audeo*).

E7. violation of the dignity of the Christian religion:

E7a. acting against the *lex Dei*: *C.Th.* 16.5.44.2 (*audacia*); 16.10.11.6 (*temerator*); *Const. Sirm.* 3.2^{2} (*temaritas*; cf. also A3); 16.18^{2} (*temeritas*; ditto); *Nov. Majo.* 11.6 (*praesumptio*); 11.[13] (*ausus*).

E7b. other incidents/riots caused by heretics: *C.Th.* 16.5.5.4 (*ausus*); 16.5.24.4 (*audeo*); 16.5.54.19^{2} (*ausus*); 16.6.4.5 (*temeritas*) (in particular, there are also numerous incidents at item A regarding heretics).

E7c. Jews: *C.Th.* 16.8.26.3 (*audacia*).

E7d. pagans: *C.Th.* 16.10.9.2 (*audacia*); 16.10.12.7 (*audeo*); 16.10.20.2^{2} (*praesumptio*).

E7f. on all non-Catholics: *Nov. Theod.* 3.11 (*audeo*).

E7g. against Christian celebrations: *Nov. Valent.* 23.23 (*audeo*).

E7h. violation of the sanctity of an asylum: *C.Th.* 9.45.4.8^{3} (*temeritas*); 9.45.4.9^{3} (*audeo*).

E7i. violation of the dignity of bishops: *C.Th.* 16.2.47.5 = *Const. Sirm.* 6.6^{2} (*praesumptor*); *Const.* 14.24 (*audacia*); 14.5^{2} (*audacia*); *Nov. Valent.* 17.7 (*praesumptio*); *Nov. Majo.* 11.15 (*praesumptio*).

---

[58] Liebs (1985: 111–112) argues that the question was the resistance in the West to accepting coins with the images of the emperors in Constantinople.

E7j. violation against the Church: *C.Th.* 16.2.34.2 (*temeritas*); 16.5.65.5 (*temeritas*); *Const. Sirm.* 11.4 (*temerarius*); 11.9 (*ausus*); 11.4[2] (*praesumptio*; see also A3); 14.6 (*temeritas*); *Nov. Valent.* 17.10 (*ausus*); 17.24 (*ausus*); 17.13 (*temeritas*).
E7k. no Jew shall dare to sell Christian slaves: *C.Th.* 16.9.5.2 (*audeo*).
E 8. (violation) against the Jewish religion: *C.Th.* 16.8.20.2 (*audeo*).
E8a. (violation) against a Jewish patriarch: *C.Th.* 16.8.11.1 (*audeo*).
F. breach of the rights:
F1. of the *Corpus naviculariorum*: *C.Th.* 13.5.30.2 (*temero*); *Nov. Valent.* 29.4 (*temeritas*).
F2. of the equites: *C.Th.* 13.5.16.4 (*ausus*).
F3. of decurions: 12.1.80.6 (*temerarius*; see also A4a); 12.1.85.2 (*temerarius*); 12.1.85.5 (*audeo*); 12.1.128.5 (*ausus*); 12.1.128.4 (*temerarius*); 12.1.186.6 (*praesumptio*); 14.1.4.5 (*audeo*).
G. a slave acting against his owner, a freedman against his patron, or a *colonus* against the landlord: *C.Th.* 4.10.2.4[2] (*praesumo*); 5.19.2.4 (*audeo*, of a *colonus* against his landlord); 5.19.2.6 (*audeo*, ditto); 9.5.1.8 (*audacia*); 9.6.4.3 (*audeo*); 9.24.2.4 (*audacia*).
G1. a slave appearing in court (no context): *Nov. Theod.* 17.1.18 (*audeo*).
H. citizens acting against other citizens: *C.Th.* 3.8.2.21 (*praesumo*); 3.18.2.[10] (*temeritas*); 4.8.5.[16] (*temero*); 4.22.2.9 (*temeritas*); *Nov. Theod.* 16.12 (*praesumptio*); *Nov. Valent.* 21.2.11 (*praesumo*).
I. protecting fugitives and keeping them from obligations: *C.Th.* 7.13.21.3 (*temerator*); 7.14.1.3 (*audeo*); 10.20.8.3 (*audacia*); 11.24.1.3 (*temeritas*); 11.24.2.3 (*audax*, seeking protection); 11.24.4.5 (*temeritas*).
J. attempting to obtain undue offices:
J1. a public official trying to assume undue office (assuming another or the same one after completion of his tenure): *C.Th.* 6.5.1.[5] (*praesumo*); 6.22.7.6 (*praesumo*); 6.27.19.3 (*audeo*); 6.30.5.3 (*audeo*); 8.1.16.4 (*audeo*); 9.26.2.3 (*audeo*).
J2. a decurion striving to change his status:
J2a. senator's rank: *C.Th.* 12.1.118.6 (*audeo*); *Nov. Theod.* 15.2.2 (*temeritas*); 15.2.3 (*audacia*); 15.2.8 (*audeo*).
J2b. imperial service, in general: *C.Th.* 8.4.28.5 (*audeo*); 8.4.30.11 (*audeo*); 12.1.168.3 (*audeo*); 12.1.188.6 (*audeo*).
J2c. state craftsman: *C.Th.* 12.1.62.3 (*audeo*).
J2d. a lower status: *Nov. Majo.* 7.9 (*praesumptio*).
K. other cases of usage as an accusation: 9.14.3.19 (*audeo*); *Const. Sirm.* 5.5 (*audeo*)

III. Positive and neutral cases of usage:
Audeo: *C.Th.* 2.17.1.6; 6.29.12.2; 9.45.4.9; 11.30.11.7; 12.6.27; *Nov. Theod.* 16.10; 16.15; *Nov. Majo.* 2.43.
other meanings of the verb *praesumo*: *C.Th.* 6.35.14.13; 7.8.11.2; 8.5.29.1; 9.42.8.23; 10.18.2.7; 11.29.6.5; 12.1.134.10; 12.1.184.2; 12.9.2.3; 15.1.18.5; 15.1.26.7; *Nov. Majo.* 1.10.
Temeratio in the sense "forgery": *C.Th.* 1.32.1.3.
Temeritas in the sense "hastiness of accusations": *C.Th.* 9.1.5.4.

tempto

I. A. indicating directly an attempt to contravene some recently issued law or the laws in general: *C.Th.* 1.9.1.14; 1.15.16.3; 1.20.1.6; 3.32.1.8; 4.13.3.4; 5.10.1.1^{2}; 6.23.4.10; 6.35.13.9; 7.4.18.3 (second appearance); 7.7.3.5; 8.4.19.4; 8.4.29.7; 9.16.11.5; 9.26.4.4; 9.30.2.5; 9.35.2.4; 9.39.3.2; 9.42.1.2^{2}; 10.1.2.4; 10.9.1.7; 10.19.9.6; 10.19.13.3; 11.16.1.4; 11.16.17.4; 11.30.6.16; 11.30.8.11; 11.36.30.3; 12.1.80.4; 12.19.2.9; 13.5.30.2; 14.1.6.4; 14.3.21.5; 14.9.3.5; 14.10.2.3; 14.11.1.4; 14.16.1.2^{2}; 15.1.31.7; 15.12.2.4; 16.1.4.8 = 16.4.1.3; 16.1.4.10; 16.5.21.3; 16.5.47.2^{2}; 16.5.59.5; 16.8.19.4^{2}; 16.10.9.5; 16.10.12.10; 16.10.13.11; 16.10.24.6; *Const. Sirm.* 11.5^{2}; 16.23^{2}; *Nov. Theod.* 5.1.25; 6.28; 10.1.37; 17.2.44; 21.28; 24.51; *Nov. Valent.* 6.1.4; 12.33; 17.10; *Nov. Majo.* 6.53.

B. other (all negative): *C.Th.* 2.14.1.9^{2}; 2.26.2.5; 3.11.1.8^{2}; 4.14.1.23^{2}; 4.23.1.3; 6.4.22.22; 6.27.3.12; 6.29.2.18; 7.4.18.3 (first appearance); 7.4.30.6; 7.18.17.5; 8.7.9.4; 9.5.1.8; 9.7.9.2; 9.10.1.9; 9.10.1.13; 9.10.1.14; 9.10.2.2; 9.14.3.14; 9.26.1.3; 9.33.1.3; 10.8.3.3; 10.20.11.3; 11.24.4.2; 11.24.6.9; 11.34.1.3; 11.36.1.8; 11.36.23.2; 12.1.12.3; 12.1.16.5; 13.5.9.4; 13.7.1.3; 14.1.4.4; 14.14.1.2; 15.1.10.4; 15.2.8.5; 15.5.3.3; 16.5.6.12^{2}; 16.5.44.4; 16.5.51.4 = 16.5.56.1^{2}; 16.5.57.4; 16.5.65.16; 16.6.4.9^{2}; 16.8.19.16; 16.8.22.7^{2}; 16.10.12.15; *Nov. Theod.* 5.3.18; 7.1.14; 18.19; 24.36; 24.65; *Nov. Valent.* 17.29; *Nov. Majo.* 6.48.

II. in an accumulation figure, alongside other terms describing *audacia*: *C.Th.* 6.35.13.9; 7.4.30.6; 8.4.29.7; 9.5.1.8; 9.10.1.13; 10.19.9.6; 11.24.4.2; 13.5.30.2; 14.1.4.4; 15.2.8.5; 16.5.51.4 = 16.5.56.1^{2}; 16.10.9.5; 16.10.24.6; *Const. Sirm.* 11.5^{2}; *Nov. Theod.* 5.1.25; 10.1.37; 18.19; *Nov. Valent.* 6.1.4.

conor

I. A. indicating directly an attempt to contravene this law or the law in general: *C.Th.* 5.7.2.15; 16.10.15.1^{2}; *Nov. Theod.* 26.57; *Nov. Marc.* 1.68.

B. other (in negative usage): *C.Th.* 6.22.1.4; 6.27.14.2; 6.30.6.4; 6.35.5.2; 6.35.14.9; 7.4.30.4; 8.4.9.3, 8.5.11.2; 8.5.66.4; 9.16.7.3; 9.45.4.8; 9.45.4.6^{3}; 10.20.8.5; 11.16.1.5; 11.28.10.1^{2}; 11.30.6.12; 11.30.31.3; 12.1.1.2; 12.1.82.2; 12.1.149.1; 12.9.1.2; 15.14.8.6; 16.4.6.3; 16.5.2.5; 16.5.19.3; 16.5.24.2; 16.8.9.5; 16.10.18.2; *Const. Sirm.* 16.18^{2}; *Nov. Theod.* 25.50; *Nov. Valent.* 12.14; *Nov. Sev.* 2.5.

C. in positive or neutral meanings: *C.Th.* 9.19.4.14^{2}; *Nov. Theod.* 3.12.

II. in an accumulation figure, alongside other terms describing *audacia*: *C.Th.* 6.35.14.9; 7.4.30.4; 8.5.66.4; 9.45.4.8; 11.28.10.1^{2}.

insolentia, insolens, insolenter

A. attitude of officials abusing their authority: *C.Th.* 1.16.11.3 (*insolenter*); 1.29.7.1 (*insolenter*); 1.29.7.4 (*insolentia*); 5.15.20.11 (*insolentia*); 6.4.22.24 (*insolenter*); 8.5.30.10 (*insolentia*); 11.7.3.2 (*insolentia*); 11.30.13.3 (*insolens*); *Nov. Majo.* 3.3 (*insolens*); 3.10 (*insolentia*).

B. other cases of the attitude based on arrogance: *C.Th.* 1.16.4.1^{2} (*insolens*; arrogant resistance to decisions of public officials); 3.16.2.20 (*insolens*; divorce demanded without any reason); 10.20.6.5 (*insolentia*; giving refuge to fugitive flax weavers

after issue of the prohibition); 13.3.7.2 (*insolenter*; usurping the post of philosophy teacher); 16.9.3.4 (*insolentia*; unjust accusations against Jews).
C. in the sense "excessive": *C.Th.* 7.13.7.6 (*insolenter*).

procax, procacitas, proterve, protervitas, petulans, petulanter
A. indicating arrogance: *C.Th.* 9.4.1.2 (imprecating the emperor's names); 11.36.14.7 (*vesania* of an unlawful appeal); 16.9.4.3 (violating an imperial prohibition); *Nov. Marc.* 1.73 (acting against an imperial constitution).
B. indicating rather shamelessness or lawlessness: *C.Th.* 3.16.2.9; 4.8.5.[7^2]; 9.7.2.16; 15.6.2.3; *Nov. Majo.* 9.19.

Furor

Similar to *audacia*, the notion of *furor* (also expressed by several terms close in meaning such as *amentia, dementia, insania, vesania*) is one of those terms which define the attitude of a person taking action rather than any specific action being undertaken. As in the case of the former term, one is confronted here with the ambiguity which can be explained by the complicated history of *furor*.

The problem of the accusation of "madness" as an invective is not that it was used as such, but that it is not obvious. As a matter of fact, accusing a person of "madness" is to give an opinion of the disability of his mind, but also of his limited capability of accounting for results of his own actions. In Rome, the *furiosi* were included in the category of the disabled people subject to guardianship and they had already appeared in that role in the XII Tablets Law. Their *furor* ruled out any validity of legal actions they would take, yet at the same time (at least since Marcus Aurelius' reign) it shielded them against liability to criminal charges.[59] It could be supposed then that bringing up metaphorical accusations of *furor* would be indicative of contempt, not condemnation. It would be even quite difficult to expect that such a metaphor could have been applied to strengthen the force of accusations; whereas in actual fact this condemnatory sense of the term can be observed in the political discourse of the late Roman Republic, in the religious discourse of early Christianity, as well as in the Late Antique constitutions. If this is really the case, we must assume that Roman politicians, Fathers of the Church, and legislators referred to a kind of *furor* different from the one that was actually characteristic of mentally impaired individuals.

---

[59] Cf. Lanza 1990: 156 ff.; Jońca 2008: 152 ff.; Rizzelli 2014. Vallar 2016: 15–23.

In the classical literature, unfortunately, the history of the term *furor* is not represented in such an extent as that of *superstitio* or even *audacia*. Otherwise, we would have been spared many superficial views on the subject. For instance, any attempts to ascribe this "invention" to M. Tullius Cicero are only partly right. There was some speculation whether the great orator had drawn here on the stoical concept of *pathos*, or rather on the term present in the XII Tablets Law.[60] Actually, it is worth noting that as early as in the classical Greek there are cases of the term *mania* (μανία) being used as an invective. Cicero thus highlighted and made popular a certain notion that had already existed in the ancient world.

It was already in the classical Greek philosophy that accusations of "madness" would become a form of political criticism. In the classical Greek tragedy, the epithet *afrōn* (ἄφρων, "senseless," which should be rendered in Latin as *amens*) is attributed to public figures such as Xerxes and tyrant Likos[61] – also in connection with their *hybris* (ὑβρίς).[62] In particular, the representation of the tyrant figure in Plato's *Gorgias* and *Republic* is a depiction of a hapless individual whose rational part of soul is controlled by his passions. In the *Republic*, the term *mainomenos* (μαινόμενος) is used.[63] Earlier, a charge of "madness" was used by the Old Oligarch with reference to the democratic politicians.[64] As a result, at least on a sporadic basis, the aspect of "madness" appears in the aristocratic criticism of popular leaders, subsequently utilized for political propaganda purposes by the Republican-era *optimates*. As we know, accusations of *tolma*/*audacia* have a similar history as well.[65]

Only some single cases of *mania* can be found as a term of invective used in orations of the Greek rhetoricians.[66] It is more widespread in the field of philosophical polemics, as an invective employed by stoical philosophers in regard to the followers of Epicure's philosophy.[67] There is no doubt that Cicero remains influenced by stoical philosophy. He also draws from tragedy; it was noticed that the *furor* of the politicians he had criticized was sometimes of a tragic character, as it served (in a manner similar to tragic protagonists) as a punishment

60 Lepore 1954: 148.

61 Salvemini 2000: 374–376.

62 It is true that the *hybris* in question was directed, in particular, against gods and it was also punished by them, yet in the sense of the Latin equivalent of *hybris*, *superbia* was an act committed against community, and punishing it was considered as a civic duty (Murphy 1997: 77).

63 Plato, *Resp.* 573 B; *Gorg.* 507 0, where the term *afrōn* is used.

64 *Athen. Polit.* I.9, cf. Weische 1966: 12–13.

65 Cf. *audacia* above.

66 E.g., Demosthenes, *De corona* 249; cf. Weische 1966: 27, note 63; also Aeschines describes criminals as insane (*Tim.* 190–191).

67 Kubiak 1989: 239, note 8.

for their crimes.[68] But, at the same time, it is represented as a consequence of exaggerating passions beyond the human measure: Verres, the iniquitous governor of Sicily, falls into *furor* when he cannot satisfy his greed, *cupiditas*.[69] Let us notice that Verres is depicted by Cicero as a peculiar "continuator" of the tradition of Syracuse tyrants.[70] Apparently, he also imitates them as regards this particular trait; his *furor* is displayed first of all in the most brazen and impious deeds, caused by his uncontrollable avarice and forming part of the tyrant's stereotypical image.[71]

This stereotypical representation must have been comprehensible to Cicero's contemporaries. He did not invent it, but he was willing to make use of the tyrant's stereotypical image in order to discredit his political opponents.[72] Likewise, Cicero did not serve as the source from which it was derived by the Roman historians,[73] who would have readily charged their negative characters with *furor* or *mania*.[74] The stereotype of a "mad" tyrant had even become prevailing in the Late Antique panegyrical writings.

Thanks to those, it is easier to understand a certain passage in the second one of the *Catilinian Orations*. In contrasting the opponents and supporters of Catiline, Cicero offers a truly ebullient litany of contradictions: *Ex hac enim parte pudor pugnat, illinc petulantia; hinc pudicitia, illinc stuprum, hinc fides, illinc fraudatio; hinc pietas, illinc scelus; hinc constantia, illinc furor; hinc honestas, illinc turpitudo; hinc continentia, illinc lubido; denique aequitas, temperantia, fortitudo, prudentia, virtutes omnes certant cum iniquitate, luxuria, ignavia, temeritate, cum vitiis omnibus; postremo copia cum egestate, bona ratio cum perdita, mens sana cum amentia, bona denique spes cum omnium rerum desperatione confligit*.[75] As much as the juxtaposition of insanity and sane mind (*mens sana cum amentia*) is understandable, the one of madness and constancy is somewhat more enigmatic (*hinc constantia, illinc furor*). Let us also note here that another pair can be found, which is far from obvious – *fortitudo*

68 Kubiak 1989: 244–245; Taldone 1993: 8; Berno 2007: 71 ff. For a list of *furor*-related accusations in Cicero's writings, cf. Berno 2007: 80–82. Likewise, *furor* is depicted as a divine punishment in the *Aeneid*, cf. Korpanty 1985: 256.

69 *Furor* of Verres is as if a "higher degree" of his vices: *In Verr.* II.4.38 – *amentiam singularem et furorem iam, non cupiditatem*, cf. Taldone 1993: 11.

70 *In Verr.* II.1.82, II.3.20–21, II.3.31, II.4.123, II.5.68, II.5.117, II.5.143 and especially II.5.145, cf. Dunkle 1967: 161.

71 E.g., *In Verr.* II.1.7: robbery at a temple; II.4.40–41: bringing a lawsuit against Diodorus, from whom he wanted to seize a vase.

72 Dunkle 1967: 163–167.

73 Dunkle 1967: 158–160; Dunkle 1971.

74 E.g., Sallust., *In Catil.* 24.2; Livius, *Ab urbe cond.* 37.25.12; Svet., *Nero* 34.4.

75 Cic., *In Catil.* 2.25.

(valour) corresponds to *temeritas*, and it could be seen as boldness not based on reason, only a step away from *audacia*.

It could be understood what kind of *furor* may become the opposite of *constantia* when one takes a closer look at the image of a tyrant: unpredictable, inspiring terror, but at the same time also terrified himself, incessantly suspended between cruelty and fear. In the Later Roman panegyrical writings, tyrant's *furor* is usually represented as ceaseless swings of moods, flinging from paroxysms of fear to acts of mindless impudence.[76] This senseless *audacia* itself, destined for failure, may be perceived as a manifestation of "madness."[77]

In Claudian's anti-panegyrics, *furor* is painted in even darker colours. Its origin is definitely of a Tartar nature; for instance, Rufinus overwhelmed by *furor* is pictured as a messenger of the Furies, who are intent on using him to destroy the well-being of the golden epoch ushered in by Theodosius I. The *furor* thus depicted becomes an ultimate motive, sufficiently accounting for all the wicked things done by Gildo and Rufinus.[78]

Let us now revert to Cicero once again. There is another very suggestive example in his *Catilinian Orations*. In defending his position against a charge of excessive severity Cicero recalls how the Senate had once dealt with followers of "bacchanal madness"– *furor bacchantis*.[79] This comparison would have been nothing more than a mere word-play, if it had not been obvious, to the audience of this speech, that there was one, or two very closely related, type of *furor* in question. Then, one should not formulate an artificial distinction between the political *furor*, which is typical of a tyranny, and the religious one, which is one of the constitutive features of *superstitio*.[80] Ultimately, it will be easier to understand the persistently repeated accusation of *mania* against the emperors persecuting Christianity.[81] In the eyes of Lactantius or Eusebius of Caesarea, they were tyrants as well as *superstitiosi*.

Superstitio, a religious aberration, is the subject of one of the following subsections. At this point, let us only briefly consider the connection between *superstitio* and *furor*. This link is a very strong one: Horace describes

---

76 Cf., e.g., Maximus' attitude, first brazenly fighting against Theodosius, then *in modum amentis* succumbing to cowardice and despair (*Paneg. Lat.* 2.38, 42), and finally reverting again to *audacia* in his act of surrendering to the Emperor (*Paneg. Lat.* 2.43.1).

77 The relationship between *furor* and *audacia* can be defined as follows: *audacia* is, as it were, a constant vice, while *furor* a paroxysm in which the former one is displayed (Taldone 1993: 12, in reference to Cicero's writings).

78 Long 1996: 104; Garambois-Vasquez 2007: 210–211. *In Ruf.* 1.96–100, *In Gild.* 180–181.

79 Cic., *In Catil.* 4.11.

80 As recently noted, cf. Escribano Paño 2008: 395; 2009: 47–48.

81 E.g., Lact., *De mort. persec.* 5.1, 6.1, 10.5, 10.6, 11.3, 25.2, 39.5; Euseb. HE IX.10.2.

the *superstitio* as *morbus mentis*, while Livy contrasts it with *mens bona*.[82] A particularly significant position is that of Livy, if we followed Denis Grodzynski in assuming that it was him who would have given the final shape to the *superstitio* as a religion both depraved and external towards the Roman civilized order (*prava* and *externa*).[83] It should be noted that the religious *furor* (as well as the political one) conveys incrimination, not justification, in its meaning. This "madness," along with *superstitio*, was blamed on Christians; this charge was sufficient to justify sentencing them to capital punishment.[84]

In consequence, "madness" is one of the principal charges formulated by the enemies of Christianity. But, on the other hand, it was also readily used by Christian polemists in reference to their opponents, with the argumentation reversed accordingly.[85] Tertullian rendered the charge into Latin again, making ample use of it in his anti-pagan, and especially anti-heretical writings.[86] As it seems, the heresy with the error and the audacity of the mind firmly at its roots was a more appropriate addressee of accusations of *furor* than the Roman and Hellenic religions. Still, in the Christian writings, the charge in question was very much used against pagans, errant Christians, as well as Jews (the latter ones refusing to accept the Revelation in its entirety).[87] Undoubtedly, the group most readily condemned as "mad" were the Manichaeans, on account of the association between the founder's name and the word *mania*.[88] As early as the mid-fourth century, a Christian writer determined that the pagans' stubborn madness called for being eradicated by means of the fear of Imperial laws.[89]

In Nathaniel Wood's documented example, the invective *furor*, as used against religious dissidents, is secondarily incorporated in a political context; in Augustine's account, the *circumcelliones* movement is characterized by the same terms (also *audaces*, *perdites*, *latrones*, *grex*) as in Cicero's description of the *populares*. The author's conclusion that Augustine of Hippo thus defines the *circumcelliones* as a movement both religious and social in its character[90] is perhaps too far-reaching, yet some borrowings from the political rhetoric of the late Roman

---

82 Hor., *Sat.* II, 3.79.80; Liv. *Ab urbe cond.* 39.16.5; *furor* as a constitutive feature of *superstitio*, cf. Janssen 1979: 138; Kahlos 2007a: 73–74.

83 Grodzynski 1974: 45–46, see Chapter VIII: 222.

84 Pliny the Younger, *Ep.* 10.97.

85 Cf. Chapter VIII: 223, Kahlos 2007a: 71.

86 Tertul., *Apolog.* 23, *Ad martyras* 4.2, *De anima* 3.8, 50.6, *Adv. Marc.* 3, *Adv Iud.* 12.

87 *ThLL* 6.1: 1630.

88 Coyle 2004: 222–223.

89 Firmicus Maternus, *De errore profanarum religionum* 28.10.

90 Wood 1986: 48.

Republic seem to be unquestionable. Most evidently, the "religious" *furor* was close enough to the "political" one to make such borrowings possible.

The terms *furor*, *furiosus*, as well as *amentia*, *dementia*, *insania*, *vesania*, *rabies*, and *mente caecitas* are mentioned many times across the analyzed material. As no discernible differences in the application of the individual terms can be found,[91] one could speak of one notion of *furor* being expressed by all these terms.

Yet is there really just **one** notion here? It is possible to easily distinguish the cases where the *furor* turns out to be a characteristic of the dissidents' religious madness (*religionis furor*[92]) from those where it is to describe other offences. Even if at its inception those concepts were related, it did not have to be so anymore in the fourth and fifth centuries. At the same time, the examination of the relevant material points to the legislator's awareness that in the both cases he would have been dealing with at least closely related (if not the same) types of *furor*, as a certain common feature can be found in the two.

Valentinian III's novel describes desecration of graves as a crime which is at the same time "barbaric," "insane," and "cruel" (*barbara et vesana crudelitas*).[93] The legislator notes that the past emperors had already issued laws making this crime punishable by death. "As the criminal minds in their blind insanity had been always drawn to wickedness and considered themselves as not liable for the penalties hitherto established, it is necessary to renew the severity [of the law]."[94] The role of "madness" (*furor*) can be seen clearly: it makes the offender blind to the effect that he is shamelessly ready to commit a deed which is proscribed by law and punishable by harsh penalties. The new constitution, and its severe sanctions, should then make him open his eyes.

The *insania* of robbers (*latrones*), "unaware of its peril," is blinded as well.[95] In the further constitutions, too, the criminal *furor* is linked with the concept of *audacia*.[96] The legislator castigates the judge who "should burst forth into such obstinate (*pertinacia*) and illicit fury (*inlicitus furor*) that he dares (*audere*) to subject to the blows of lashes tipped with lead a chief decurion or a decurion and a senator of his own municipal council, if it may be so called, … ."[97] In this constitution, *furor* is linked with *audacia* as well as the obstinacy (*pertinacia*) of the judge.

---

91 Such distinctions are present, nonetheless, in depictions of the various types of mental illness in Roman juristic texts, cf. Renier 1950; Lanza 1990: 114–116.

92 *C.Th.* 16.5.25.

93 *Nov. Valent.* 23.

94 *quoniam noxiae mentes caeco semper in facinus furore rapiuntur et se ad poenas dudum statutas existimant non teneri, necesse est severitatem novare.*

95 *C.Th.* 1.29.8: *periculi sua nescia.*

96 *C.Th.* 4.22.3; 15.2.4.

97 *C.Th.* 12.1.85: *in hanc pertinaciam inliciti furoris eruperit, quos audeat principalem ac decurionem et suae, si sic dici oportet, curie senatorem plumbatarum ictibus subdere.*

In the case of religious offences as well, impudence is primarily displayed in obduracy. Let us recall that *audere* in Theodosius' Third Novel refers to the blindness to God's revelation in the world, whereas the Emperor is compelled to resort to *medicina legum* by religious dissidents' obstinacy (*durae frontis obstinatio*). *C.Th.* 15.5.5 makes a juxtaposition of ***stolidae paganitatis error atque insania*** and the Jewish *amentia*, in a similar way as *Const. Sirm.* 12 does with *Donatistarum pertinacia* and *furor gentilium*. *C.Th.* 16.5.6 condemns *animi obstinatioris dementia* of heretics. Certainly, this is a key term here. It is exactly against *pertinax spiritus haereticorum*,[98] against *consuetudo obstinationis et pertinax natura* of the Manichaeans,[99] that the Imperial laws are promulgated. This *obstinatum piaculum* does not leave any room for the Emperor's leniency.[100] *C.Th.* 16.5.32 is issued *ne Eunomianorum tanta dementia perseveret*, while penal sanctions of *C.Th.* 16.10.24 are to target those who celebrate Easter at the wrong date *si in eadem amentia perseverant*. Let us also remember that the "pertinacity of the depraved mind" (*pertinacia pravae mentis*) had induced Diocletian to apply the most severe measures against Manichaeans;[101] likewise, in the pagan emperors' suppressions of Christians the argument of "obduracy" is of particular significance.[102]

If the offences labelled in the language of the Late Antique constitutions as *furor* are arranged in order, some noteworthy results can be seen. The first group to be identified is that of the *furor* characteristic of the Roman Empire's domestic *hostes*. With no ambiguity, the instances such as the *tyrannicus furor* of Attalos as well as Eutropius' *rabies* can be included here. The charge also serves to build the metaphor of "enemy" in *C.Th.* 9.45.5, where it is used to refer to a slave drawing his weapon at a place of asylum. One may also infer it probably in some other similar cases: *latrones* accused of *insania*,[103] slave-owners using violence,[104] and judges interrogating decurions by torture that are accused of *furor*.[105] In all these cases, the *furor* highlights the aspect of violence.

This element of violence can also be seen where the term *furor* pertains to serious crimes (grave robbery, *parricidium*, Jews using violence against those compatriots who converted to Christianity, the only exception here being

---

[98] *C.Th.* 16.5.25.

[99] *C.Th.* 16.5.7.

[100] *Nov. Theod.* 3.

[101] *Coll.* 15.3.3 (= *FIRA* 2: 580–581).

[102] Let us recall *qui in exsecranda superstitio duraverunt* from a constitution of Maximinus Daia (Mitchell 1988: 108).

[103] *C.Th.* 1.29.8.

[104] *C.Th.* 9.10.4; *Nov. Theod.* 15.2.

[105] *C.Th.* 12.1.85; 15.9.2.

an accusation of *furor* levelled against the authors of *famosi libelli*[106]). Also in the further cases, it is possible to link *furor* with accusations of *audacia*, obduracy, or the absurdity of thinking that consents to a given type of conduct.[107]

A separate treatment should be given to the most frequent case of *furor* as used in the material in question, i.e., in reference to religious dissidents. It is levelled at heretics in general[108] or individual heretical sects,[109] as well as pagans, including those who apostatized back to paganism.[110] In the case of pagans, it may refer to both making offerings[111] and religious views.[112] The "madness" seems to have a strong connection with the error of the mind, that is, heretical doctrine. *C.Th.* 16.5.31 (*gemina* – *C.Th.* 16.5.32, 396) provides for punishing *auctores*, *doctores*, and *clerici* (clergymen) of Eunomians, "whose madness induced them to such false doctrine" (*quorum furor tantum suasit errorem*). The Eunomians, who were particularly readily portrayed by the contemporary Church historians as victims of excessive confidence in their own reason, are also particularly often pictured as "mad" in the Imperial constitutions.

Another example confirming that "madness" pertains to views can also be found in the *praefatio* of *Nov. Theod.* 3 (438). All the beauty and perfection of the world point to their Creator. Who is so "demented" (*mente captus*) as to be unable to see it? But there are indeed such individuals "with blinded senses" (*sensibus exactos*), who "dare" (*audere*) to fail to draw the obvious conclusions; the emperor lists them as follows: *Iudeos Samaritas paganos et cetera haereticorum genera portentorum*. They ought to be recalled "to the sanity of an excellent mind" (*ad sanitatem mentis*), as their obstinacy (*durae frontis obstinatio*) makes it necessary, *lege medica*.

Another constitution, in which "religious madness" is ascribed to the Jews, is the *C.Th.* 15.5.5 (425). It mentions individuals afflicted with *Iudaeae impietatis amentia* and *stolidae paganitatis error atque insania* as those who fail to understand the order of abstaining from attending theatre and circus

---

106 *C.Th.* 9.34.8.3.

107 Connections with *audacia*: *C.Th.* 4.22.3.9; 6.4.22.16; 15.2.4.2; *Nov. Theod.* 3.68; with *pertinacia*: "madness" linked to *pertinacia*: *C.Th.* 11.36.14; 12.1.85.5; 16.5.38.2; 16.5.60.5; 16.10.24.3; *Const. Sirm.* 12.9; *Nov. Theod.* 3.63; the absurdity of accusations being made by the people who have been indicted themselves: *C.Th.* 9.1.12.8.

108 *dementia* (*C.Th.* 16.1.2; 16.5.6; 16.5.24), *furor* (*C.Th.* 16.5.6; 16.5.60; 16.6.2), *vesania* (*C.Th.* 16.1.2; 16.5.15; 16.6.6), *insania* (*C.Th.* 16.5.65).

109 Most frequently, Eunomians (*dementia* – *C.Th.* 16.5.32; *furor* – *C.Th.* 16.5.25; 16.5.31; 16.5.32; 16.6.7; *vesania* – *C.Th.* 16.5.25), also *amentia* of Manichaeans and Pepysites (*C.Th.* 16.10.24), "raving" (*furere*) Manichaeans and Donatists (*C.Th.* 16.5.38).

110 *mente caecati* (*C.Th.* 16.7.5).

111 *vesanus ac sacrilegius* (*C.Th.* 16.10.7), *insania* (*C.Th.* 16.10.2).

112 *furor*, *dementia*, and *vesania* (*Nov. Theod.* 3.8), *furor* (*Const. Sirm.* 12), *insania* (*C.Th.* 15.5.5).

performances on Sundays. Describing the adherents of Judaism, whose religion was tolerated and protected by the state, as "mad" indicates that the "religious madness" cannot be identified with the religious *crimen*. On the other hand, unlike *superstitio*, the accusation of "madness" is not distributed "fairly," as most frequently it is used with reference to heretics, less often applied to pagans, and only twice to Jews.[113]

amentia, dementia, furor, insania, mente caecitas, mente captus, rabies, vesania

I. A. "madness" in the sense of mental illness: *C.Th.* 9.4.1.5 (*insania*); 9.43.1.11 (*furiosus*); 9.43.1.11 (*demens*).

B. "madness" of "enemies": *C.Th.* 1.29.8.2 (*insania*, brigands); 6.4.22.16 (*insania*; with regard to calling an official *hostis publicus*); 6.4.22.18 (*furor*, ditto); 7.16.2.9 (*furor*, tyrant); 9.45.5.10 (*furiosus*, an armed slave at a place of asylum treated as *hostis*); 9.45.5.12 (*insania*, ditto); *Nov. Theod.* 15.2.14 (*vesania* of a decurion who had used a garrison of armed slaves against tax-collectors).

C. "madness" of public officials: *C.Th.* 9.40.17.14 (*rabies* of Eutropius); 12.1.85.5 (*furor*); 15.9.2.4 (*insania*).

D. "madness" of offenders: *C.Th.* 4.22.3.9 (*furor*, taking a contested property by force before the verdict); 9.10.4.6 (*furor*, violence); 9.34.8.3 (*furor*, *libelli famosi*); 9.38.6.5 (*furor*, *parricidium*); 9.38.6.7 (*caecus*, incest); 15.2.4.2 (*furor*, appropriation of public water); Nov. Valent. 23.4 (*furor*, tomb robbery); 23.4 (*caecus*, ditto); 23.17 (*vesanus*, ditto).

E. other cases of "madness": *C.Th.* 2.33.2.4 (*furor*, exceeding allowed interest rates on loans); 9.1.12.8 (*furor*, accusations by persons who are already indicted themselves); 11.36.14.7 (*vesania* of a person making an unlawful appeal); 11.39.12.3 (*amentia*, the plaintiff demanding that the defendant provide evidence of ownership).

F. "madness" of acting against the Catholic Church: *C.Th.* 16.2.12.3 (*furialis*, accusing a bishop in court); 16.8.1.3 (*furor*, Jews persecuting those who converted to Christianity); *Const. Sirm.* 15.14[2] (*vesania*, accusing clergymen without any proof of guilt).

G. "madness" of non-Catholics:

G1. heretics: *C.Th.* 16.1.2.9 (*demens*); 16.1.2.9 (*vesanus*); 16.5.6.2 (*dementia*); 16.5.6.13[2] (*furor*); 16.5.15.2 (*vesania*); 16.5.24.2 (*dementia*); 16.5.38.2 (*furo*); 16.5.60.5 (*furor*); 16.5.65.2 (*insania*); 16.6.2.2[2] (*furor*); 16.6.6.18 (*vesania*); 16.10.24.3 (*amentia*), including Eunomians: *C.Th.* 16.5.25.3[2] (*vesania*); 16.5.25.5[2] (*furor*); 16.5.31.2 = 16.5.32.3 (*furor*); 16.5.32.1 (*dementia*); 16.6.7.1[2] (*furor*).

G2. pagans: *C.Th.* 15.5.5.12 (*insania*); 16.7.5.2 (*caeco*, apostasy); 16.10.2.2 (*insania*); 16.10.7.2 (*vesanus*); *Const. Sirm.* 12.9 (*furor*); *Nov. Theod.* 3.63 (*vesania*); 3.68 (*furor*); 3.71 (*dementia*).

[113] This third case deals with a different matter, namely the violence used by Jews against those who abandoned their Jewish religion and converted to Christianity.

G3. Jews: *C.Th.* 15.5.5.11 (*amentia*).

G4. all non-Catholics: *Nov. Theod.* 3.6 (*mente captus*).

II. "madness" linked with *audacia*: *C.Th.* 4.22.3.9 (*furor* with *audacia*); 6.4.22.16 (*insania* with *praesumptio*); 15.2.4.2 (*furor* with *audacia*); *Nov. Theod.* 3.68 (*furor* with *audacia*).

"madness" linked with *pertinacia*: *C.Th.* 11.36.14.7 (*procax vesania*); 12.1.85.5 (*furor* with *pertinacia*); 16.5.38.2 (*furere non desistunt*); 16.5.60.5 (*si in eodem furore permanserit*); 16.10.24.3 (*si in eadem amentia perseverant*); *Const. Sirm.* 12.9 (*Donatistarum pertinacia, furore gentilium*); *Nov. Theod.* 3.63 (*naturali vesania et licentia pertinaci*).

Pertinacia, obstinatio

Pertinacia and *obstinatio*, both referring to hard-hearted obstinacy, as terms with a definitely negative overtone, can be often found especially in the language used by the Church Fathers.[114] They are relatively seldom seen in the Imperial documents, and there can be no doubt they serve as elements of the language of invective. This is corroborated by both their joint appearance as part of accumulation figures[115] and their association, or equivalence, with *furor*.[116] They also remain in connection with *audacia*.[117] Nonetheless, infrequent instances of their usage make it hard to determine any application rules for this invective: it is quite often used in reference to heretics, and non-Catholics in general, as well as abuses of authority on the part of the state administration apparatus, but it also happens to appear in other contexts.[118]

[114] E.g., Ambrose, *De bono mortis* 7.29: *erroris pertinacia*; *Ep.* 77.18: *Iudeorum pertinacia*; August. Hipp., *De moribus ecclesiae catholicae et Manicheorum* 1: *impudentissima pertinacia*.

[115] *C.Th.* 11.38.1; 16.5.7.

[116] *C.Th.* 12.1.85; *Const. Sirm.* 12; *Nov. Theod.* 3. Associations with *furor* can also be observed in the Church Fathers' language, cf. August. Hipp., *Ep.* 139.1: *insana pertinacia*; Cypr. Carthag., *Ep.* 54: *superba est ista obstinatio et sacrilega praesumptio, quam sibi furor pravus adsumit* (the sentence is repeated almost verbatim by August. Hipp., *Contra Gaudentium* 2.13, with only *obstinatio* and *praesumptio* interchanged).

[117] *Nov. Theod.* 7.2.

[118] *Const. Sirm.* 9: a stubborn sinner divested of his clerical rank; *C.Th.* 11.38.1: making an appeal after two lost lawsuits; *Nov. Valent.* 31: causing the divorce of a pair of *coloni* with two different landlords; *Nov. Majo.* 6: the obstinacy of childless widows who would not remarry.

obstinatio, obstinatus

A. non-Catholics: *C.Th.* 16.5.6.2; 16.5.7.16; *Nov. Theod.* 3.13 (in the latter case, with reference to all non-Catholics, in other cases – to heretics).

B. officials: *Nov. Valent.* 7.1.3.

C. other (negative): *C.Th.* 11.38.1.2; *Nov. Valent.* 31.22; *Nov. Majo.* 6.54.

pertinacia, pertinaciter, pertinax

A. non-Catholics: *C.Th.* 16.5.7.16; 16.5.25.3; 16.5.53.6; *Const. Sirm.* 12.9; *Nov. Theod.* 3.63 (in the latter case, with reference to pagans, in other cases – to heretics).

B. officials: *C.Th.* 11.30.58.12; 12.1.85.5; 12.1.85.10; *Nov. Theod.* 7.2.31; *Nov. Valent.* 1.3.28.

C. other (negative): *C.Th.* 10.26.1.11; 12.1.16.1; *Const. Sirm.* 9.7.

Subreptio

A particularly harsh manner of discrediting a person has been to compare them to some seemingly despised animal, such as a pig, donkey, dog, snake, etc. This technique was not used very often by classical authors,[119] and tended to appear more frequently in the language of the Church Fathers as corresponding to the idea of Biblical invective.[120] In the language of the Imperial documents, on the other hand, no obvious metaphor based on animal imagery can be found. Still, one may wonder if certain expressions are not indicative of likening the accused person to a snake.

I shall also refer, if only in passing, to the metaphor of poison, which can be found three times in the constitutions of the Theodosian Code (alongside the more frequent cases mentioning poison or poisoning in literal terms[121]). It refers once to *famosi libelli*[122] and twice to heresy.[123] In the latter case, it is possible to discern associations with the typical metaphor of heresy as the venom of serpents or scorpions, best known from the introduction to the *Panarion* by Epiphanius of Salamis.[124]

---

119 Hoffmann 1892: 22–31; Opelt 1965a: 143–144.

120 Opelt 1980: 252–254; Wissemann 1992: 99 ff.

121 *C.Th.* 4.6.3.16 (alluding to a love potion); 9.12.1.7; 9.19.4.3^{2}; 9.38.1.2; 9.38.3.3; 9.38.4.4; 9.38.6.8; 9.38.7.5; 9.38.8.10; 11.36.1.5; 11.36.1.10; 11.36.7.3; *Const. Sirm.* 8.26.

122 *C.Th.* 9.34.10.2.

123 *C.Th.* 16.5.6.8; 16.6.2.6^{2}.

124 Epiph., *Panarion*, Proem. II.3.

Once, in Theodosius II's novel discussed above, there appears the verb *serpo* related to the term *serpens*.[125] It alludes to a certain decurion's "slithering" into a public office which he was not entitled to assume. Similar insidious actions are ordinarily described in the Code as a *subreptio*. They are sometimes used to signify some sort of a devious slipping into Imperial service, but much more often in reference to insidiously obtaining some Imperial decision (usually in the form of a rescript), or even attempting to do so. There is no doubt that in the both cases *subreptio* and other related terms possess their own peculiar and specific tones of condemnation.

subreptio, subrepo, subrepticus, subreptivus
A. "slipping" insidiously into imperial service: *C.Th.* 8.4.28.2[2] (*subreptio*); 10.20.11.3 (*subreptivus*); 10.22.4.4 (*subreptio*); *Nov. Theod.* 3.23 (*subreptivus*); 15.2.6 (*subreptio*); 15.2.23 (*subreptio*).
B. using devious means to obtain an imperial decision or attempting to do so: *C.Th.* 1.2.9.2 (*subreptio*); 1.11.2.2 (*subrepo*); 2.23.1.4 (*subreptio*); 3.10.1.8 (*subreptio*); 5.12.2.3 (*subreptivus*); 6.28.5.4 (*subreptivus*); 9.26.3.3 (*subrepticus*); 10.3.7.5 (*subreptio*); 11.23.3.2 (*subreptio*); 12.6.25.5 (*subreptio*); 12.16.1.2 (*subreptivus*); 13.3.13.2 (*subrepticus*); 13.11.10.5 (*subrepticus*); 14.3.20.2 (*subrepticus*); 14.3.21.4 (*subreptio*); 14.15.5.6 (*subreptio*); 14.23.1.2 (*subreptio*); 15.1.43.5 (*subrepticus*); 16.8.8.5 (*subreptio*); 16.9.3.5 (*subreptio*); *Nov. Theod.* 8.15 (*subreptio*); 17.1.21 (*subreptio*); 19.6 (*subreptio*); 26.60 (*subrepticius*); *Nov. Valent.* 19.5 (*subreptio*); 27.51 (*subreptio*); *Nov. Majo.* 4.16 (*subreptio*).
C. other: *Const. Sirm.* 9.4 (*subrepo*, metaphorically: vices slither into ranks of clergy); *Nov. Valent.* 1.3.9 (*subreptio*, on tax-collectors' activity); *Nov. Majo.* 6.84 (*subrepo*, a mother deceived by a different heir to inheritance).

Features contrary to *humanitas*

The ideal of *humanitas* ("humanity") was, at least as viewed by some authors of the late Roman Republic, the fundamental requirement that any educated Roman citizen was supposed to fulfil.[126] It did not disappear during the Principate, and subsequently would even become an important element of the ruler's public propaganda image in the Late Antique Imperial constitutions. The emperor made reference to his *humanitas* in his justification of many legal

[125] *Nov. Theod.* 15.2.4. See Chapter IV: 106–110.
[126] Schadenwaldt 1973; Korpanty 1979: 99–115.

provisions enacted for the benefit of his subjects.[127] Yet there appeared a significant change in the content of this term as compared with the one to be found in, for instance, Cicero's writings. As much as in his time the concept of *humanitas* comprised two components: the kind attitude to others (*philanthropia*) and living in accordance with classical education (*paideia*),[128] in the later period the meaning *philanthropia* would begin to come into prominence.[129] There would also appear some new meanings, e.g., the weakness seen as an inherently human trait.[130] Yet the most important component was the one that was characteristic of legal texts. As Richard Honig argues, in almost all the passages where the idea of *humanitas* appears in the Late Antique Imperial constitutions, one may observe, besides various aspects of the "kind-heartedness to others," the idea of "righteousness," consisting in the conformity with the natural sense of justice, *aequitas*. Nearly all legal solutions justified through *humanitas* can be explained in two ways: by appealing either to *philanthropia* or to *aequitas*.[131] The terms derived from *inhumanus*, appearing infrequently in the Late Antique texts, should be explained exactly as pertaining to situations where the law in question would have been interpreted contrary to the principle of *aequitas*.[132] As a result, they are technical terms intended to serve the purpose of the criticism of a legal provision, not of a person or a deed, and they are never used to function as terms of invective.

It is quite different in the case of a number of terms which can be understood as contrary to the "philanthropic" aspect of *humanitas*. Among them, there are terms such as *immanitas* ("inhumanity"), *crudelitas* ("cruelty"), and some others ones that indicate more poignantly the inhuman, even savage, aspect of cruelty – *saevitia*, *feritas*.

At the same time, the criticism of "cruelty" does not signify a similar criticism of "severity." In fact, the "severity" as such does not have to stand in contradiction to the ideal of *humanitas* – in one of the amnesty constitutions (*C.Th.* 9.38.10) it is even considered as contrary to that ideal to apply amnesty to those who had managed to evade punishment (it would have

127 Honig 1960: 72–80.

128 Honig 1960: 28; Korpanty 1979: 107–112.

129 Honig 1960: 29; Korpanty 1979: 115.

130 Honig 1960: 34. In this sense, the term *humanitas* appears at *C.Th.* 9.17.6.

131 Honig 1960: 81–84. The sentences in the Digests, in which the *humanitas* appears as *aequitas*, were sometimes regarded as interpolations of Late Antique provenance, cf. Krüger 1898.

132 Palma 1992. It turns out that "inhuman" are situations arising from a literally correct interpretation of some valid provision, yet still in contradiction with the principal ideal of *humanitas*, leading to the Emperor's decision (or the *iurisconsulti* interpretation) precluding the possibility of such an interpretation.

been at variance with the natural sense of justice).[133] In the entire Theodosian Code, there are only several instances of the criticism of severity (*acerbitas*), and even then (with one exception) it refers to abuses of power within the framework of the valid legal system. If the "severity" could be contrasted with "humanity," it would be first of all the case when it denoted a feature characteristic of the *barbaricum*, alien to the Roman world.

Saevitia, in itself, does not appear to be such a trait, as it can be attributed to both just penalties and the castigated cruelty of officials or barbarians. The term *crudelitas* does not possess this neutral character. It is noteworthy in that *saevitas* in the Roman historiography points to the ferocity characteristic of wild animals and it is a definitely stronger term than *crudelitas*.[134] However, it is also typical of just penalties in the Later Roman legislation. It may be recognized as an aspect of the brutalization affecting the language of the legislation in Late Antiquity, whose one of the functions is to be deterrence.

A term which is perceived to be particularly characteristic of barbarians is *feritas* – "bestiality." In this case, the language of the law strictly follows in the footsteps of traditional depictions of the barbarian, as *feritas* is the most frequent charge levelled at barbarians in literary sources as well.[135] Still, in the Imperial documents, *feritas* is all the more striking as it is their sole characteristic. As opposed to the ubiquitous *furor haereticorum*, there is no trace of *furor barbarorum* in the constitutions, even though the latter charge would be entirely justified in the tradition of barbarian depictions.[136] On the contrary, two citations point to the distinction between *feritas barbarorum* and "non-barbaric" *furor*:

- *C.Th. 7.16.2.9: tyrannici furoris et **barbaricae** feritatis (it is the usurper – that is, Atticus – who is "mad," while the barbarian – Alaric – "bestial");*

- *Nov. Valent. 23.17 (metaphorically, on the crime of tomb robbery): **barbara** et vesana crudelitas (on the one hand, the cruelty here is "barbaric," on the other – "mad").*

Which does not mean that the "madness" itself cannot contain an element of *feritas*![137]

---

[133] *Indignum est enim humanitate, qui post damnationem commisit in legem.* Cf. Honig 1960: 81. Also in *Const. Sirm.* 8, *humanitas* delimits the extent: *quatenus tamen iusta humanitas patitur.*

[134] Dunkle 1971: 14–15.

[135] Dauge 1981: 428–429.

[136] Dauge 1981: 430–431.

[137] *Fera et periculi sui nescia latronum insania* (*C.Th.* 1.29.8); *Quis enim tam mente captus, tam novae feritatis immanitate damnatus est* (*Nov. Theod.* 3).

Apart from the barbarians, *feritas* (as well as *crudelitas* and *saevitas*) is, in particular, the feature of public officials guilty of authority abuses (this charge is a serious one, as because of their cruelty they stand in opposition to the ideal of the Roman *humanitas*). In one instance, they are charged as *latrones*. Referring twice to non-Catholics deserves our attention, as in the both cases the point is not a "positively" professed false doctrine or a cult-related practice, but the true faith being rejected. An apostate, as the legislator points out in *C.Th.* 16.7.5, thus places himself beyond the limits of the human *communio* – and this allows the legislator to justify a very specific order depriving him of the rights connected with drafting and accepting testaments and donations.[138]

We must be cautious in interpretations of the adjective *feralis* and the adverb *feraliter*. They may have been derived from *fera* ("wild beast") or *feralia* ("funeral"). It may also happen that in a given context both interpretations are possible (e.g., *feralis pestis* in *C.Th.* 9.16.5 may be construed as the penalty of being torn to pieces by wild animals, or also simply as a metaphor of capital punishment associated with the magician's necromantic practices;[139] *antra feralia*, which the legislator uses to describe in *C.Th.* 16.5.57 churches of the heretics, may be both caves of wild beasts and subterranean tombs). This ambiguity may explain the ambivalence in how the adjective was used. It is undoubtedly negative when it refers to barbaric cruelty. For a Roman, the term "sepulchral" may carry even more negative overtones than "bestial," but it does not have to be linked with any condemnation. It can be found, in particular, where it is used in reference to a person being locked in the dark, especially in prison. Frequently, it is also a just punishment. The actual intention behind the term is particularly clearly discernible in the text of the Easter amnesty, preserved as *Const. Sirm.* 8. The joyous and serene atmosphere of the Resurrection holiday cannot be disturbed by the anguished wailing of prisoners. This circumstance urges the emperor to release from the sepulchral darkness of prisons those who had been convicted for some less serious crimes. It is one of the most vivid justifications in the Later Roman law.[140] It could even be argued that the adjective *feralis*, mentioned several

---

138 Baccari 1996: 283 ff.

139 Cf. Chapter IV: 90–91.

140 "For in the midst of festive ceremonies and the venerable rites of a sacred season it is not seemly that the dissonant voices of the unfortunate should resound; that accused persons, with their disheveled hair in deathly disorder should be dragged as objects of common pity, that groans brought from the depths of the heart should be heard, although sacred and joyful occasions are in harmony with each other; and it is not fitting, in the midst of the serene words of the prayers and the pious voices dedicated to the eternal Divinity, to feel, to hear, or to see anything sad. Whence We do not suppress Our well known clemency as shown by Our benefits, but We open also the prisons, We lay aside the chains, and We properly abolish the occasion for uncombed hair in the prison that is dark with filth. We snatch all persons from the death penalty ..." [lit-

times in the passages devoted to the anti-heretical criticism, makes reference to the darkness of the grave, rather than to bestial cruelty – it may be indicated by the absence in that criticism of the terms such as *crudelitas*, whereas, on the other hand, let us note the presence of some terms such as *dirus*, and so forth, and especially the ubiquity, in this section of the Later Roman legislation, of the term *contagium*, primarily associated with the touching of mortal remains.[141]

A separate, and also quite special, case is the ambiguous adjective *immanis*. It may simply, in its neutral sense, point to a huge amount of something, or it may also be treated as opposite to *humanitas*. In the source material in question, *immanis* preserves this ambiguity, yet it always carries a negative overtone. Only in a couple of cases is this "negativity" of a purely contextual character: with regard to enormous amounts of profits obtained unlawfully.[142] But when we read that the bulk of the outstanding tax payments, now (unlawfully) collected, oppresses the provinces,[143] it is possible to discern an element of "cruelty," as *immanis* often amplifies the cruelty inherently typical of barbarians,[144] especially the atrocity of torture. A further motive is the *immanitas* of offences – it is used readily, in particular, with regard to the most serious crimes,[145] e.g., in amnesties.[146]

inhumanus

C.Th. 3.5.3.4; *Nov. Theod.* 11.7; *Nov. Theod.* 22.2.36.

saevitia, saevus, saevio

A. as a feature of barbarians: *C.Th.* 9.12.1.10.

B. as a feature of public officials: *C.Th.* 9.3.2.3^2; 11.7.11.3; *Nov. Majo.* 2.44.

C. weight of a crime: *C.Th.* 9.38.7.4.

D. severity of the sentence and (just) punishment: *C.Th.* 9.1.2.3; 9.40.11.2.

erally: sepulchral penalties] (*Neque enim convenit inter festivas caeremonias et venerabiles sacri temporis ritus strepere infelicium dissonas voces, trahi ad communem misericordiam horrentibus passis feraliter crinibus reos, audiri tractos ex imo pectore gemitus, cum utique bene sibimet sacra et laeta conveniant et non deceat inter serena votorum ac dicatas aeterno numini pias voces aliquid triste sentire audire conspicere. Unde notam beneficiis nostris non supprimimus lenitatem, aperimus quin etiam carcerem, vincla deponimus, inpexos tenebrosae pedore custodiae crines decenter amovemus. Eripimus omnes feralibus poenis…*) Transl. Pharr 1952: 480–481.

141 Cf. Chapter VII: 199–200.

142 *Nov. Majo.* 2.75; *C.Th.* 7.13.7.5.

143 *C.Th.* 5.14.31.3.

144 *Nov. Valent.* 12 – literally (*immanitas hostilis*); metaphorically: *Nov. Theod.* 3 (*novae feritatis immanitate damnatus*), *C.Th.* 9.12.1: *saevitia immanum barbarorum.*

145 *C.Th.* 11.36.4.4, 9.40.16.3 = 11.30.57.2.

146 *Const. Sirm.* 7.6^2, 9.38.8.10, 9.38.7.5.

E. on imprisonment: *Nov. Valent.* 1.3.25; *Nov. Majo.* 2.47 (as a result of a public official's lawlessness).
F. as a feature of fate (*fortuna*, contrasted with the Imperial *humanitas*): *Const. Sirm.* 13.2.

crudelitas, crudeliter, crudelis
A. as a feature of barbarians: *Nov. Valent.* 23.17 (metaphorically on grave robbery).
B. as a feature of a public official: *C.Th.* 8.1.15.2; 9.3.1.17; *Nov. Valent.* 1.3.26 (twice).
C. suffering in prison: *C.Th.* 9.1.18.2 (caused by a public official).
D. torture: *Nov. Majo.* 2.48 (due to the lawlessness of an official).

feritas, feralis, fera, ferus, ferocitas
A. as a feature of barbarians: *C.Th.* 5.7.2.2; 7.16.2.9, *Const. Sirm.* 16.7; *Nov. Valent.* 2.3.4.
B. as a feature of *latrones*: *C.Th.* 1.29.8.1.
C. as a feature of public officials: *C.Th.* 9.3.6.6; *Const. Sirm.* 13.15 (prison guards); *Nov. Majo.* 2.27.
D. on religious dissidents: *C.Th.* 16.5.7.6^{2} (religious practices of heretics); 16.6.4.17 (ditto); 16.5.57.10 (*antra feralia* – their churches); 16.7.5.5 (minds of apostates, contrasted with the human *communio*); 16.8.1.2 (*secta* – on the Jews who persecute their brethren in faith converting to Christianity); *Nov. Theod.* 3.6 (on the minds of non-Catholics); 3.15 (*sectae* – on non-Catholics).
E. punishment : *C.Th.* 9.15.1.3^{2}; 9.16.5.3 (*feralis pestis*); *Const. Sirm.* 8.21.
F. imprisonment: *C.Th.* 6.29.1.3; *Const. Sirm.* 8.16 (ref. to the hair of the incarcerated).
G. wild animals (*fera*): *C.Th.* 9.12.1.8; 15.5.2.3; 15.11.R; 15.11.1.6; 15.11.1.7; 15.11.2.2.
H. harshness of winter: *Nov. Theod.* 3.78.

acer, acerbitas, acerbus
A. just severity: *C.Th.* 1.2.8.2^{2}; 1.10.4.3; 4.20.1.2^{2}; 8.5.41.2; 9.19.2.3^{2}; 9.24.2.6; 9.42.13.2; 10.10.32.11; 11.1.35.6; 11.7.20.6; 13.11.4.9; 16.5.38.6; 16.5.54.1^{2}; 16.6.6.17; 16.10.9.3; *Nov. Theod.* 3.71; 15.2.14; 24.51; *Nov. Valent.* 7.2.21.
B. castigated severity: *C.Th.* 11.30.11.18; *Nov. Valent.* 12.2; 12.7; *Nov. Majo.* 2.28 (of public officials); 2.36 (ditto).
C. injustice of the situation: *Nov. Theod.* 22.1.6.
D. weight of a crime: *C.Th.* 9.25.1.3; *Const. Sirm.* 7.2^{2}.
E. heavy insult: *C.Th.* 8.14.1.3.
F. harshness of winter: *C.Th.* 6.29.12.3.

immanis, immanitas
A. large quantity: *C.Th.* 5.14.31.3; 7.13.7.5; *Const. Sirm.* 14.11 (on *flagitium*); *Nov. Majo.* 2.75.
B. cruelty contrasted with *humanitas*:

B1. of barbarians: *C.Th.* 9.12.1.10; *Nov. Valent.* 12.12.

B2. as a feature of crimes: *C.Th.* 9.38.7.5 (tomb robbery); 9.38.8.10 (tomb robbery); 9.40.16.3 = 11.30.57.2; 11.36.4.4 (adultery); 13.5.16.4; 16.6.7.1² (rebaptism); *Const. Sirm.* 7.6²; *Nov. Theod.* 3.62 (of pagans, may refer to sacrifices and views as such).

B3. as a feature of torture: *C.Th.* 9.35.2.5²; 11.36.7.14.

B4. as a feature of non-Catholics: *Nov. Theod.* 3.7.

Perfidia

Fides was one of the prominent values for the Romans of the Republican period. It encompassed practically all the important areas of life. In international relations, it was to signify fulfilment of obligations, loyalty of the subordinated party to those who have the upper hand and, conversely, protecting those in inferior positions; it was similarly construed in patron-client and family relationships, relations between gods and citizens, as well as gods and the whole community. Just as important was the *fides* in relations between equal citizens, as the loyalty forming the basis of mutual trust. It also found its way into the system of private law, as *bona fides* – assumed in all matters related to concluding contractual agreements or within the framework of *fideicomissum*.[147] Obviously, from the perspective of a Roman, the attitude contrary to *fides*, i.e., *perfidia* (perfidiousness), must have been something that is not only exceptionally revolting but also undermining the foundations of all social order. It is no surprise then that on the level of international relations, among other things, it was exactly *perfidia* that had been perceived as a feature typical of Rome's worst enemies, the Carthaginians. It is to be found on some other levels as well, e.g., in a guardian's breach of trust in relation to a person in his charge, in a breach of faith between lovers (on the other hand, *perfidia* can also be possibly discerned in an act of rape); *perfidia* could even have been metaphorically attributed to objects.[148]

There are multiple references to *fides* in the documents of the Later Roman Empire. These are primarily some traditional appeals to *fides* as loyalty, in the case of private law contracts. Yet there also appears a new and distinct meaning of the term *fides*. It also begins to be applied to the content of the orthodox Christian faith (and not, as could be expected, a Christian's

[147] Korpanty 1979: 32–36.

[148] Opelt 1965a: respectively, 31, 203, 208, 254; in general, instances of *pefidia* in the classical Latin literature – cf. Opelt 1965a: 282.

individual stance which is beyond the scope of the legislator's interest, or even an individual act of confession, defined as a *confessio*).[149]

The term *perfidia* is relatively rare in the texts of the Imperial constitutions. There are only six instances of the terms *perfidia* and *perfidus*, which can be found as contrasted with the concept of the ancient Roman *fides*. Three cases concern violations of *fides* towards private persons,[150] one refers to concealing the fact of another person's apostasy,[151] while another one deals with insidiously hiding free young men involved in some illicit service for Roman soldiers whereas they should have been recruited as army conscripts.[152] The sixth case is somewhat enigmatic, referring to some vague offences committed by the administrative staff, *apparitores*, which are described as *prava admodum venalisque perfidia*, whose severity (*desaevire*) must be stopped and for this reason they ought to be prosecuted *in absentia* as well.[153] This is the only example where a term of invective is used explicitly.

More often, the term *perfidia* appears in religious contexts, where it may be contrasted with the orthodox *fides*. Interestingly, in as much as *fides* serves, most of all, as a contrast to the beliefs of Jews and heretics,[154] *perfidia* is used only with reference to heretics and pagans. It appears that *perfidia* is not symmetrical with *fides* here. It would rather signify the criminal character of a specific heretical doctrine, and it may be, as a result, characteristic of each heretical doctrine individually.[155] It may be used in plural,[156] but it could as well be said that all the heresies share in fact one common feature of *perfidia*.[157]

fides

A. Catholic faith: *C.Th.* 9.16.12.3; 11.39.11.2 = 16.7.4.2; 15.7.4.4; 15.7.9.4; 16.1.R; 16.1.3.13; 16.1.3.15; 16.1.4.3; 16.2.16.3; 16.4.3.2; 16.5.6.5; 16.5.6.2²; 16.5.6.6²; 16.5.6.14²; 16.5.7.9²; 16.5.12.3; 16.5.24.4; 16.5.41.4; 16.5.41.7²; 16.5.42.3; 16.5.44.2; 16.5.58.8; 16.5.65.32; 16.6.2.5; 16.6.2.6; 16.6.2.8; 16.6.4.1; 16.6.4.8²; 16.6.4.16²; 16.6.7.1²; 16.7.4.10; 16.7.5.2; 16.7.7.4; 16.8.18.3; 16.8.18.4; 16.8.19.7; 16.8.19.20; 16.8.23.4; 16.8.23.7; 16.8.26.8; 16.9.2.7; 16.11.2.3; *Const. Sirm.* 6.18²; *Nov. Theod.* 3.27; 3.47; *Nov. Valent.* 3.21; 17.4; 18.3; 23.9; *Nov. Majo.* 6.22.

---

149 Stachura 2007a: 38–39.

150 *C.Th.* 2.17.1.30²; 3.5.5.3; *Nov. Majo.* 6.98.

151 *C.Th.* 16.7.3.14².

152 *C.Th.* 7.1.10.6.

153 *C.Th.* 9.40.14.2.

154 Stachura 2007a: 39.

155 *C.Th.* 16.5.6; 16.5.37.

156 *C.Th.* 16.5.63.

157 *C.Th.* 16.5.60: *diversa sunt nomina, sed una perfidia.*

B. with regard to the Empire: *C.Th.* 4.4.6.5 (our love of *fides*); 16.5.55.5 (*fides publica*); *Nov. Valent.* 17.25 (*fides nostri imperii*); 32.14 (*fides publica*).
C. as a feature of officials (or of their conduct): *C.Th.* 1.1.5.21; 1.7.3.5; 1.28.1.1; 6.28.8.2; 6.35.7.5; 7.4.24.7; 8.1.1.5; 8.1.9.15; 8.1.10.1^2; 8.5.36.7; 10.2.2.4; 11.7.14.3; 12.1.75.7 (of decurions); 12.1.97.4; 12.6.4.3 (of decurions); 12.6.9.3; 12.6.29.3; 12.7.2.6; 12.7.2.8; 13.5.22.2; *Const. Sirm.* 14.24; *Nov. Theod.* 1.10; 24.67; *Nov. Valent.* 8.1.7; 15.26.
D. as a feature of other individuals (or of their conduct): *C.Th.* 3.7.3.5; 4.4.3.7; 8.5.3.5; 8.12.1.13^2; 8.12.2.10; 12.12.16.4; 13.5.26.6^2; *Nov. Theod.* 16.9; *Nov. Valent.* 21.2.8; 21.2.9.
E. other: *C.Th.* 1.1.5.5^2; 1.10.8.7^2; 1.34.3.1^2; 2.4.2.4; 2.27.1.16; 2.27.1.7^2; 2.27.1.19^2; 2.29.2.7; 3.1.1.2; 3.4.1.2; 3.5.7.2; 3.5.11.6; 3.30.3.22; 3.32.2.5; 4.8.7.2; 4.19.1.7; 4.19.1.8; 4.22.3.10; 4.23.1.2; 4.23.1.3; 6.30.15.6; 8.12.2.6; 9.1.9.2; 9.1.19.3^2; 9.7.8.2; 9.7.8.5; 9.19.4.7; 9.28.2.2; 9.34.3.2; 9.34.7.10; 9.42.10.7; 10.1.15.5; 10.2.2.5; 10.8.5.10; 10.11.1.1; 10.11.1.3; 10.12.2.7^2; 10.15.2.4; 10.15.3.2; 10.17.R; 10.18.1.4; 10.24.2.6; 10.25.1.3; 10.25.1.6; 11.5.1.3; 11.8.3.13^2; 11.20.6.1^2; 11.22.5.4; 11.26.1.2; 11.28.13.4; 11.28.13.13; 11.39.R; 11.39.2.1; 11.39.3.2; 11.39.13.3; 12.3.1.13; 12.12.5.2; 13.5.14.7^2; 13.5.32.8; 13.9.2.7; 13.9.5.4; 13.10.7.5^2; 13.11.1.1^2; 13.11.13.2; 14.4.9.6; 15.14.9.6; 16.9.3.4; *Nov. Theod.* 9.33; 18.1; 22.1.70; 22.2.39; *Nov. Valent.* 7.2.17; 14.9; 19.11; 21.2.27; *Nov. Marc.* 3.14.

perfidia, perfidus
A. in opposition to the Christian *fides*: *C.Th.* 16.5.6.8; 16.5.12.6; 16.5.15.1; 16.5.25.1^2; 16.5.37.5; 16.5.60.4; 16.5.63.1; 16.5.63.5; 16.7.7.13; *Nov. Theod.* 3.76; *Nov. Majo.* 6.25 (the attitude of Catholics contrary to the faith).
B. other cases: *C.Th.* 2.1.17.30^2; 3.5.5.3; 7.1.10.6; 9.40.14.2; 16.7.3.14^2; *Nov. Majo.* 6.98.

Impietas

The third of the Roman values, violations of which are condemned in the Late Antique constitutions, is *pietas*. For the Romans, it signified diligent fulfilment of obligations towards the family, country, and gods.[158] Accordingly, failing to fulfil obligations in relation to family, country, or gods was called *impietas*.[159] In our material, the terms *pietas* and *impietas* are relatively rare (aside from the Emperor referring to himself as *pietas nostra* or *mea*), yet all the three

[158] Obligations are thus ranked in Cic., *De off.* 1.45.160, although the term *pietas* as such is not mentioned; for more on *pietas* in Cicero, cf. Gertrude Emilie 1944.
[159] Ulrich 1930: 1–9; Wagenvoort 1980a; Champeux 1989; Kowalski 2002: 107, 109. On *impietas* as a charge Cicero used against the enemies, cf. Achard 1981: 289–315.

meanings can be found therein. It is noteworthy that the *pietas* towards the country (which is mentioned only twice) designates decurions' attitude to their city, not citizens' to the Empire. Much more frequently, charges of *impietas* are used in the context of children's attitude to their parents or vice versa. *Pietas* is also understood as Christians fulfilling their duties in relation to God. At the same time, *impietas* is used with reference to non-Catholics as well as in the context of transgressing against injunctions related to sexual purity. Finally, there is one case which is not very clear. Namely, after stipulating penalties for *violatio sepulchri*, the Emperor reminds the recipient of the constitution of his love for *pietas* and *religio*, and further on recalls the duties of public officials in relation to both the living and the dead.[160] It may be seen, possibly, as a reference to the most ancient sense of *pietas* – the respect for the ancestors' spirits.[161]

impius, impietas
A1. of children towards their parents (or grandchildren towards grandparents): *C.Th.* 5.1.4.14; 8.13.1.2; 8.13.1.13; 8.13.2.2; 8.13.4.2.
A2. of parents towards their children: *Nov. Valent.* 31.20 (separating children from parents); *Nov. Majo.* 6.19 (assigning daughters for virginity – ambiguous).
B. of *curiales* towards the city: *C.Th.* 12.18.2.4.
C. in relation to God, Christian religion: *C.Th.* 15.5.5.11; 16.5.15.2^2; 16.5.66.4; 16.5.66.6; 16.6.2.6^2; 16.7.6.2; 16.9.5.2; *Nov. Theod.* 3.79; 18.20 (on prostitution); *Nov. Majo.* 6.19 (assigning daughters for virginity – ambiguous); 6.116. D. other: *C.Th.* 6.24.11.8 (a case of misfortune).

pietas
A1. of children towards their parents: *C.Th.* 8.13.2.3; *Nov. Majo.* 6.84; 6.118.
A2. of parents towards children: *C.Th.* 3.8.2.32^2; 8.13.6.2^2; 8.18.1.2; *Nov. Valent.* 33.10; *Nov. Majo.* 6.73 (here, also a wife's *pietas* for the remembrance of her late husband).
B. of *curiales* towards the city: *Nov. Theod.* 22.1.8.
C. in relation to God, Christian religion: *C.Th.* 9.45.4.13; *Const. Sirm.* 3.5^2 (*pietas* of bishops); 11.23; *Nov. Valent.* 23.52 (in the context of a grave desecration, the attitude of *pietatis et religionis amor* mentioned).
D. as the emperor's attribute: *C.Th.* 5.12.3.9; 6.10.1.2; 10.26.1.4; 11.1.34.5; 11.1.36.1; 13.1.21.5; 14.16.2.4; 14.26.2.4; 15.1.37.2; *Const. Sirm.* 8.4; *Nov. Theod.* 2.3; *Nov. Valent.* 2.3.11; 7.2.1; 8.1.31; 10.11; 10.15; 13.16; 13.31; 15.1; *Nov. Marc.* 1.6; 1.13; 1.21; 1.45; 1.70; 2.36; 2.40; 5.7; *Nov. Anth.* 3.6.

---

160 … *ut criminosis poena reddatur, innocenter viventibus gratulatio, pax sepultis* (*Nov. Valent.* 23).
161 Korpanty 1979: 196.

pius
A1. of children towards their parents: *C.Th.* 8.12.2.[5^2].
A2. as a mutual relation between children and parents: *Nov. Majo.* 6.5.
C. towards God, Christian religion: *C.Th.* 7.20.12.12 ("on the pretext of pious religion"); *Const. Sirm.* 8.18; 9.3; *Nov. Majo.* 11.6.
D. as the emperor's characteristic: *C.Th.* 1.12.5.4; 12.1.90.1; *Nov. Theod.* 3.5; Nov. Valent. 1.1.4; 27.29; *Nov. Majo.* 2.12; *Nov. Anth.* 3.5.
D1. as a characteristic of an Imperial official: *Nov. Theod.* 18.11.
D2. as a characteristic of an Imperial disposition: *C.Th.* 16.5.60.3; *Nov. Theod.* 17.1.3; 26.64.
E. other: *C.Th.* 16.1.2.7 (on the Holy Trinity).

Improbitas

Unlike the characteristics discussed above, the term *improbitas* is more ambiguous, as it does not indicate transgressing against any specific value.[162] Following the *Thesaurus Linguae Latinae*, one could point to such meanings of the word *improbus* as "unjust" (opposition to *aequitas*), but also more suggestive of arrogance (*insolentia*) or other vices (*aviditas*, *crudelitas*) of the perpetrator.[163] In the Imperial documents, no specific sense can be assigned to this particular term, as it conveys some rather general indication of certain forms of arrogance which happen to overlap with some cases of *insolentia* or *audacia*. Still, the most frequent case, i.e., the explicit criticism of violations of the Imperial law, cannot be found here. Unjustified petitions addressed to the emperor are particularly often referred to as *improbae*. In addition, it is possible to identify a number of cases characteristic of the charge of *audacia*: abuses related to the use of the Imperial Post, breach of privileges, violent crimes, unjust efforts to join the Imperial service, religious dissidents' illegal activities. Several times, associations between *improbitas* and *temeritas* as part of accumulation figures can be found. Finally, *improbitas*, in a way similar to *insolentia*, is particularly often used to characterize actions of public officials.

improbe, improbitas, improbus
I. A. petitions: *C.Th.* 2.26.4.3; 4.18.1.15; 5.12.2.[5^2]; 10.10.26.4; 14.15.4.1; 14.15.4.2^2; *Const. Sirm.* 1.8^2.
B. misuse of the Public Post: *C.Th.* 6.29.2.18; 8.5.4.6.

---

162 Which is exactly why Cicero could apply it as a general term, used in reference to all enemies, cf. Achard 1981: 221–355.

163 *ThLL* 7.1: 690–691.

C. crimes: *C.Th.* 2.4.5.3 (*invasio*); *Nov. Valent.* 23.50 (grave robbery); *Nov. Majo.* 6.48 (*raptus*).
D. unlawful efforts to join the imperial service : *C.Th.* 12.1.45.2 (decurions); 16.2.39.1[2] = *Const. Sirm.* 9.18 (discharged from priesthood); *Nov. Theod.* 15.2.2 (decurion).
E. religious dissidents' activity: *C.Th.* 16.5.53.7 (heretics); *Nov. Theod.* 3.69 (pagans).
E1. other actions against Divine and human rights: *Const. Sirm.* 3.2[2] (unlawful use of bishop's title).
F. offences committed by public officials: *C.Th.* 2.1.3.4; 5.14.33.5; 6.4.22.12; 6.29.2.23, 9.27.6.5; 10.1.16.2; 10.8.5.22, 16.2.14.2; 16.5.4.5 (*profanorum improbitas* contrasted with *dissimulatio iudicium* as a cause of moderation towards heretics); *Nov. Valent.* 1.3.10; 1.3.24; 7.1.32; *Nov. Majo.* 2.49.
G. decurions' attitudes: *C.Th.* 1.29.7.4.
H. other offences against the emperor or a public official: *C.Th.* 1.5.3.5 (against judicial decisions); 9.4.1.2; 10.19.9.3; 13.3.14.4 (breach of privileges); 13.11.10.7.
I. injustice against private individuals: *C.Th.* 3.5.12.2[2]; 4.22.2.5; 9.6.4.2 (unlawful voices of freedmen against their patrons); 13.6.7.4[2]; *Nov. Valent.* 12.5; 27.9; 32.43; *Nov. Majo.* 3.3; 6.113.
J. the Senate council always opposes *improbis rebus*: *Nov. Valent.* 14.3.

II.

associations with *temeritas*: *C.Th.* 4.22.2.5; *Const. Sirm.* 3.2[2]; *Nov. Theod.* 15.2.2.
associations with *insolentia*: *C.Th.* 1.29.7.4; *Nov. Majo.* 3.3.

Chapter VII: Terms indicating the nature of a criminal act

After discussing the terms directly describing the hostile relation towards the Roman or ecclesiastical communities, as well as those concerning attitudes of the "enemies," I shall now focus on the terms which represent, in aggressive manner, the nature of offences committed by those enemies. Still, we should be cautious in classifying them as terms of invective, as the negative contents they conveyed were not necessarily intended to refer to the perpetrator in an offensive manner. It may be assumed that in many cases the point was simply to describe a given act in adequate terms, even if the designation in question would have carried some negative content in itself. For instance, the term *crimen* as such contains this sort of message. Nevertheless, defining a specific act in this particular way does not have to involve any extraordinary condemnation, only the information that such an action constitutes an offence liable to penal sanction. In turn, I shall concentrate on those terms of invective where the notion of "offence" is apparently amplified, in particular when an expression which is stronger than technically necessary is used.[1] Next, I shall look through some terms making the character of a criminal act more specific, indicating a violation of religious order, i.e., *piaculum*, *profanatio*, and *contagium*. Finally, I will consider some instances of words by which the legislator may point to some infringements of public order.

---

1 The notion of "offence" is, just as obviously, the fertile ground that serves to elaborate diverse amplification figures. We could refer here to a *comparatio*, when a criminal act is designated with the name of a much more serious crime, an act which is condemned even more. Amplifying an offence may also involve application of *ratiocinatio* (demonstrating the magnitude of a crime through the value of the good being violated) or *congeries* (names of the condemned offence accumulated in a sequence). But the most frequent type of rhetorical figure here is, similarly to some other cases of amplification encountered in the Late Antique constitutions, the simple figure of *incrementum*, consisting in referring to a specific criminal act with a possibly most intensely charged negative term.

Terms describing offences in amplificatory manner

The Romans had used a number of terms to refer to offences judged according to the penal procedure. In the Late Antique constitutions, the most frequently applied term was *crimen*; some other relatively often used terms were *facinus*, *scelus*, less frequently *flagitium*, *comissum*, incidentally *nefas*. Likewise, *delictum* was used sometimes, though incorrectly, as a synonym.[2] These should be distinguished from some others terms, such as *piaculum*, conveying the notion of transgressing against the *sacrum* (which will be discussed in the next subsection), and especially from the names of individual offences, e.g., *parricidium* or *adulterium*.

On the level of legal discourse, *crimen*, *facinus*, *scelus*, *flagitium* are synonyms,[3] and there are numerous cases where the same offence is designated within the same constitution with one and then some other of these terms. Differences can be seen at the level of the ideological message of the text, as the individual terms carry various emotional weights. The most neutral one is, evidently, *crimen*. It may be expected to be seen where the discourse is of a purely technical nature,[4] e.g., when it refers to the type being specified by the concrete crime name, such as *crimen maiestatis*, *crimen sacrilegii*.[5] It is also preferred in those statements where the nature of a given offence is not taken into consideration at all, as they deal instead with regulating the provisions concerning issues such as treatment of convicted individuals[6] or, in general, penal proceedings.[7]

---

2 Although the distinction into offences judged according to penal or civil procedures remains valid in the post-classical period, it is not accompanied in the contemporary Imperial constitutions with the distinction between the terms used in the both cases. The term *delictum*, which in its technical sense is ascribed to offences judged according to the civil procedure, is regarded, in the Late Antique documents, as practically a synonym of *crimen*, a crime against public law – cf., e.g., *C.Th.* 2.1.3.3; 7.8.19.4; 9.3.6.8. A clear division into the terms *crimina* and *delicta* had already become blurred during the Principate period due to the introduced category of *crimina extraordinaria*, encompassing a number of offences previously judged under civil law. For a discussion, cf. Tellegen 1979: 393–394.

3 They may be treated as synonymous, apart from their original "moral or religious tone" (Mommsen 1899: 9, note 4). I do not mention the term *comissum* in this subchapter, because its infrequent use in the *Codex Theodosianus* does not give us the possibility to make an analysis as in the cases of the other terms mentioned.

4 According to Mommsen (1899: 9–10), this particular term is the closest one to the accuracy required of *terminus technicus*.

5 E.g., *C.Th.* 9.5.1.1: *crimen maiestatis*; *C.Th.* 3.7.2.4: *crimen adulterium*; *C.Th.* 6.29.9.3: *crimen sacrilegii*; *C.Th.* 9.10.3.3: *crimen violentiae*.

6 E.g., *C.Th.* 9.40.8.2: *Quicumque Christianus sit in quolibet crimine deprehensus, ludo non adiucetur*.

7 Especially as regards a distinction between civil and penal proceedings (*civiliter/criminaliter agere*; *civilis/criminalis causa*) – for instance, *C.Th.* 1.7.4.6; 1.12.3.1 and dozens of further ex-

Where the stress in a given statement is laid upon the fact of the criminal act itself, more often various terms tend to be applied interchangeably. These may be subject to gradation. An example, and at the same time a key to discern the weight of individual terms, is provided in the passage of Cicero's oration against Verres, as cited in Chapter III: *facinus est vincere civem Romanum, scelus verberare, prope parricidium necare.*[8] The lowest rank here is given to *facinus.* Also in the language of the Late Antique Imperial documents, this term does not appear to be much different, in its application, from *crimen*, with an exception that it tends to be avoided in the most neutral and technical expressions. It is noteworthy that *facinus* had originally denoted a vehement and bold action, and may have conveyed some positive overtone in that earlier period.[9]

The term ***scelus*** paints a completely different picture. It is clearly connected with moral condemnation,[10] not very far from our modern understanding of the word "felony," marked by a particularly heavy negative emotional charge, and also amplifying the "magnitude," or "weight," of the criminal act.[11] As such, it was already used widely as an "offensive word" in Latin comedy.[12]

It should be noted that within the juristic discourse the term *scelus* must be recognized as equivalent to *crimen*, as it simply refers to a crime and does not convey any additional content compared with *crimen*. Each act defined as *scelus* can also be technically called *crimen*. Even if the term *scelus* is a preferred one for the *crimina atrocia* (felonies), it actually extends far beyond that group, and it is impossible, in my opinion, to determine a subset of crimes beyond which the term *scelus* would be regarded as wrong. This is not to say it would have been correct, as applying this equivalent of our modern "felony" to minor offences would have been simply ridiculous. Yet this impropriety is due to the inapplicability of the magnification (which this particular term conveys) to any acts of very little weight.

---

amples; moreover, also when the public character of accusation is emphasized (*crimina accusatio, C.Th.* 5.19.2.14), with the accusation itself also defined as *crimen* (e.g., *C Th.* 9.1.3.1), in conformity with the original sense of this word (*ThLL* 4: 1190–1193).

8 Cic. *In Verr.* II.5.170, cited in Quint., *Inst. Orat.* VIII.4.4 as an instance of *incrementum.*

9 *ThLL* 6.1: 77.

10 Particularly evident in derivative words: *scelerosus* means "penetrated with evil," "oriented towards crime," *sceleratus* – "tainted with crime," *scelestus* – "evil by nature," "oriented to commit *scelus*" (Thome 1993: 330–331; Riess 2001: 33). In literary texts, a man encumbered with *scelus* may, through *contagium*, carry misfortune over to others (Thome 1992: 77, note 19).

11 According to Thome (1993: 330), from the beginning *scelus* had been connected in Latin with particularly serious crimes, often with some part-magical part-religious aura in the background.

12 Müller 1913: passim.

Let us refer to a number of examples to examine this aspect further. *Crimina atrocia* tend to be defined as *scelera.*[13] The legislator contrasts *crimina leviora* with *scelera saeviora,*[14] and refers to perpetrators of the latter as *criminosissimi.*[15] The extensive amnesty constitution preserved as *Const. Sirm.* 8 mentions, for several times, both the offences subject to amnesty and those most serious ones (beyond the scope of the amnesty); for the former, only the term *crimen* is used, whereas in the latter case, *crimen* and *scelus* are applied interchangeably.

When a juxtaposition of various offences within particular types is made, *scelus* is fairly often a degree higher than *crimen* or *facinus.* As regards the crime of heresy, the Manichaeans, who were persecuted the most, are those who had reached *ad imam scelerum nequitiam.*[16] Whereas a common *adulterium* is referred to as *crimen* or *facinus*, the term *scelus* appears to be characteristic of homosexual prostitution. A very similar case is *crimen raptus*; *scelus* is applied here to more drastic incidents of abduction: once, kidnapping someone's wife, in another case – abducting a virgin consecrated to God. Illegal appropriation of payments due to the City of Rome by governors and their officials is called *facinus* and it is punishable by the injunction to return the appropriated amount fourfold. Still, if the same offence were committed again, it would be judged as a *scelus* and punished by exile (the governor) and death penalty (members of his *officium*). Although one could cite multiple cases where such gradation does not exist, and the term *scelus* is treated as equivalent with the other designations of "crime," one could not juxtapose such cases with even one where the *scelus* would stand for the "slightest" one of the several crimes mentioned in the constitution.

All these things considered, one could agree to recognize the usage of *scelus* in the Imperial documents as a sort of amplification known as *incrementum*, i.e., amplification by referring to a specific item with some term which is itself used to "magnify" the thing in question. It seems reasonable then to make a survey of the crimes which the legislator decides to define as *scelus.*

As already noted, the term tends to be used as a common name for a group of crimes defined as *crimina atrocia*, among which the most frequently mentioned are *maiestas*, *homicidium*, *adulterium*, *veneficium*, and *maleficium*, but sometimes also desecration of graves, forgery, *latrocinium.* These offences are most often listed in the context of amnesty, as exceptions from the amnesty constitution. In two of the amnesty laws, the crimes in question are designated as *scelera.*[17]

[13] *C.Th.* 1.11.2.

[14] *C.Th.* 9.3.7; also, *C.Th.* 16.2.23 contrasts *scelus* with *levis delictum.*

[15] *C.Th.* 9.40.4.

[16] *C.Th.* 16.5.65, the sole instance of *scelus* in this constitution.

[17] *C.Th.* 9.38.7; *Const. Sirm.* 8.

The term *scelus* is applied both to *crimina atrocia* in general and specific offences within that group: tomb desecration, magic, monetary counterfeit, and (most often) sex crimes and various forms of *latrocinium*. Among "sex crimes," the term is used to refer to male homosexuality, more drastic cases of abduction (*raptus*), incest, as well as forbidden marriage between a decurion and a slave. It is only once that the "common" *adulterium* is called *scelus* – yet the relevant constitution provides for punishing it in the same way as *parricidium* (burning alive in a sack). As regards *latrocinium*, there are no grounds for gradation: the crime of *scelus* is both participation in brigandage perpetrated by barbarian invaders and providing refuge to deserters, who are treated "as" *latrones* in some cases. Once, *scelus* is also mentioned to refer to Heraclianus and his unsuccessful usurpation attempt in Africa in 413, also once directly to the crime of *maiestas*.

Another group of crimes designated as *scelus* are offences connected with religion, specifically such as heresy (both heresy as such and heretical practices). It is worth noting that the term is applied particularly often with regard to the Manichaeans, i.e., the religious group most vehemently condemned, and also in the constitutions which provide for particularly severe sanctions. Furthermore, apostasy and encouraging someone to commit it, as well as making offerings to gods, are also defined as *scelus*. The fact that the use of the term *scelus* is more frequent than that of the other ones with reference to offences committed by religious dissidents[18] is noteworthy; as early as the writings of classical authors, the term in question was being used to denote offences against religion.[19]

The third, perhaps the most interesting, group of crimes described as *scelus* are abuses of authority perpetrated by public officials. It is not always stated explicitly what kind of criminal acts are being referred to, and there may be an impression that the very fact of a crime being committed by an official deserves such a hard censure. Among the ones which are mentioned there are: extortion of duties, *superexactiones*, appropriation (by officials) of payments due to the city, as well as diverse incidents related to bribery (*ambitus*, *peculatus*, trading in opportunities for dereliction of decurion's service). The penalties, if specified, are very severe.[20] Thus, here as well, the crimes in question are regarded as most serious.

---

[18] In the entire Theodosian Code, the term *crimen* is used 195 times (64%), *facinus* – 40 (13%), *scelus* – 56 (18%), *flagitium* – 15 (5%); whereas in chapters 5–10 of Book 16, on religious dissidents and their offences, these terms are used, respectively: *crimen* – 27 times (45%), *facinus* – 10 (17%), *scelus* – 18 (30%), *flagitium* – 5 (8%).

[19] Ferrini 1976: 18, n. 1.

[20] Death penalty (*C.Th.* 11.8.1; 14.15.6; *Nov. Majo.* 7), proscription (*C.Th.* 9.26.1; *Nov. Valent.* 7.1), exile (*C.Th.* 9.26.1; 14.15.6), infamy (*C.Th.* 8.4.16; 9.27.1).

Twice, the term *scelus* is used to refer to a criminal offence against the *fiscus* committed by a common citizen. Just once, the word is applied to a very peculiar event: Catholic priests being assaulted and beaten up by a riotous mob. In turn, the term *scelesta* is used once to describe the *impietas* of children towards their parents; in this particular matter, the strong words are employed to buttress the emperor's decision in an otherwise civil case.[21]

scelus, sceleratus, scelerate, scelerosus, scelestus

A. offence: *C.Th.* 2.1.1.3 (punishable by death); *C.Th.* 9.40.18.2; 15.12.1.5; 16.8.21.4; *Nov. Majo.* 5.4.

B. offences characterized as serious: *C.Th.* 1.11.2.2[2]; 9.38.7.3; 9.40.4.11; 11.36.7.5; *Const. Sirm.* 8.21; 8.23; 8.24.

C1. use of barbarians against fellow citizens or officials: *C.Th.* 7.1.1.1; 9.14.3.2; 9.14.3.5; *Nov. Theod.* 15.2.11.

C2. *latrocinium*: *C.Th.* 1.29.8.4; 1.29.8.5; 9.30.3.4 (cattle theft, treated as *latrocinium* in certain cases); 9.30.3.6 (ditto); 9.35.7.4; 9.42.24.3.

C3. protecting *latrones*, deserters: *C.Th.* 7.18.4.4; 7.18.6.5 (twice); 7.19.1.12.

D. sexual offences:

D1. incest: *C.Th.* 3.12.3.5[2].

D2. homosexuality: *C.Th.* 9.7.3.2; 9.7.6.3.

D3. *raptus*: *C.Th.* 9.24.3.2 (of another man's spouse); 9.24.3.3[3] (of another man's spouse); 9.25.1.3 (of a virgin consecrated to God); *Nov. Majo.* 6.50.

D4. adultery: *C.Th.* 11.36.4.4.

D5: marriage between a decurion and a slave: *C.Th.* 12.1.6.13[2].

E. tomb robbery: *C.Th.* 9.17.3.3; 9.38.8.9; *Nov. Valent.* 23.19; 23.35.

F. sorcery: *C.Th.* 9.38.4.4.

G. monetary counterfeit: *C.Th.* 9.21.2.2; 9.21.2.19; 9.21.2.2[2].

H1. *maiestas*: *C.Th.* 9.42.23.4.

H2. tyranny: *C.Th.* 15.14.13.4.

I. abuse of authority by officials: *C.Th.* 7.8.10.18; 8.1.11.7; 8.4.15.6; 8.4.16.7; 9.26.1.6 (twice); 9.27.1.2; 9.28.2.2; 11.8.1.6; 14.15.6.7; *Nov. Valent.* 7.1.4; *Nov. Majo.* 7.54.

J. fraudulent contracts: *C.Th.* 10.1.10.1.

K. concealment of property belonging to proscribed persons: *C.Th.* 9.42.5.1.

L. *impietas* of children towards their fathers: *C.Th.* 8.13.2.3.

M. offences related to religion:

---

21 On precluding the possibility to file a complaint against the annulment of a donation by way of *praescriptio fori*, i.e., of proceedings in an incompetent court of law; such a complaint was precluded in criminal cases.

M1. heresy: *C.Th.* 16.5.7.13^{2}; 16.5.34.10; 16.5.36.4^{2}; 16.5.51.3 = 16.5.56.1^{2} (gatherings); 16.5.65.21; 16.5.66.5; 16.6.4.4; 16.6.4.3^{2} (rebaptism); 16.6.6.2 (rebaptism); 16.6.7.5 (gatherings); *Nov. Valent.* 18.8; 18.10.
M2. apostasy: *C.Th.* 16.7.3.4; 16.7.3.3^{2}; 16.7.3.12^{2}; 16.7.3.14^{2}; 16.9.4.1^{2} (persuading to apostatize to Judaism).
M3. making pagan sacrifices: *C.Th.* 16.10.7.3; 16.10.12.21; 16.10.25.2; *Nov. Theod.* 3.66.
M4. acts of assault and battery against clergymen: *Const. Sirm.* 14.11.

The term *scelus* is not the sole amplificatory designation of "crime" in the Late Antique documents. Another one that can be found is ***flagitium***, which was applied definitely less often. In Latin, this term comprises two meanings, among others, pertaining to "crime": a more particular one – pointing to sex crimes, and a general one – which signifies *crimen*, irrespective of its character.[22] Nonetheless, in the collection of the texts under examination, the semantic scope of *flagitium* seems to be close to that of *scelus* – it is used to refer to *crimina atrocia*, encompassing male homosexuality and more drastic cases of *raptus*, a specific type of desertion "recidivism" (namely, refusing to obey the emperor's order to return to military service), as well as acts of assault and battery against clergymen, apostasy, offences committed by public officials, *impietas* of children towards their father. Yet the most interesting fact is that *flagitium*, similarly to *nefas* and some other derivative words, is mentioned several times in the same texts where *scelus* also appears. Juxtapositions of a few synonyms referring to serious offences make up amplificatory rhetorical figures of accumulation (*congeries*).[23]

flagitium, flagitiosus
A. offences: *C.Th.* 9.1.19.13; 9.38.6.2 (contrasted with serious crimes, *nefaria crimina*).
B. serious crimes: *C.Th.* 9.40.1.5.
C4. desertion: *C.Th.* 7.18.4.4^{2}.
D2. homosexuality: *C.Th.* 9.7.6.1.
D3. *raptus*: *C.Th.* 9.24.3.1^{2} (of another man's spouse).
D4. adultery: *Nov. Majo.* 9.17.
D5. marriage between a decurion and a slave: *C.Th.* 12.1.6.8^{2}.
G. monetary counterfeit: *C.Th.* 9.21.4.5.

---

22 *ThLL* 6.1: 839–840; the original meanings of *flagitium* refer to "public disgrace."

23 *C.Th.* 8.13.2 (*scelus, flagitium* – *impietas* of children towards parents); *C.Th.* 9.24.3 (*scelus, flagitium* – abducting someone's wife); *C.Th.* 9.28.1 (*crimen, flagitium, nefas* – crime of *peculatus*); *C.Th.* 16.6.4 (*scelus, facinus, flagitium, piacularis* – rebaptism); *C.Th.* 16.7.3 (*crimen, scelus, flagitium* – apostasy); *Const. Sirm.* 14 (*nefas, scelus, flagitium* – priests assaulted and beaten); *Nov. Majo.* 9 (*flagitium, nefarius* – adultery).

I. abuses of authority committed by officials: *C.Th.* 1.14.2.2; 1.34.3.5[2]; 9.28.1.3[2]; *Nov. Theod.* 24.24; *Nov. Marc.* 1.11.

L. *impietas*: *C.Th.* 8.13.2.4.

M. offences related to religion:

M1. heresy: *C.Th.* 16.6.4.5[2] (rebaptism).

M2. apostasy: *C.Th.* 16.7.3.2; 16.7.3.12[2]; 16.7.4.8; 16.8.6.3 (Jewish *flagitia*, in the context of possible acts of apostasy – Christian wives apostatizing to the religion of their husbands).

M4. acts of assault and battery against clergymen: *Const. Sirm.* 14.11.

Besides *scelus* and *flagitium*, another noteworthy synonymous term is ***nefas***. This third term is ambiguous, as it is often simply applied in the legislator's justification of his decision, such as when it is just "not right" to choose a different course of action. Much less frequently is the term *nefas* employed in reference to a crime, but then, as can be seen, it turns out to be a very strong one. Curiously, *nefas* is used, in this sense, almost exclusively to describe offences committed by public officials. In turn, the derivative adjectives: *nefarius*, *nefandus* appear to have been frequently used in cases of religious offences. In a way similar to *scelus*, it seems to be a justified term here. Likewise, in Latin literature, *nefas* puts a particular emphasis on the religious aspect of a crime, "godlessness" of the offender.[24]

Nefandus is related to the adjective *infandus*. The latter one is a very strong term of invective, referring to something "monstrous," "hideous," "too terrible to talk about it."[25] It is mentioned twice in the Theodosian Code. *C.Th.* 15.14.7 depicts tyrant Maximus as *infandissimus tyrannus*. At *C.Th.* 16.7.5, *infandes* and *ferales* are used in reference to the apostates' minds, which had induced them to depart from the human community.

nefas (in the sense: a crime, not "it is not right"/"it does not befit")

D6. procuration: *Nov. Theod.* 18.21.

I. offences committed by public officials: *C.Th.* 7.4.21.1[2]; 9.28.1.4[2]; 14.17.6.9.

M4. acts of assault and battery against clergymen: *Const. Sirm.* 14.11.

nefarius, nefarie, nefandus

B. serious crimes: *C.Th.* 9.38.6.4; 9.40.18.3.

C2. *latrocinium*: *C.Th.* 9.42.24.2.

---

[24] Riess 2001: 33; Thome 1993: 325, 328 draws our attention in particular to the "repulsion" aspect, associated with the adjectives *nefarius* and *nefandus*.

[25] *ThLL* 7.1: 1344–1346.

D3. *raptus*: *C.Th.* 9.24.1.8 (urging to commit this crime).
D4. adultery: *Nov. Majo.* 9.3; 9.12.
E. tomb robbery: *Nov. Valent.* 23.19.
F. magic: *C.Th.* 9.16.7.2; 9.35.2.4.
I. abuses committed by officials: *C.Th.* 1.16.7.8²; 2.29.1.6; 10.10.16.7; *Nov. Theod.* 24.35.
M1. heresy: *C.Th.* 16.5.5.7 (rebaptism); 16.5.6.8; 16.5.15.1²; 16.5.48.2; 16.5.57.4 (gathering); 16.5.58.2 (gathering); 16.5.58.6 (rebaptism); 16.5.66.4; 16.5.66.6 (heresiarch); 16.6.7.1 (gathering); 16.7.3.4; *Const. Sirm.* 6.14².
M2. apostasy: *C.Th.* 16.7.3.3² (those who persuaded others to apostatize); 16.8.1.5 (Jews in the context of apostasy).
M3. offerings: *C.Th.* 16.10.5.2 (permission to make nocturnal offerings); *Nov. Theod.* 3.63.
M5. Jews: *C.Th.* 16.9.4.6 (contrasted with Christians); *Nov. Theod.* 3.35 (contrasted with Christians).
N. unjustified denunciation or accusation: *C.Th.* 9.6.1.2; 9.6.1.3; 9.6.2.3.
O. homicide: *Nov. Valent.* 19.15.
P. other: *C.Th.* 10.10.24.5 (*petitio* constituting *sacrilegium*); 11.39.7.3 (documents used to authenticate what is false).

infandus
H2. tyrant: *C.Th.* 15.14.7.2.
M2. apostasy: *C.Th.* 16.7.5.5.

Piaculum

The terms that denote serious crimes, such as *scelus* and *nefas*, may have directly indicated the religious dimension of a criminal act. In consequence, they would be readily applied to describe offences against religion. Still, our source material also contains a group of several terms which tend to point to the violation of the *sacrum* more explicitly. As we shall see, referring to a given act as *piaculum*, *sacrilegium*, or *profanatio* defines this sort of infringement in various ways.

Applying *piaculum* and other related terms in reference to criminal acts draws on the archaic conception of punishment as an expiatory sacrifice, freeing the community from the contamination, *contagium*, brought on by someone's reprehensible action.[26] Although the term cannot be found very often in the Late Antique documents, all the instances of its application deserve our attention exactly due to the preservation of that component of the archaic perception

26 Ehlers 1941: 1181; Voci 1953: 55.

concerning the nature of the incurred guilt. *Nov. Valent.* 18 condemns Manichaeism as a felony (*scelus*), which not only exposes the body to the danger of punishment, but also taints the soul "in a way impossible to be expiated" (*inexpiabiliter*). In two cases, *piaculum* is linked directly with *contaminatio*, which takes place upon perpetrating a criminal act of tomb desecration.

The sinister context in which these terms are mentioned can also be seen in some of the cases further on. In total, out of 14 mentions in the relevant material, three cases refer to crimes of sepulchral desecration, six – to crimes related to religious matters (including three – to offences of rebaptism, which also entails *contagium*). In one case, *piaculum* concerns the crime of infanticide. It is also noteworthy that the term is applied as part of a metaphor – if a decurion's duties are considered as *mysteria*, refusing to fulfil them constitutes a *piaculum*.[27]

expiatio, inexpiabilis, inexpiabiliter, piaculum, piacularis

A. abuse of authority: *C.Th.* 7.13.9.5 (*inexpiabilis*); 13.5.16.4 (*expiatio*).

B. abandoning a decurion's post [the duties described as *mysterium*]: *C.Th.* 12.1.122.7 (*piaculum*).

C. infanticide: *C.Th.* 9.14.1.2 (*piaculum*).

D. tomb robbery: *C.Th.* 9.17.2.8 (*piaculum*); 9.17.5.4 (*piaculum*); *Nov. Valent.* 23.18 (*inexpiabilis*).

E. heretics: *C.Th.* 16.5.9.9 (*inexpiabilis*); 16.6.2.3^2 (*piacularis*); *Nov. Valent.* 18.11 (*inexpiabiliter*).

E1. rebaptism: *C.Th.* 16.6.4.5^2 (*piacularis*); 16.6.6.8 (*piacularis*).

F. pagans: *C.Th.* 16.10.12.5 (*piaculum*).

G. all non-Catholics: *Nov. Theod.* 3.13 (*piaculum*).

Profanatio

Even though the noun *profanatio* is not mentioned in the relevant source material, the notion of "profanation" is present here through the verb *profanare*, adjective and noun *profanus*, and one *nomen agentis profanator*. All these terms always appear in contexts related to religion. *Profanus* denotes "godlessness," not a purely negative one, but evoked by the positive presence of the element

[27] *C.Th.* 12.1.122: ...*maneant in sinu patriaeet veluti dicati infulis mysterium perenne custodiant; sit illis piaculum inde discedere.*

opposed to religion. *Profanus* did not indicate a simple lack but rather depriving some entity of "sacredness" via (at least strictly ritual) contagion (*contagium*).[28]

In the Imperial constitutions, *contagium* is alluded to by expressions such as *caenum profanatarum religionum* ("filth of profaned religions," *C.Th.* 16.6.6), or *contagium profanae repetitionis* (*C.Th.* 16.6.4, with reference to rebaptism). Active profanation through "corruption" is also indicated by referring to a Manichaean as *profanator atque corruptor catholicae disciplinae* (*C.Th.* 16.5.7). In turn, a stark contrast with the Catholic religion can be seen in describing the apostates as those who *prodentes divinum mysterium in profana migrarunt* ("who have betrayed the divine mystery and have gone over to profane doctrines" – *C.Th.* 16.7.4). At the same time, the profanation may refer not only to the religion but also, indirectly, to God Himself.[29]

Generally speaking, these terms are used to refer to heretics (their teachings, gatherings) or pagan worship practices. It is noteworthy that Judaic practices, permitted by law, are never called *profanae*. Thus, the term *profanatio* would only come up where a religious offence took place.[30]

The term *profanus* is mentioned in different contexts in three other cases. In Majorian's Sixth Novel, *profana cupiditas* guides the abductor of a virgin consecrated to God; at *C.Th.* 9.38.7, incest violates "the revered bond of cognate blood" in an "unholy" (*profano*) way. Still, the most interesting is the metaphor which can be found at *C.Th.* 1.15.8 – the emperor's majesty is called "sanctuaries" (*adyta*), whereas requests of those not entitled to be granted direct access to the emperor are compared with *preces profanorum*, prayers of the people who are so far away from sanctity that they ought to be removed from those "sanctuaries."[31]

profanus, profano, profanator

A1. incest: *C.Th.* 9.38.6.7.

A2. abducting a virgin consecrated to God: *Nov. Majo.* 6.48.

B1. heresy:

B1a. as a characteristic of schism: *C.Th.* 16.1.3.3.

B1b. on heretics: *C.Th.* 16.5.4.5; 16.5.5.4; 16.5.9.2; 16.5.41.9^2; *Const. Sirm.* 12.1.

B1c. as a characteristic of heretical teachings: *C.Th.* 16.5.3.4; 16.5.24.3; 16.5.26.2.

---

28 Benveniste 1960; Wagenvoort 1980b; and esp. Caseau 2008.

29 *C.Th.* 16.10.7.6.

30 Stachura 2004: 228–231.

31 Specifically, attention is focused on the possibility of direct access to the emperor of the Praetorian Prefect's vicars, whose requests should not be treated as the above-mentioned "prayers of the profane."

B1d. as a characteristic of heretical gatherings: *C.Th.* 16.5.7.18; 16.5.30.9; 16.5.36.2^2; 16.5.41.4.
B1e. rebaptism: *C.Th.* 16.6.4.6; 16.6.6.2.
B2. paganism:
B2a. as a characteristic of pagan worship: *C.Th.* 16.7.4.11 (in the context of apostasy); 16.7.7.10 (pagan existence, in the context of apostasy); 16.10.7.6; 16.10.10.4; 16.10.17.1; 16.10.21.1.
B2b. access to pagan temples: *C.Th.* 16.10.11.3.
B2c. profanation of baptism through apostasy: *C.Th.* 11.39.11.2 = 16.7.4.3; 16.7.4.13.
B3. metaphorically, on access of unauthorized people to the emperor: *C.Th.* 1.15.8.1^2 (*profanus* as a noun).

Contagium

In order to explain the term *contagium* to the modern reader, we should avoid from drawing simplistic analogies with the modern-day world-view. It is tempting to interpret the ancient classical "contagion," expressed by means of the terms such as *contagium*, *contagio*, *contaminatio*, *pollutio*, *macula*,[32] or – in Greek – *miasma* (μίασμα), through comparing with our modern obsessive fears of "infectious disease."[33] The fears connected with those terms were different. *Contagium* referred, above all, to contamination with evil or tribulation. Although, as the word suggests, it would have been transferred via physical contact, it did not assume any belief in material factors carrying over or spreading the evil. As Robert Parker points out, what actually contaminated was the mourning, not touching of the deceased person.[34] "Infectiousness" of the disease was questioned by philosophers; simultaneously, they were afraid of touching what was "defiling" in the face of the supernatural.[35] It is only in late Platonism that we come across the idea of some evil demons transferring *contagium*, which on a very superficial interpretation may resemble germs

32 In one of its meanings, cf. *ThLL* 8: 24–25.

33 As suggested in Zuccotti 1992; Grout-Gerletti 1998.

34 Parker 1983: 41.

35 Gregory of Nyssa may also be fearful of a heresy "infection" even by touching the heretical writings and argues at the same time, citing the ancient medical knowledge, that leprosy is not an infectious disease, cf. Holman 1999: 294–295. In Antiquity, if an individual was afraid of being "infected" by physical contact with a sick person, at the source of their fear was not some image of germs moving swiftly from one person to another, but rather the apprehension of being touched with the misery suffered by the ill person (Parker 1983: 219).

as they are now envisioned.[36] Effects of "contamination" may have affected the whole of a community as an epidemic sent down by gods, a natural disaster, or even a military defeat – all of them are designated with the same Greek term *loimos* (λοιμός).[37]

The terms expressing the idea of *contagium* began to enter the language of invective in a relatively late period. The one that had appeared the earliest is the charge of contamination by crime.[38] They came to be used extensively only in patristic polemical writings.[39] Here, they are constituent parts in descriptions of *superstitio*, which can be already noticed in some works by pagan authors.[40]

In the texts under consideration, one shall find examples of *contagium* used as a metaphor conveying a given accusation as well as the literal understanding of this idea. It is certainly the latter case where a reference is made to the *contagium* caused by one specific crime: *violatio sepulchri* (violation of a grave). This criminal offence, which had been punishable by severe penalties in Rome for a long time,[41] was very clearly connected with the *contagium* perpetrated by the criminal.[42] There is no difference here between the constitutions issued by the pagan[43] and Christian emperors.[44] There can be no doubt that the *contagium* was recognized as real, and this is exactly why acts of grave robbery were considered to have been among the worst crimes.[45] Constantius II had prohibited any reuse of materials from tombs for construction purposes, as all those who attempted to do so "both despoil the buried dead by the destruction of the tombs, and they contaminate (*polluere*) the living by the use of this material in building."[46]

---

36 Parker 1983: 55.

37 Parker 1983: 257.

38 *Contagio sceleris*, see Cic., *Pro L. Murena oratio* 78, *Pro P. Cornelio Sulla oratio* 6, *In Verr.* II.5.183.

39 Cf. *ThLL* 4: 625–629, e.g., Tert., *Idol.* 8: *contagio idolatriae*; Firm. Matern., *Err.* 16.4: *ne diutius Romanum orbem praesumptionis istius error funestus immaculet.*

40 Let us mention here, for instance, *superstitionis istius contagio* in Pliny the Younger (*Ep.* 10.96.9) and Firmicus Maternus (*Err.* 12.1).

41 De Visscher 1963: 152–155.

42 It was already in the sphere of Greek beliefs that any confusion or blurring of the boundary between the worlds of the living and the dead would have entailed "contamination," cf. Parker 1983: 59.

43 The fear of *pollutio*, with which the presence or sight of the body of a deceased person may taint the community is present in the constitutions of the pagan Emperors Diocletian *C.* 3.44.12 (290) and Julian *C.Th.* 9.17.5 (363).

44 Constans *C.Th.* 9.17.2 (349), Constantius II *C.Th.* 9.17.4 (356), Gratian *C.Th.* 9.38.6 (381), Valentinian III *Nov. Valent.* 23 (447).

45 The act of *violatio sepulchri* can be found listed among the most serious crimes at *C.Th.* 3.16.1; 9.38.3; 9.38.7; *Const. Sirm.* 8.

46 *et sepultos spoliant destruendo, et vivos polluunt fabricando* (*C.Th.* 9.17.4.3, 356).

Julian the Apostate's constitution provides regulations against the crime of defiling (*contaminare*) the sanctity of tombs.[47] Valentinian III castigates priests guilty of tomb robbery, as they subsequently "bring to the sacred altars of the Church hands that are polluted by the contagion of the ashes of the dead" (*cinerum contagione pollutas*).[48]

There is no doubt that *contagium* is linked with incest, as in a few cases the verb *incestare* is used as a synonym of *contaminare*. They are, nonetheless, metaphorical uses,[49] similarly as when *contagium* is associated with a "plague" (*pestis*).[50] In the case of the most serious crimes, *contagium* is connected, as may be expected, with homicide,[51] magic,[52] adultery, and abduction of a woman. Several times, a person's "contamination" with crime is generally mentioned, without discussing its nature. It is difficult to ascertain, based on the above-mentioned applications of the term, if this is only a metaphor drawing on the original idea, or perhaps one with some actual fear of being "contaminated." Apparently, this latter possibility could be surmised in the case of magic practices, described as causing confusion among the natural elements.[53] But the metaphorical character of the charge can be seen where the "contamination" or "contagion" accusations are levelled at corrupted officials and decurions. A reference is made to the "contagion of the office" on account of the crimes they had committed during their tenure.[54] Two constitutions against individuals undoubtedly perceived as *hostes publici* seem to be particularly interesting cases here. The legislator states that during Heraclianus' consulship all

---

47 *C.Th.* 9.17.5 (363).

48 *Nov. Valent.* 23 (447).

49 *C.Th.* 9.17.5 (363) with reference to violations of burial sites; *C.Th.* 16.6.2 (377) referring to being rebaptized; *C.Th.* 7.1.13 (391), as it concerns "polluting" the eyes with the view of naked bodies.

50 An actual metaphor of the plague is present at *C.Th.* 9.28.2, where the Emperor announces that the criminal offences (here: *peculatus*, embezzlement of public funds) ought to be eliminated: *velut contagium quoddam funestae pestis*. Likewise, at *C.Th.* 16.5.44, heresies spreading like "the pest" are to be the result of neglecting the laws in force (*Quae pestis cave contagione latius emanet ac profluat*). One could ask a sarcastic question here: what kind of measures did officials of the Later Roman Empire use to eliminate "the pest." It would not seem to be fair, though. The legislator applies this plague metaphor in order to communicate a message to the effect that if some remedial measures are not undertaken, crime will be spreading like the plague. Cf. also *pestifer dogma* (*C.Th.* 16.5.58), *Fotinianae labes contaminatio* (*C.Th.* 16.5.6).

51 *humano cruore pollutus* (*Nov. Valent.* 19).

52 *maleficiorum labe pollutus* (*C.Th.* 9.16.11).

53 The constitution *C.Th.* 9.16.5 – discussed in Chapter IV: 89–91.

54 *C.Th.* 9.40.17 and *C.Th.* 2.1.3 point to the public official's being "tainted" with abuses.

the acts of slave emancipation had been tainted to such an extent that they must be repeated in order to be valid.[55] Another constitution, already discussed in Chapter IV, following the condemnation of Eutropius, who *morum sceleritate dignitates polluit*, orders, among other things, that all his statues be destroyed, as they may pollute (*polluere*) the eyes of those who look at them. The same constitution also mentions the crimes with which Eutropius had tainted his consulship – *prodigium contagione foedavit*. The accumulation of various invectives in connection with the charge of *contagium* is so "thick" in this constitution that one may speak of a consciously constructed amplification figure of *congeries*.[56]

Contagium is connected with being touched by dirt (*caenum*, *sordes*, *macula*). It is rarely understood in its literal sense (and even then it may be used to build a metaphor). In principle, "dirt" or "filth" is everything that is "disgraceful," e.g., contrary to the dignity of the senator's or decurion's rank, indicating infamy, low birth, or simply living in poverty.[57] Generally speaking, the "contagion" took place as a result of a given offence being committed, e.g. marrying a person of a lower status illegally. Nevertheless, there are also statements to the effect that those who leave their position at the *curia* taint with poverty their relatives who continue to remain there. Similarly, *macula* (disfavour) resting on the Lycians is unfair as it results (in some unspecified way) from the hostility between Tatianus and his successor as Praetorian Prefect, Rufinus.[58] To put it in more general terms, the legislator readily uses the metaphor of *contagium* when he wishes to communicate the "disfavour" (infamy, the brand of a criminal, degradation in the social status) falling on someone, with or without that person's wilful action.

Multiple instances of the *contagium* metaphor appear in the penal constitutions referring to religion. They are part of the *superstitio*-related descriptions here. Still as much as the charge of *superstitio* concerns all the religious minorities, *contagium* apparently indicates only those cases where religious dissidents commit an act recognized as *crimen*.[59] Only those who apostatize

---

55 *C.Th.* 15.14.13: *Libertates quoque, quoniam certum est scelere eius sollemnitatem consulatus esse polutam, in melius revocamus* ("We also revoke for the better all grants of freedom, since it is certain that the legal formalities of the consulship were polluted by his criminality").

56 *C.Th.* 9.40.17, cited and discussed in its entirety in Chapter IV: 94–98.

57 On the "contagion" metaphor in the context of the disfavour falling on the members of the senatorial order, see Schlinkert 1996: 118.

58 On this subject, see Barr 1979: 181.

59 Stachura 2004: 250.

to Judaism may be deemed as contaminating themselves with the dirt.[60] Paganism involves more possibilities: the contamination may be caused by apostasy,[61] as well as by making pagan sacrifices.[62] *C.Th.* 16.10.11 (391) forbids public officials from entering pagan temples as they are *polluta loca* (most certainly tainted by pagan offerings). In the case of heresies, the characteristic of tarnishing lies in the doctrines themselves,[63] as well as in heretical religious practices, especially rebaptism.[64] It is also significant that the "contamination" concerns criminals,[65] as well as heretical sects[66] and places where pagan rituals are performed.[67] Less often (but still) does the "contagion" affect the Catholic religion[68] or the Roman community. The latter possibility even becomes a justification for banishing heretics from the cities: "in order that they may not be contaminated with the contagious presence of the criminals."[69]

Expelling an offender from the city is a typical response of the community intending to prevent the *contagium*,[70] yet let us not forget that the presence of any kind of criminal, not just a religious one, is considered as "contagion." The Easter Amnesty of 385 (*C.Th.* 9.38.8) encompasses all the prisoners except for those whose release would rather "contaminate" the common joy and good cheer (*quibus contaminari potius gaudia laetitiamque communem*) – namely, perpetrators of the most serious crimes (felonies). It does not seem to be justified to divide the meaning of *contagium* into "secular" and "religious," or "pagan" and "Christian."

Contagio, contagium, contaminatio, polluo, attingo, contamino, macula, maculo, sordes
A. non-Catholics:

---

60 *C.Th.* 16.7.3.3: *polluere semet Iudaicis contagiis*; *C.Th.* 16.8.19.20: *si quis ex Christiana fide incredulitate Iudaica polluantur.*

61 *C.Th.* 16.7.4; 16.7.6.

62 *C.Th.* 16.10.10; *Nov. Theod.* 3.8.

63 *C.Th.* 16.5.40; 16.5.20; 16.5.26; *Nov. Valent.* 18.

64 *C.Th.* 16.5.52: *ritu sacrilegia polluerunt*; on rebaptism – *C.Th.* 16.6.2; 16.6.4; 16.6.3; 16.6.5.

65 *C.Th.* 16.7.3; 16.10.10; 16.5.26; 16.7.6; 16.6.3; 16.6.4; 16.5.40; 16.8.19; 16.5.52; *Const. Sirm.* 6; *Nov.Theod.* 3; *Nov. Valent.* 18.

66 *C.Th.* 16.5.20; 16.6.5.

67 *C.Th.* 16.10.11.

68 Its rites – *C.Th.* 16.5.26; the sacrament of baptism – *C.Th.* 16.6.1; 16.6.2; 16.6.4; the religion itself – *C.Th.* 16.7.4; 16.5.56. At *C.Th.* 16.5.19, instances of heretics usurping the clerical titles proper for the Catholic clergy described as *religionis macula.*

69 *ut nec praesentiae criminosorum contagione foedetur* – *C.Th.* 16.5.62, cf. also the further versions of this constitution, *C.Th.* 16.5.64 and *Const. Sirm.* 6.

70 Parker 1983: 118, 386 ff.

A1. heretics: 16.5.6.7 (*contaminatio*); 16.5.19.3 (*macula*); 16.5.20.1 (*contagium*); *C.Th.* 16.5.20.1 (*pollutus*); 16.5.26.3 (*contamino*); 16.5.26.5 (*pollutus*); 16.5.40.7^{2} (*polluo*); 16.5.44.3 (*contagio*); 16.5.52.17 (*polluo*); 16.5.56.2^{2} (*contagio*); 16.5.62.4 = 16.5.64.3 = Const. Sirm. 6.23^{2} (*contagio*); 16.5.62.4 = 16.5.64.3 = *Const. Sirm.* 6.23^{2} (*foedo*); Const. Sirm. 6.19^{2} (*macula*); *Nov. Valent.* 18.11 (*polluo*); 18.24 (*polluo*).
A2. rebaptism: *C.Th.* 16.6.1.4 (*contamino*); 16.6.2.4 (*polluo*); 16.6.4.6 (*contagio* + *infacio*); 16.6.4.11 (*polluo*); 16.6.5.2 (*pollutus* + *violare*); 16.6.6.2 (*caenum*); 16.6.6.3 (*polluo*); 16.6.6.3 (*sordes*).
A3. pagans: *C.Th.* 16.10.10.1 (*polluo*); 16.10.11.5 (*pollutus*); 16.10.21.2 (*polluo*); *Nov. Theod.* 3.72 (*contamino*); 3.72 (*polluo*).
A4. apostasy to paganism: *C.Th.* 16.7.4.10 (*polluo*); 16.7.6.2 (*maculo*).
A5. apostasy to Judaism: *C.Th.* 16.7.3.3 (*polluo*); 16.7.3.4 (*contagium*); 16.8.19.10 (*foedus*); 16.8.19.20 (*polluo*); 16.8.22.7^{2} (*foedo*); 16.9.4.8 (*caenum*).
B1. sepulchral violation: *C.Th.* 9.17.2.8 (*attingo*); 9.17.2.21 (*attingo*); 9.17.4.3 (*polluo*); 9.17.5.4 (*contamino*); 9.38.6.5 (*maculo*); *Nov. Valent.* 23.7 (*cinis*); 23.21 (*contagio*); 23.21 (*polluo*); 23.21 (*cinis*); 23.25 (*foeditas*); 23.25 (*maculo tempora nostra*).
B2a. adultery: *C.Th.* 2.1.3.4 (*polluo*); 9.38.4.3 (*foeditas*); *Nov. Majo.* 9.5 (*macula*). At *C.Th.* 9.7.2.3, *foedo* is used in the sense: accusing of adultery.
B2b. *raptus*: *Nov. Majo.* 6.50 (*polluo*).
B2c. other sexual offences: *C.Th.* 15.6.2.3 (*foedus*); 15.8.2.16 (*sordes*); *Const. Sirm.* 10.8 (*contamino*).
B3. theft: *C.Th.* 14.15.3.6 (*attingo*, here: the touch, in literal sense).
B4. magic: *C.Th.* 9.16.6.5 (*contamen*); 9.16.11.2 (*pollutus*).
B5. murder: *C.Th.* 9.38.6.5 (on *parricidium*: *sanguine proprio manum tinxit*); *Nov. Valent.* 19.2 (*polluo*).
B6a. contaminating oneself with crimes: *C.Th.* 10.10.30.7 (*polluo*).
B6b. a cleric tainted with crimes: *C.Th.* 16.2.41.7^{2} (*maculo*); *Const. Sirm.* 15.1^{2} (*maculo*); 15.9^{2} (*pollutus*); 15.13^{2} (*polluo*).
B6c. releasing a criminal taints the common joy of celebration: *C.Th.* 9.38.8.4 (*contamino*).
C1. marrying a person of a lower status: *C.Th.* 2.1.3.4 (*macula*); 4.6.3.[5] (*macula*); 4.12.5.[4] (*pollutus*); 12.1.6.2 (*sordidus*); *Nov. Majo.* 7.6 (*polluo*); 7.8 (*contagio*); 7.19 (*polluo*); *Nov. Marc.* 4.26 (*contamino*); 4.26 (*polluo*); *Nov. Anth.* 1.34 (*foeditas*).
C2. brand of a low status: *C.Th.* 6.35.14.12 (*macula*); *Nov. Marc.* 4.31 (*macula*); 4.31 (*sordeo*).
D. brand of a punishment, or disfavour: *C.Th.* 7.13.10.2 (*macula*); 8.4.8.13^{2} (*macula*); 9.14.3.13 (*sordeo*); 9.38.9.7 (*macula*); 9.40.2.5 (*maculo*, here: the brand, in literal sense); 15.14.11.6 (*polluo*); 15.14.12.2 (*macula*); *Nov. Majo.* 6.93 (*macula*); *Nov. Marc.* 4.31 (*polluo*).
E. abuses of authority:
E1. acts of emancipation effected under a tyrant's rule: *C.Th.* 15.14.13.4 (*polluo*).
E2. contagion of the offices held by Eutropius *C.Th.* 9.40.17.3 (*caenosus*); 9.40.17.3 (*sordes*); 9.40.17.7 (*contagio*); 9.40.17.7 (*foedo*); 9.40.17.8 (*polluo*); 9.40.17.12 (*polluo*).

E3. abuses of authority committed by officials: *C.Th.* 9.28.2.3 (*contagium, peculatus*); 9.27.1.2 (*maculo, repetundae*).
F. contagion of a decurion's rank related to his departure from this post: *C.Th.* 2.29.1.1 (*foedus*); 12.1.26.5 (*foedo*); 12.1.27.3 (*foedus*); 12.1.50.6 (*foedus*); 16.2.39.8 = *Const. Sirm.* 9.17 (*foedus*).
G. metaphor: *Const. Sirm.* 14.9 (*foedo*, bishops tainted by violent acts such as their hair having been pulled out); 16.12 (*maculo*; "may the avarice not contaminate the glory of a good deed").
H. literally: *C.Th.* 7.1.13.3 (*polluo*); 7.1.13.3 (*sordidatus*); 7.1.13.5 (*caenum*); 15.2.1.3 (*sordes*).

In the Late Antique Imperial constitutions, there are several terms quite clearly related to the notion of *contagium* – *funestus, dirus, infaustus, labes, pestis.*

The adjective ***funestus*** refers directly to funeral, and thus to being contaminated with the ashes of a deceased person. In this more narrow sense, it has a definitely negative overtone, and even more so in its broader meaning when it is rendered as "deadly" or at least "bringing misfortune."[71] In the source material under consideration, clear references to the former sense can be found, connecting *funestus* with the idea of *pollutio* – by the ashes of the dead, incestuous marriage, or the crime of *peculatus*,[72] whereas there is no doubt that we are dealing with a more narrow sense when "deadly" would refer to the voice of a slave or a family member accusing someone of a crime (which is forbidden except for the crime of *maiestas*). Referring to the usurper Eugenius' consuls as *funesti* should be considered as a metaphor, but most frequently this specific adjective is used to describe the denounced religions of pagans or heretics: heretical gatherings, places of pagan worship, night offerings, or, in general, "errors" of pagan *superstitio*.

funestus
A. *pollutio*: *C.Th.* 3.12.3.5 (*funesto*, on incestuous marriage); 9.28.2.3 (*velut contagium quoddam funestae pestis*); *Nov. Valent.* 23.6.
B. other cases in a non-religious sense: *C.Th.* 9.6.3.3[2] (deadly); 15.14.9.18 (*funesti* – referring to tyrant Eugenius' consuls).
C. related to religion:
C1. heretics: *C.Th.* 9.16.7.3; 16.5.19.4; 16.6.7.1.
C2. pagans: *C.Th.* 16.10.19.7[2]; *Const. Sirm.* 12.1[2]; *Nov. Theod.* 3.64.

---

[71] *ThLL* 6.1 (1913): 1584–1586.
[72] For more on this crime, cf. Gnoli 1979.

The adjective ***dirus*** was used by the Romans to refer to things and phenomena perceived as terrible or eerie, bringing death and misfortune, and thus naturally applied in characteristics of the underworld.[73] In the relevant material, it is mentioned only five times, each time in its more narrow, religious meaning: "fatal, sinister, bringing disaster."[74] It is used twice in a manner indicating magic or pagan incantations, twice with reference to heresies, once – tomb desecration, which is certainly due to the accompanying *contagium*.

dirus

A. incantations: *C.Th.* 9.38.6.8 (in sorcery); 16.10.7.6 (pagan).

B. heresy: *C.Th.* 16.5.12.6; 16.5.54.5.

C. tomb desecration: *Nov. Valent.* 23.33.

The primary meaning of the word ***infaustus*** is "ill-boding," "bringing misfortune," although it may also simply mean "unfortunate."[75] Specific instances in the material point to an intense negative charge behind this term. It is used in clearly negative contexts also when it refers to the *pollutio* associated with interment. Moreover, it indicates the tyrant's figure, abuses committed by public officials, or heresy.

infaustus

A. tyrant: *C.Th.* 9.40.21.2; 15.14.9.14; 16.2.47.5 = *Const. Sirm.* 6.6[2]

B. abuses committed by officials: *C.Th.* 7.8.12.[2]; 7.18.17.4.

C. funerals (*pollutio*) : *C.Th.* 7.20.12.13; 9.17.5.8.

D. heretics: *C.Th.* 16.5.34.5; 16.5.64.4 = *Const. Sirm.* 6.26[2].

The terms ***labes, pestis*** indicate a disaster which may also be possibly linked with the idea of *contagium*. As a matter of fact, such a relation can be noted in a great part of the instances from the constitutions.[76] A listing of offences liable for such harshly phrased censure is similar to those in the previous cases: usurpation, dishonesty of public officials, magic, heresy; in addition, also "the stigma and

[73] Thome 1993: 81.

[74] *ThLL* 5.1 (1910): 1268–1270.

[75] *ThLL* 7.1 (1934–1964): 1355–1356.

[76] *C.Th.* 9.16.11.2: *maleficiorum labe pollutum*; *C.Th.* 9.40.17.5: *saeculi nostri labes appareat* (on Eutropius, who in this constitution is described in the language replete with references to *contagium*); *C.Th.* 15.14.12.1: *His, quos tyrannici temporis labes specie dignitatis infecerant, inustae maculae omnem abolemus infamiam*; *C.Th.* 16.5.6.7: *Fotinianum labe contaminatio*; *C.Th.* 9.28.2.3: *velut contagium quoddam funestae pestis*; 16.5.44.3: *Quae pestis cave contagione latius emanet ac profluat*; cf. also a mention of *pestis* in the Emperor Justin's constitution – *C.J.* 9.18.6, concerning sepulchral violation.

ignominy of disgraceful turpitude" (*pudendae turpitudinis labes atque ignominia*), with which the activity of procurers affected the state (*Nov. Theod.* 18).

labes, pestis
A. tyrants : *C.Th.* 15.14.12.1 (*labes*).
B. officials: *C.Th.* 1.5.9.5 (*labes*); 9.28.2.3 (*pestis*, comparison); 9.40.17.5 (*labes*).
C. witchcraft: *C.Th.* 9.16.5.3 (*pestis*, as a punishment for witchcraft); 9.16.11.2 (*labes*).
D. heretics: *C.Th.* 16.5.6.7 (*labes*); 16.4.2.1[2] (*pestifer*); 16.5.44.3 (*pestis*); 16.5.58.11 (*pestifer*).
E. prostitution: *Nov. Theod.* 18.7 (*labes*).
F. other: *C.Th.* 8.4.16.5 (*labes*, disease).

Adjectives ending with -bilis as terms of invective

A number of adjectives used in the Imperial documents refers to being guilty, deserving punishment. Among these terms, there is a small group of verbal adjectives ending with -*bilis*, marked by negative emotions. In Honig's view, they serve as one of the means, in the texts of the Theodosian Code, to augment the force of expression;[77] thus, they also turn out to be a suitable material for constructing invective. *Exsecrabilis* and *abominabilis* express, at the same time, an aspect of the emperor's personal disgust, whereas *culpabilis*, *damnabilis*, *detestabilis*, *plectibilis*, and *reprehensibilis* all demonstrate the objective dimension of the act for which the offender is brought to justice. With the exception of *detestabilis*, the other four forms were not known in classical Latin, Honig states that they had found their way into the language of the Code from Patristic writings, at times with obviously transformed meanings – as they do not depict the condition of being guilty in relation to God, but transgressions of provisions of the law.[78] Furthermore, the Code's texts also contain the adjective *notabilis* (deserving infamy), as well as some negative ones: *inexpiabilis*, *inexcusabilis*, *implacabilis* (in the sense: unpardonable), *intolerabilis* (intolerable).

The above-mentioned adjectives possess the feature of instilling negative overtones even into neutral expressions when the both are present together. Negative concepts, such as *audacia*[79] or *coniventia*,[80] are thus reinforced even

[77] Honig 1960: 145.
[78] Honig 1960: 148–186.
[79] *C.Th.* 7.8.5: *reprehensilbilis temeritas*; *C.Th.* 16.4.2: *ausu grave atque damnabili*; *C.Th.* 16.5.5: *plectibili ausu*; *Nov. Valent.* 6.1.2: *inexpiabilis culpa atque temeritas plectenda*.
[80] *C.Th.* 11.30.8; 11.36.10; *Const. Sirm.* 14.

more. Unfortunately, a survey of the circumstances in which they appear gives us an impression of confusion. The adjectives indicating the penal sanction for a given act are mentioned in reference to offences committed by private persons, as well as officials and, very frequently, non-Catholics. A rule can be found only in the case of the two most emotionally charged adjectives: *exsecrabilis* and *abominabilis*, as well as the verbs from which they had been derived (*exsecro* and *abomino*). They refer in particular to heretics and pagans; consequently, they even tend to have been identified with the revulsion motivated by religious considerations.[81] Still, the verbs *abomino* and *exsecro* also appear in the context of sexual offences, denunciation, and the crime of grave robbery; in one case, *exsecro* is used in a much more lenient way (the owner who treated his slaves in a given manner ought not to be castigated). It is evident then that it is not the religious background of *exsecrabilis* that is decisive as to whether or not to use it against the non-Catholics; one could rather say that the offences connected with religion arouse the strongest verbal outrage of the legislator, even if they do not necessarily involve the harshest penalties.

intolerabilis
abuses of authority: *C.Th.* 7.13.7.4; *Nov. Valent.* 12.11.
dereliction of duties at the *curia*: *Nov. Valent.* 15.15

inexcusabilis
breach of imperial constitutions: *Nov. Valent.* 6.1.2.
other (neutral): *C.Th.* 11.16.7.3; *C.Th.* 12.12.15.4.

implacabilis
meaning: "unforgivable," against religion: *Nov. Theod.* 17.2.44.
meaning: "implacable": *C.Th.* 4.8.5.16.

notabilis
against religion: *C.Th.* 2.8.18.5 = 8.8.3.4 = 11.7.13.4; 16.5.7.12[2].
other crimes: *C.Th.* 8.5.37.2 (plunder).
on infamy: *C.Th.* 9.14.3.13; 11.30.34.5; *Const. Sirm.* 2.4[2].

damnabilis
against a given Imperial law: *C.Th.* 16.4.2.3.
abuse of authority: *C.Th.* 11.30.8.13.

[81] Honig 1960: 146.

against religion: *C.Th.* 16.10.17.3.
other crimes: *C.Th.* 1.9.2 = 11.1.20.2 (obtaining a rescript under false pretences); 9.39.1.4 (unjust accusation); *Nov. Theod.* 18.8 (evasion of regulations by procurers).

culpabilis
abuses of authority: *C.Th.* 6.27.18.2; 6.29.3.8; 11.36.10.3; *Const. Sirm.* 14.2.

reprehensilibilis
abuses of authority: *C.Th.* 7.8.5.1^{2}.

plectibilis
departure from the *curia*: *C.Th.* 12.1.161.1.
against religion: *C.Th.* 16.5.5.4.
other crimes: *C.Th.* 14.3.16.2 (illegal appropriation of grain from public granaries).

detestabilis
crimes: *C.Th.* 9.24.1.7 (aiding to commit *raptus*); *C.Th.* 14.3.1.4 (transfer of property in order to avoid decurion's service).
infamy: *C.Th.* 2.19.1.6.

execrabilis, execror, execratio, execrabiliter
against religion: *C.Th.* 16.5.7.12^{2} (*execror*); 16.5.35.1 (*execrabilis*); 16.5.51.3 (*execror*); 16.5.57.6 (*execrabilis*); 16.5.60.2 (*execror*); 16.5.61.3 (*execrabilis*); 16.6.6.11 (*execror*); 16.10.9.3 (*execrabilis*); 16.10.23.2 (*execror*); 16.10.25.2 (*execror*); *Nov. Valent.* 18.4 (*execrabilis*).
tomb robbery: *Nov. Valent.* 23.36 (*execrabilis*).
denunciation: *C.Th.* 10.10.2.2 (*execror*); 10.10.12.10^{2} (*execror*).
attempting to effect proscribed marriages: *Nov. Anth.* 1.40 (*execrabiliter*).
castigation: *C.Th.* 3.16.2.13 (*execratio* of a spouse-criminal); 3.30.3.15 (*execror*, deserving to be praised, not stigmatized).

abominabilis, abominanter, abomino
incest: *C.Th.* 3.12.1.2 (*abominanter*).
against religion: *C.Th.* 16.8.26.2 (*abomino*); 16.10.13.2 (*abomino*); *Nov. Valent.* 17.11 (*abominabilis*).

Terms indicating disturbances of public order

Among the terms used in the language of the Late Antique constitutions, there is a considerable group of those which point to some sort of disturbance in the proper status quo – in various ways and on various levels. In some cases, reference is made to the peace in relation to an individual, while others, which are of particular interest in the context of our analysis, concern disturbances of the peace as related to the community or violations of public order. Some of the terms discussed below can be clearly assigned to a specific type of disturbance, whereas for the other ones it is necessary to embrace the whole context in order to determine what kind of "turmoil" is being referred to. In a majority of cases, it is also difficult to identify, without any ambiguity, the intention behind a particular invective being expressed; it may be argued that the legislator simply refers to things as they are. One could even speak of their use as technical terms, e.g., with regard to crimes such as abduction (*raptus*), robbery (*rapina*), or a wide range of criminal offences involving use of violence, all subsumed under the designation *crimen vis*,[82] in relation to which the word *violentia* is apparently obvious. Still, some instances of the metaphorical usage of the terms conveying unquestionably negative weight indicate that they may at least potentially have fulfilled the relevant function in the normative texts under discussion.

As it seems, the softest of the terms referring to disturbances of the order in the Roman Empire are the words derived from the noun ***inquietudo*** ("disquiet", "perturbation") – *inquieto, inquietus, inquietator*, which can be often found in the language of the Imperial documents. They comprise a variety of cases almost always concerned with the peace of private individuals being disturbed (possibly, individuals as members of corporate bodies), not the peace in the state in general. The most frequent source of the said "perturbation" is the state apparatus itself, and the most typical case of *inquietudo* is the "disquiet" caused by the threat of definite forensic or administrative measures effected by the state. In view of such circumstances, the Emperor's role is to act in favour of relieving all his subjects, or a specific group of them, of the "perturbation" in question. To put it simply, the Emperor revokes the law causing inconvenience to the subjects or suspends the enforcement thereof in specific cases, each time justifying such a move with his wish to spare the subjects this sort of "disquiet."

Aside from the letter of the law, another potential source of "perturbation" may be actions of public officials, both legitimate and those considered as abuses

---

[82] Cf. Robinson 1995: 29–30, 79–81.

of official authority, e.g., committed by tax-collectors.[83] Another denounced practice is provincial governors' encroaching upon the competences of central offices.

Besides, there are also some rare cases of *inquietudo* which cannot be possibly included within the above scheme, such as harassing the Jewish Christian converts by their former Judaic fellow believers, disturbances caused by deposed members of clergy, or tumults instigated among barbarians by Stilicho. Only in the two last cases could we speak of "disturbances" in the sense of *seditio*, i.e., riots perilous to the public law and order.

inquieto, inquietudo
A. disturbing with the threat of legal or administrative action – the emperor eliminates perturbations: *C.Th.* 4.3.1.4; 4.8.7.2; 5.9.1.5; 5.12.3.[16]; 6.23.4.18; 6.35.8.2; 7.8.10.2; 7.11.1.5; 7.20.2.21; 8.7.5.5; 9.42.1.15; 10.1.5.1; 10.1.5.2; 10.8.3.3; 10.12.2.2; 10.18.1.3; 11.7.1.5; 11.15.1.3; 11.16.17.4; 12.1.30.2; 12.1.81.3; 12.1.177.13; 12.1.181.10; 12.6.6.5; 13.1.10.3; 13.3.10.2; 13.5.8.4; 13.5.9.4; 13.5.20.2; 13.6.4.4; 14.3.9.4; 14.25.1.3; 15.1.41.2²; 15.7.2.2; 16.2.3.1²; 16.2.9.1; 16.2.11.4; 16.2.15.1²; 16.5.2.3; *Nov. Theod.* 26.9; *Nov. Valent.* 1.1.16; 12.20.
(including) A1. the emperor acting in opposition to those officials who disturb the subjects: *C.Th.* 6.10.1.7; 6.35.8.2; 6.35.14.10; 7.20.2.21; 10.1.5.1; 10.1.5.2; 10.8.3.3; 10.18.1.3; 11.7.1.5; 11.16.17.4; 13.5.9.4.
B. other: *C.Th.* 6.35.14.10 (not clear if the "perturbation" is caused by actions of some official, or not); 9.42.22.3 (inciting disturbances among barbarians); 15.7.2.2 (forcing the children of actors to remain in profession); 16.8.5.2 (Jews disturbing Jewish Christian converts); *Const. Sirm.* 2.2 (disturbances incited by deposed clergymen); 4.4²
inquietudo (Jews harassing Jewish Christian converts, a different version at *C.Th.* 16.8.5).

A group of words connected with the term ***vastatio*** ("devastation") is much less represented in the Code. In most instances, it describes the devastating of the Roman territories by barbarians,[84] while in two cases the damage was done as a result of Roman officials' actions. Namely, the constitution *C.Th.* 7.7.3 condemns the negligence leading to the devastation of pastures by the livestock kept by the military, while the *C.Th.* 7.18.17 refers to the specially appointed tribunes who use the pretext of tracking down army deserters to ravage (*vastat*) the province – this enigmatically designated abuse of power provides a sufficient justification for liquidating this office.

---

83 *C.Th.* 7.20.2; 10.1.5; 10.18.1; 11.7.1.

84 In one case, a reference is made to a Roman citizen who had used the barbarians to gain the senatorial rank – in attempting to reach his goal, the decurion from Emesa (*Nov. Theod.* 15.2) left "everything" *vasta et sola* ("devastated and desolated"). Cf. Chapter IV: 106–110.

devasto, vastatio, vastitas, vasto, vastus

A. barbarians: *C.Th.* 7.13.20.1[2]; 11.28.12.2; 12.1.177.4; *Nov. Theod.* 15.2.10 (here: metaphorically on the effects of actions of some decurion who raided the governor's *officium* with barbarians' aid); *Nov. Valent.* 1.2.1; 1.2.7; 34.6; 34.15; 34.18.

B. officials: *C.Th.* 7.7.3.6 (damage caused by livestock kept by the army); 7.18.17.2.

C. other (neutral): *C.Th.* 15.3.4.3; 16.3.1.2; *Nov. Theod.* 3.9.

Depraedatio ("depredation") is of course the term derived from *praedo* ("predator"), which may be treated as a synonym of *latro* ("robber"). Its scope, nevertheless, would not correspond with several instances of the word *praedo* as mentioned in Chapter V. Similarly to *vastatio*, the noun *depraedatio* is naturally linked with the activity of barbarians and *latrones*. *Depraedatio* may be the effect of actions of both foreign invaders and Romans: there are references to *depraedationes* and *latrocinium* perpetrated by deserters, twice to (voluntary and involuntary) participation of some Roman citizens in *depraedationes* committed by the barbarians. Much more often than *vastatio* is the term applied metaphorically to the practices of dishonest public officials. As might be expected, the practices of tax-collectors abusing their official authority are represented as "depredation"; the term is mentioned many times in the Emperor Majorian's Second Novel, which is concerned with this specific problem. *Depraedatio* is also used in reference to the officials' practice of charging illegal payments,[85] i.e., simply, bribes.[86] In such cases, the related accusation is usually a component of a more elaborate invective.[87]

depraedatio

A. barbarians: *C.Th.* 7.1.1.1; *Nov. Valent.* 9.6.

B. robbery: *C.Th.* 7.18.15.2; 15.14.14.6 (in connection with a barbarian raid).

C. officials: *C.Th.* 1.16.7.3[2]; 10.4.1.5; *Nov. Valent.* 7.2.17; *Nov. Majo.* 7.52 (chief decurions, *principes*).

C1. in connection with tax-collecting: *C.Th.* 8.10.3.2; *Nov. Valent.* 1.3.23; *Nov. Majo.* 2.31; 2.37; 2.44.

D. internal tax in Jewish communes: *C.Th.* 16.8.14.7.

The nouns ***discursus***, ***excursus***, ***incursus*** are used to refer to various barbarian raids (once, a Roman raid on barbarian territories). The metaphorical use

85 *C.Th.* 1.16.7

86 *C.Th.* 9.3.6; *Nov. Majo.* 7.

87 *C.Th.* 1.16.7, cf. Chapter IV: 81–83; *C.Th.* 9.3.6: officers in charge of the prison called *ministri ferales*.

in Majorian's Second Novel may be considered as analogous to the one in which the term *depraedatio* appears in this constitution. Also, in the Ninth Novel of the same Emperor, the term *incursus* is applied in reference to the appearance, in any province of the Roman Empire, of a fugitive already sentenced to life-time exile for adultery; wherever such a person might be identified, he ought to be killed. Let us note that the fugitive is treated here in the same way as a *hostis*.

discursus, excursio, excursus, incursio, incursus

A. by barbarians: *C.Th.* 7.12.1.1²; 10.10.25.2; 11.28.12.2; *Const. Sirm.* 16.7; *Nov. Theod.* 4.9; *Nov. Valent.* 9.5; 13.47; 13.58.

A1. against barbarians: *C.Th.* 7.17.1.18.

B. metaphorically: *Nov. Majo.* 2.30 (travelling across the province with the aim of exacting excessive taxes); 9.16 (wherever throughout the Empire an individual convicted for adultery may be found, he ought to be killed).

C. other meanings: *C.Th.* 8.5.16.2; 9.1.7.4; 9.24.1.7; 15.1.45.6.

Unlike the previously discussed terms, ***invasio*** (verb – *invadere, nomen agentis – invasor*) is not used in the normative texts even once in reference to a raid or an invasion from the outside. Its primary meaning denotes taking someone's property by force, which may be an act of *crimen vis* or a lawful act,[88] as well as confiscation of property. *Invado* is consequently a neutral term and may become an element of the invective language only when accompanied by other, more explicit, expressions.[89] Some metaphorical uses of the term also display the characteristics of invective, as at *C.Th.* 9.38.6, where the adulterer is described as *genialis tori ac lectuli invasor alieni*, and *Nov. Valent.* 17, which gives an account, sentence by sentence, of how the unworthy bishop Hilary incited disturbances among the Churches of Gaul and usurped the authority to ordain bishops (contrary to the will of the people in those Churches) – in the both cases, the verb *invadere* is used.

invado, invasor, invasio

A. taking someone's, or disputed, property by force: *C.Th.* 2.1.3.6; 2.26.1.3; 2.26.1.17 (*invasor*); 2.26.1.18; 2.29.1.4; 2.29.2.4²; 4.18.1.2 (*invasor*); 4.18.1.8; 4.22.3.3; 9.1.1.3; 9.10.2.1; 10.10.12.3²; 12.9.1.2 (both instances); 16.2.28.3; 16.5.65.5; *Nov. Valent.* 8.R (*invasor*); 8.1.15 (*invasor*); 8.1.27; 8.1.33 (*invasio*).

---

88 *C.Th.* 3.16.1.

89 *C.Th.* 2.1.3: along with the term *direptio* (plunder); *C.Th.* 2.29.1 (*inpudentius* and *inhonestius*); *C.Th.* 2.29.2 (described as *temeritas* and *violentia*); *C.Th.* 4.18.1 (*invasor* simultaneously called *praedo*); *C.Th.* 9.10.2 (*temptare*); *C.Th.* 16.5.65 (*temeritas*).

A1. in accordance with the law: *C.Th.* 3.16.1.9[2].

A2. forfeiture: *C.Th.* 4.6.3.22; 4.6.3.[25]; 10.10.15.3; 12.1.92.4.

B1. assuming the post of a deceased official: *C.Th.* 6.27.14.2.

B2. usurping the right to ordain bishops: *Nov. Valent.* 17.13.

C. forced entry into a place of asylum and arresting the fugitive: *C.Th.* 9.45.4.7[3].

D. adultery: *C.Th.* 9.38.6.6 (*invasor*).

E. instigating riots in the Churches: *Nov. Valent.* 17.11.

The semantic scope of the terms derived from the verb ***violo***, and used in the language of the Imperial documents, is very extensive. Two principal semantic areas can be identified: one refers to a group of criminal offences, the other – to violation of the Imperial law.

In the former field, *violentia* is primarily a technical term used to express *crimen vis*. In a majority of cases, it refers to taking the contested real estate by force prior or contrary to a court verdict.[90] But, incidentally, the term is also used to refer to other cases of *vis*, such as using violence to extort a certificate of purchase, maintaining a private prison, and twice – *violentia* is used to indicate religious disturbances. A particularly noteworthy expression is *congressus violentiae*; taking part in this "gathering with the aim of violence" is listed along with such crimes as *latrocinium*, *homicidium*, and serious sex crimes (*raptus*, *stuprum*, *adulterium*).[91]

Another criminal offence with the term *violatio* in its name is *violatio sepulcri*, the crime of tomb desecration, regarded as one of the most serious due to the *contagium* involved. Apart from these two crime types, there are also some single cases when *violatio* is used to describe other, always most serious, crimes (treason, abduction, incest, adultery).

The other of the two semantic fields is the one where *violatio* is used in reference to violation of a certain value, not a specific criminal act. In most cases, the value in question is the Imperial law. *Violatio* indicates then a distinct offence: the lack of respect for Imperial decrees – *legis violatio*, which is the most frequent case of *sacrilegium*.[92] In this particular sense, *violatio* becomes closely related to the rhetoric pointing to the offender's *audacia*.

This sense of *violatio* is transferred over to the religion supported by the emperor. A person guilty of making pagan sacrifices is, according to Theodosius I, *reus violatae religionis*[93] – which is coined by analogy with

---

[90] Harries 2006: 92–99.

[91] *C.Th.* 9.2.5.

[92] See Chapter IX: 233–237.

[93] *C.Th.* 16.10.12.15.

violatio legis. In another constitution by the same Emperor, a violation of *divinae legis sanctitas* is mentioned.[94] Had it not been for the context provided by the constitution *Cunctos populos*,[95] which was issued on the same day, one could even argue on whether the reference is made to the Divine law or that of the divine emperor (the emperor's *divinitas* is still present in the rhetoric of the Christian Roman Empire). Yet this connection should give more justification to the assumption that here as well the Emperor extends the protection of his *leges* on to the *lex Dei*, ruling that in the latter case it is the question of a *sacrilegium*, too. At the same time, it is notable that the term *violatio* is used only once to refer to the "violation" of a Christian doctrine,[96] never becoming an element of the language used to describe heresy in the Imperial law, while rather tending to indicate a breach of the principles of the Christian religion on a more general level, the cases in point being rebaptism and infringement of the clerical privileges.

violo, violentia, violator, violentus

A. *crimen vis*, in general : *C.Th.* 9.10.1.3; 9.10.1.8; 9.10.4.2; 9.10.4.4; 9.10.4.8; 9.10.4.10.
A1. taking the disputed property by force: *C.Th.* 2.4.6.2²; 2.29.2.3²; 4.22.1.3²; 4.22.2.4; 4.22.3.8; 9.10.2.1; 9.10.2.2; 9.10.3.3; 9.10.3.5; 9.10.3.8; 9.10.3.13; 11.36.14.4; 11.36.14.5.
A2. other violent crimes: *C.Th.* 3.1.1.2 (use of violence at a purchase transaction); 9.2.5.4 (*congressus violentiae*); 16.2.31.22 = *Const. Sirm.* 14.6² (violence against bishops); *C.Th.* 16.8.20.2 (violence against Jews); 16.10.24.8 (assault on peaceful pagans or Jews); *Nov. Valent.* 32.16 (private prison; cf. Pharr 1952: 542, note 6).
B. *violatio sepulchri*: *C.Th.* 9.17.R; 9.17.2.25; 9.17.4.1; 9.17.4.2²; 9.38.7.6; *Nov. Valent.* 23.R; 23.3; 23.6; 23.26; 23.37; 23.46; 23.49.
C. other crimes: *C.Th.* 9.8.1.7 (adultery); 9.37.2.9² (*maiestas*); 9.38.4.4 (*raptus*); 9.38.6.7 (incest); *Nov. Majo.* 6.48 (*raptus*); 9.20 (adultery).
D. violation of the Imperial law: *C.Th.* 1.9.1.14; 1.15.16.3; 6.4.22.16; 6.23.4.10; 6.35.13.9 (*sacrilegium*); 7.4.30.[8] (*sacrilegium*); 7.8.13.4; 7.8.5.1²; 7.9.1.4; 8.1.16.5; 8.7.16.12; 8.11.3.2²; 8.11.4.8 (*sacrilega dissimulatio*); 9.30.2.5; 10.10.15.4; 10.10.24.6; 11.16.1.4; 11.30.8.16; 11.30.29.5²; 11.30.60.5; 12.1.176.8; 13.5.5.8; 14.11.1.4; 14.16.1.5²; 15.5.3.6; 15.5.3.6; 16.2.42.16; 16.5.66.6²; 16.8.14.9; 16.8.20.8; 16.9.4.1²; *Nov. Valent.* 17.36.
D1. other adverse action affecting values related to the Empire: *C.Th.* 10.1.9.2 (*res privatae*); 15.1.25.5 (public ornaments on private houses); *Nov. Theod.* 24.23 (money – *sacrae pecuniae*); *Nov. Valent.* 17.25; (*ausibus enim talibus fides et reverentia nostri*

94 *C.Th.* 16.2.25.2.
95 *C.Th.* 16.1.2, cf. n. 772.
96 *C.Th.* 16.5.6.6².

violatur imperii – on bishop Hilary's disobedience towards the Pope; here: projection from Church to state).
E. by analogy with the Imperial law – violations of the principles of the Catholic religion: *C.Th.* 16.2.25.2 (*sacrilegium*); 16.2.34.2; 16.5.6.6[2] (of the Holy Spirit); 16.6.5.2; 16.7.3.7[2]; 16.10.12.15; *Nov. Majo.* 11.19.
F. other: *C.Th.* 2.24.1.13[2]; 13.9.3.10; *Nov. Majo.* 11.5.

A number of terms derived from the verb ***rapio*** (*rapacitas*, *rapax*, *rapina*, *raptor*, *raptus*) have three basic technical meanings in the Theodosian Code. The first one refers to abducting a woman (*crimen raptus*), one of the most serious crimes;[97] the second one is used to denote a different crime committed with the use of violence, a robbery, i.e., taking someone's property by force (*rapina*). Other instances of the term's use with regard to serious cases of theft, e.g., connected with sepulchral violations, would draw on this specific sense. Finally, the third one refers to carrying out a verdict (*rapere ad supplicium*). It should be noted that in its metaphorical sense the term is only used to signify a "robbery." It then refers to unlawful extortion of payments or other benefits by officials. In this metaphorical use, it may also be regarded as a term of invective.

rapacitas, rapax, rapina, rapio, raptor, raptus
A. *rapere ad supplicium*: *C.Th.* 1.10.4.2; 1.16.11.4; 9.42.10.4; *Nov. Majo.* 2.70.
B. abduction of a woman (the crime of *raptus*): *C.Th.* 9.1.1.2; 9.2.5.4; 9.8.1.10; 9.24.R; 9.24.1.2; 9.24.1.9; 9.24.1.10; 9.24.1.11; 9.24.1.14; 9.24.1.16; 9.24.1.1[2]; 9.24.2.2; 9.24.3.2; 9.25.R; 9.25.1.1; 9.25.1.3; 9.25.1.4; 9.25.2.2; 9.25.3.2; 9.38.3.4; 9.38.4.4; 9.38.6.6; 9.38.7.6; 9.38.8.7; 11.36.7.4; *Const. Sirm.* 10.13[2]; *Nov. Majo.* 6.48.
C. other criminal acts:
C1: robbery: *C.Th.* 2.1.8.3 (taking property by force); 9.30.3.2 (cattle theft); 9.42.21.2 (if anybody stole anything from Stilicho's property); 13.5.29.5 (if anybody robbed the *navicularii* – *poena in raptores constituta*); 13.5.29.6 (caught in an act of robbery); 16.10.24.9 (robbery in result of an attack on peaceful Jews or pagans).
C2: tomb robbery: *Nov. Valent.* 23.4.
C3: *crimen peculatus*: *C.Th.* 9.28.2.2; 9.28.2.4; 9.28.2.5 (twice).
C4: metaphorically on *parricidium*: *C.Th.* 9.38.6.5 (*qui parricidali furore raptus*).
C5: bishops kidnapped by a mob: *Const. Sirm.* 14.7.

[97] As such excluded from the amnesty, cf. *C.Th.* 9.38.3; 9.38.4; 9.38.6; 9.38.7; 9.38.8. Cf. Robinson 1995: 71–73. On this crime, see Evans-Grubbs 1989; Haase 1994: 458–462; Puliatti 1995; Botta 2004.

D. actions of public officials: *C.Th.* 1.16.7.1; 6.35.11.2; 8.1.10.4²; 8.5.21.2; 9.27.3.8; 13.11.11.6; *Nov. Valent.* 7.1.22.

E. other: *C.Th.* 2.10.2.[2]; 11.28.10.3.

The verb ***turbare*** and some related derivative terms should be considered alongside the word families stemming from the nouns ***seditio*** and ***tumultus***.[98] As we shall see, in all the three cases the related meanings tend to prevail. On the other hand, the sense of the noun ***turba*** is somewhat different, as it expresses contempt towards the "rabble" rather than fear of riots.

Turbare may be the term that points to disturbing the law and order. It is used then to refer to various acts of violence: brigandage, the use of violence at places of asylum, or the unlawful use of force by officials and decurions. The Emperor Majorian's novel *De aurigis et seditiosis*, which all we know of is the title, may have possibly concerned the question of disturbances in connection with activities of the circus factions.

Moreover, in two of the Post-Theodosian Novels the verbs *turbare* and *perturbare* are used in direct reference to disturbances against law and order.[99] In the further two cases, *turbulentus* apparently refers to the way in which the law is violated, not the fact of the violation itself.[100]

Most frequently, when the words related to the verb *turbare* or the noun *seditio* are mentioned, reference is being made to disturbances connected with religion. Significantly, the riots in question are always those caused by the Christians, more precisely by the adherents of the Church officially recognized by the state: either incited by deposed bishops or in connection with demolishing pagan temples or synagogues. In such cases, there is no doubt that it is first and foremost the public order which is made the subject of particular protection.

The words used in the constitutions against heretics are of particular interest. According to the *Const. Sirm.* 14, even though the disturbance affects *quies publica*, it takes place *in contemptum Christianae religionis*, whereas the *C.Th.* 16.5.44 speaks of disturbing (*turbare*) the faith and Catholic sacraments. In consequence, the public order is affected rather indirectly here, by way of a specific hostile action against the Catholic religion. Likewise, the *C.Th.* 16.5.38, which describes heretical gatherings as *turbae seditionis*, does not seem to refer to some actual *seditio*; the name is used here metaphorically in order to justify the repressive measures against heretics. As Laurence Guichard points out, the metaphor of "disturbances" is habitually used in religious

---

[98] On the meanings of these terms in the Republican period, see Osthoff 1952.

[99] *Nov. Valent.* 32; *Nov. Marc.* 1.

[100] *C.Th.* 16.1.4 = 16.4.1; 16.10.24.

polemical writings, regardless of the actual occurrence of religious riots.[101] The term *turba*, which is actually not always a negative one in literary Latin,[102] appears regularly in reference to heretical communities, yet it is not the only one for that purpose. As evident in the analyzed material, this noun assumes a negative aspect of meaning in all the instances of its usage.

A special mention should be made of the constitution against magic practices, with some references to disturbing the elements (*elementa*), not the law and order. In turn, the *C.Th.* 9.6.1 uses the term *tumultus* to describe an impermissible situation where a freedman accuses his patron of a crime punishable by death. In the former case, the natural order is being violated, while in the latter – the social one.

Another, somewhat softer, meaning of *turbare* is identical with *inquietare* – it is applied when some legitimate actions would have a negative impact on Roman citizens; in consequence, a change or a reinterpretation of thc law in their favour is bound to take place.

tumultuosus, tumultus, turbulentus, turbide, turbo, proturbo, seditio

A. actions against public order: *C.Th.* 7.20.7.4^{2} (*perturbo*, on army veterans who had turned into brigands); 8.15.5.[17] (*turbide* – a sale effected under threat of violence); 10.26.1.9 (*conturbo* – a decurion's attempt to interfere with trial proceedings); 10.26.1.9 (*turbulentus*, as above); 11.36.31.5 (*perturbatio*; brigands); *Const. Sirm.* 14.3 (*turbo*, action against both public order and the Christian religion); *Nov. Valent.* 1.3.27 (*turbulentus* – disturbance during tax collection, here: unjust taxes); *Nov. Majo.* 12.R (*seditiosus* – mentioned in the title of the lost constitution: *De aurigis et seditiosis*).

B. disturbing public order in connection with actions against pagans or Jews: *C.Th.* 16.8.22.2^{2} (*seditio*); 16.10.16.2 (*tumultus, turba*, cf. below); 16.10.24.6 (*turbulentus*, here: unlawful action mentioned directly, cf. item D).

C1. actions against the peace in the Church: *C.Th.* 9.45.4.8^{3} (*turbo*); 16.1.4.8 = 16.4.1.4 (*seditio, turbo*); *Const. Sirm.* 2.7^{2} (*turbator*); 2.8^{2} (*tumultus*); *Nov. Valent.* 17.11 (*tumultus*).

C2. illegal gatherings of John Chrysostom's followers: *C.Th.* 16.2.37.3^{2} (*tumultosus*); 16.2.37.4^{2} (*seditio*); 16.4.3.2 (*turbo*); 16.4.4.2 (*tumultosus*); 16.4.5.2 (*tumultosus*).

C3. illegal gatherings of heretics: *C.Th.* 16.5.38.6 (*seditio, turba* cf. below); 16.5.44.2 (*turbo*).

D. actions aimed directly against the imperial law: *C.Th.* 16.1.4.7 = 16.4.1.2 (*turbulentus*); 16.10.24.6 (*turbulentus*); *Nov. Valent.* 32.44 (*turbo*); *Nov. Marc.* 1.68 (*perturbo*, here: also in the meaning characteristic of *inquietare*, cf. item G).

E. disturbing the elements with magic practices: *C.Th.* 9.16.5.2 (*turbo*).

---

101 Guichard 2008: 165.

102 E.g., Jerome, *Ep.* 78.18: *turba credentium*.

F. disturbing social order, a freedman's denunciation of his patron: *C.Th.* 9.6.1.2 (*tumultus*).
G. perturbation caused by the threat of court or administrative action: *C.Th.* 3.1.1.3 (*turbo*); 4.22.2.3 (*turbo*); 4.22.4.2 (*perturbo*); 5.12.2.[7^{2}] (*perturbo*); 5.14.31.2 (*turbo*); 13.11.6.2 (*turbo*); 13.11.16.9^{2} (*turbo*); 15.1.42.4 (*perturbo*); 15.2.7.2 (*turbo*); *Nov. Marc.* 1.68 (*perturbo*).
H. other: *C.Th.* 7.1.13.5 (*turbidus*, contamination of water); 9.4.1.3 (*turbulentus*, perturbation caused by intoxication); 16.5.20.2 (*proturbo*, chase away).

turba
A. as related to heretics: *C.Th.* 16.5.3.2; 16.5.6.5; 16.5.9.2; 16.5.10.3; 16.5.12.8; 16.5.38.5.
B. other cases: *C.Th.* 1.9.3.6 (*turba ignobili* contrasted with *agentes in rebus*); 12.1.176.4 (*sacerdotalium superflua turba*); *Nov. Valent.* 24.5 (*turba mercantum*, negative context).
C. in the sense: religious disturbance/riots: *C.Th.* 16.10.16.2; *Const. Sirm.* 2.7^{2}; *Nov. Valent.* 17.26.

Chapter VIII: Terms indicating deviation (particularly in relation to religion)

As a separate category, one should distinguish those insulting terms which do not refer directly to the person of a perpetrator, his attitude, or the nature of a criminal act. In religious polemical works, there are terms of invective directly concerned with religions other than that supported by state authorities. Among such terms, let us mention *furor* and *contagium*, already discussed in the previous chapters, simultaneously pointing to a dissident's stance and the consequences caused by his religious activity. Nonetheless, one should set apart the words relating to the religion they professed and to the fact that it was wrong, at the same time implying the author's orthodox position.

Superstitio

First of all, it is fitting to begin here with the term which the ancient Romans had already considered as synonymous with religious error, i.e., *superstitio*.

In the constitutions dealing with religious dissidents, *superstitio* becomes a principal term defining any religion which is different from the version of Christianity regarded as orthodox by the state. In one of Constantine's constitutions, as preserved in Greek, the respective term is *deisidaimonia* (δεισιδαιμονία).[1] This rendering is the most correct of all possible terms. However, it should be noted that the meanings of the two terms are not overlapping in full. *Superstitio* appears to be a term much richer in its meanings and also expressing a negative content which is stronger than that of *deisidaimonia*, rather ridiculed than opposed by Greek philosophers.

The two words are different even in their etymologies. *Deisidaimonia* is a compound term whose etymology is relatively simple: *deidō* (δείδω) means

1 Euseb., *Vita Const.* III. 65–66.

"to be afraid," *daimonion* (δαιμόνιον) – a divine being. This "fear of god" is simply godliness, perceived either positively or impartially; only towards the close of the fourth century BC had that "fear of gods" become, in the philosophers' view, a contemptible superstition, which from then on would be consistently described with the formerly respectable term. This position stems from certain axiomatically accepted assumptions, which Dale Martin has called *Grand Optimal Illusion*. The identification of ontological and ethical hierarchies or, more trivially speaking, a conviction that the entities ontologically higher than Greek aristocrats (i.e., gods and *daimones*) must act in conformity with the ethical ideals held by the Greek elite was not based on anything more than the optimistic belief that the world *ought to be* so. With nothing more than that optimistic assumption at their disposal, the philosophers recognized manifestations of the fearful religious attitude to be ridiculous superstitions, as it appealed to the insight, characteristic of the Greeks, intimating that the gods were volatile, moody, and biased. Martin notes prudently that the position derided by the philosophers had yet offered significant psychological benefits, as it afforded some kind of opportunity to manipulate the gods through pious religious practices in times of danger. Philosophers and physicians may have ridiculed or stigmatized them as expressions of *deisidaimonia*, yet what they had to offer instead would not have to be necessarily more effective or convincing.[2]

The etymology of the word *superstitio* is more mysterious and apparently no scholar, ancient or modern, has satisfactorily managed to resolve this question to date.[3] As a matter of fact, it should be noted that even in Antiquity

---

2 For fundamental hypotheses of the work, see Martin 2004: 227–236.

3 Cicero's definition (*De nat. deorum* 2.71), treated with attention and cited as authoritative by Isidore of Seville (*Etimol.* 10.244, cf. Herrera 1993: 531–532) links *superstitio* with *superstes* (descendants): *qui totos dies precabantur et immolabant, ut sibi sui liberi superstites essent, superstitiosi sunt apellati.* Yet this definition is in fact pseudo-etymological, as it is not the object of the efforts (taking care that the descendants should outlive them – i.e., become *superstes*), but exaggerated forms of piety in the efforts to ensure protection for their descendants from the gods that play a decisive role in transforming religion into *superstitio*. Among the scholars who attempted to explain the etymology of the word, only Janssen followed in the footsteps of Cicero's definition, showing the anti-Roman selfish attitude of those who placed the survival of their offspring, or their own, above the well-being of their country, by appealing to foreign religions (Janssen 1975: 161 ff.). Other explanations derived from *superstes* are equally risky, e.g., the opinion that the term had once signified "spirit of the dead" (unfortunately, this is not an attested meaning of the word), thus *superstitiosus* – believing in spirits (Müller-Graupa 1931); deriving *superstes* from the "advantage" of a soothsayer who knew what was to happen in the future, and of a magus wielding control over spirits (Linkomies 1931: 79 nn.). Aside from *superstes*, other explanations are just as controversial. For instance, Otto argued that *superstitio* was a notion analogous to the Greek *eksstasis*, which should be understood as *eksstasis psyche* – the state of going

the origin of this word was not entirely clear anymore, leading to various attempts to define it or trace back its etymology. Furthermore, the word was more ambiguous than the Greek *deisidaimonia*.

Since as early as the third century BC, the term *superstitio* (as the adjective *superstitiosus*) had been attested in reference to divination practices. *Superstitiosus*, e.g., in Plautus' comedies, is simply a person who is able to predict the future. This, most likely original, meaning of the term is completely void of any negative connotation.[4]

The next phase in the development of the concept of *superstitio*, which may be dated to the close of the Republican period, is the identification of the term with *deisidaimonia*, the latter being condemned by the Greek philosophers.[5] This fact, tremendously important for a better understanding of the idea of religious error, has been overlooked, to the data, by the scholars concerned with the research of this subject, as they have concentrated on the history of Latin. In fact, there can be no doubt that the use of the term *superstitio* in a manner similar to the Greek *deisidaimonia* should be attributed exactly to the influence of Greek culture. The Romans searched for a counterpart of this philosophical concept in their language and in their choice of the term *superstitio* may have been guided by one of the fundamental constituent elements of the image of a "superstitious man," namely the inclination to see omens in all sorts of phenomena.

The identification of *superstitio* with *deisidaimonia* caused that, under some specific circumstances, *superstitio* may have been also applied in a positive sense, as a synonym of *religio* (the Greeks would still use the term *deisidaimonia* in a similar sense).[6] Nevertheless, the prevailing trend was to contrast the both concepts: *religio* and *superstitio*. As L. F. Janssen argues, on the religious level it would correspond to the contrast between the Roman *humanitas* and the barbarian *immanitas*.[7] From the perspective of the Roman elite, *superstitiones* were considered as anti-state, or at least predisposed to express

---

out of (*eks-*) or above (*super-*) one's own body. The word describes a religious experience which may be understood quite broadly, to embrace going "beyond oneself" both in an act of prophetic rapture and religious fear (Otto 1909: 551–552). The question is that this kind of experience was completely alien to Romans (Janssen 1975: 137–138). Likewise, a hypothesis proposed by Calderone, deriving *superstitiosus* from *ἀναθηματικός* (supposedly, a servant of the priest explaining words of the oracle, cf. Calderone 1972: 292) has not been accepted. As a matter of fact, all of the examples listed here would demonstrate that each scholar involved in the examination of this subject offered their own hypotheses, with none of them regarded as universally acceptable.

4 Plautus, *Curculio*, v. 397; *Rudens* v. 1139. Cf. Grodzynski 1974: 37.

5 Martin 2004: 127.

6 E.g., *D.* 12.2.5.1; *D.* 50.2.3, cf. Salzman 1987: 174.

7 Janssen 1979: 146–152.

the "egotism" of their believers.[8] The threat was compounded by the fact that those religions had come from the outside and the views they championed were often openly hostile to the Roman state.[9]

The consequence of this approach to *superstitio* was its definition as a religion which is not only depraved (*prava*) but also originating on the outside of the Roman community (*externa*). Denis Grodzynski, whose research on the history of the term *superstitio* was based on the particularly solid foundations (the hitherto unpublished material collected for the entry *superstitio* in the *Thesaurus Linguae Latinae*)[10], found that the latter meaning was given to the term *superstitio* by Livy. It may be conjectured that it was the author's conscious move, aiming to condemn the alien religious cults and demonstrate their sinister role in the history of the Roman Republic. In any case, beginning from Livy, one could speak of these two aspects of *superstitio*: perversion (*pravitas*) which also pertains to the Greek *deisidaimonia*, and "outwardness" (*externitas*), a strictly political charge.[11]

To sum up, unlike *deisidaimonia*, *superstitio* contains a clearly political aspect – it refers not only to perverting the religion but also to transgressing against the Roman community. Moreover, *superstitio* is a less distinct term, and thus it has a broader semantic scope. The inability to define the limits and determine the characteristics of *superstitio* would lead some scholars to argue that the term did not possess any content, only denoting a negative value attributed to a certain phenomenon in religion.[12] It may be a somewhat exaggerated claim, as besides *pravitas* and *externitas* it is also possible to point to a number of definite associations connected with the notion of *superstitio* (*furor*, *vanitas*, *contagium*, as well as the stereotype linking *superstitio* with old women),[13] yet the fact remains that there existed a fairly free manipulation of this particular content in how specific manifestations of *superstitio* are described.

---

8 Janssen 1975: 173. It is notable that the Church Fathers had maintained, to a certain extent, the distinction between *superstitio*, centred on individual benefit, and *religio*, serving the common good, simultaneously drawing the line between miracles of the Old Testament prophets and Christian saints, which were performed for the good of the community, and wonders of pagan magicians, intended to benefit their own glory (Kahlos 2007a: 111).

9 Janssen 1979: 149–151.

10 Grodzynski 1974: 36, note 3.

11 Grodzynski 1974: 45–46.

12 Harmening (1979: 40) points out that *superstitio* had never been a term defining objective characteristics of things or relations (*Sachbegriff*), but only indicated a negative value ascribed to some religious phenomenon.

13 It was deconstructed into these constituent parts by Kahlos 2007a: 103–109 and 2007b: 397–404; earlier, this observation can be found in Grodzynski 1974: 40; Janssen 1979: 138.

Thus conceived *superstitio* becomes a main weapon of both pagan intellectuals and state officials in their struggle against Christianity. Perhaps due to the fact that the discussion (as opposed to the verdicts being passed) was held in Greek, the emphasis was placed on the religious, not political, aspect of *superstitio/deisidaimonia*. In that dispute, as we know, the Christian authors made a reversal (*retorsio*) of the charge, applying the designation *deisidaimonia* to the pagan religion. The reversal was based on a solid intellectual justification; Clement of Alexandria, Origen, as well as Eusebius of Caesarea, had all demonstrated that it was precisely the Christian religion which best fulfilled the conditions pagan philosophers had set out for religion, and that it rejected everything they had condemned in the religion practised by the simple pagans, generally labelled as *deisidaimonia*. As opposed to the philosophers' teachings, Christianity had turned out to be an efficient way of overcoming the perverted popular pagan religion (even though at the expense of a significant concession in the form of acknowledging the thoroughly evil will of the demons).[14] Still, the interpretations in question are only sufficient for reversing the charge of *pravitas*, as the Christian apologists would tend to overlook the political aspect of *superstitio*. Although they had indeed attempted to prove that Christianity was not only harmless to but even favourable to the existence of the Roman community, they had not yet sufficiently demonstrated the adverse political impact of practising the pagan religion. It is significant in that it may help to explain why the fourth- and fifth-century legislators would also have problems with the *externitas* of "false religions" in relation to the Roman community. Among all the *superstitiones*, only heresies imply that their followers are being put beyond the pale of the Roman community, whereas the status of pagans and Jews is more difficult to define, and the legislator is definitely more ambivalent in this respect.[15]

The term *superstitio* is mentioned many times in our source material. The contemporary constitutions would apply it to Judaism, heresy, and paganism in equal measure, while *superstitiones* may have also been used to refer to all these "false religions" together. *Superstitiones* are then all religions except for the one professed by the Christian Church supported by the emperor. At the same time, their legal status is of no significance, as the term pertains

---

14 Martin 2004: 162 ff. Simultaneously, within the Christian literature in Latin, *retorsio* is implemented in Tertullian's writings, where Christianity becomes *vera religio*, whereas pagan religions – automatically *superstitiones* (Grodzynski 1974: 48; Sachot 1991: 388–389).

15 Baccari (1996: 291–300) argues that pagans and Jews were not excluded from the Roman civic community; on the other hand, it may be puzzling to find such expressions as *Romanis legibus inimici* with reference to Jews and Samaritans (*Nov. Theod.* 3) or referring to the Jewish religion as *aliena Romano imperio* (*C.Th.* 16.8.19).

to both heresy in general, condemned as *crimen*, and Judaism (permitted, and even protected by the state). For the first time, the term appears in reference to the Jewish religion in the year 392, at *C.Th.* 16.8.8 (392), which orders Imperial officials to respect decisions of the superiors of the Jewish communities. For that reason, if any expressions pointing to the criminal nature of *superstitio* can be found in the constitutions (for instance, at *C.Th.* 16.8.19 (409), where *crimen superstitionis* is explicitly mentioned), the "criminality" does not result analytically from *superstitio*, but is "added" thereto. In the case mentioned above, a reference is made to the *crimen* of heresy, which is defined here as *superstitio*.[16]

The application of *superstitio* with regard to Judaism demonstrates that the term cannot be simply contrasted with *religio*, as based on the Late Antique legal texts, either. In fact, the term *religio* is used on a regular basis in the contemporary constitutions in reference to both orthodox Christianity and the Jewish religion. Conversely, the heretics are never mentioned simply as *religio*, without one of the discrediting epithets (*criminosa*, *damnata*, *execrabilis*, *falsa*, *prava*, *scaeva*). In the constitutions prior to the reign of Theodosius I, the term *religio* is even used twice in reference to pagans – at *C.Th.* 16.2.5 (323), they are contrasted with Christians as the *diversarum religionum homines* ("men of different religions"), while in *C.Th.* 9.16.9 (371), the haruspicies are referred to as a *concessa a maioribus religio* ("worship allowed by our elders").[17]

In the latter case, the term *superstitio* may be interpreted in two ways: with regard to divination practices or pagan rituals in general. Such an ambiguity in the use of the term is a feature characteristic of the legislations of Constantine and, perhaps, Constans. At *C.Th.* 9.16.1 (320), Constantine gives permission for public haruspicies to those who "wish to serve their own *superstitio*" (*suae superstitioni servire cupientes*),[18] while at *C.Th.* 16.2.5 (323) he prohibits forcing Christians to participate in *superstitio aliena*. Finally, in his order preserved in the form of an inscription, Constantine permits the construction of the *gens Flavia* temple on the condition that it not be tainted by *superstitio*.[19] In turn, Constans proscribes *superstitio* with his constitution *C.Th.* 16.10.2 (341, citing the prohibition issued by his father), and at *C.Th.* 16.10.3 (342) he restates

---

16 The constitution applies the term "heresy" to a new sect, *caelicoli*, and just as a result also charges them with *crimen superstitionis*. On recognizing the heresy itself (and not only heretical acts) as a *crimen*, see Stachura 2004: 228.

17 One could possibly argue for adding the phrase *religio bustorum* ("sanctity of tombs"), as mentioned by the Emperor Julian in the constitution *C.Th.* 9.17.5, 363.

18 It may well be an example of the application of another (older) meaning of *superstitio*, as the word could have been used simply to denote divination practices (cf. Calderone 1972: 387–390; Grodzynski 1974: 39, 59).

19 The inscription of Hispellum: *CIL* XI.5265 = *ILS* 705.

his will to eradicate it. Michelle R. Salzman puts forward her hypothesis that this ambivalence was intentional, especially as regards Constans' legislation. According to her view, the emperors used the term *superstitio* in such a way as to communicate two different messages by means of one constitution. While their Christian subjects were to favour the interpretation that the designation in question referred to any sort of pagan worship and believed that the emperor had proscribed it outright, the pagan communities, still strong and influential in some places, continued to recognize as *superstitio* only those forms of pagan religion which had been already denounced before the advent of Christianity and may have thought that nothing had really changed in that respect. As a result, the both parties accepted the religious legislation of the emperors and were content with it, while the rulers gained their opportunity to pursue a flexible religious policy, i.e., suppressing any pagan cults at the places where pagan communities were weak and, conversely, tolerating them where they were strong. Constans II and the emperors of the Theodosian dynasty had no longer needed this ambivalent approach, and consequently in their constitutions the term *superstitio* would clearly referred to paganism in general, not the divination practices.[20]

Without any intention to deny this interesting, though quite risky, hypothesis, I think that assuming the ambivalence of *superstitio* is not necessary to substantiate it. A simpler explanation is possible. As indicated by the use of the term in reference to Judaism, *superstitio* itself is applied as a term of invective, and has no real significance for the legal contents of the constitution. The mere usage of the word does not mean that a given manifestation of a specific religious cult becomes acknowledged as *crimen* and banned.[21] In contrast with the term *superstitio*, particular elements of its description correspond, to a certain extent, to the religious scope of *crimen*. It should be emphasized that this is only a tendency, not a rule – elements of that description applied to the Jews are very rare in the constitutions; they are used infrequently and usually when Jews are mentioned within the same category as pagans or heretics.[22]

---

[20] Salzman 1987: 377–383.

[21] In the case of Constans' constitutions, as analyzed by Salzman, let us note that *C.Th.* 16.10.2 assumes elimination of the *superstitio* connected with pagan sacrifices (*sacrificii*) and the extent of the concept depends on what kind of sacrifices are meant by the legislator. On the other hand, *C.Th.* 16.10.3 assumes that all *superstitiones* ought to be eradicated (*Quamquam omnis superstitio penitus eruenda sit*), but only indirectly implies the possible existence of the orders to do so, allowing (implicitly: contrary to those orders) the preservation of temples in the rural areas.

[22] Stachura 2004: 243–251.

superstitio

A. heretics: *C.Th.* 16.5.5.7; 16.5.10.2; 16.5.34.1; 16.5.34.7; 16.5.39.1; 16.5.48.2;16.5.49.8; 16.5.51.2 = 16.5.56.1; 16.5.53.5 (*superstitiosus*); 16.5.54.5; 16.5.65.8; 16.5.65.26²; 16.5.66.1; 16.8.19.3 (with regard to *caelicoli*, treated as heretics); 16.11.3.3; *Nov. Valent.* 18.2; 18.24.

B. pagans: *C.Th.* 2.8.22.2; 9.16.1.7; 16.2.5.3; 16.5.63.2; 16.7.6.2; 16.10.2.2; 16.10.3.1; 16.10.12.16; 16.10.16.2; 16.10.17.3; 16.10.18.5; 16.10.20.1; 16.10.20.8; 16.10.20.17; *Const. Sirm.* 12.2; *Nov. Theod.* 3.64.

C. Jews: *C.Th.* 2.1.10.4; 12.1.158.2; 16.8.8.4; 16.8.14.1; 16.8.24.1; 16.8.28.3; 16.9.4.6.

D. all non-Catholics: *C.Th.* 12.1.157.2 = 12.1.158.4²; 16.5.63.4; *Const. Sirm.* 6.20².

Error, devio, pravitas, depravatio, perversitas, scaevus

The aforementioned elements of the description of *superstitio* in the Late Antique laws are primarily *furor*, *contagium*, and *error*. While the first two terms are used quite extensively and have already been discussed in one of the previous chapters, *error*, as used in our source material as a term conveying a negative content, is characteristic of "false" religions.

In the Christian authors' writings, *error* may have indicated each of the "false" religions, i.e., heresy, Judaism, paganism.[23] On the other hand, when applied in this specific religious meaning in the Theodosian Code, it refers first of all to heresy (in particular, the doctrine of rebaptism[24]), and seldom, perhaps only by analogy, to paganism.[25] Moreover, the most notable fact here is that the term *error* is also used to describe the craft of divination practised by astrologers, i.e., *ars mathematica*,[26] thus juxtaposed with heretical doctrines.[27] *Error* is not applied to any doctrine whose practices are permissible, whereas the *C.Th.* 16.10.21 (416) points to those who tarnish themselves with *profano pagani ritus errore seu crimine*, as if the both terms were equivalent in this case.

---

23 *ThLL* 5.2, 818. The examples presented here point to the usage of *error* in these meanings by the Church Fathers, beginning from Irenaeus and Tertullian (the second century AD).

24 *C.Th.* 16.6.2; 16.6.3; 16.6.4.

25 The expression *error veterum* from *C.Th.* 16.10.20 may point out that the pagan *error* was mentioned by analogy with the *error* proper, i.e., heresy.

26 This *ars* had already been proscribed by Diocletian (*C.* 9.18.2, 294) and described as *damnabilis*.

27 Desanti 1995: 691 f. In a close affinity to the astrologers' "error" may also be the *prava confessio* of augurs and soothsayers (*augures et vates*) in one of Constantius II's constitutions (*C.Th.* 9.16.4). In the further three constitutions (*C.Th.* 9.16.8; 16.10.9; 16.10.12) the craft of divination is defined as a forbidden doctrine, in the same way as heresy is.

error

A. heretics: *C.Th.* 16.5.11.2; 16.5.13.2; 16.5.19.3; 16.5.20.4; 16.5.21.1; 16.5.31.2 = 16.5.32.3; 16.5.41.4[2]; 16.5.54.17; 16.5.54.16[2]; 16.5.60.2; 16.5.63.3; 16.5.63.5; 16.5.64.4; 16.6.2.2; 16.6.2.5; 16.6.2.5[2]; 16.6.3.2; 16.6.4.8; 16.6.4.15[2]; *Const. Sirm.* 6.15[2]; 6.19[2]; 6.26[2]; furthermore, *Const. Sirm.* 2.2[2] (on relegated bishops).

B. pagans: *C.Th.* 16.5.63.3; 16.5.63.5; 16.10.20.6; 16.10.20.20; 16.10.21.2; *Nov. Theod.* 3.64.

C. astrologers (*mathematici*): *C.Th.* 9.16.8.2; 9.16.12.2; 9.16.12.3; 9.16.12.6.

D. heretics, pagans, Jews, and astrologers: *Const. Sirm.* 6.26[2].

E. on apostasy: *C.Th.* 16.7.3.2[2]; 16.7.7.11.

The idea of leaving the path of the Catholic religion is also expressed by means of several other terms: ***devio***, ***pravus***, ***pravitas***, ***depravare***, ***depravatio***, ***perversitas***, ***perversus***. The verb *deviare* refers, as may be expected, to apostates[28] and heretics,[29] once, it is used to refer to both heretics and pagans.[30] The terms *pravitas*, *pravus*, *depravare* are reserved for heresy, whereas *perversitas* and *perversus* concern heretics and adherents of Judaism. Yet, in contrast with *error*, these terms are connected not only with errors of the non-Catholics. The *C.Th.* 11.7.3 mentions *perversi iudices*, who unjustly decide to use torture in tax-related cases. As regards the terms derived from *pravus*, there are even more of the non-religious meanings. Let us mention here those cases where the terms in question are applied to condemn Imperial officials (both judges and lower-ranking personnel) on account of their prejudiced decisions[31] and corrupt practices.[32]

devio, *devius*

abandoning the faith:

A1. on heresy: *C.Th.* 16.5.28.3 (*devio*); 16.6.3.2 (*devius*).

A2. on paganism: *C.Th.* 16.7.5.2 (*devius*); 16.7.7.4 (*devio*).

A3. on both heresy and paganism: *C.Th.* 16.10.13.4 (*devio*); *Const. Sirm.* 12.5 (*devio*).

---

[28] *C.Th.* 16.7.5: *qui fide devii et mente caecati sacrosanctae religionis cultu et reverentia descivisset*; *C.Th.* 16.7.7: *postquam a fide deviaverint*.

[29] *C.Th.* 16.5.28: *qui vel levi argumento iudicio catholicae religionis et tramite detecti fuerint deviare*; *prefatio Const. Sirm.* 12 makes a distinction between *devinantes* (heretics) and *ignari* (pagans), whereas *C.Th.* 16.5.52 states that the Donatists "have sacrilegiously withdrawn" (*sacrilege descivere*) from the Catholic Church.

[30] *universi, qui a catholicae religionis deviare contendunt* (*C.Th.* 16.10.13) – this sentence should be construed in the context of the verb *contendere*, indicating religious dissidents' stubborn refusal to accept and follow the right way.

[31] *C.Th.* 3.11.1; 6.29.1; 8.1.15; 12.1.61; 13.5.16.

[32] *C.Th.* 1.16.3; 7.13.9; 9.40.14.

B. literally (to deviate; straying off the path): *C.Th.* 8.5.25.3 (*devio*); 12.19.1.4 (*devius*); 13.5.33.2 (*devius*).

depravatio
A1. on heresy: *C.Th.* 16.6.4.15.
A2. on paganism: *C.Th.* 16.2.18.2^{2}.

depravo
A1. on heresy: *Const. Sirm.* 6.21^{2}.
B. perverting the imperial law: *C.Th.* 8.5.14.3^{2}; 9.45.5.18.
C. abuses committed by officials: *C.Th.* 1.16.3.6.
D. other: *C.Th.* 1.4.1.3; 12.1.1.3; *Nov. Valent.* 12.34; *Nov. Majo.* 6.104.

prave, pravitas, pravus
A1. on heresy: *C.Th.* 16.5.41.2; 16.5.41.4; 16.5.40.17^{2}; 16.5.52.14; 16.5.52.1^{2}; 16.5.58.3^{2}; 16.5.62.4; 16.6.4.14; 16.6.4.15^{2}; 16.6.6.5; *Const. Sirm.* 12.7 (heretics and pagans).
A1a. on augurs and soothsayers (*vates*): *C.Th.* 9.16.4.2.
A4. false accusations against clergymen: *Const. Sirm.* 10.7.
B. perverting the imperial law: *C.Th.* 5.15.17.4; *Nov. Valent.* 27.31.
C. abuses committed by officials: *C.Th.* 1.12.8.[1]; 1.16.5.2; 3.11.1.13^{2}; 6.29.1.6; 7.10.1.9; 7.13.9.3; 8.1.15.3; 9.40.14.2; 11.30.31.3; 12.1.61.3; 13.5.16.5.
D. other: *C.Th.* 3.16.1.2; 9.24.1.6; 9.43.1.9; 11.36.18.8; 13.9.5.2; *Nov. Valent.* 10.37; 31.21; *Nov. Majo.* 6.106; *Nov. Sev.* 1.8.

perversitas, perversus, perverto
A1. on heresy: *C.Th.* 16.5.5.7; 16.5.20.3; 16.5.58.3^{2}; 16.6.5.2^{2}; *Nov. Valent.* 18.25.
A3. on Jews: *C.Th.* 16.8.19.4; 16.8.24.6; *Nov. Theod.* 3.47.
C. abuses committed by officials: *C.Th.* 11.7.3.2.
D. other: *C.Th.* 8.18.3.4.

One more term to be mentioned here is ***scaevus***, indicating perversion and perfidiousness. It also comprises an "ominous" element and can be linked with the idea of *contagium* in two of the cases where it appears.[33] The term does not possess a distinct semantic field in the texts of the Code; it may be used with reference to perversions related to the heretics' faith as well as, for instance, perverted interpretations of Imperial laws. Just once, the term *scaevi* refers to the tyrant's reign.[34]

[33] *C.Th.* 9.40.17; 16.2.44.
[34] *C.Th.* 15.14.9.

scaevus, scaevitas

A1. heretics' perversion of faith *C.Th.* 16.5.19.1 (*scaevus dogma*); 16.5.43.9 = *Const. Sirm.* 12.20 (*scaeva religio*); *C.Th.* 16.6.4.15 (*scaevitas paternae depravationis*).

B. perversion of the imperial law: *Nov. Theod.* 9.6; *Nov. Valent.* 25.25.

D. other: *C.Th.* 3.8.2.3^{2} (bad intention); *C.Th.* 9.40.17.9 (*scaevitas* of the mores, referring to Eutropius); 15.14.9.9 (time of the tyrant's reign); 16.2.44.5 = *Const. Sirm.* 10.7^{2} (*crimen* of a clergyman's illicit extraneous liaison with a woman).

Part III: Synthesis

Chapter IX: Categories of enemies

As stated in Chapter I, the use of the language of invective always points to the speaker's hostility in relation to the person subjected to condemnation. Thus far, I have analyzed a number of elements of the language of invective as used in the sources of a specific nature, i.e., official documents of the Empire. The statement is formulated here on behalf of the ruling emperor and conveys his official position. The aggressive content present in such statements indicates the hostile relation existing between the legislator and those considered as targets of the invective. In consequence, if we were to ask the question who was officially regarded as enemy in the Later Roman Empire, the answer, as simple as it may seem, is that the enemies were those described in terms of invective in the contemporary official documents.

The listing of the elements of that language, as presented in the previous chapter, facilitates the next step, a sort of introduction to the conclusions section of the present study. Notably, it is now possible to identify the groups of "enemies of the Roman order," in reference to whom these expressions with negative content were applied. One may also be tempted to make certain distinctions among these groups of enemies on account of a variety of charges against them.

Sacrilegium

At the beginning, let us focus on the situations where some specific terms of invective are not evoked as much by the type of the enemies denounced as the type of the values being infringed. This value is primarily the Imperial law or, more broadly, all the things which are particularly associated with the figure of the emperor (for instance, property of the Imperial *res privata* or the emperor's image on coins). In the same way, the Divine law becomes an object of protection as well. In both cases, reference is made to the crime of *sacrilegium*.

Sacrilegium is a term used to refer to several offences. In the constitutions of the period, one cannot see any clear mention of *sacrilegium* as a "theft of a sacred object."[1] The offences defined as *sacrilegium* are of a different character. In those referring to secular issues, there is usually some common feature to be found, namely showing disrespect to Imperial laws.[2] This offence may also involve some extra penalty, in addition to the one ordinarily dispensed for a specific act. This additional penalty is mostly designated as *poena sacrilegii*. Antoni Dębiński, in his analysis of the relevant mentions, concludes that the punishment in question is a fixed penalty (even though it is not explicitly stated in the texts), not the one dispensed arbitrarily by the judge.[3] Yet some known laws expressly mention penalties for *sacrilegium* several times, and those are very different, e.g., capital punishment[4] and fines to be paid in pounds of gold.[5] Also *Const. Sirm.* 11 clearly indicates that (at least in this case) the penalty for *sacrilegium* could not have been excessively harsh, as it was to be followed by the *exilium* (exile, banishment) of the perpetrator.[6] Most evidently, the legislator differentiates among various penalties depending on the weight of the violation. There is nonetheless one common name for the offence, as each individual case involves the breach of the *sacrum* characteristic of Imperial constitutions. The motive can be found so frequently that even when it is not identified explicitly, it may be supposed it was precisely the violation of the Imperial constitution that was the reason for defining the act as a *sacrilegium*.[7]

This sense is in a close affinity with the third one, frequently found in the Imperial constitutions: violation of the Divine law, the orthodox

---

1 The sole exception here are only the words of Julian the Apostate's constitution *C.Th.* 9.17.5, according to which "our ancestors considered" grave violation as the crime "closest to *sacrilegium*" (*proximum sacrilegio maiores semper habuerint*).

2 Most of the constitutions indicate, directly or indirectly, that the crime of *sacrilegium* is the very violation of a specific constitution, regardless of its object (cf. Maiuri 2005: 149). In consequence, attempting to make a further systematization, depending on what the violated Imperial injunctions had exactly referred to, appears to be a pointless task. Such a systematization has already been made by Dębiński 1995: 121–145, Cañizar Palacios 2009: 137–138.

3 Dębiński 1995: 159–161.

4 *C.Th.* 9.23.1, where the death penalty is designated as *sacrilegii sententia*; *C.Th.* 13.11.1.

5 *C.Th.* 15.1.27 – in this case, it is clearly stated that the said 10 pounds of gold is added as a penalty for *sacrilegium* in addition to the required return of the unlawfully expended amount; *Nov. Valent.* 3 – 25 pounds of gold; *Nov. Valent.* 27 – 30 pounds of gold.

6 *post debitae ultionis acrimoniam, quae erga sacrilegos iure promenda est, exilio perpetuae deportationis utantur.*

7 Cf. *sacrilegium*: *C.Th.* 6.5.2.5; 6.29.9.3; 6.35.13.9; 7.4.30.8; 7.8.10.8; 10.10.16.4; 10.10.24.6; 11.29.5.8; 11.30.6.5; 16.2.47.4 = *Const. Sirm.* 6.12[2]; *C.Th.* 16.5.7.19; *Nov. Theod.* 17.1.22; *Nov. Valent.* 3.45; *sacrilegus*: *C.Th.* 8.11.4.7; 11.28.10.1[2]; 13.4.4.13; 15.1.27.7; 16.4.4.2; 16.9.3.6; *Const. Sirm.* 16.18[2]; *Nov. Theod.* 18.19; *Nov. Valent.* 27.51.

Christian religion.[8] Apparently, *sacrilegium*, which is mentioned in the Late Antique constitutions dealing with religious issues, is not derived from the concept of "stealing a sacred object" (despite the fact that the process of transferring this sense of *sacrilegium* on to the theft of church property had already taken place in Late Antiquity[9]), but exactly from the analogy between infringements of the inviolability of the Imperial and Divine laws.[10] This type of *sacrilegium* is attributed to those who transgress against the sanctity of Sunday as well as that of church asylum, but above all – non-Catholics. Still, one could wonder if in the latter case the adjective and the noun *sacrilegus*, in particular, are used as terms of invective, considering the fact that not only heretical gatherings, pagan offerings, or the heretical doctrine, but also even the heretics as individuals are thus defined. On the other hand, *Nov. Valent.* 18 clearly points out that the Manichaeans are to be subjected to *poenas, quas in sacrilegos iura sanxerunt* – "the penalties which the laws have sanctioned against persons guilty of sacrilege." At least in this case, the use of *sacrilegus* is clearly related to the classification of the offence as *sacrilegium* and the application of *poena sacrilegii*. Accumulation of various disparate provisions by Justinian's compilers in the chapter *C.J.* 9.29 *De crimine sacrilegii* (offences against the Catholic religion, questioning Imperial appointments, undertaking any employment at the governor's *officium* in one's native province without the emperor's permission) makes it clear that in all the cases reference was made to the same offence.[11]

---

8 *Sacrilegium*: *C.Th.* 16.2.25.2; 16.2.31.1 = *Const. Sirm.* 14.33; *C.Th.* 16.5.6.8; 16.6.4.11; 16.6.4.17; 16.7.3.8[2]; 16.7.7.7; *Const. Sirm.* 13.6; *sacrilegus*: *C.Th.* 2.8.18.5 = 8.8.3.1[2] = 11.7.13.4; 9.45.4.9; 16.5.52.4; 16.5.8.5; 16.5.20.2; 16.5.40.18[2]; 16.5.41.6[2]; 16.5.52.17; 16.5.53.1; 16.5.63.4; 16.5.66.6; 16.7.7.2; 16.8.7.2; 16.8.18.3; 16.10.7.2; 16.10.11.6; 16.10.19.6[2]; *Const. Sirm.* 12.1[2]; *Nov. Valent.* 18.15; 23.8; *Nov. Majo.* 6.37.

9 Mordek 1987: 457.

10 It can be seen at *C.Th.* 16.2.25, which almost certainly had been, in its original form, one with *C.Th.* 16.1.2 (Di Mauro Todini 1990: 120–121, note 8; more sceptically, Noethlichs 1971: 132). The constitution states that "those persons who through ignorance confuse or through negligence violate and offend the sanctity (*sanctitas*) of divine law (*lex divina*) commit sacrilege" (*Qui divinae legis sanctitatem aut nesciendo confudunt aut neglegendo violant et offendunt, sacrilegium committunt*). The key to the understanding of this text is the term *lex divina*, which might have also referred to the Imperial law. Still, it is the *C.Th.* 16.1.2 that makes a distinction between our (*nostrae*) and Divine (*divinae*) penalties, and also refers to the orthodox Christian religion as *lex*. It can be assumed then that with the statement cited above the legislator had consciously built an analogy between the offences against the Imperial and Divine laws. At *Const. Sirm.* 11, the term *sacrilegium* is applied in reference to *temeraria praesumptio* perpetrated *in iniuriam ecclesiarum nostrique praecepti* ("to the injury of the Church and of Our regulation").

11 The infringement of the Imperial and Divine law is indicated by *sacrilegus*: *C.Th.* 16.2.2.3; 16.2.40.13 = *Const. Sirm.* 11.8[2].

Except for just one case where *sacrilegium* is applied in a clearly metaphorical sense, as a term of invective,[12] all the other instances of *sacrilegium* can be considered as violations of the *sacrum* of the Imperial authority, as it is in the case of acting in overt defiance of the Imperial law. The same designation can also be applied to the crime of *maiestas*[13] – due to the inviolability of the Imperial authority being infringed, or the crime of coinage counterfeit[14] – as it is a grave offence against the image of the reigning ruler. Another noteworthy situation, and similarly perceived as a case of *sacrilegium*, is any deliberation over Imperial appointments.[15] Other offences indirectly against the emperor are: failing to honour the hierarchy of offices,[16] violating Imperial constitutions,[17] exorting additional payments by tax collectors,[18] and tax evasion attempts.[19]

Interestingly, all these cases of *sacrilegium* may entail the use of some characteristic invective. As regards acts committed against the Imperial and Church values, "violation" (*violatio*) is the case.[20] The attitude of the person acting in defiance of the Imperial law is commonly described as *audacia* (*temeritas*, *praesumptio*). This particular invective is definitely most often used in reference to the situation when the *sacrum* of the Imperial law is violated, which only sporadically is explicitly called *sacrilegium*.[21] Less

---

12 At *C.Th.* 11.36.4, the legislator replaces *adulteres* ("adulterers") with the descriptive expression *sacrilegii nuptiarum* ("sacrilegious violators of marriage"). The harsh tone of this phrase is meant to justify the penalty being made equal with that meted out to the *parricidi*.

13 *C.Th.* 9.38.3.3; 9.42.6.4.

14 *C.Th.* 9.23.1.2; 9.38.6.10

15 *C.Th.* 1.6.9.2.

16 *C.Th.* 6.24.4.3.

17 *C.Th.* 10.10.16.1.

18 *Nov. Valent.* 7.1.16.

19 *C.Th.* 13.11.1.3.

20 Violation of the Imperial law: *C.Th.* 1.9.1.14; 1.15.16.3; 6.4.22.16; 6.23.4.10; 6.35.13.9 (in combination with *sacrilegium*); 7.4.30.[8] (*sacrilegium*); 7.8.13.4; 7.8.5.1²; 7.9.1.4; 8.1.16.5; 8.7.16.12; 8.11.3.2²; 8.11.4.8 (*sacrilega dissimulatio*); 9.30.2.5; 10.10.15.4; 10.10.24.6; 11.16.1.4; 11.30.8.16; 11.30.29.5²; 11.30.60.5; 12.1.176.8; 13.5.5.8; 14.11.1.4; 14.16.1.5²; 15.5.3.6; 15.5.3.6; 16.2.42.16; 16.5.66.6²; 16.8.14.9; 16.8.20.8; 16.9.4.1²; *Nov. Valent.* 17.36. Other acts against Imperial values: *C.Th.* 10.1.9.2 (*res privatae*); 15.1.25.5 (public ornaments on private houses); *Nov. Theod.* 24.23 (money – *sacrae pecuniae*); *Nov. Valent.* 17.25 (*ausibus enim talibus fides et reverentia nostri violatur imperii* – on bishop Hilary's disobedience to the Pope; here – projection from the Church on to the state). By analogy with the Imperial law – violation of the principles of the Catholic religion: *C.Th.* 16.2.25.2 (*sacrilegium*); 16.2.34.2; 16.5.6.6² (of the Holy Spirit); 16.6.5.2; 16.7.3.7²; 16.10.12.5; *Nov. Majo.* 11.19.

21 Only the constitutions directly linking *audacia* with the breach of a specific constitution: *C.Th.* 4.22.2.6; 6.18.1.5–6; 6.27.11.3; 6.29.5.6; 6.29.12.5; 6.35.13.8 (*sacrilegium*); 7.4.30.6 (*sacrilegium*); 7.8.5.1²; 8.1.16.7; 8.2.3.4; 8.4.30.11; 8.5.30.4; 8.5.54.5; 8.5.57.3; 8.5.66.6;

frequently, but still beyond any doubt, acting against the *lex Dei* is described as *audacia*.[22]

It is not very difficult to explain why the most frequently protected value is the Imperial law just being issued. The legislator thus communicates a clear message: while the breaking of a given regulation is always a criminal offence, now that it is reissued as a new edict the violation becomes an act of flagrant insolence towards the emperor – and as such it is often subject to a more severe punishment. But still any act of disregard for the Imperial law, or any act perpetrated in defiance of Imperial values or against the Church, deserves being designated as *audacia*. In this way, those who dare to commit such an offence are considered equally with the enemies of the state, already regarded as the *audaces* in the late Roman Republic.

It is notable that such efforts are focused on protecting not so much the order as enforced by the law but the law in itself, invested with a peculiar sense of inviolability, "sanctity" resting on either the "sanctity" of the Imperial authority or, in the case of Divine law, of God Himself. Consequently, a great part of the invective present in our source material serves, in effect, the purpose of denouncing the very fact of breaking the law, without entering into the content thereof.

Hostes rei publicae

Even though the *sacrum* related to the emperor and the Christian religion turn out to be so close to each other, the legislator makes a clear distinction between the enemies of the state and those of the Church. It can be seen in the division into *hostes* and *inimici*. The former term has a fairly limited range of usage, only where direct confrontation between the Roman state and its external or domestic enemies (*hostes publici*) takes place, whereas when enemies of the Church are mentioned, the term *inimicus* is applied. As we shall see, sets of invectives used to denounce the adversaries of the Church and the state are different as well. Nonetheless, we should make some further distinction here to identify various categories of *hostes*.

8.8.1.3; 8.8.2.3–4; 8.8.4.6; 9.38.9.4; 10.19.9.6; 10.26.1.10; 11.7.10.3; 11.14.2.4; 11.30.11.7; 12.1.9.3; 12.1.176.8; 12.1.182.2; 12.1.188.6; 12.6.32.10[2]–11[2],15[2]; 14.16.3.8; 16.4.2.1[2]; 16.5.8.3; 16.5.51.4 = 16.5.56.1[2]; 16.8.1.4; 16.8.10.4; 16.10.2.3; *Const. Sirm.* 6.3[2]; *Nov. Theod.* 5.1.25; 10.1.37; 18.19; 20.24; 24.23; 24.53; *Nov. Valent.* 6.1.2; 27.52.

22 *C.Th.* 16.5.44.2; 16.10.11.6 (*sacrilegus*); *Const. Sirm.* 3.2[2] (*contra legem non minus divinas quam humanas*); 16.18[2] (*sacrilegus*); *Nov. Majo.* 11.6.

The obvious enemies of the Roman Empire, as attested in the constitutions, are **barbarians**[23] – as a general rule, they are referred to as *hostes*, usually without any adjective. Similarly, the situations where they appear are ordinarily those connected with direct confrontation and conflict, less frequently references are made to trade relations with barbarians, and even then the legislator is concerned with restrictions imposed on trading with potential enemies.[24] Although the extant constitutions may be usually assigned to specific historical events,[25] all of them do not even begin to depict the real significance of alien invasions for the history of the Later Roman Empire. Still, they make it possible to notice that the Roman authority was particularly affected by two invaders, also on account of the fact that they had forced it to issue a number of constitutions aimed to resolve specific problems caused by the incursions in question. These dramatic events are: Alaric's invasion of Italy,[26] Vandal invasion of Africa, and the ensuing attacks on the coasts of Italy.[27]

The barbarians are represented in a definitely one-dimensional way. It is easy to understand why the only barbarian activity being castigated are raids (*incursus*) and devastation of the Roman territories (*vastatio*);[28] after all, the legislator is practically not concerned with any other aspects of their actions. It is still more curious that they are only guided by one motive described with the terms such as *immanitas*, *crudelitas*, *saevitas*, and, in particular, *feritas*.[29] In this way, reference is always made to the savagery characteristic of wild animals and contrasted with the classical *humanitas* also propagated as the ideal of the Imperial authority in the period of the Later Roman Empire. It is of course the most popular of the charges levelled against barbarians in Classical literature. Nonetheless, let us note that this is not the only one; for instance, it may be surprising that the concept of *furor barbaricus* is not mentioned even once in the texts of the laws under consideration.[30] The image of the barbarian in the source material is, for this reason, not so much a traditional one as reduced to the very essence of that tradition:

23 On the subject of the Romans' attitude towards barbarians, especially in the period of the Later Roman Empire, see Dauge 1981; Rugullis 1992; Chauvot 1998; Ohnacker 2003.

24 Stachura 2010: 615.

25 Cf. Rugullis 1992: 58–85, 89.

26 *Const. Sirm.* 16 = *C.Th.* 5.7.2 (408), 7.16.1 (408), 7.16.2 (410), 7.13.20 (410); *Nov. Valent.* 32 (451) – the latter constitution concerns of course the long-term effects of the destruction caused by the invasion.

27 *Nov. Valent.* 9 (440); 1.2 (440/441); 2.3 (443); 12 (443); 6.3 (444); 13 (445); 34 (451); 35 (452).

28 *C.Th.* 7.13.21.2^2; 11.28.12.2; 12.1.177.4; *Nov. Theod.* 15.2.10 (metaphorically); *Nov. Valent.* 1.2.1; 1.2.7; 34.6; 34.15; 34.18; furthermore, *depraedatio*: *C.Th.* 7.1.1.1; *Nov. Valent.* 9.6.

29 *Feritas*: *C.Th.* 5.7.2.2; 7.16.2.9; *Const. Sirm.* 16.7; *Nov. Valent.* 2.3.4; *saevitas*: *C.Th.* 9.12.1.10; *crudelitas*: *Nov. Valent.* 23.17 (metaphorically); *immanitas*: *C.Th.* 9.12.1.10; *Nov. Valent.* 12.12.

30 Ambros. Med., *Exameron* 3.5; Amm. Marc. 16.12.31.

as a dangerous alien invader whose motivating factors behind their actions are reduced to the cruelty seen as alien to the Roman culture and statehood (as the approved "severity" thereof is usually expressed by means of other terms).[31]

While the foreign invaders are defined in the Late Antique legislation as *hostes*, **domestic enemies**[32] are generally referred to as *hostes publici*. This particular expression is used in reference to Gildo, Stilicho, and Heraclianus. Much more frequently, usurpers are simply designated as *tyrannus*; the fact that synonyms or at least some terms very close in meaning are the case in point here is attested by the presence of another constitution against Heraclianus in the chapter *De infirmandis his quae sub tyrannis aut barbaris gesta sunt* (*C.Th.* 15.14). We should also be aware of the fact that the term *hostis* refers to an external enemy in the first place, as can be seen in the distinction between *externo hoste* and *domestica clade* in *Nov. Majo.* 1.

A list of usurpers consisting of the names which can be found in the relevant Late Antique documents (even though some of them may have played only a fairly marginal role) is quite extensive. Apart from those who were definitely intent on taking over Imperial power, such as Maxentius,[33] Magnentius,[34] Magnus Maximus,[35] Eugenius,[36] Gildo,[37] Attalus,[38] Heraclianus,[39] and John,[40] let us also mention several legitimate emperors vanquished by their political opponents (Licinius,[41] Constantine II[42]), as well as some officials who were accused of tyrannical tendencies only following their deposition (e.g., Stilicho;[43] also, as already noted in Chapter IV, the constitution against Eutropius represents certain parallels with the constitutions promulgated against the deposed usurpers[44]). It can be seen that although it would be impossible to recreate the history of the internal struggles for

31 *Acerbitas*, sometimes *saevitas*, see Chapter VI: 175–176.

32 Wardman 1984, Delmaire 1997, Escribano Paño 1997, Neri 1997, Leszka 1999.

33 *C.Th.* 5.8.1; 8.4.1 (or on Licinius, see Pharr 1952: 190, note 3).

34 *C.Th.* 9.38.2 (or on Gallus, cf. Pharr 1952: 253, note 5); 15.14.5.

35 *C.Th.* 15.14.6; 15.14.7; 15.14.8; 15.14.10 (or on Eugenius, cf. Pharr 1952: 438, note 16).

36 *C.Th.* 7.18.9; 15.14.9; 15.14.10 (or on Maximus, cf. Pharr 1952: 438, note 16); 15.14.11; 15.14.12.

37 *C.Th.* 7.8.7.

38 *C.Th.* 7.16.2; 9.38.11; 9.38.12.

39 *C.Th.* 9.40.21; 15.14.13.

40 *C.Th.* 16.2.47 = *Const. Sirm.* 6.

41 *C.Th.* 8.4.1 (or on Maxentius, see Pharr 1952: 190, note 3); 15.14.1; 15.14.2; 15.14.3; *C.Th.* 15.14.4.

42 *C.Th.* 10.8.4; 11.12.1.

43 *C.Th.* 7.16.1; 9.42.21; 9.42.22.

44 *C.Th.* 9.40.17. The fact that it can be found in the chapter *C.Th.* 9.40 does not contradict this, as it is there that the constitution against Heraclianus can be found as well.

power in the Later Roman Empire on the basis of the Imperial constitutions alone, there is much more factual information here than can be possibly obtained from the constitutions concerning barbarian raids.

The reason is that the deposed tyrant had left many more problems to resolve than a barbarian raid. Foreign invaders may have wreaked much havoc during their raids, yet after the tyrant's defeat there still remained the question of his followers and this particular issue had to be handled in one way or another. The most serious problem, nevertheless, was the fact that the tyrant had exercised his (usurped) Imperial authority over a specific territory throughout a definite period of time, which had not been limited to official appointments, but also involved promulgation of many legal acts, from constitutions to rescripts; moreover, verdicts and decisions were issued by state officials subordinated to the tyrant's rule. The period of the tyrant's reign, *tempus tyrannicum*,[45] thus singled out, was given special treatment after his deposition. It was necessary to decide which legal acts must be made null and void, which endorsed by the legitimate Imperial authority, and on what terms. The chapter *C.Th.* 15.14 deals with this specific question.

In total, the number of texts in various constitutions relating to usurpers is fairly limited. Nevertheless, it allows one to find out that the invective used to stigmatize tyrants would differ from the one depicting the ferocity of the barbarians. The tyrants are charged with *audacia*[46] and *furor*,[47] yet let us also take note of some rare terms, such as *infandissimus tyrannorum*[48] and *vafra mens*.[49] The usurper John is charged with the *invidia* towards the benefits of the time under the Theodosian emperors' rule.[50] In the context of the problems created by the *tempus tyrannicum*, the most noteworthy is the use of the words comparing the tyrants' reigns to calamities – *incendium* or *labes*.[51] Let us not forget that according to the contemporary view such disasters may have been manifestations of *contagium*. If my hypothesis put forward in Chapter IV is correct, the idea of *contagium*, with which the constitution against Eutropius is permeated, and which can be only marginally identified in the two constitutions issued after the deposition of Eugenius, was much more strongly represented in the complete texts of the constitu-

45 The phrase used at *C.Th.* 7.18.9; 9.38.2; in the title of *C.Th.* 5.8 – *tempora tyranni*.

46 *C.Th.* 15.14.6.2; 9.38.11.2; 15.14.6.3; 16.2.47.5 = *Const. Sirm.* 6.6[2].

47 *C.Th.* 7.16.2.9.

48 *C.Th.* 15.4.2.7.

49 *C.Th.* 15.14.7.2.

50 *Const. Sirm.* 6.4.

51 *C.Th.* 9.38.11.3; 15.14.12.1.

tions concerning tyrants. As a result, the combination of the two elements, *labes* and *contagium*, would have been, in these constitutions, similar to that at *C.Th.* 9.40.17.[52] The time of the tyrant's rule would have been thus perceived as the touching of its sanctity by an ignoble person, whereas Imperial decisions ensuing after the overthrow of the tyrant would have been intended to cleanse the Roman world of the related contamination.

The crime of ***latrocinium***[53] is only sporadically mentioned in the Late Antique legislation. However, in spite of such sparse evidence, it is still possible to obtain a certain general view of the brigandage practices of the period. Individual constitutions point to Isaurian,[54] Berber,[55] Italic,[56] and Egyptian[57] brigandage. They also show the tendency among *latrones* and deserters to join forces and form bands of brigands together.[58] That would give rise to Vincenzo Giuffrè's common sense deliberations on the two groups largely overlapping with one another: what else could a deserter have done to survive than resort to *latrocinium*, and vice versa, who would have joined the ranks of *latrones*, if not deserters?[59] While one could reasonably agree with the former suggestion, it must be noted that the ranks of *latrones* were apparently joined by individuals from a wider spectrum of society (e.g., shepherds were viewed as potential *latrones*[60]).

The invective directed at brigands is close to the one used to describe external and domestic *hostes*. In a way similar to barbarians, they are driven by savage cruelty (*feritas*),[61] but also, as in the case of tyrants, charges of *audacia*[62] and *furor* are mentioned.[63] If one could venture a far-reaching conclusion on the basis of our limited source material, it could be said that the brigands would tend to act in ways similar to barbarians, yet their wicked motivations were be more complex.

---

52 Cf. Chapter IV: 98.

53 McMullen 1966: 255–268; Hobsbawn 1969; Shaw 1984; Herz 1988; Shaw 1990; Sanchez Leon 1996; Neri 1998: 367–417.

54 *C.Th.* 9.35.7. On the Isaurian brigandage, see Shaw 1990; Lenski 1999; Feld 2005.

55 *C.Th.* 7.19.1.

56 *C.Th.* 7.20.7; 9.30.2.

57 *C.Th.* 11.36.31.

58 *C.Th.* 7.18.7; 7.18.14. Besides deserters and robbers, measures are also taken against those who provide them with shelter and protection; for more on the phenomenon, see Krause 1987: 218–223.

59 Giuffrè 1981: 216.

60 *C.Th.* 9.31.1. On the question of associations between *latrocinium* and cattle theft in the Roman Empire, see Herz 1988.

61 *C.Th.* 1.29.8.1.

62 *C.Th.* 7.19.1.17; and for deserters: *C.Th.* 7.13.10.4; 7.18.14.2; 7.18.11.7.

63 *C.Th.* 1.29.8.2.

Inimici ecclesiae

As regards enemies of the Church, the term *inimicus*, relevant for the relations between citizens, is mentioned. This deliberate choice on the part of the legislator seems to unveil a certain idea: the state enters into the relations between the Church and its opponents in a way analogous to disputes between citizens, thereby protecting the Church against the "enemies."[64] On the other hand, some orthodox believers may be guilty of specific *crimina*, such as the very participation in a heretical congregation, definite forbidden cult practices, or apostasy from the faith regarded as orthodox by the state.[65] This explains the fact that the invective used to censure them is varied as well.

Heretics in the Later Roman Empire are of course a heterogeneous group, as members of various Churches and communities outside the Church supported by the Roman state.[66] On the other hand, both the Church and the state define heresies as a certain single entity,[67] which allows the authorities to pursue a homogeneous policy towards them. The separate chapters created in the *C.Th.* and *C.J.*, with the constitutions aimed at heretics, are precisely the manifestations of that policy.[68]

Obviously, in the course of the further development of the Church and state relations, the structure of the group defined by law as "heretics" must have been gradually changing as well. This was due to the fact that not all the emperors had given their support to the same party within the Church. Nonetheless, with the advent of Theodosius I's reign, one could speak of the Imperial religious policy becoming more stabilized; the overwhelming majority of the anti-heretical laws can be dated to the period commenced by his reign.[69] The term "heretics" is applied in effect to members of various Christian churches as well as Manichaeans[70] (during Justinian's reign, the definition of "heresy" became

---

64 Stachura 2004: 233–235, cf. Chapter V: 122.

65 Stachura 2004: 262–265.

66 Noethlichs 1971; De Giovanni 1980: 81–112; 157–166; Bucci 1986: 409–417; Falchi 1986; Di Mauro Todini 1990; Dębiński 1990: 59–116; Gaudemet 2000; Stachura 2000a: 51–134; Noethlichs 2006.

67 For the methods of defining heresy by indicating the content of the orthodox teachings (e.g., *C.Th.* 16.5.6) or orthodox bishops (e.g., *C.Th.* 16.1.2), cf. Stachura 2000b: 65–68. The legislator's position is well attested by the statement that there are many names given to heresy, *sed una perfidia* (*C.Th.* 16.5.60).

68 *C.Th.* 16.5; *C.J.* 1.5.

69 Out of 66 constitutions under the chapter *C.Th.* 16.5, only 4 come from the time before Theodosius I's reign.

70 Although some of the constitutions appear to have treated the Manichaeans separately, cf. Stachura 2000a: 24.

extended to encompass all non-Catholics[71]). Conversely, there may be some doubt if the followers of the schismatic churches (i.e., not much different from the Catholic Church in doctrinal issues) were considered as "heretics" according to the law. When the anti-heretical legislation comes to encompass the Luciferians, Donatists, and Sabbathians, it is always accompanied with the explanation that in actual fact the issue is not only the schism but also heresy,[72] whereas the constitution *C.Th.* 16.5.28 (428) deals with the schismatic Novatians and Sabbathians more leniently than all the other heresies mentioned further on.

In accordance with the law, the heretics are given a very rough treatment. Heresy itself is designated as "crime" (*crimen* as well as the stronger term *scelus*).[73] Even the very act of professing a heresy may involve some consequences (usually restrictions and limitations related to the inheritance law) resulting from the heretic's expulsion beyond the Roman civic community.[74] Nevertheless, the legislator's attention is focused in particular on punishing those who violate the prohibitions against attending heretical services, ordaining clergymen, and performing rebaptism.[75] It is notable that death penalty is very rarely mentioned among the various punishments,[76] as the most frequent penal sanctions concern exile and fines. In view of this relative leniency, one should be aware of the fact that unlike pagans and Jews, the heretics were considered as offenders not in consequence of the prohibitions they may have violated, but due to the very fact of belonging to a heretical community.[77]

This conspicuous position of the heretics is also reflected in the terms of invective used in reference to that group. As I have noted before, both the term *haereticus* itself and a listing of designations referring to heresy may be treated as invective.[78] The listing of invectives applied to heretics may appear as particularly lengthy and varied, yet it is by no means a random

71 *C.J.* 1.5.18; *C.J.* 1.5.20; cf. Berger 1953: 359 ff.; Baccari 1991: 270.

72 *C.Th.* 16.5.28 (against Luciferians) explains that straying from the path of the Catholic religion even in a minor matter is heresy; *C.Th.* 16.6.4 refers to the Donatists as: the sect which prefers the name "schism" as they do not wish to be called "heresy"; *C.Th.* 16.6.6 explains that the Sabbathians, celebrating Easter not on the day when it is celebrated by the Church, act as if they worshipped a different Son of God.

73 Cf. Stachura 2004: 228.

74 Prior to *C.Th.* 16.5.65 (428), this provision concerned only Manichaeans (cf. Stachura 2007b) and Eunomians (cf. Stachura 2006a).

75 Stachura 2004: 252–253.

76 *C.Th.* 16.5.9, 16.5.36, 16.5.51 = 16.5.56; 16.5.53.

77 Stachura 2004: 257 ff.

78 See Chapter V: 134–137.

one.[79] Similarly to paganism and Judaism, heresy is called *superstitio*[80] as well. Yet it is only with regard to heresy that all the elements of the description of *superstitio – pravitas*,[81] *furor*,[82] *contagium*,[83] are consistently applied. Each one of these notions is of course expressed by means of a number of various terms (*pravitas* also as *error*,[84] *perversitas*,[85] *scaevitas*,[86] while in the case of "madness," there appears a derivative idea of "pertinacity" – *pertinacia*[87]). The heretics are treated as a menace to public order, which is expressed by referring to their gatherings as *turbae*.[88] They are regarded as "enemies," *inimici* of the Church and Christianity,[89] and, as noticed before, the state should undertake to defend these superior values in the struggle. They are also contrasted with the true religion through the use of the terms *perfidia*[90] and *profanus*.[91] Finally, let us note that in reference to them the emperor-legislator makes use of the verb *execror*, expressing the utmost revulsion.[92]

---

79 For a more extensive discussion, see Escribano Paño 2009: 47–51.

80 *C.Th.* 12.1.157.2 = 12.1.158.4^{2}; 16.5.5.7; 16.5.10.2; 16.5.34.1; 16.5.39.1; 16.5.48.2; 16.5.49.8; 16.5.51.2 = 16.5.56.1; 16.5.53.5 (*superstitiosus*); 16.5.54.5; 16.5.63.4; 16.5.65.8; 16.5.65.26^{2}; 16.5.66.1; 16.8.19.3 (with reference to the *caelicoli*, treated as heretics); 16.11.3.3; *Nov. Valent.* 18.2; 18.24; *Const. Sirm.* 6.20^{2}.

81 *C.Th.* 16.5.41.2; 16.5.41.4; 16.5.40.17^{2}; 16.5.52.14; 16.5.52.1^{2}; 16.5.58.3^{2}; 16.5.62.4; 16.6.4.14; 16.6.4.15^{2}; 16.6.6.5; *Const. Sirm.* 12.7 (heretics and pagans), moreover, *depravatio*: *C.Th.* 16.6.4.15; *depravo*: *Const. Sirm.* 6.21^{2}.

82 *C.Th.* 16.1.2.9; 16.1.2.9; 16.5.6.2; 16.5.6.13^{2}; 16.5.15.2; 16.5.24.2; 16.5.25.3^{2}; 16.5.25.5^{2}; 16.5.31.2 = 16.5.32.3; 16.5.32.1; 16.5.38.2; 16.5.60.5; 16.5.65.2; 16.6.2.2^{2}; 16.6.6.18; 16.6.7.1^{2}; 16.10.24.3; *Nov. Theod.* 3.6.

83 *C.Th.* 16.5.6.7; 16.5.19.3; 16.5.20.1; 16.5.26.3; 16.5.26.5; 16.5.40.7^{2}; 16.5.44.3; 16.5.52.17; 16.5.56.2^{2}; 16.5.62.4 = 16.5.64.3 = *Const. Sirm.* 6.23^{2}; 16.6.1.4; 16.6.2.4; 16.6.4.6; 16.6.4.11; 16.6.6.3; 16.6.5.2; 16.6.6.2; 16.6.6.3; *Const. Sirm.* 6.19^{2}; *Nov. Valent.* 18.11; 18.24; moreover, *funestus*: *C.Th.* 9.16.7.3; 16.5.19.4; 16.6.7.1; *dirus*: *C.Th.* 16.5.12.6; 16.5.54.5; *infaustus*: *C.Th.* 16.5.34.5; 16.5.64.4 = *Const. Sirm.* 6.26^{2}; *labes*: *C.Th.* 16.5.6.7; *pestis*: *C.Th.* 16.4.2.1^{2}; 16.5.44.3; 16.5.58.11.

84 *C.Th.* 16.5.11.2; 16.5.13.2; 16.5.19.3; 16.5.20.4; 16.5.21.1; 16.5.31.2 = 16.5.32.3; 16.5.41.4^{2}; 16.5.54.17; 16.5.60.2; 16.5.63.3; 16.5.63.5; 16.5.64.4; 16.6.2.2; 16.6.2.5; 16.6.3.2; 16.6.4.8; 16.6.4.15^{2}; *Const. Sirm.* 6.15^{2}; 6.19^{2}; 6.26^{2}.

85 *C.Th.* 16.5.5.7; 16.5.20.3; 16.5.58.3^{2}; 16.6.5.2^{2}; *Nov. Valent.* 18.25.

86 *C.Th.* 16.5.19.1; 16.5.43.9 = *Const. Sirm.* 12.20; *C.Th.* 16.6.4.15.

87 *C.Th.* 16.5.6.2; 16.5.7.16; 16.5.25.3; 16.5.53.6; *Const. Sirm.* 12.9; *Nov. Theod.* 3.18.

88 *C.Th.* 16.5.3.2; 16.5.6.5; 16.5.9.2; 16.5.10.3; 16.5.12.8; 16.5.38.5.

89 *C.Th.* 16.5.42.2; 16.5.51.2; 16.5.56.2; 16.5.62.2; 16.5.53.2; 16.5.64.2; *Const. Sirm.* 6.22^{2}.

90 *C.Th.* 16.5.6.8; 16.5.12.6; 16.5.15.1; 16.5.25.1^{2}; 16.5.37.5; 16.5.60.4; 16.5.63.1; 16.5.63.5.

91 *C.Th.* 16.1.3.3; 16.5.3.4; 16.5.4.5; 16.5.5.4; 16.5.7.18; 16.5.9.2; 16.5.24.3; 16.5.26.2; 16.5.30.9; 16.5.36.2^{2}; 16.5.41.4; 16.5.41.9^{2}; 16.6.6.2. *Const. Sirm.* 12.1.

92 *C.Th.* 16.5.7.12^{2}; 16.5.35.1; 16.5.51.3; 16.5.57.6; 16.5.60.2; 16.5.61.3; 16.6.6.11; 16.10.9.3; 16.10.23.2; 16.10.25.2; *Nov. Valent.* 18.4.

Among numerous heretical practices, the legislator turns his particular attention to rebaptism (in each Code, there is even a separate chapter dealing with the problem[93]). In certain heretical and schismatic churches, it was granted to those believers who had converted from other Christian confessions whose baptism was not recognized by the former. As a matter of fact, also the Catholic Church did not acknowledge the validity of the sacrament of baptism performed by the Churches with different baptismal formulas.[94] In any case, the practice of rebaptism in other Churches was considered by Catholics as an offence against the sacrament. This particular affront would lead to the response in the form of penal sanctions and many terms of invective. As could be expected, the generic accusation here is that of *contagium*, which is committed in defiance of the original and legitimate baptism.[95]

Followers of the traditional pagan cults had not been persecuted for their religious beliefs or directly forced to convert to Christianity under the Christian Roman emperors (at least until Justinian's reign),[96] but they were forbidden to make offerings to gods, even though the exact date of such a prohibition, its extent as well as the will to enforce it remain a subject of scholarly dispute.[97] Whatever the situation during the period of the second Flavian dynasty, the watershed moment came later on with the promulgation of the constitution *C.Th.* 16.10.12 (392), which placed a prohibition on blood sacrifices as well as offerings in any form in general. Nonetheless, at no later moment were any legal injunctions issued on prohibiting activities connected with the worship of ancient gods, except for the prohibition on celebrating the Maiuma feast, but in this particular case the reason for the proscription was the celebration's alleged indecency, not its religious context.[98]

---

93 *C.Th.* 16.6, *C.J.* 1.6.

94 Canon 8 of the Arles synod, canons 7 and 8 of the Laodicea synod, canon 7 of the Council of Constantinople.

95 *C.Th.* 16.6.1.4; 16.6.2.4; 16.6.4.6; 16.6.4.11; 16.6.6.3; 16.6.5.2; 16.6.6.2; 16.6.6.3.

96 In his constitution *C.J.* 1.11.10, the emperor orders pagans and their families to attend Holy Mass. On the anti-pagan legislation in Late Antiquity: Noethlichs 1971; De Giovanni 1980: 136–150, 170–172; Bucci 1986: 389–396, 403–409; Falchi 1986; Dębiński 1990: 117–173; Gaudemet 1990; Gaudemet 2000; Kahlos 2009: 64–66; 88–92; 106–108.

97 Particularly controversial is the mention in Eusebius (*Vita Const.* II.45), possibly confirmed by *C.Th.* 16.10.2 (341), on the Emperor Constantine's general prohibition on pagan sacrifices. Sceptical views with regard to the prohibition in question were expressed, among others, by Barnes 1984 (in a discussion with the critics of the view); a moderate position is held by Errington 1988 (the proscription was very soon repealed); for arguments in favour of the existence of this prohibition, at least in papyrii, see Bradbury 1994.

98 *C.Th.* 15.6.2.

Of course, by preventing the adherents of the traditional ancient religions from making any offerings, the most significant constituent element of their worship was taken away from them. Still, it does not change the fact that the Imperial law explicitly condemned only sacrifice as an offence, remaining neutral towards the pagans as long as they did not attempt to realize it. One of the constitutions even provides for a category of "peacefully living pagans," who "do nothing against the law."[99] In the case of heresy, such words would have been a contradiction in terms, as even "being a heretic" was in itself treated as a criminal offence. The "anti-pagan" laws, collected in Chapter 10, Book XVI of the Theodosian Code, essentially refer to two questions: pagan sacrifices and temples, but at the same time it is worth stressing that the latter were demolished primarily as places contaminated by pagan ritual offerings.[100] It should be also added that as a general rule practices related to pagan sacrifices were punished more severely than offences committed by heretics, i.e., they were punishable by death (under the Constantinian dynasty, and then again beginning from Theodosius II's reign).[101]

There is no doubt that pagans are described in terms of invective in the Late Antique constitutions. The name *pagani* itself seems to be contemptuous, while their beliefs are depicted as *superstitio* with no question at all.[102] Nevertheless, the individual elements of the description of *superstitio* – *pravitas*,[103] *furor*,[104] and *contagium*[105] – are evidently less ascribed to pagans than to heretics. This tendency would begin to change over time, as the anti-pagan policy was becoming more and more rigorous.[106] One should also note that the term *superstitio* often pertains not so much to pagans' religious views as sacrificial practices they would perform, that

---

99 *C.Th.* 16.10.24.

100 *C.Th.* 16.10.16; 16.10.19 = *Const. Sirm.* 12; *C.Th.* 16.10.25.

101 *C.Th.* 16.10.6 (356), 16.10.25 (435); *Nov. Theod.* 3 (438).

102 *C.Th.* 2.8.22.2; 9.16.1.7; 12.1.157.2 = 12.1.158.4²; 16.2.5.3; 16.5.63.2; 16.7.6.2; 16.10.2.2; 16.10.3.1; 16.10.12.16; 16.10.16.2; 16.10.17.3; 16.10.18.5; 16.10.20.1; 16.10.20.8; 16.10.20.17; *Const. Sirm.* 12.2; *Nov. Theod.* 3.64; *Const. Sirm.* 6.20².

103 *Pravitas*: *Const. Sirm.* 12.7 (heretics and pagans); *depravatio*: *C.Th.* 16.2.18.2²; *error*: *C.Th.* 16.5.63.3; 16.5.63.5; 16.10.20.6; 16.10.20.20; 16.10.21.2; *Const. Sirm.* 6.26²; *Nov. Theod.* 3.64.

104 *C.Th.* 15.5.5.12; 16.7.5.2; 16.10.2.2; 16.10.7.2; *Const. Sirm.* 12.9; *Nov. Theod.* 3.6; 3.63; 3.68; 3.71, moreover, *pertinacia*: *Nov. Theod.* 3.18; 3.63.

105 *C.Th.* 16.10.10.1; 16.10.11.5; *Nov. Theod.* 3.72; moreover, *funestus*: *C.Th.* 16.10.19.7², *Const. Sirm.* 12.1²; *Nov. Theod.* 3.64.

106 The laws as cited in the previous three notes are dated as follows: *C.Th.* 16.10.2 (341); 16.2.18 (370); 16.10.7 (381); 16.7.5 (391); 16.10.10 (391); 16.10.11 (391); 16.10.19 (407); *Const. Sirm.* 12 (407); *C.Th.* 16.10.20 (415); 16.10.21 (415); 15.5.5 (425); 16.5.63 (425); *Nov. Theod.* 3 (438).

is, the actual criminal offence.[107] The terms *perfidia*[108] and *profanus*[109] put the pagans in opposition to the true religion (as envisioned by the legislator).

While the very fact of being a pagan would not constitute an offence, abandoning the Christian faith in order to join a traditional pagan religion, i.e., committing the apostasy – did. As a result, an apostate was regarded as an offender, which would put him closer to the status of a heretic. Just like a heretic, he was to be excluded from the human community, which entailed specifically being stripped of the right to bequeath and inherit property by way of testament.[110] Apostatizing to pagan religions is particularly often defined as *profanatio*[111] and *contagium*[112] (just as rebaptism and conversion from Christianity to Judaism). Very frequently, considering a fairly modest body of texts dealing with the issue, the crime of apostasy is harshly designated as *scelus*.[113]

In the Later Roman Empire, **Judaism** was permitted but subjected to certain restrictions.[114] It also determines the possibility of the invective applied in reference to its adherents. To contrast it with the "true" religion, Judaism is described as *superstitio*.[115] Still, elements of the *superstitio* description are exceptionally rare in the criticism aimed at Judaism, as are any other terms of invective.[116] Exceptions are made to situations when Jews enter into some sort of negatively viewed interaction with Christians, e.g., selling Christian slaves,[117] attempting to persecute a Jew converting to Christianity,[118] or in cases of the conversion from Christianity to Judaism.[119] Especially in the latter case, the legislator depicts the Jewish religion using a full spectrum of terms marked by negative content, among which the most characteristic one is the charge of *contagium*.[120] In this relatively rare example of such criticism, the description

107 Stachura 2008: 182, note 18.

108 *C.Th.* 16.7.7.13; *Nov. Theod.* 3.76.

109 *C.Th.* 11.39.11.2 = 16.7.4.3; 16.7.4.11; 16.7.4.13; 16.7.7.10; 16.10.7.6; 16.10.10.4; 16.10.11.3; 16.10.17.1; 16.10.21.1.

110 *C.Th.* 16.7.1, 16.7.2; 16.7.3; 16.7.4; 16.7.6; 16.7.7; cf. Baccari 1996: 283 ff.

111 *C.Th.* 11.39.11.2 = 16.7.4.3; 16.7.4.11; 16.7.4.13; 16.7.7.10.

112 *C.Th.* 16.7.6.2; 16.7.4.10.

113 *C.Th.* 16.7.3.4; 16.7.3.3^2; 16.7.3.12^2; 16.7.3.14^2.

114 Noethlichs 1971; De Giovanni 1980: 117–136, 166–170; Rabello 1980; Bucci 1986: 396–402; Falchi 1986; Linder 1987; Dębiński 1990: 175–201; Martin, Namo-Pekelman 2008.

115 *C.Th.* 2.1.10.4; 12.1.157.2 = 12.1.158.4^2; 12.1.158.2; 16.8.8.4; 16.8.14.1; 16.8.24.1; 16.8.28.3; 16.9.4.6; *Const. Sirm.* 6.20^2.

116 *Perversitas*: *C.Th.* 16.8.24.6; *Nov. Theod.* 3.47; *furor*: *C.Th.* 15.5.5.11; *Nov. Theod.* 3.6; *obstinatio*: *Nov. Theod.* 3.18.

117 *Audacia*: *C.Th.* 16.9.5.2.

118 *Furor*: *C.Th.* 16.8.1.3.

119 *Scelus*: *C.Th.* 16.9.4.1^2.

120 *C.Th.* 16.7.3.3–4; 16.8.19.10,20; 16.8.22.7^2; 16.9.4.8.

of Judaism is close to that of heresy; expressions typical of the latter one also appear, namely *perversitas*[121] or contemptuous diminutives: *conciliabulum*, *conventiculum*[122] to denote congregations gathering for prayers.

On the other hand, Judaism was subject to protection from overzealous Christians; it was prohibited to disturb Jewish religious meetings and demolish synagogues.[123] The Christians attempting to carry out such actions are accused of *seditio*[124] – the expression is characteristic of religious disturbances, also in conflicts among Christians or in connection with demolishing pagan temples.[125]

Corrupted officials

A great deal of the criticism encountered in the normative documents of Late Antiquity is concerned with the state apparatus itself. It has been traditionally interpreted as an expression of the helplessness of the Later Roman Empire in the face of many abuses and corrupt practices of the state bureaucracy.[126] As noted before, the British scholar Jill Harries proposed a different interpretation of these parts. Through his critical view of real or imagined abuses of his officials, the emperor made it known that he never ceased to watch over the quality of the performance of the state apparatus in his control.[127] In this way, the hitherto commonly accepted interpretation of this motif was contrary to the legislator's intentions: he wished to create an impression of absolute control over actions of the administration. Expressions of that control are both severe penalties for abuses and stern words used to describe them.

Obviously, the picture that can be seen is very much influenced by the work of the compilers of the Theodosian Code. For instance, in reference to the *palatini*,[128] who were acting in the provinces without the governor's permission, only

---

121 *C.Th.* 16.8.19.4

122 *C.Th.* 16.8.1.6; 16.8.20.1; cf. Stachura 2007a: 42, 55, Escribano Paño 2008: 396.

123 *C.Th.* 16.8.9; 16.8.12; 16.8.20; 16.8.21; 16.8.25; 16.8.26; 16.8.27; 16.10.24.

124 *C.Th.* 16.8.22.2[2].

125 Cf. Chapter VII: 216.

126 Such a suggestion is mentioned repeatedly in Pharr's commentary to the English translation of the Theodosian Code; Veyne 1981: 355 even assumes the legislator's conscious helplessness, issuing declarations rather than laws; on corruption in the Later Roman Empire, see also MacMullen 1988: 137–170.

127 Harries 1999a: 59, 96–98.

128 The general name for those serving at the *officium* of the central administrative bodies, cf. Delmaire 1995: 122–127; Palme 1999: 102.

one charge is levelled – *audacia*.[129] Among the Novels of Valentinian III, two constitutions condemn the *palatini*'s practice of unlawful tax collection in the provinces.[130] The texts are rife with invective. The incriminated officials are accused of *depraedatio*[131] and *rapina*,[132] their obstinacy in disobeying the Imperial orders is castigated (*obstinatio*, *pertinacia*),[133] their actions are described as having been motivated by avarice (*avaritia*, *aviditas*, *cupiditas*);[134] moreover, their *audacia* is also condemned.[135] As all these charges are clearly redundant for the content of the disposition, it may be conjectured that similar terms of invective had disappeared from many extant constitutions in the Code. In consequence, the source material at our disposal ought to be examined and evaluated with particular caution.

One should be also aware of the fact that while some of the charges concern all the Imperial *militia*, others are specific for certain groups that are distinguished therein. An example of the criticism directed against the palace officials, *palatini*, has been already cited above. The distinction which can be well drawn on the basis of the results of our analysis, is primarily between the *iudices*, "judges," ordinarily provincial governors, and their subordinate personnel (*officium*). In reality, there would have been such a gap between the status of the former (dignitaries appointed to a given office for a brief tenure) and the latter (career officials attached to their profession) that they could be regarded as two distinct groups, and I shall only venture to consider them as a single entity for the sake of the subject matter of this chapter.[136] It is also possible to make a distinction between the civil and military officials.[137]

---

[129] *C.Th.* 1.5.13.5; 12.6.32.15².

[130] *Nov. Valent.* 7.1; 7.2. Described as *scelus*: *Nov. Valent.* 7.1.4.

[131] *Nov. Valent.* 7.2.17.

[132] *Nov. Valent.* 7.1.22.

[133] *Nov. Valent.* 7.1.3; 7.2.31.

[134] *Nov. Valent.* 7.1.8,16,21; 7.2.2,14,23.

[135] *Nov. Valent.* 7.1.4; 7.1.32.

[136] This particular distinction is illustrated by the two significant terms – *dignitas* and *militia*. The latter one is applied to any official in the Imperial service, from the provincial governor to his administrative personnel; whereas not all the office positions in the administration are associated with *dignitas*, and, in turn, not all the offices endowed with *dignitas* are distinguished by its external attribute, the belt called *cingulum* (cf. Noethlichs 1981: 22–23). A somewhat different view of the question can be found in Palme 1999, who contrasts the offices linked to *dignitas* with the *militia* proper, the latter name being applicable only to those serving at the *officia* (Palme 1999: 117); he also notes that the *cingulum* had been primarily a token of the *militia* (Palme 1999: 101). It should be also noted, nonetheless, that the gap between the official and his *officium* had diminished by Late Antiquity as compared with the Principate period (Rosen 1990: 283).

[137] It is controversial to what extent the distinction between the civil and military administrations in the Later Roman Empire is the result of the actual division into two paths, as regards the course of a given career, or only of the strict differentiation between the functions

On the other hand, it is not easy to differentiate between the functions performed by the *militia* and the decurions, especially on account of the fact that tax collectors (*exactores*) could have been appointed from the ranks of city councillors or personnel of the *officium*.[138]

Charges against high-ranking civil officials, in particular provincial governors, are most frequently related to their judicial function. Among various abuses being denounced are: passing unjust verdicts,[139] disregarding certain privileges of interrogated persons, such as immunity from the use of torture,[140] refusing the right to appeal from the verdict.[141] Extorting unjustified duties is also subject to criticism,[142] whereas appointing one's own servants to offices is described as *audacia*.[143] The behaviour of unjust *iudices* is at times also described with the verb *inquietare*,[144] while the motives for their actions are *insolentia*,[145] *furor*,[146] and *pertinacia*,[147] as well as variously expressed greed[148] and sloth.[149] Unjust verdicts and other wrong practices of the judges are censured as *pravitas*.[150] At last, let us note that diverse offences of both *iudices*[151] and subordinate *officiales*[152] are quite often defined as particularly serious crimes, which is indicated by the use of such terms as: *scelus*, *flagitium*, *nefas* as well as derivative words.

---

of the particular offices. The former position is advocated by Nesselhauf 1938: 48–49; MacMullen 1963a, and contested by Noethlichs 1981: 25.

138 Seeck 1909: 1544; Karayannopoulos 1958: 183–184; Jones 1986: 727–729 (cf. also the study Thomas 1959 on the development of the office of *exactor* in Late Antique Egypt). The proximity as well as the difference in status between the two groups are discussed in Palme 1999: 118–119.

139 *C.Th.* 1.16.3.6; 3.11.1.13²; 6.4.22.24; 9.27.6.4; 13.5.16.5; *Nov. Marc.* 11.

140 *C.Th.* 10.18.1.3; 11.7.3.2, 12.1.85.5.

141 *C.Th.* 11.30.30.8; 11.30.58.12.

142 *C.Th.* 7.10.1.9; 11.16.17.4; 12.1.61.3; 13.5.9.4; 15.9.2.4.

143 *C.Th.* 1.34.3.2.

144 *C.Th.* 6.35.8.2; 10.8.3.3; 10.18.1.3; 11.16.17.4; 13.5.9.4.

145 *C.Th.* 6.4.22.24; 11.7.3.2; 11.30.13.3.

146 *C.Th.* 12.1.85.5; 15.9.2.4.

147 *C.Th.* 11.30.58.12; 12.1.85.5; 12.1.85.10.

148 *C.Th.* 1.5.9.4; 9.27.6.4; 12.1.61.3 (it is not entirely clear here if *libido* does not rather refer to arbitrary behaviour); *Nov. Valent.* 28.14.

149 *C.Th.* 1.5.9.3; 1.10.7.7; 1.11.1.9; 1.15.17.4; 2.6.2.3; 6.4.13.17; 8.8.5.5; 9.1.7.3; 9.1.18.1; 10.1.16.12; 15.1.2.3; *Const. Sirm.* 12.10; *Nov. Theod.* 3.84.

150 *C.Th.* 1.12.8.1; 1.16.3.6; 3.11.1.13²; 7.10.1.9; 11.30.11.3; 12.1.61.3; 13.5.16.5 and *perversitas*: *C.Th.* 11.7.3.2.

151 *C.Th.* 1.14.2; 1.34.3; 2.19.1.6; 9.27.1.2; 14.15.6; *Nov. Marc.* 1.11.

152 *C.Th.* 1.16.7.8²; 8.4.15.6; 8.4.16.7; 10.10.16.7; 14.17.6.9.

Particularly emphatic charges are applied in reference to the crime of embezzling public funds – *peculatus*.[153] It is referred to as a felony (*scelus*, *flagitium*, *nefas*),[154] robbery (*rapina*),[155] and also likened to *contagium funestae pestis*.[156]

A different method of description is applied to the offences committed by *officiales*. They have, of course, fewer opportunities for independent decisions that may be considered as *pravae*.[157] In principle, they are jointly responsible for decisions of the judge they are subordinate to. Very often, in the cases where unlawful decisions are involved, fines are stipulated separately for the judge and his *officiales*.[158] On the other hand, *officiales* may attempt to obtain illegal duties from their intermediate position between their high-ranking superior and citizens, as attested by the above-mentioned constitution *C.Th.* 1.16.7. It is not concerned with some isolated incident only, as the Code provides more examples of the accusations of avarice – *avaritia*, *aviditas*, *cupiditas* with reference to that particular staff level.[159]

As I have noted in Chapter IV, the constitution *C.Th.* 1.16.7 compares dishonest officials of the *officium* to *latrones*. On a regular basis, similar charges are aimed at the tax collectors accused of *depraedatio*[160] and *rapacitas*,[161] as well as of causing unrest – *inquietas*.[162] Likewise, fairly similar are the charges against military officials, most frequently in the context of extorting undue benefits as well.[163]

Finally, let us make a note of the fact that the most frequently used invective in the Code, i.e., *audacia*, is not only aimed at dishonest officials, but it also protects their authority from the citizens' contempt.[164] Nonetheless, the same protection of the dignity of the office also appears in the context of the criticism referring to officials – namely, *audacia* is ascribed to those officials who infringe on the competence of other offices.[165]

---

[153] *C.Th.* 9.28.1; 9.28.2; the fundamental study on this offence is Gnoli 1979.

[154] *C.Th.* 9.28.1.3²–4²; 9.28.2.2.

[155] *C.Th.* 9.28.2.2,4–5.

[156] *C.Th.* 9.28.2.3.

[157] *C.Th.* 9.40.14.2 (*ne diu apparitorum prava … venalisque pefidia … desaeviret*).

[158] Noethlichs 1981: 223–225; Rosen 1990.

[159] *C.Th.* 1.16.3.5; 1.16.7.6²; 1.32.2.6; 6.30.17.6; 7.4.32.5; 8.1.16.6; 8.10.2.8; 11.4.1.6; *Nov. Majo.* 2.49; *Nov. Marc.* 2.32.

[160] *C.Th.* 8.10.3.2; *Nov. Valent.* 1.3.23; *Nov. Majo.* 2.31,37,44.

[161] *C.Th.* 13.11.11.6.

[162] *C.Th.* 7.20.2.21; 10.1.5.1–2; 11.7.1.5.

[163] *Rapina*: *C.Th.* 6.35.11.2; 8.1.10.4²; 9.27.3.8; *avaritia*: *C.Th.* 4.13.3.4; *Nov. Majo.* 2.49; *crudelitas*: *C.Th.* 8.1.15.2; *nefas*: *C.Th.* 7.4.21.1²; *Nov. Theod.* 24.35.

[164] *C.Th.* 1.14.1.9; 4.22.3.6,9,1²; 9.14.3.19; 9.40.16.19; 11.22.4.2; 12.1.173.4²; *Nov. Valent.* 7.3.2,4; *Nov. Majo.* 9.7.

[165] *C.Th.* 1.5.13.5; 1.6.11.2; 1.28.3.3; 6.22.7.6; 8.8.7.5; 11.7.17.4; 12.10.1.2²; 14.15.6.4; 15.1.41.6².

Criminosi

A great number of acts described in the previous subsections are obvious criminal offences within the system of the Later Roman order – to name only robbery and heresy. Yet it appears that another separate subsection ought to comprise all the "remaining" crimes which cannot be linked with hostile attitudes towards the Church or state, with acting against the *sacrum*, or perversions in the conduct of the Imperial administration. One could rightly expect that the constitutions dealing with penal issues should contain not just penalties but also multiple terms of invective directed at offenders. Is not the censure of the offender an opportunity to pay homage to the values, to communicate the emperor's self-presentation as a defender of those values, the public order and rule of law, and thus to attain the indirect goals of inserting invective in the normative documents? Yet our expectations would turn out to be confirmed in the actual evidence only in part. As a matter of fact, only certain specific crimes, such as magic and tomb robbery, are denounced by means of an ample variety of invective, whereas the other ones are accompanied by terms of invective on a sporadic basis, as if condemning them were so obvious that it would not require any further rhetorical justification.

It is obvious that magic (in its wider sense, encompassing also, or perhaps in particular, divination practices) would deserve the designation *scelus*, as it was perceived as one of the most serious crimes. It had been regarded as a very serious offence since the Republican period.[166] In the Late Antique constitutions, magic is almost always mentioned among the gravest crimes.[167]

The crime of magic becomes somewhat similar to that of heresy in Late Antiquity. It is most evident in the listing of soothsaying crafts, corresponding to the enumerations of particular heresies,[168] referring to *ars mathematica* with the heresy-specific term *error*,[169] entrusting the surveillance over adequate measures against this "error" to bishops,[170] as well as in the same treatment being applied to heretical and magic writings.[171] Another similarity, this time more evocative of paganism, also refers to the divination practices

[166] Desanti 1990: 11–139, Rives 2006. This commonly accepted view was strongly criticized by Fögen 1993: 54 ff. For the Late Antique laws against magic and divination, cf. Desanti 1990: 133–201; Fögen 1993; Haack 2003: 186–194, 199–209; Hano 2005.

[167] *C.Th.* 9.38.3; 9.38.4; 9.38.6; 9.38.7; 11.36.1; 11.36.7; *Const. Sirm.* 8.

[168] Cf. Chapter V: 142.

[169] *C.Th.* 9.16.8.2; 9.16.12.2–3.6; *Const. Sirm.* 6.26[2].

[170] *C.Th.* 9.16.12.

[171] *C.Th.* 16.5.34.

as *superstitio*.[172] Nevertheless, the character of the crimes is clearly different: those who engage in magic crafts are called *hostes communis salutis*[173] and *inimici humani generis*,[174] and they are represented, in consequence, as the enemies of the whole humanity, not of the Christian religion. In the constitution *C.Th.* 9.16.5 discussed above, there is even a reference made to disturbing the natural order of the elements.[175] It is no surprise then that the legislator perceives such a practice as *audacia*.[176]

The most significant charge against magic practices seems to have been the one expressed by the term *contagium*[177] and some derivatives (such as calling magic *labes*,[178] wishing the magicians were affected by *feralis pestis*,[179] or using the term *dirus* in reference to magic incantations[180]). If the magic is indeed perceived as interfering with the natural order, the charge of *contagium* appears here in its most basic meaning.[181]

Although in the Emperor Valentinian's Novel 23 the legislator attempts to indicate the religious motivations for penalties against persons **guilty of tomb violations**,[182] the tone of the entire constitution rather remains in line with the traditional view of this crime as a special kind of *contagium*. At least the Emperor Julian the Apostate is very much aware of this tradition,[183] yet it is also undeniable that the Christian emperors have a similar view of grave robbery – as one of the most serious crimes, along with magic practices, murder, adultery, and *maiestas*.[184]

The severity in dealing with this particular crime can be explained by the relevant passage in the aforementioned Valentinian's Novel, calling the perpetrator *violator quietis et luce ipsius hostis*.[185] Not only does he desecrate the mortal remains of the deceased resting in peace, but he also acts in contravention of the natural order through committing an act of *contagium*,

---

172 *C.Th.* 9.16.1.7.

173 *C.Th.* 9.16.11.3.

174 *C.Th.* 9.16.6.3.

175 This particular accusation rebounds on the Manichaeans (*C.Th.* 16.5.65), who had been, after all, also accused of magic practices (Procop., *Hist. Arc.* 22.25).

176 *C.Th.* 9.16.5.1–2; cf. Chapter IV: 89–91.

177 *C.Th.* 9.16.6.5; 9.16.11.2.

178 *C.Th.* 9.16.11.2.

179 *C.Th.* 9.16.5.3.

180 *C.Th.* 9.38.6.8.

181 Cf. Chapter VII: 200.

182 De Visscher 1963: 139–158.

183 *C.Th.* 9.17.5.

184 *C.Th.* 3.16.1; 9.38.3; 9.38.7; 9.38.8; *Const. Sirm.* 8. Designated as *scelus* in *C.Th.* 9.17.3.3; 9.38.8.9; *Nov. Valent.* 23.19, 35.

185 *Nov. Valent.* 23.26.

contaminating the world of the living with the ashes of the dead (*defunctorum cineres*).[186] Particularly horrifying is the case of clergymen who touch the holy altars with their hands stained with the ashes from the graves they had previously violated and robbed.[187] This is not a view that could be found only in this one constitution of Valentinian III, as preserved in full and very rich in rhetorical figures. Also, Constantius II makes the charge concerning those who take the construction materials from tombs and reuse them in building their houses – *et sepultos spoliant destruendo, et vivos polluunt fabricando*.[188]

The amount of invective used in reference to the offenders guilty of sepulchral violations is astonishing indeed; the "accumulation" is incomparable with any other offence, perhaps except for penal provisions on religious issues. They are charged with *audacia*[189] and *furor*,[190] while their acts are called *piaculum*;[191] besides, they are described in the terms close to religious offenders, although the foundations of the description are completely different as this is the case of drawing on the idea of *superstitio*. Only this crime, alongside the religious offences, deserves the adjective *execrabilis*,[192] expressing the Emperor's utmost outrage. This act is beneath the dignity of a civilized man, as expressed by the charge of *immanitas*[193] and the phrase *barbara et vesana crudelitas*.[194] On the other hand, the proper name of the crime (*violatio sepulchri*) contains the element of *violatio*, characteristic of the description of a violent act. Both *audacia* (applied, in case of the criminal offences, most frequently to violent crimes[195]) and *furor* may refer to the *violatio* in question.[196]

As noted in one of the previous chapters, the term *scelus* may be applied to all serious crimes. Still, apart from magic and tomb robbery, it is mostly **sex crimes** that involve the use of the elaborate invective expressed by means of a wide variety of terms.[197] It is possible to notice a certain gradation among them: homo-

186 *Nov. Valent.* 23.6.

187 *Nov. Valent.* 23.20–24.

188 *C.Th.* 9.17.4.3. The term *contagium* in the context of this crime: *C.Th.* 9.17.2.8,21; 9.17.4.3; 9.17.5.4; 9.38.6.5; *Nov. Valent.* 23.7,21,25,33 (*dirus*).

189 *C.Th.* 9.17.2.8; *C.Th.* 9.17.5.1; *Nov. Valent.* 23.6,8,29,31.

190 *Nov. Valent.* 23.4.17.

191 *C.Th.* 9.17.2.8; 9.17.5.4; *Nov. Valent.* 23.18 (*inexpiabilis*).

192 *Nov. Valent.* 23.36.

193 *C.Th.* 9.38.7.5; 9.38.8.10.

194 *Nov. Valent.* 23.17.

195 Cf. Chapter VI: 159.

196 *Nov. Valent.* 23.4 describes a grave robber as "driven into crime by madness," in a similar way to the description of *parricidium* in *C.Th.* 9.38.6: *parricidiali furore raptus*.

197 Ankum 1985; Rilinger 1988: 170–178; Robinson 1995: 54–73; Arjava 1996; Rizzelli 1997; Mentxalca 1998; on the Constantinian legislation concerning *adulterium*, see Venturini 1988.

sexual relations and incest are censured more harshly than common adultery.[198] The latter is described primarily as a contamination of purity, i.e., *contagium*.[199] Some interesting metaphors can also be found, drawing a comparison between this crime and *sacrilegium*[200] or "invading" (*invadere*) the marital bed.[201]

A similar array of invective can be seen where the question of forbidden marriage is concerned. Roman law proscribed relationships between members of the senatorial class or *curiales* and "unworthy" persons.[202] Not only are penal sanctions provided to prevent such marriages, but also they are depicted as *contagium*[203] or even *scelus*.[204] On one occasion, such a marriage is described by the term expressing the most intense outrage, that is *execrabiliter*.[205] With a similar sense of revulsion, the adverb *abominanter* is used to depict incest.[206]

Abduction of a woman is one of the most serious crimes in the Later Roman Empire.[207] In a way similar to adultery, it is subject to gradation as well: kidnapping a virgin consecrated to God[208] or someone's wife[209] are perceived as the gravest cases of this offence. *Raptus* is described by means of a particularly rich vocabulary of invective. It can be explained by the fact that this crime combines elements of adultery and violence. In consequence, terms of invective typical of the description of sex offences (*contagium*)[210] as well as those relating to *crimen vis* (*violatio*,[211] *audacia*[212]) appear to be adequate, even though the offence itself did not fall within the category of *crimen vis*.[213]

---

198 See Chapter VI: 192, on the terms *scelus*, in reference to incest and homosexual relations. On the status of the latter in the Later Roman law, see Manfredini 1985: 267–271; Dalla 1987: 167; Cantarella 1999: 224–231; on the legal consequences of incest, see Misztal-Konecka 2007: 161–206.

199 *C.Th.* 2.1.3.4; 9.38.4.3; *Nov. Majo.* 9.5. Other sex offences: *C.Th.* 15.6.2.3; 15.8.2.16; *Const. Sirm.* 10.8.

200 *C.Th.* 11.36.4.7.

201 *C.Th.* 9.38.6.6.

202 Evans-Grubbs 1995. On the prohibition against marriages between highborn women and slaves, see Evans-Grubbs 1993: 140–154.

203 *C.Th.* 2.1.3.4; 4.6.3.[5]; 4.12.5.[4]; 12.1.6.2; *Nov. Marc.* 4.26; *Nov. Majo.* 7.6,8,19; *Nov. Anth.* 1.34.

204 *C.Th.* 12.1.6.13.

205 *Nov. Anth.* 1.40.

206 *C.Th.* 3.12.1.2.

207 Evans-Grubbs 1989; Haase 1994: 458–462; Puliatti 1995; Botta 2004.

208 *C.Th.* 9.25; *Nov. Majo.* 6.

209 *C.Th.* 9.24.3.

210 *Nov. Majo.* 6.50.

211 *C.Th.* 9.38.4.4; *Nov. Majo.* 6.48.

212 *C.Th.* 9.24.1.12; 9.24.2.4; 9.24.3.1^2; 9.25.2.1^2.

213 Harries 2006: 90.

As a result, the constitutions against abductors abound in instances of the invective language to an extent comparable only to those dealing with magic, sepulchral robbery, or offences committed by non-Catholics.

A specific type of invective is also aimed at criminal acts committed with the use of **violence**. As one of the constitutions in the Theodosian Code points out, various offences, including homicide, are subsumed under the category of *crimen vis*.[214] Yet the most frequent case in the legislation being considered here is where one of the parties to a dispute takes the contested property by force while the case has not yet been resolved in court.[215] Such acts are described by the terms *invasio*[216] and *violatio*,[217] as well as *furor*.[218] However, it is notable that among many criminal offences the charge of *audacia* is most often used with regard to this particular crime.[219] There can be no doubt that the above-mentioned violent resolution of the dispute is indicative of the disregard towards the judicial authority, hence referring to such an act as "insolence" is by all means adequate. As the above case of *raptus* clearly points out, the association between *audacia* and violence is no coincidence.

---

214 *C.Th.* 9.10.1. Cf. Harries 2006: 91–92.

215 Harries 2006: 92–99. This crime came to be tried in court according to criminal law only during the period of the Dominate. Cf. also Pottier 2012.

216 *C.Th.* 2.1.3.6; 2.26.1.3,17; 2.26.1.18; 2.29.1.4; 2.29.2.4^2; 4.18.1.2,8; 4.22.3.3; 9.1.1.3; 9.10.2.1; 10.10.12.3^2; 12.9.1.2; 16.2.28.3; 16.5.65.5; *Nov. Valent.* 8.R; 8.1.15,27,33.

217 *C.Th.* 2.4.6.2^2; 2.29.2.3^2; 3.1.1.2; 4.22.1.3^2; 4.22.2.4; 4.22.3.8; 9.2.5.4; 9.10.1.3,8; 9.10.2.1,2; 9.10.3.3,5,8,13; 9.10.4.2,4,8,10; 11.36.14.4,5; 16.2.31.22; 16.8.20.2; 16.10.24.8; *Const. Sirm.* 14.6^2 (= *C.Th.* 16.2.31); *Nov. Valent.* 32.16.

218 *C.Th.* 4.22.3.9; 9.10.4.6.

219 *C.Th.* 2.29.2.3^2; 4.22.3.6,9,1^2; 9.10.1.13; 10.1.15.4; *Nov. Valent.* 8.1.2,3,16,33.

Chapter X: Conclusions. The hierarchy of "enemies" in Imperial documents

There is still one more element to make this study complete. In the examinations of the source material so far I have generally omitted the quantity aspect, as long as making references to arguments related to the frequency of the application of a given term marked by a negative content had not been necessary for drawing conclusions as to its prevailing meaning. Yet this work cannot be concluded without asking the question: what was the extent of the phenomenon in question? Does the language of invective appear in the Imperial documents only exceptionally, or, on the contrary, are they perhaps filled with it? In Chapter IV, I presented examples of ten texts containing entire structures of invective, yet I was also aware of the fact that they were exceptions in the present source material. Two of those examples are especially instructive: an analysis of Theodosius' Novel 15.2 and Valentinian's Novel 18 has shown how much invective-laden language can be found exactly in those parts of the constitutions which the codification commission had been obliged to remove. It is now possible to draw some more solidly substantiated conclusions from the listing of all the enumerated terms present in the relevant research material. As a matter of fact, the terms I have listed throughout Chapters V–VIII, which can be recognized as marked by their negative contents,[1] appear in 737 constitutions of the Theodosian Code (29.3%), whereas they can be found in as many as 76 Novels (76%) and all the 16 Sirmondian Constitutions. It confirms my observation that the abridgement of the texts for the purpose of the Code deprives them of a considerable portion of their ideological content expressed through the use of the invective language.

[1] Of course, excluding the terms or meanings clearly neutral or positive, which are not cited in the listing. On the other hand, it is enough to refer once again to the analysis in Chapter IV to be able to find out that the list of the terms with negative content could have been made longer, especially by the words which take on negative shades of meaning within the context of a concrete text, and the terms only once or twice appearing throughout the source material in question (e.g., *serpo* in *Nov. Theod.* 15.2), which in consequence have not been subjected to further analysis.

Nonetheless, the greater part of both the constitutions in the Theodosian Code and the complete ones contains only some single instances of terms with negative overtones. Counting mentions of individual words is indeed a very precarious method of distinguishing constitutions with the presence of stronger ideological content, e.g., due to their very diverse sizes. In fact, counting words with no regard for their context may prove to be misleading.[2] With this particular caveat, I believe that it is worthwhile presenting the results of our statistical research with indications on what kind of "enemies" are the most numerous invectives aimed at. As can be seen, there are very few of such examples. If we set apart the constitutions which contain at least five instances of the relevant terms, it turns out that there are 24 Novels (24%), 9 Sirmondian Constitutions (56.3%) and only 77 constitutions of the Code (3.1%). It is also notable that the constitutions more "abundant" in terms laden with negative contents are concerned with a fairly limited amount of themes.

Among them, the most frequent are those which pertain to heretics (45).[3] It should be no surprise as I have taken into consideration the proper names of heresies, but also the terms *haeresia*, *haereticus*, and *schisma*, as marked by their negative contents. But even with these being removed, in Chapters 5 and 6 of Book XVI of the Code, there would still remain 19 constitutions with at least five mentions of other negative terms (26% of the constitutions present here).[4] Not as frequent in the distinguished group are the texts of the constitutions against pagans (15 – of which 11 also concern heretics)[5], with the consideration that the greatest number of the terms identified can be found in the constitutions aimed at many non-Catholic groups: heretics, pagans, and also, frequently, Jews.[6] In total, adding the *C.Th.* 16.8.19 against the *caelicoli* (treated as heretics) and the *C.Th.* 16.9.4 against the Jews selling Christian slaves, and individually

2 Cf. the invective in Fögen 1998 directed at Honoré, where the latter scholar's method is called "mass murder on texts."

3 *C.Th.* 16.5.5; 16.5.6; 16.5.7; 16.5.9; 16.5.11; 16.5.12; 16.5.13; 16.5.19; 16.5.20; 16.5.24; 16.5.25; 16.5.26; 16.5.32; 16.5.34; 16.5.38; 16.5.40; 16.5.41; 16.5.43; 16.5.44; 16.5.51; 16.5.52; 16.5.54; 16.5.56; 16.5.57; 16.5.58; 16.5.59; 16.5.60; 16.5.62; 16.5.63; 16.5.64; 16.5.65; 16.5.66; 16.6.6.2; 16.6.4; 16.6.6.5; 16.6.6; 16.6.7; 16.7.3; 16.10.13; 16.10.24; *Const. Sirm.* 6; 12; 14; *Nov. Theod.* 3; *Nov. Valent.* 18.

4 *C.Th.* 16.5.5; 16.5.6; 16.5.7; 16.5.19; 16.5.24; 16.5.26; 16.5.41; 16.5.51; 16.5.54; 16.5.56; 16.5.57; 16.5.58; 16.5.63; 16.5.65; 16.5.66; 16.6.6.2; 16.6.4; 16.6.6; 16.6.7.

5 *C.Th.* 16.5.43; 16.5.62; 16.5.63; 16.5.64; 16.7.3; 16.7.7; 16.10.12; 16.10.13; 16.10.20; 16.10.21; 16.10.24; *Const. Sirm.* 6; 12; 14; *Nov. Theod.* 3. Only *C.Th.* 16.7.7; 16.10.12; 16.10.20, and 16.10.21 refer to pagans exclusively; in *C.Th.* 16.7.3; 16.10.24; *Const. Sirm.* 6, and *Nov. Theod.* 3 Jews are mentioned alongside heretics and pagans.

6 The record number can be found in *Nov. Theod.* 3, with 46 relevant words; next in line are *Const. Sirm.* 6 (25); *Const. Sirm.* 12 (25); among the constitutions of the Theodosian Code, let us mention *C.Th.* 16.7.3 (15) and *C.Th.* 16.10.24 (11 terms).

counting those which concern many religious groups simultaneously, makes up a set of 51 constitutions against non-Catholics in the distinguished group.

The fact that among the completely preserved texts there are quite a number of those concerned with the matters of the Church (Sirmondian Constitutions) explains why there are many constitutions referring to the relations between the state and the Church in the collection of the texts I have selected. It is notable that only one of the constitutions in this matter stands out due to its particularly harsh language – *Nov. Valent.* 17, dealing with the specific case of a rebellious bishop guilty of inciting riots.

Following the constitutions referring to penalties for offences connected with religion, another group we have distinguished in the collection is comprised of the constitutions against certain criminal offences; among them, *latrocinium*,[7] desertion,[8] *invasio* of disputed property[9] and other violent crimes,[10] magic,[11] violation of a tomb,[12] abduction of a woman,[13] procurement[14] and adultery[15] – 19 constitutions, in all. Of course, this listing is random to a certain extent, as it is clear that there are also long series of terms with negative contents directed at false accusers in Constantine's edict *De accusatiobus*[16] and homosexuals in one of Theodosius' constitutions, the latter known from the *Collatio legum Mosaicarum et Romanorum* 5.3,[17] whereas the fragments of these constitutions in the Theodosian Code (*C.Th.* 9.5.1[18] and *C.Th.* 9.7.6[19]) do not contain many instances of negative vocabulary. This list would basi-

7 *C.Th.* 1.29.8.

8 *C.Th.* 7.18.4; 7.18.11.

9 *C.Th.* 4.18.1; 4.22.2; 4.22.3; *Nov. Valent.* 8.1.

10 *C.Th.* 9.10.1; 9.10.4; 9.14.3.

11 *C.Th.* 9.16.4; 9.16.5; 9.16.6.

12 *C.Th.* 9.17.2; *Nov. Valent.* 23 (as many as 34 terms!).

13 *C.Th.* 9.24.1 (the crime's proper name is repeatedly mentioned there); 9.24.3; *Nov. Majo.* 6 (fragment).

14 *Nov. Theod.* 18. On the legislation concerning procurers, see Formigoni Candini 1990; Rizzelli 1990; Neri 1998: 213–223.

15 *Nov. Majo.* 9.

16 *CIL* 5.2781 (= *FIRA* 1: 458–461): 19 *temeritas* (on groundless accusations); 27 *scelus* (on informers); 27 *audacia* (ditto); 29 *tempto* (on accusations against owners by their slaves or against patrons by freedmen); 31 *atrox* (ditto); 31 *audacia* (ditto); 34 *audacia* (ditto); 44 *ausus* (preparing *libelli famosi*); 45 *temeritas* (ditto). On the rhetoric of the edict, see Rivière 2002: 131–137.

17 *Coll.* 5.3 (= *FIRA* 2: 557) 4 *contaminatio*; 4 *foedo*; 9 *flagitium*; 11 *flagitium*, 12 *immanitas*, 14 *expio*.

18 The complex question of the affinity between the edict *De accusationibus* and *C.Th.* 9.5.1 is related by Matthews 2000: 254–270, though without any final conclusion, and only indicating that the constitution from the Theodosian Code had not been drawn up, in all certainty, on the basis of the known version of the edict.

19 Probably, *Coll.* 5.3 and *C.Th.* 9.7.6 had been drawn up on the basis of different versions of the same constitution, cf. Matthews 2000: 279.

cally confirm my observation from Chapter IX: only certain specific offences warranted the legislator's need to apply the language of invective. There are also greater numbers of terms charged with negative content in the three amnesty constitutions[20] and also another one,[21] in which all the most serious crimes are enumerated.

The third group is composed of abuses of authority committed by officials and tax collectors. 13 texts can be assigned to this group.[22] Not many, considering that – as Karl Leo Noethlichs estimates – about 900 constitutions of the Theodosian Code deal with infringements of duties by officials.[23] Among them, only one concerns a specific official treated with hostility – the aforementioned *C.Th.* 9.40.17 regarding Eutropius. This is the only one that can be compared with the much more concise constitutions against the domestic *hostes*. On the other hand, the foreign enemies, i.e., barbarians, do appear in several constitutions we have noted,[24] yet they are accompanied with a fairly modest number of negative designations. It would be even difficult to call it a language of aggression in this particular case, as what can be found there is more like a brief note referring to the destruction caused by the enemy or to the existing threat.

This brief survey makes it possible to demonstrate what were the primary goals of the more elaborate invective in the texts of the Imperial documents. As regards the almost eight times more numerous cases when only one or several identified terms can be found in a given constitution, it is impossible to make a generalization other than the one employed throughout Chapters V–IX. There is no doubt that there may have been some occasionally random references to vices, or not necessarily intentionally used harsh expressions. Still, the consistent approach can be seen as well, e.g., in many references to the idea of *audacia* where the possibility of the Imperial constitution being disregarded is foreseen. It is impossible to balance the proportions between the deliberate and not-fully-intentional uses of the "offensive words," especially as in many individual cases one cannot possibly guess the intentions of the author. Nonetheless, one should be always aware of the fact that the ideological message of the text (which a specific negative term may have

---

20 *C.Th.* 9.38.6; 9.38.8; *Const. Sirm.* 8.

21 *C.Th.* 11.36.7 forbidding these offenders to appeal.

22 *C.Th.* 1.16.7; 2.1.3; 6.4.22; 9.28.2 (the crime of *peculatus*); 9.40.17; 12.1.85; 13.5.16; *Nov. Theod.* 24; *Nov. Valent.* 1.3; 7.1; 7.2; 27 (the fragment castigating the breach of law by an official); *Nov. Majo.* 2; moreover, the constitutions *C.Th.* 10.26.1 and *Nov. Theod.* 15.2 censure the cases of individuals unlawfully attempting to enter the Imperial service.

23 Noethlichs 1981: 228.

24 *Nov. Valent.* 9; 13; 34.

been a part of) was, in its principle at least, consciously formulated or assumed by the successive individuals involved in its creation.

Is it true then that in each particular case where a specific word marked by a potentially negative content can be found, there is indeed an invective (in our broad understanding of the term)? And is, for this reason, a statement of blame constructed here deliberately in all such cases (which, as a whole, constitutes a specific triangle among the person condemning, the one being condemned, and the audience listening to the statement)? Certainly, such an assumption would be a fallacy. But much more incongruous, even absurd, would be, in my opinion, perceiving in all of the relevant instances the language of invective as having been applied unconsciously. Let us recall the key statement that the ideological message of the Imperial documents was their significant objective, and thus the language of invective had been intentionally utilized as well for the purpose of its formulation.

This language, it seems, reveals a list of those to whom the legislator would have ascribed the role of "enemies" of the Empire's law and order. I would not argue, of course, that there should have existed any coherent thought behind the list, transmitted by the successive generations of Imperial officials. What is there is rather a certain general idea which may be found and identified thanks to the extant body of the Imperial documents. The list is not very surprising in itself; if anything, it is its priority order. The most sweeping range of invective is applied in order to target the heretics and, more broadly, all those considered as *inimici* of the Church. With no doubt, the case in point here is the influence of the language used in the religious polemic of Late Antiquity. The next one, but still figuring very prominently, are certain categories of offenders (not necessarily those one may have expected here – e.g., murderers and the guilty of the crime of *maiestas* are not included here) as well as officials abusing their authority. The domestic and foreign enemies seem to occupy more remote positions in the order of priority, perhaps owing to the occasional character of the critical situations they had caused, but in the case of barbarians – also due to the emotional distance to their actions maintained by the legislator (it is enough to compare the criticism directed at them with the one concerning the emperor's own officials). The language of invective, as present in the Imperial documents, reveals quite an interesting hierarchy employed by the authors to arrange the order of the emperor's "enemies."

The method I have chosen to distinguish the groups of "enemies" of the Roman order is entirely different from the one utilized by Ramsay MacMullen in his study. It is no wonder then that the listing of the enemies I have compiled does not tally altogether with the one encountered in his work. The language of the Imperial constitutions uses the harshest terms in reference to heretics and pagans, yet they are envisaged as "*inimici* of the Church," not as enemies of the state or the Roman community. The heretics are indeed, according to MacMullen's insight, "outsiders" to that community,[25] in so far as they are excluded from it on the strength of the Imperial law. Further positions among those affected by the language of aggression as used in the constitutions are occupied by perpetrators of certain offences, criminals, and corrupt officials. And once again, I do not agree with MacMullen's findings, as he assigns the status of "enemies" to magicians and brigands alone.[26] He also fails to notice that Imperial officials may be subjected to condemnation as well. As it appears, the American scholar has focused his attention, perforce, on the conspicuous and exceptional cases, while the present analysis makes it possible to single out those who were regarded as a threat to the Imperial order in the ordinary correspondence between the Imperial authority and state functionaries.

Let us now sum up the results of the present survey. In the methodology part, I have shown, with the aid of the modern research on the language of the constitutions, the actual role played there by the phenomenon of language aggression, which I have decided (very well aware of all the difficulties involved) to place within the tradition of invective in Antiquity. I have also adopted a method allowing me to examine the language in question. In the analysis part, I first demonstrated how the language of invective functioned as exemplified by a selection of 10 Imperial constitutions; next, I proceeded to analyze a set of terms marked by their negative contents, present in all the constitutions within the selected collections. As much as necessary, I have indicated their origin, various shades of meaning present in literary language, but in particular their semantic fields throughout the relevant material. It is my heartfelt hope that this research shall prove to be of independent value as a resource for scholars concerned with the studies of the Theodosian Code, Post-Theodosian Novels, and Sirmondian Constitutions, i.e., historians, Romanists, and philologists. Nevertheless, it has been my ambition to create something more than a mere resource book. This study has consistently attempted to reach a synthesis answering the following questions: which groups of "enemies of the Roman order" were stigmatized by the Late Antique constitutions, with what intensity, and how?

As it turns out, the most stigmatized group are heretics, described by a full range of terms indicative of *superstitio*. The offensive language is also used in reference to pagans involved in making forbidden sacrifices, and all the non-Catholics in connection with apostatizing from the state-supported Church. In the latter case, the metaphor of *contagium* is particularly readily used.

---

25 MacMullen 1966: 200–210.

26 MacMullen 1966: 95–162, 255–268.

Unlike the "*inimici* of the Church," enemies of the state are mentioned less frequently and the censure directed at them is less intense. It refers especially to terse descriptions of barbarians; in the constitutions concerning domestic enemies, certain elements characteristic of the tyrant description in Antiquity can be found.

A relatively intense level of stigmatization affects some other categories of offenders, primarily magicians and perpetrators of sepulchral violations. At times, Imperial officials prove to be convenient targets of invective as well, yet not very often, considering that one-third of the Code's constitutions deal with their offences.

The language of invective, as I have chosen to name the phenomenon in question, always indirectly points to the values being infringed by the individual at whom the invective is addressed. If one takes a closer look at this hierarchy, it becomes clear that the specifically protected value is not the state, but the state-supported Church and the orthodoxy thereof. But there is one more aspect of the activity of the state which appears to be particularly stressed by the invective as present in the constitutions. It is ... the Imperial constitutions themselves, the transgressions of which are described as *audacia* and *violatio*. In this way, a large percentage of the terms of invective that can be found in the constitutions turn out to defend the very contents of the Imperial orders. In consequence, it can be said that the value, whose violations would arouse the emperor's most intense outrage, is the "inviolability" of his own constitutions, that of the Christian religion, sepulchres, as well as that which is infringed by individuals involved in magic practices. Any acts against other aspects of the Roman order are only of secondary significance.

A listing of the relevant terms with possibly negative emotional content as present in the individual constitutions

C.Th. 1.2.9.2 *subreptio*
C.Th. 1.4.1.3 *depravo*
C.Th. 1.5.3.5 *improbus*
C.Th. 1.5.9.3 *desidia*; 4 *aviditas*; 5 *labes*
C.Th. 1.5.13.5 *audeo*
C.Th. 1.6.11.2 *praesumo*; 15 *temeritas*
C.Th. 1.9.1.14 *tempto*; 14 *violo*
C.Th. 1.9.2 *damnabilis*

C.Th. 1.9.3.3 *segnis*; 6 *turba*
C.Th. 1.10.4.2 7 *invidia*
C.Th. 1.10.7.7 *desidia*
C.Th. 1.11.1.9 *desidia*
C.Th. 1.11.2.2 *subrepo*; 2^{2} *scelus*
C.Th. 1.12.6.4 *temeritas*
C.Th. 1.12.8.[1] *pravus*
C.Th. 1.14.1.9 *audax*
C.Th. 1.14.2.2 *flagitium*
C.Th. 1.15.8.1^{2} *profanus*
C.Th. 1.15.16.3 *tempto*; 3 *violo*
C.Th. 1.15.17.4 *desidia*
C.Th. 1.16.3.5 *avaritia*; 6 *depravo*
C.Th. 1.16.4.1^{2} *insolens*
C.Th. 1.16.5.2 *prave*
C.Th. 1.16.6.8 *maleficus*; 10 *libido*
C.Th. 1.16.7.1 *rapax*; 3^{2} *depraedatio*; 6^{2} *aviditas*; 8^{2} *nefarius*; 12^{2} *latrocinium*
C.Th. 1.16.11.3 *insolenter*
C.Th. 1.20.1.6 *tempto*
C.Th. 1.28.3.3 *praesumo*; 4 *temerarius*; 5 *audacia*
C.Th. 1.29.5.6 *avarus*
C.Th. 1.29.7.1 *insolenter*; 4 *improbus*; 4 *insolentia*; 4 *temeritas*
C.Th. 1.29.8.1 *ferus*; 2 *insania*; 2 *latro*; 4 *scelerosus*; 5 *scelus*
C.Th. 1.31.1.2^{2} *invideo*
C.Th. 1.32.2.6 *avaritia*
C.Th. 1.32.5.3 *hostilis*
C.Th. 1.34.3.2 *audeo*; 5^{2} *flagitium*
C.Th. 2.1.1.3 *sceleratus*
C.Th. 2.1.3.4 *improbe*; 4 *macula*; 4 *polluo*; 4 *libido*; 6 *invado*
C.Th. 2.1.8.3 *rapio*
C.Th. 2.1.10.4 *superstitio*
C.Th. 2.1.17.30^{2} *perfidia*
C.Th. 2.4.5.3 *improbus*
C.Th. 2.4.6.2^{2} *violo*
C.Th. 2.6.2.3 *desidia*
C.Th. 2.8.18.5 *notabilis*
C.Th. 2.8.22.[2] *paganus*; 2 *superstitio*
C.Th. 2.14.1.9^{2} *tempto*
C.Th. 2.19.2.13^{2} *inimicus*; 14^{2} *inimicus*
C.Th. 2.23.1.4 *subreptio*; 5 *audeo*; 10 *audeo*

C.Th. 2.26.1.3 *invado*; 17 *invasor*; 18 *invado*
C.Th. 2.26.2.5 *tempto*
C.Th. 2.26.4.3 *improbus*; 4 *invidia*
C.Th. 2.29.1.1 *foedus*; 4 *invado*; 6 *nefarie*
C.Th. 2.29.2.3^{2} *temeritas*; 3^{2} *violentia*; 4^{2} *invado*
C.Th. 2.33.2.4 *furor*
C.Th. 3.1.1.2 *violentia*; 3 *turbo*
C.Th. 3.4.1.4 *barbarus*
C.Th. 3.5.5.3 *perfidia*
C.Th. 3.5.13.2^{2} *improbitas*
C.Th. 3.8.2.21 *praesumo*; 3^{2} *scaevus*
C.Th. 3.10.1.8 *subreptio*
C.Th. 3.11.1.8^{2} *tempto*; 13^{2} *pravitas*
C.Th. 3.12.1.2 *abominanter*
C.Th. 3.12.3.5 *funesto*; 5^{2} *scelus*
C.Th. 3.13.3.4 *audeo*
C.Th. 3.14.1.2 *barbarus*
C.Th. 3.16.1.2 *cupiditas*; 2 *pravus*; 9^{2} *invado*
C.Th. 3.16.2.9 *procacitas*; 13 *execratio*; 20 *insolens*
C.Th. 3.18.2.10 *avaritia*; [10] *temeritas*
C.Th. 3.32.1.8 *tempto*
C.Th. 4.3.1.4 *inquietudo*
C.Th. 4.4.5.5^{2} *audeo*
C.Th. 4.6.3.[5] *macula*; 22 *invado*; [25] *invado*
C.Th. 4.8.5.[16] *temero*; 5^{2} *hostis*; [7^{2}] *petulanter*
C.Th. 4.8.7.2 *inquieto*
C.Th. 4.10.2.4^{2} *praesumo*
C.Th. 4.12.5.[4] *pollutus*
C.Th. 4.12.6.[2] *libidinosus*; 2 *cupiditas*
C.Th. 4.13.3.4 *avaritia*; 4 *tempto*
C.Th. 4.14.1.2 3^{2} *tempto*
C.Th. 4.18.1.2 *invasor*; 2 *praedo*; 8 *invado*; 8 *praedo*;15 *improbus*
C.Th. 4.20.1.3^{2} *latrocinium*
C.Th. 4.22.1.3^{2} *violentia*
C.Th. 4.22.2.3 *turbo*; 4 *violentia*; 5 *improbus*; 6 *audeo*; 6 *temeritas*; 9 *temeritas*
C.Th. 4.22.3.3 *invado*; 6 *audacia*; 8 *violentus*; 9 *audacia*; 9 *furor*; 1^{2} *praesumptio*; 1^{2} *temero*
C.Th. 4.22.4.2 *perturbo*
C.Th. 4.23.1.3 *tempto*
C.Th. 5.1.4.14 *impius*

C.Th. 5.6.2.2 *barbarus*; 4 *hostis*
C.Th. 5.6.3.1 *barbarus*
C.Th. 5.7.1.[2] *hostilis*; [8] *barbarus*
C.Th. 5.7.2.[2] *barbaricus*; 2 *feritas*; 6 *barbarus*; 15 *conor*
C.Th. 5.8.1.[2] *tyrannus*; 3^{2} *avaritia*
C.Th. 5.9.1.5 *inquietudo*
C.Th. 5.10.1.1^{2} *tempto*
C.Th. 5.12.2.3 *subreptivus*; [5^{2}] *improbus*; [7^{2}] *perturbo*
C.Th. 5.12.3.[16] *inquietudo*
C.Th. 5.14.31.2 *turbo*
C.Th. 5.14.33.[5] *cupiditas*; 5 *improbus*
C.Th. 5.15.17.4 *prave*
C.Th. 5.15.20.11 *insolentia*
C.Th. 5.15.21.3 *temeritas*
C.Th. 5.19.2.4 *audeo*; 6 *audeo*
C.Th. 6.4.13.17 *segniter*; 22 *segnities*
C.Th. 6.4.22.12 *improbus*; 16 *insania*; 16 *praesumptio*; 16 *violo*; 17 *hostis*; 18 *furor*; 18 *temeritas*; 22 *tempto*; 24 *insolenter*
C.Th. 6.5.1.[5] *praesumo*
C.Th. 6.10.1.6 *temerarius*; 7 *inquietator*
C.Th. 6.18.1.5 *temeritas*; 6 *audeo*
C.Th. 6.22.1.4 *conor*
C.Th. 6.22.7.6 *praesumo*
C.Th. 6.23.4.10 *tempto*; 10 *violo*; 18 *inquietudo*
C.Th. 6.24.11.8 *impius*
C.Th. 6.27.3.12 *cupiditas*; 12 *tempto*
C.Th. 6.27.11.3 *audeo*
C.Th. 6.27.14.2 *conor*; 2 *invado*
C.Th. 6.27.15.3^{2} *desertor*
C.Th. 6.27.18.2 *culpabilis*
C.Th. 6.27.19.3 *audeo*
C.Th. 6.28.5.4 *subreptivus*
C.Th. 6.29.1.3 *feralis*; 6 *pravus*
C.Th. 6.29.2.18 *improbus*; 18 *tempto*; 23 *improbe*
C.Th. 6.29.3.8 *culpabilis*
C.Th. 6.29.4.3^{2} *audeo*
C.Th. 6.29.5.2 *avaritia*; 6 *audeo*
C.Th. 6.29.9.[2] *praesumo*
C.Th. 6.29.12.5 *audeo*
C.Th. 6.30.5.3 *audeo*

C.Th. 6.30.6.4 *conor*
C.Th. 6.30.7.5 *praesumo*
C.Th. 6.30.16.8 *desertor*
C.Th. 6.30.17.4 *desertor*; 6 *avaritia*
C.Th. 6.35.4.1^2 *temeritas*
C.Th. 6.35.5.2 *conor*
C.Th. 6.35.8.2 *inquieto*
C.Th. 6.35.10.5 *temero*
C.Th. 6.35.11.2 *rapax*
C.Th. 6.35.13.8 *temerarius*; 9 *tempto*; 9 *violo*
C.Th. 6.35.14.9 *conor*; 10 *inquietudo*; 12 *macula*; 13 *praesumo*
C.Th. 7.1.1.1 *barbarus*; 1 *depraedatio*; 1 *sceleratus*
C.Th. 7.1.7.4 *cupiditas*
C.Th. 7.1.10.6 *perfidus*
C.Th. 7.4.18.3 *tempto* (2 ×)
C.Th. 7.4.21.1^2 *nefas*
C.Th. 7.4.30.4 *conor*
C.Th. 7.4.30.6 *audeo*; 6 *tempto*; [8] *violator*
C.Th. 7.4.32.5 *aviditas*; 4^2 *audacia*; 4^2 *temero*
C.Th. 7.4.35.3 *cupiditas*; 4 *libido*
C.Th. 7.4.36.4^2 *temerator*
C.Th. 7.7.2.2 *libido*
C.Th. 7.7.3.5 *tempto*; 6 *devasto*
C.Th. 7.7.4.4 *praesumo*
C.Th. 7.8.5.1^2 *temeritas*; 1^2 *reprehensibilis*; 1^2 *violo*
C.Th. 7.8.7.1 *hostis*
C.Th. 7.8.10.2 *inquietudo*; 18 *sceleratus*
C.Th. 7.8.12.[2] *infaustus*
C.Th. 7.8.13.4 *violo*
C.Th. 7.9.1.4 *violenter*
C.Th. 7.10.1.9 *praesumo*; 9 *temeritas*; 9 *pravus*
C.Th. 7.11.1.5 *inquietudo*
C.Th. 7.12.1.5 *audeo*; 1^2 *barbarus*; 1^2 *incursio*
C.Th. 7.12.2.7 *desidia*
C.Th. 7.13.7.4 *intolerabilis*; 6 *insolenter*
C.Th. 7.13.9.3 *pravitas*; 5 *inexpiabilis*
C.Th. 7.13.10.2 *macula*; 4 *audeo*
C.Th. 7.13.16.1 *hostilis*
C.Th. 7.13.20.1^2 *barbarus*; 1^2 *vastitas*
C.Th. 7.13.21.3 *rebellis*; 3 *temerator*

C.Th. 7.14.1.3 *audeo*
C.Th. 7.15.1.1[2] *cupiditas*
C.Th. 7.16.1.1 *hostis*
C.Th. 7.16.2.9 *furor*; 9 *barbaricus*; 9 *feritas*; 9 *tyrannicus*
C.Th. 7.16.3.3 *barbarus*
C.Th. 7.17.1.18 *discursus*
C.Th. 7.18.1.2 *desertor*; 5 *deserto*
C.Th. 7.18.3.1 *desertor*
C.Th. 7.18.4.1 *desertor*; 4 *scelus*; 5 *desertor*; 1[2] *desertor*; 4[2] *flagitiosus*
C.Th. 7.18.5.1 *desertor*; 4 *desertor*
C.Th. 7.18.6.1 *desertor*; 4 *desertor*
C.Th. 7.18.6.5 *scelus*; 5 *scelus*
C.Th. 7.18.7.1 *desertor*; 2 *latro*
C.Th. 7.18.8.1 *desertor*; 11 *desertor*
C.Th. 7.18.9.2 *desertor*; 7 *desertor*; 5[2] *desertio*; 5[2] *tyrannicus*
C.Th. 7.18.10.3 *desertor*
C.Th. 7.18.11.1 *desertor*; 3 *desertio*; 7 *rebellis*; 7 *temeritas*; 10 *desertio*; 11 *desertor*
C.Th. 7.18.12.1 *desertor*
C.Th. 7.18.13.1 *desertor*; 2 *desertor*
C.Th. 7.18.14.1 *desertor*; 2 *audeo*; 3 *latro*; 3 *desertor*
C.Th. 7.18.15.2 *latrocinium*; 2 *depraedatio*
C.Th. 7.18.16.1[2] *desidiosus*
C.Th. 7.18.17.2 *desertor*; 2 *vasto*; 4 *infaustus*; 5 *tempto*
C.Th. 7.19.1.12 *scelus*; 14 *latro*; 17 *temeritas*
C.Th. 7.20.2.21 *inquieto*
C.Th. 7.20.7.2 *latrocinium*; 4[2] *perturbo*
C.Th. 7.20.12.13 *infaustus*
C.Th. 7.21.2.1 *paganus*
C.Th. 8.1.9.3 *segnitia*
C.Th. 8.1.10.4[2] *rapina*
C.Th. 8.1.11.7 *scelus*
C.Th. 8.1.15.2 *crudeliter*; 3 *pravitas*
C.Th. 8.1.16.4 *audeo*; 5 *violo*; 6 *avaritia*; 7 *temero*
C.Th. 8.2.3.4 *audeo*
C.Th. 8.4.1.2 *tyrannus*
C.Th. 8.4.8.13[2] *macula*
C.Th. 8.4.9.3 *conor*
C.Th. 8.4.15.6 *scelus*
C.Th. 8.4.16.7 *scelus*
C.Th. 8.4.19.4 *tempto*

C.Th. 8.4.28.5 *audeo*; 2^{2} *subreptio*
C.Th. 8.4.29.3 *praesumo*; 7 *tempto*
C.Th. 8.4.30.11 *audeo*
C.Th. 8.5.4.6 *improbus*
C.Th. 8.5.6.2 *praesumo*
C.Th. 8.5.11.2 *conor*
C.Th. 8.5.12.2 *praesumptio*
C.Th. 8.5.14.3^{2} *depravo*
C.Th. 8.5.15.2 *audacia*; 3 *audeo*
C.Th. 8.5.21.2 *rapina*
C.Th. 8.5.22.11 *praesumo*
C.Th. 8.5.30.4 *audeo*; 10 *insolentia*
C.Th. 8.5.37.2 *notabilis*
C.Th. 8.5.47.3 *libido*
C.Th. 8.5.54.5 *praesumo*; 5 *temeritas*
C.Th. 8.5.55.1 *praesumo*
C.Th. 8.5.57.3 *temeritas*
C.Th. 8.5.59.2 *praesumo*
C.Th. 8.5.61.1 *praesumptio*; 2 *temeritas*
C.Th. 8.5.62.2 *praesumo*; 4 *temero*
C.Th. 8.5.63.2 *praesumptio*
C.Th. 8.5.65.2 *praesumptio*
C.Th. 8.5.66.4 *conor*; 6 *temerarius*
C.Th. 8.7.5.5 *inquieto*
C.Th. 8.7.7.4 *audeo*
C.Th. 8.7.9.4 *tempto*
C.Th. 8.7.16.12 *violo*; 2^{2} *desertor*
C.Th. 8.7.20.5 *praesumo*
C.Th. 8.7.23.7 *temerarius*
C.Th. 8.8.1.3 *audeo*
C.Th. 8.8.2.3 *praesumptio*; 4 *temero*
C.Th. 8.8.3.4 *notabilis*
C.Th. 8.8.4.6 *temero*
C.Th. 8.8.5.5 *desidia*; 6 *invidia*
C.Th. 8.8.7.5 *praesumo*
C.Th. 8.10.2.8 *avaritia*
C.Th. 8.10.3.2 *depraedatio*
C.Th. 8.10.4.3 *temeritas*
C.Th. 8.11.2.3 *audeo*
C.Th. 8.11.3.3 *hostis*; 2^{2} *violo*

C.Th. 8.11.4.8 *violo*
C.Th. 8.13.1.2 *impius*; 13 *impietas*
C.Th. 8.13.2.2 *impius*; 3 *scelestus*; 4 *flagitiosus*
C.Th. 8.13.4.2 *impius*
C.Th. 8.15.5.[17] *turbide*
C.Th. 8.18.3.4 *perverto*
C.Th. 9.1.1.2 *rapio*; 3 *invado*
C.Th. 9.1.7.3 *segniter*
C.Th. 9.1.12.6 *invidiosus*; 8 *furor*
C.Th. 9.1.18.1 *desidia*; 2 *crudelis*
C.Th. 9.1.19.13 *flagitium*; 14 *inimicus*
C.Th. 9.2.5.3 *latrocinium*; 4 *raptus*; 4 *violentia*
C.Th. 9.3.1.17 *crudelitas*
C.Th. 9.3.2.3^{2} *saevio*
C.Th. 9.3.6.5 *praedor*; 6 *feralis*
C.Th. 9.4.1.2 *improbus*; 2 *petulans*
C.Th. 9.5.1.5 *temeritas*; 8 *audacia*; 8 *tempto*
C.Th. 9.6.1.2 *tumultus*; 2 *nefarius*; 3 *nefandus*
C.Th. 9.6.2.3 *nefandus*
C.Th. 9.6.3.3^{2} *funestus*
C.Th. 9.6.4.2 *improbus*; 3 *audeo*
C.Th. 9.7.2.3 *foedo*; 16 *proterve*
C.Th. 9.7.3.2 *scelus*
C.Th. 9.7.6.1 *flagitium*; 3 *scelus*
C.Th. 9.7.9.2 *tempto*
C.Th. 9.8.1.7 *violo*; 10 *raptor*
C.Th. 9.10.1.3 *violentia*; 8 *violentia*; 9 *tempto*; 13 *temero*; 13 *tempto*; 14 *tempto*
C.Th. 9.10.2.1 *invado*; 1 *violentia*; 2 *tempto*; 2 *violentia*
C.Th. 9.10.3.3 *violentia*; 5 *violentia*; 8 *violentus*; 13 *violentus*
C.Th. 9.10.4.2 *violentia*; 4 *violentia*; 6 *furor*; 8 *violentia*; 10 *violentia*
C.Th. 9.12.1.10 *barbarus*; 10 *immanis*; 10 *saevitia*
C.Th. 9.14.1.2 *piaculum*
C.Th. 9.14.2.7 *latro*
C.Th. 9.14.3.2 *barbarus*; 2 *scelestus*; 5 *scelus*; 13 *sordeo*; 14 *tempto*; 19 *audeo*
C.Th. 9.15.1.3^{2} *feralis*
C.Th. 9.16.1.1 *haruspex*; 4 *haruspex*; 7 *superstitio*
C.Th. 9.16.2.1 *haruspex*
C.Th. 9.16.3.3 *libido*
C.Th. 9.16.4.1 *haruspex*; *mathematicus*; 2 *augur*; 2 *hariolus*; 2 *magus*; 2 *pravus*; 2 *vates*; 3 *maleficus*

C.Th. 9.16.5.1 *audeo*; 2 audeo; 2 *turbo*; 3 *pestis*; 3 *feralis*; 3 *inimicus*
C.Th. 9.16.6.3 *inimicus*; 3 *magus*; 5 *contamen*; 5 *magus*; 5 *maleficus*; 6 *augur*; 6 *hariolus*; 6 *haruspex*; 6 *mathematicus*
C.Th. 9.16.7.2 *nefarius*; 3 *conor*; 3 *funestus*
C.Th. 9.16.8.1 *mathematicus*; 2 *error*
C.Th. 9.16.10.2 *invidia*
C.Th. 9.16.11.2 *labes*; 2 pollutus; 3 *hostis*; 5 *tempto*; 6 *maleficus*; 8 *inimicus*
C.Th. 9.16.12.1 *mathematicus*; 2 *error*; 3 *error*; 6 *error*
C.Th. 9.17.2.8 *attingo*; 8 *audeo*; 8 *piaculum*; 21 *attingo*; 25 *violator*
C.Th. 9.17.3.1 *cupidus*; 3 *scelus*
C.Th. 9.17.4.1 *violo*; 3 *polluo*; 2^2 *violo*
C.Th. 9.17.5.1 *audacia*; 4 *contamino*; 4 *piaculum*; 8 *infaustus*
C.Th. 9.17.6.5 *audeo*
C.Th. 9.21.2.2 *scelus*; 19 *scelus*; 2^2 *scelus*
C.Th. 9.21.4.5 *flagitium*
C.Th. 9.23.2.1^2 *audeo*
C.Th. 9.24.1.2 *rapio*; 6 *pravus*; 7 *detestabilis*; 8 *nefarius*; 9 *raptor*; 10 *rapio*; 11 *raptor*; 12 *audacia*; 14 *raptor*; 16 *rapio*; 1^2 *raptor*
C.Th. 9.24.2.2 *raptor*; 4 *audacia*
C.Th. 9.24.3.2 *raptus*; 2 *scelus*; 1^2 *audacia*; 1^2 *flagitium*; 3^3 *scelus*
C.Th. 9.25.1.1 *raptor*; 3 *raptus*; 3 *scelerosus*; 4 *rapio*
C.Th. 9.25.2.2 *rapio*; 1^2 *audeo*
C.Th. 9.25.3.2 *raptor*
C.Th. 9.26.1.3 *tempto*; 6 *scelus*; 6 *scelus*
C.Th. 9.26.2.3 *audeo*
C.Th. 9.26.3.3 *subrepticus*
C.Th. 9.26.4.4 *tempto*
C.Th. 9.27.1.2 *maculo*; 2 *scelus*
C.Th. 9.27.3.8 *rapio*
C.Th. 9.27.6.4 *cupiditas*; 5 *improbus*
C.Th. 9.28.1.3^2 *flagitium*; 4^2 *nefas*
C.Th. 9.28.2.2 *rapina*; 2 *scelus*; 3 *contagium*; 3 *pestis*; 3 *funestus*; 4 *rapio*; 5 *rapio*; 5 *rapio*
C.Th. 9.29.2.2 latro; 6 *latro*
C.Th. 9.30.2.1 latro; 5 *tempto*; 5 *violo*
C.Th. 9.30.3.2 rapina; 4 *scelus*; 6 *scelus*
C.Th. 9.31.1.4 *latro*
C.Th. 9.33.1.3 *tempto*
C.Th. 9.34.6.3 *inimicus*
C.Th. 9.34.8.3 *furor*

C.Th. 9.34.10.2 *inimicus*; 2 *venenatus*
C.Th. 9.35.2.4 *nefandus*; 4 *tempto*; 5^{2} *immanitas*
C.Th. 9.35.7.2 *latro*; 4 *latro*; 4 *sceleratus*
C.Th. 9.37.2.9^{2} *violo*
C.Th. 9.38.2.2 *tyrannicus*
C.Th. 9.38.3.4 *maleficus*; 4 *raptor*
C.Th. 9.38.4.3 *foeditas*; 4 *raptus*; 4 *scelus*; 4 *violentia*
C.Th. 9.38.6.2 *flagitium*; 4 *nefarius*; 5 *furor*; 5 *maculo*; 5 *tango*; 5 *rapio*; 6 *invasor*; 6 *raptor*; 7 *caecus*; 7 *profanus*; 7 *violo*; 8 *dirus*
C.Th. 9.38.7.3 *cupiditas*; 3 *scelus*; 4 *saevus*; 5 *immanitas*; 6 *raptus*; 6 *violatio*
C.Th. 9.38.8.4 *contamino*; 7 *raptor*; 9 *scelus*; 10 *immanitas*; 10 *maleficus*
C.Th. 9.38.9.4 *audeo*; 7 *macula*; 7 *inimicus*
C.Th. 9.38.11.2 *praesumptio*; 2 *tyrannicus*; 3 *tyrannis*
C.Th. 9.38.12.1 *tyrannis*
C.Th. 9.39.1.4 *damnabilis*
C.Th. 9.39.2.2 *praesumo*
C.Th. 9.39.3.2 *tempto*
C.Th. 9.40.1.5 *flagitium*
C.Th. 9.40.4.11 *scelerosus*
C.Th. 9.40.14.2 *perfidia*; 2 *pravus*
C.Th. 9.40.16.3 *immanitas*; 19 *audacia*
C.Th. 9.40.17.3 *caenosus*; 3 *sordes*; 5 *labes*; 7 *contagio*; 7 *foedo*; 8 *polluo*; 9 *scaevitas*; 12 *polluo*; 14 *rabies*
C.Th. 9.40.18.2 *scelus*; 3 *nefarius*
C.Th. 9.40.21.1 *hostis*; 2 *infaustus*
C.Th. 9.40.24.2 *barbarus*
C.Th. 9.41.1.9 *praesumo*
C.Th. 9.42.1.15 *inquietudo*; 2^{2} *tempto*
C.Th. 9.42.5.1 *scelerate*
C.Th. 9.42.21.2 *rapio*
C.Th. 9.42.22.1 *praedo*; 3 *barbaries*; 3 *inquieto*
C.Th. 9.42.23.4 *scelus*
C.Th. 9.42.24.2 *latro*; 2 *nefarius*; 3 *scelus*
C.Th. 9.43.1.9 *pravitas*; 11 *libido*
C.Th. 9.44.1.3 *invidia*; 7 *inimicus*; 7 *invidia*
C.Th. 9.45.4.8 *conor*; 6^{3} *conor*; 7^{3} *invado*; 8^{3} *temeritas*; 8^{3} *turbo*; 9^{3} *audeo*
C.Th. 9.45.5.10 *furiosus*; 12 *insania*; 15 *hostilis*; 18 *depravo*
C.Th. 10.1.2.4 *tempto*
C.Th. 10.1.5.1 *inquietudo*; 2 *inquieto*; 10 *temero*
C.Th. 10.1.9.2 *violo*

C.Th. 10.1.10.1 *scelestus*
C.Th. 10.1.15.4 *temeritas*
C.Th. 10.1.16.2 *improbus*; 12 *segnitia*
C.Th. 10.3.7.5 *subreptio*
C.Th. 10.4.1.5 *depraedatio*; 10 *audeo*
C.Th. 10.8.3.3 *inquietudo*; 3 *tempto*
C.Th. 10.8.4.2 *hostis*
C.Th. 10.8.5.22 *improbe*
C.Th. 10.9.1.7 *tempto*
C.Th. 10.10.2.2 *execror*; 3 *invidia*
C.Th. 10.10.4.2 *audacia*
C.Th. 10.10.10.1 *inimicus*
C.Th. 10.10.11.2 *aviditas*
C.Th. 10.10.12.3^2 *invado*; 10^2 *execror*
C.Th. 10.10.15.3 *audeo*; 3 *invado*; 4 *audeo*; 4 *violo*
C.Th. 10.10.16.7 *nefarius*
C.Th. 10.10.24.5 *nefarius*; 6 *violator*
C.Th. 10.10.25.1 *barbaricus*; 2 *incursus*; 3 *libido*
C.Th. 10.10.26.4 *improbus*
C.Th. 10.10.29.1^2 *cupiditas*
C.Th. 10.10.30.7 *polluo*
C.Th. 10.10.33.3 *rebellis*
C.Th. 10.11.1.8 *inimicus*
C.Th. 10.12.2.2 *inquietudo*; 4^2 *invidia*
C.Th. 10.15.1.3 *audeo*
C.Th. 10.18.1.3 *inquietudo*
C.Th. 10.19.2.1 *cupiditas*
C.Th. 10.19.9.3 *improbus*; 6 *audacia*; 6 *tempto*
C.Th. 10.19.13.3 *tempto*
C.Th. 10.20.6.5 *insolentia*
C.Th. 10.20.8.3 *audacia*; 5 *conor*
C.Th. 10.20.11.3 *subreptivus*; 3 *tempto*
C.Th. 10.20.12.2 *audeo*
C.Th. 10.20.13.5 *temero*
C.Th. 10.22.4.4 *subreptio*
C.Th. 10.26.1.4 *invidia*; 9 *conturbo*; 9 *turbulentus*; 10 *audeo*; 11 *pertinacia*
C.Th. 11.1.20.2 *damnabilis*
C.Th. 11.1.30.2 *audeo*
C.Th. 11.2.2.2 *praesumptio*
C.Th. 11.4.1.6 *avaritia*

C.Th. 11.7.1.5 *inquietudo*
C.Th. 11.7.3.2 *insolentia*; 2 *perversus*
C.Th. 11.7.10.3 *audeo*
C.Th. 11.7.11.3 *saevio*
C.Th. 11.7.13.4 *notabilis*
C.Th. 11.7.17.4 *audeo*
C.Th. 11.8.1.5 *cupiditas*; 6 *scelus*
C.Th. 11.12.1.1 *inimicus*
C.Th. 11.14.2.4 *temero*
C.Th. 11.14.3.2 *temerator*; 3 *audeo*
C.Th. 11.15.1.3 *inquietudo*
C.Th. 11.16.1.4 *tempto*; 4 *violo*; 5 *conor*
C.Th. 11.16.3.3 *libido*
C.Th. 11.16.11.4 *temeritas*; 7 *temeritas*
C.Th. 11.16.16.5 *audeo*
C.Th. 11.16.17.3 *temero*; 4 *inquietudo*; 4 *tempto*
C.Th. 11.18.1.5 *hostis*; 3^2 hostis
C.Th. 11.22.4.2 *temeritas*
C.Th. 11.22.5.6 *temero*
C.Th. 11.23.3.2 *subreptio*
C.Th. 11.24.1.3 *temeritas*
C.Th. 11.24.2.3 *audax*
C.Th. 11.24.4.2 *tempto*; 5 *temeritas*
C.Th. 11.24.6.9 *tempto*
C.Th. 11.28.10.1^2 *temero*; 1^2 *conor*
C.Th. 11.28.12.2 hostis; 2 *incursio*; 2 *vasto*
C.Th. 11.30.6.12 *conor*; 16 *tempto*
C.Th. 11.30.8.11 *tempto*; 13 *damnabilis*; 16 *violo*
C.Th. 11.30.11.18 *acerbus*
C.Th. 11.30.13.3 *insolens*
C.Th. 11.30.29.5^2 *violo*
C.Th. 11.30.30.8 *audeo*
C.Th. 11.30.31.3 *conor*; 3 *pravus*
C.Th. 11.30.34.1 *audeo*
C.Th. 11.30.57.2 *immanitas*
C.Th. 11.30.58.12 *pertinaciter*
C.Th. 11.30.59.2 *audeo*
C.Th. 11.30.60.5 *violo*
C.Th. 11.31.5.8 *desidia*
C.Th. 11.31.7.3 *hostis*

C.Th. 11.34.1.3 *tempto*
C.Th. 11.36.1.4 *maleficus*; 8 *tempto*
C.Th. 11.36.4.4 *immanitas*; 4 *scelus*
C.Th. 11.36.7.3 *maleficus*; 4 *raptor*; 5 *scelus*; 11 *audacia*; 14 *immanitas*
C.Th. 11.36.10.3 *culpabilis*
C.Th. 11.36.13.2 *audeo*
C.Th. 11.36.14.4 *violentia*; 5 *violentia*; 7 *procax*; 7 *vesania*
C.Th. 11.36.18.8 *pravus*
C.Th. 11.36.23.2 *tempto*
C.Th. 11.36.26.5 *audeo*
C.Th. 11.36.30.3 *tempto*
C.Th. 11.36.31.5 *perturbatio*; 5 *rebellis*
C.Th. 11.38.1.2 *obstinatus*
C.Th. 11.39.7.3 *nefarius*
C.Th. 11.39.11.2 *profano*
C.Th. 11.39.12.3 *amentia*
C.Th. 12.1.1.2 *conor*; 3 *depravo*
C.Th. 12.1.6.2 *sordidus*; 8 *libido*; 8^2 *flagitium*; 13^2 *scelus*
C.Th. 12.1.9.3 *audacia*
C.Th. 12.1.12.3 *tempto*
C.Th. 12.1.16.1 *pertinacia*; 5 *tempto*
C.Th. 12.1.26.5 *foedo*
C.Th. 12.1.27.3 *foedus*
C.Th. 12.1.29.1 *desertor*
C.Th. 12.1.30.2 *inquietudo*
C.Th. 12.1.45.2 *improbe*
C.Th. 12.1.50.6 *foedus*
C.Th. 12.1.61.3 *libido*; 3 *prave*
C.Th. 12.1.62.3 *audeo*
C.Th. 12.1.69.2 *cupiditas*
C.Th. 12.1.80.4 *tempto*; 6 *temerarius*
C.Th. 12.1.81.3 *inquietudo*
C.Th. 12.1.82.2 *conor*
C.Th. 12.1.84.5 *desertio*
C.Th. 12.1.85.2 *temerarius*; 5 *audeo*; 5 *furor*; 5 *pertinacia*; 10 *pertinacia*
C.Th. 12.1.92.4 *invado*
C.Th. 12.1.118.6 *audeo*
C.Th. 12.1.122.7 *piaculum*
C.Th. 12.1.128.4 *temerarius*; 5 *ausus*
C.Th. 12.1.149.1 *conor*

C.Th. 12.1.157.2 *superstitio*
C.Th. 12.1.158.2 *superstitio*; 4^{2} *superstitio*
C.Th. 12.1.161.1 *plectibilis*; 10 *cupiditas*
C.Th. 12.1.168.3 *audeo*
C.Th. 12.1.173.4^{2} *audeo*
C.Th. 12.1.176.4 *turba*; 8 *audeo*; 8 *violo*
C.Th. 12.1.177.4 *vasto*; 13 *inquietudo*
C.Th. 12.1.181.10 *inquietudo*
C.Th. 12.1.182.2 *audeo*
C.Th. 12.1.186.6 *praesumptio*
C.Th. 12.1.188.6 *audeo*
C.Th. 12.6.6.5 *inquietudo*
C.Th. 12.6.25.5 *subreptio*
C.Th. 12.6.32.10^{2} *ausus*; 11^{2} *audeo*; 15^{2} *temeritas*
C.Th. 12.7.2.2 *cupiditas*
C.Th. 12.8.1.2 *praesumo*
C.Th. 12.9.1.2 *conor*; 2 *invado* (2 ×)
C.Th. 12.10.1.2^{2} *praesumo*
C.Th. 12.16.1.2 *subreptivus*
C.Th. 12.18.2.4 *impius*
C.Th. 12.19.2.9 *tempto*
C.Th. 13.1.10.3 *inquieto*
C.Th. 13.1.20.6 *audeo*
C.Th. 13.3.7.2 *insolenter*
C.Th. 13.3.10.2 *inquietudo*
C.Th. 13.3.13.2 *subrepticus*
C.Th. 13.3.14.4 *improbitas*
C.Th. 13.4.4.5 *barbarus*
C.Th. 13.5.5.8 *violo*
C.Th. 13.5.8.4 *inquietudo*
C.Th. 13.5.9.4 *inquieto*; 4 *tempto*
C.Th. 13.5.13.5 *invideo*
C.Th. 13.5.16.3 audeo; 4 ausus (2×); 4 *expiatio*; 4 *immanis*; 5 *pravus*
C.Th. 13.5.20.2 inquietudo
C.Th. 13.5.29.5 *audacia*; 5 *raptor*; 6 *rapina*
C.Th. 13.5.30.2 *temero*; 2 *tempto*
C.Th. 13.6.4.4 *inquietudo*
C.Th. 13.6.7.4^{2} *improbus*
C.Th. 13.7.1.3 *tempto*
C.Th. 13.8.1.2 *audeo*

C.Th. 13.9.5.2 *pravitas*
C.Th. 13.11.6.2 *turbo*
C.Th. 13.11.10.5 *subrepticus*; 7 *improbe*
C.Th. 13.11.11.6 *rapacitas*
C.Th. 13.11.16.9^2 *turbo*
C.Th. 14.1.4.4 *tempto*; 5 *audeo*
C.Th. 14.1.6.4 *tempto*
C.Th. 14.3.1.4 *detestabilis*
C.Th. 14.3.9.4 *inquietudo*
C.Th. 14.3.16.2 *praesumo*; 2 *plectibilis*
C.Th. 14.3.20.2 *subrepticus*
C.Th. 14.3.21.4 *subreptio*
C.Th. 14.3.21.5 *tempto*
C.Th. 14.9.3.5 *tempto*
C.Th. 14.10.2.3 *tempto*
C.Th. 14.11.1.4 *tempto*; 4 *violo*
C.Th. 14.14.1.2 *tempto*
C.Th. 14.15.3.6 *audeo*
C.Th. 14.15.4.1 *improbus*; 2 *audeo*; 2^2 *improbus*; 5^2 *audeo*
C.Th. 14.15.5.6 *subreptio*
C.Th. 14.15.6.4 *praesumo*; 7 *scelus*
C.Th. 14.16.1.2^2 *tempto*; 5^2 *violo*
C.Th. 14.16.3.8 *audeo*
C.Th. 14.17.5.8^2 *temeritas*
C.Th. 14.17.6.3 *temeritas*; 9 *nefas*
C.Th. 14.19.1.3 *audeo*
C.Th. 14.23.1.2 *subreptio*
C.Th. 14.25.1.3 *inquietudo*
C.Th. 15.1.2.3 *desidia*
C.Th. 15.1.10.4 *tempto*
C.Th. 15.1.12.4 *audeo*
C.Th. 15.1.14.1 *praesumptio*
C.Th. 15.1.25.4 *aviditas*; 5 *violo*; 6 *praesumptio*; 6 *temero*
C.Th. 15.1.27.8 *audacia*
C.Th. 15.1.28.2 *audaciter*
C.Th. 15.1.31.7 *tempto*
C.Th. 15.1.33.4 *praesumo*
C.Th. 15.1.37.1 *temeritas*; 3^2 audeo
C.Th. 15.1.41.2^2 *inquieto*; 6^2 *praesumo*
C.Th. 15.1.42.4 *perturbo*

C.Th. 15.1.43.5 *subrepticus*
C.Th. 15.2.2.2 *aviditas*
C.Th. 15.2.4.2 *audacia*; 2 furor
C.Th. 15.2.6.8 *avidus*; 8 *cupiditas*
C.Th. 15.2.7.2 *turbo*
C.Th. 15.2.8.2 *praesumo*; 4 *audeo*; 5 *tempto*
C.Th. 15.5.3.3 *tempto*; 6 *violator*; 6 *violo*
C.Th. 15.5.5.11 *amentia*; 11 *impietas*; 11 *paganitas*; 12 *insania*
C.Th. 15.6.2.3 *foedus*; 3 *procax*
C.Th. 15.7.2.2 *inquieto*
C.Th. 15.7.3.2 *invideo*
C.Th. 15.8.2.16 *sordes*
C.Th. 15.9.2.4 *insania*
C.Th. 15.12.1.5 *scelus*
C.Th. 15.12.2.4 *tempto*
C.Th. 15.14.1.1 *tyrannus*
C.Th. 15.14.2.1 *tyrannus*
C.Th. 15.14.3.1 *tyrannus*
C.Th. 15.14.4.1 *tyrannus*
C.Th. 15.14.5.2 *tyrannus*
C.Th. 15.14.6.2 *audacia*; 2 *audeo*; 2 *tyrannicus*; 3 *praesumptio*
C.Th. 15.14.7.2 *infandus*; 2 *tyrannus*
C.Th. 15.14.8.1 *tyrannus*; 6 *conor*
C.Th. 15.14.9.2 *tyrannicus*; 9 *scaevus*; 14 *infaustus*; 18 *funestus*
C.Th. 15.14.10.1 *tyrannus*
C.Th. 15.14.11.4 *tyrannus*; 6 *polluo*; 7 *tyrannicus*
C.Th. 15.14.12.1 *labes*; 1 *tyrannicus*; 2 *macula*
C.Th. 15.14.13.4 *polluo*; 4 *scelus*
C.Th. 15.14.14.1 *barbaricus*; 2 *invidiose*; 6 *depraedatio*
C.Th. 16.1.2.9 *demens*; 9 *vesanus*; 9 *haereticus*
C.Th. 16.1.3.3 *profanus*; 13 *haereticus*
C.Th. 16.1.4.7 *turbulentus*; 8 *seditio*; 8 *turbo*; 8 *tempto*; 10 *tempto*
C.Th. 16.2.1.1 *haereticus*
C.Th. 16.2.3.1^2 *inquieto*
C.Th. 16.2.5.3 *superstitio*
C.Th. 16.2.7.2 *haereticus*
C.Th. 16.2.9.1 *inquietudo*
C.Th. 16.2.11.4 *inquieto*
C.Th. 16.2.12.3 *furialis*
C.Th. 16.2.15.1^2 *inquietudo*

C.Th. 16.2.18.1^2 *paganus*; 2^2 *depravatio*
C.Th. 16.2.25.2 *violo*
C.Th. 16.2.28.3 *invado*
C.Th. 16.2.31.22 *violentus*
C.Th. 16.2.32.3 *invidia*
C.Th. 16.2.34.2 *temeritas*; 2 *violo*; 5 *haereticus*
C.Th. 16.2.37.3^2 *tumultosus*; 4^2 *seditio*
C.Th. 16.2.39.8 *foedus*; 1^2 *improbus*
C.Th. 16.2.41.7^2 *maculo*
C.Th. 16.2.42.16 *violo*
C.Th. 16.2.44.5 *scaevus*
C.Th. 16.2.47.2 *invideo*; 2 *tyrannus*; 5 *praesumptor*; 5 *infaustus*
C.Th. 16.4.1.2 *turbulentus*; 3 *tempto*; 4 *seditio*; 4 *turbo*
C.Th. 16.4.2.3 *ausus*; 3 *damnabilis*; 1^2 *audeo*; 1^2 *pestifer*
C.Th. 16.4.3.2 *turbo*
C.Th. 16.4.4.2 *tumultosus*; 3 *audeo*
C.Th. 16.4.5.2 *tumultosus*
C.Th. 16.4.6.3 *conor*
C.Th. 16.5.1.2 *haereticus*; 3 *schismaticus*
C.Th. 16.5.2.1 *Novatianus*; 3 *inquietudo*; 5 *conor*
C.Th. 16.5.3.2 *Manichaeus*; 2 *turba*; 4 *profanus*
C.Th. 16.5.4.2 *haereticus*; 5 *improbitas*; 5 *profanus*
C.Th. 16.5.5.3 *haeresis*; 4 *ausus*; 4 *plectibilis*; 4 *profanus*; 7 *nefarius*; 7 *perversus*; 7 *superstitio*
C.Th. 16.5.6.1 *haereticus*; 2 *dementia*; 2 *obstinatus*; 4 *haereticus*; 5 *turba*; 7 *contaminatio*; 7 *labes*; 7 *Fotinianus*; 8 *Arrianus*; 8 *Eunomianus*; 8 *nefandus*; 8 *perfidia*; 8 *venenum*; 6^2 *violo*; 11^2 *haereticus*; 12^2 *tempto*; 13^2 *furor*
C.Th. 16.5.7.1 *Manichaea*; 1 *Manichaeus*; 16 *obstinatio*; 16 *pertinax*; 18 *profanus*; 3^2 *Manichaeus*; 6^2 feralis; 10^2 *Apotactita*; 10^2 *Encratita*; 10^2 *Hydroparastata*; 10^2 *Saccoforus*; 12^2 *notabilis*; 12^2 *execror*; 13^2 *scelus*
C.Th. 16.5.8.1 *Arrianus*; 1 *Eunomianus*; 3 *praesumo*
C.Th. 16.5.9.1 *Manichaeus*; 2 *profanator*; 2 *turba*; 7 *Encratita*; 8 *Hydroparastata*; 8 *Saccoforus*; 9 *inexpiabilis*
C.Th. 16.5.10.1 *Tascodrogita*; 2 *haereticus*; 2 *superstitio*; 3 *turba*
C.Th. 16.5.11.2 *Arrianus*; 2 *error*; 2 *Eunomianus*; 2 *haeresis*; 2 *Macedonianus*; 2 *Pneumatomachus*; 3 *Apotactita*; 3 *Encratita*; 3 *Hydroparastata*; 3 *Manichaeus*; 3 *Saccoforus*
C.Th. 16.5.12.2 *Apollinarianus*; 2 *Arrianus*; 2 *Eunomianus*; 2 *Macedonianus*; 5 *praesumo*; 6 *dirus*; 6 *perfidia*; 8 *turba*
C.Th. 16.5.13.1 *Arrianus*; 1 *Eunomianus*; 1 *Macedonianus*; 2 *Apollinarianus*; 2 *error*
C.Th. 16.5.14.1 *Apollinarianus*; 2 *haeresis*; 2 *improbitas*

C.Th. 16.5.15.1 *perfidus*; 2 *vesania*; 1^{2} *nefarius*; 2^{2} *impius*
C.Th. 16.5.16.1 *Arrianus*
C.Th. 16.5.17.2 *Eunomianus*
C.Th. 16.5.18.1 *Manichaeus*
C.Th. 16.5.19.1 *scaevus*; 3 *macula*; 3 *conor*; 3 error; 3 *haeresis*; 4 *funestus*
C.Th. 16.5.20.1 *contagium*; 1 *pollutus*; 1 *haereticus*; 3 *perversitas*; 4 *error*
C.Th. 16.5.21.1 *error*; 1 *haereticus*; 3 *tempto*
C.Th. 16.5.22.1 *haereticus*
C.Th. 16.5.23.1 *Eunomianus*
C.Th. 16.5.24.1 *haereticus*; 2 *dementia*; 2 *conor*; 3 *profanus*; 4 *audeo*; 7 *audacia*
C.Th. 16.5.25.2 *haereticus*; 3 *pertinax*; 1^{2} *Eunomianus*; 1^{2} *perfidus*; 3^{2} *vesania*; 5^{2} *furor*
C.Th. 16.5.26.1 *haereticus*; 2 *audeo*; 2 *profanus*; 3 *contamino*; 4 *audeo*; 5 *pollutus*
C.Th. 16.5.27.2 *Eunomianus*
C.Th. 16.5.28.1 *haereticus*; 3 *devio*; 4 *haereticus*
C.Th. 16.5.29.2 *haereticus*; 3 *audeo*
C.Th. 16.5.30.2 *haereticus*; 7 *haereticus*; 9 *profanus*
C.Th. 16.5.31.1 *Eunomianus*; 2 *furor*; 2 *error*
C.Th. 16.5.32.1 *dementia*; 1 *Eunomianus*; 2 *Eunomianus*; 3 *furor*; 3 *error*
C.Th. 16.5.33.1 *Apollinarius*
C.Th. 16.5.34.1 *Eunomianus*; 1 *superstitio*; 2 *Montanista*; 5 *infaustus*; 7 *superstitio*; 10 *scelus*
C.Th. 16.5.35.1 *execrabilis*; 1 *Manichaeus*
C.Th. 16.5.36.1 *Eunomianus*; 2^{2} *profanus*; 4^{2} *scelus*
C.Th. 16.5.37.1 *Donatista*; 4 *Donatista*; 5 *perfidia*
C.Th. 16.5.38.1 *Donatista*; 1 *Manichaeus*; 2 *furo*; 4 *audeo*; 5 *turba*; 6 *seditio*; 6 *acer*
C.Th. 16.5.39.1 *haereticus*; 1 *superstitio*
C.Th. 16.5.40.2 *Donatista*; 3 *Fryga*; 3 *Manichaeus*; 3 *Priscillianista*; 7^{2} polluo; 13^{2} *Manichaeus*; 14^{2} Fryga; 14^{2} *Priscillianista*; 17^{2} *pravitas*
C.Th. 16.5.41.2 *pravus*; 3 *Donatista*; 3 *haereticus*; 3 *Manichaeus*; 4 *pravus*; 4 *profanus*; 4^{2} *error*; 9^{2} *profanus*
C.Th. 16.5.42.2 *inimicus*
C.Th. 16.5.43.1 *Donatista*; 1 *Montenses*; 2 *gentilis*; 2 *Manichaeus*; 2 *Priscillianista*; 5 *Caelicola*; 8 *Donatista*; 9 *scaevus*
C.Th. 16.5.44.1 *Donatista*; 1 *haereticus*; 2 *audacia*; 2 *turbo*; 3 *contagio*; 3 *pestis*; 4 *tempto*
C.Th. 16.5.45.5 *audeo*
C.Th. 16.5.46.1 *Donatista*; 2 *haereticus*; 3 *gentilis*; 3 *paganus*
C.Th. 16.5.47.1^{2} *haereticus*; 2^{2} *tempto*
C.Th. 16.5.48.1 *Montanista*; 1 *Priscillianista*; 2 *nefarius*; 2 *superstitio*
C.Th. 16.5.49.1 *Eunomianus*; 8 *superstitio*

C.Th. 16.5.51.2 *haereticus*; 2 *inimicus*; 2 *superstitio*; 3 *execror*; 3 *scelus*; 4 *temeritas*; 4 *tempto*
C.Th. 16.5.52.3 *Donatista*; 14 *pravus*; 17 *polluo*; 1^2 *haereticus*; 1^2 *pravus*
C.Th. 16.5.53.5 *superstitiosus*; 6 *pertinax*; 7 *improbitas*
C.Th. 16.5.54.1 *Donatista*; 1 *haereticus*; 5 *dirus*; 5 *superstitio*; 17 *error*; 1^2 *acerbus*; 3^2 *Donatista*; 6^2 *haeresis*; 16^2 *error*; 19^2 *ausus*
C.Th. 16.5.55.3 *Donatista*
C.Th. 16.5.56.1 *haeresis*; 1 *superstitio*; 2 *inimicus*; 1^2 *temeritas*; 1^2 *scelus*; 1^2 *tempto*; 2^2 *contagio*; 2^2 *temero*
C.Th. 16.5.57.1 *Montanista*; 4 *audeo*; 4 *nefarius*; 4 *tempto*; 6 *execrabilis*; 10 *feralis*; 12 *Montanista*
C.Th. 16.5.58.1 *Eunomianus*; 2 *nefarius*; 4 *haereticus*; 5 *haereticus*; 6 *nefarie*; 9 *Eunomianus*; 10 *audeo*; 11 *pestifer*; 12 *Eunomianus*; 13 *Eunomianus*; 3^2 *Eunomianus* (2×); 3^2 *perversitas*; 3^2 *pravitas*; 4^2 *Eunomianus* (3×); 12^2 *Eunomianus*; 14^2 *Eunomianus*
C.Th. 16.5.59.1 *Fryges*; 1 *Manichaeus*; 2 *Arrianus*; 2 *Pepyzita*; 2 *Priscillianista*; 3 *Eunomianus*; 3 *haereticus*; 3 *Macedonianus*; 3 *Novatianus*; 3 *Protopaschita*; 5 *tempto*
C.Th. 16.5.60.1 *haereticus*; 2 *execror*; 2 *Arrianus*; 2 *error*; 2 *Eunomianus*; 2 *Macedonianus*; 4 *perfidia*; 5 *furor*
C.Th. 16.5.61.2 *Eunomianus*; 3 *execrabilis*
C.Th. 16.5.62.1 *Manichaeus*; 2 *haereticus*; 2 *inimicus*; 2 *mathematicus*; 2 *schismaticus*; 4 *contagio*; 4 foedo; 4 pravus; 5 *schisma*
C.Th. 16.5.63.1 *haeresis*; 1 *perfidia*; 2 *gentilis*; 2 *inimicus*; 2 *schisma*; 2 *superstitio*; 3 *error* (2×); 4 *superstitio*; 5 *error* (2×); 5 *perfidia*
C.Th. 16.5.64.1 *haereticus*; 1 *Manichaeus*
C.Th. 16.5.64.2 *inimicus*; 2 *schismaticus*; 3 *contagio*; 3 *foedo*; 4 *error*; 4 *infaustus*
C.Th. 16.5.65.1 *haereticus*; 2 *insania*; 5 *temeritas*; 5 *invado*; 8 *superstitio*; 10 *Arrianus*; 10 *Macedonianus*; 11 *Apollinarianus*; 14 *Novatianus*; 14 *Sabbatianus*; 16 *Eunomianus*; 16 *tempto*; 16 *Valentinianus*; 17 *Fryges*; 17 *Marcianista*; 17 *Montanista*; 17 *Priscillianista*; 18 *Borborianus*; 18 *Enthusiasta*; 18 *Euchita*; 18 *Messalianus*; 19 *Audianus*; 19 *Donatista*; 19 *Hydroparastata*; 20 *Fotinianus*; 20 *Marcellianus*; 20 *Paulianus*; 20 *Tascodrogita*; 21 *scelus*; 22 *Manichaeus*; 24 *Manichaeus*; 3^2 *haereticus*; 21^2 *haereticus*; 23^2 *haereticus*; 26^2 *superstitio*
C.Th. 16.5.66.1 *superstitio*; 3 *Arrianus*; 4 *impietas*; 4 *nefarius*; 4 *Porfyrianus*; 5 *scelus*; 5 *Simonianus*; 6 impius; 6 nefandus; 2^2 *audeo*; 6^2 *violator*
C.Th. 16.6.1.4 *contamino*
C.Th. 16.6.2.2 error; 4 *polluo*; 5 *error*; 2^2 *furor*; 3^2 *piacularis*; 5^2 *error*; 6^2 *impius*; 6^2 *virus*
C.Th. 16.6.3.2 *devius*; 2 *error*
C.Th. 16.6.4.1 *adversarius*; 3 *haeresis*; 3 *schisma*; 4 *Donatista*; 4 *scelus*; 5 *temeritas*; 6 *contagio*; 6 *profanus*; 7 *haeresis*; 7 *schisma*; 8 *error*; 11 *polluo*; 14 *pravitas*;

15 *depravatio*; 15 *scaevitas*; 17 *feralis*; 3^2 *scelus*; 5^2 *piacularis*; 5^2 *flagitium*; 8^2 *fides*; 9^2 *tempto*; 15^2 *error*; 15^2 *pravus*

C.Th. 16.6.5.2 *pollutus*; 2 *Donatista*; 2 *Montanista*; 2 *violo*; 2^2 *perversus*

C.Th. 16.6.6.2 *caenum*; 2 *profano*; 2 *scelus*; 3 *polluo*; 3 *sordes*; 3 *haereticus*; 5 *pravus*; 8 *piacularis*; 11 *execror*; 12 *desertor*; 12 *Novatianus*; 13 *Sabbatianus*; 14 *Novatianus*; 18 *vesania*; 18 *haereticus*

C.Th. 16.6.7.1 *Eunomianus*; 1 *funestus*; 1 *nefarius*; 4 *Eunomianus*; 5 *scelus*; 1^2 furor; 1^2 *fides*; 1^2 *immanis*

C.Th. 16.7.1.2 *paganus*

C.Th. 16.7.2.1 *paganus*

C.Th. 16.7.3.2 *flagitium*; 3 *polluo*; 4 *contagium*; 4 *Manichaeus*; 4 *nefandus*; 4 *scelerosus*; 2^2 *error*; 3^2 *scelus*; 3^2 *nefarius*; 7^2 *violo*; 8^2 *Manichaeus*; 12^2 *flagitium*; 12^2 *scelus*; 14^2 *perfidia*; 14^2 *scelus*

C.Th. 16.7.4.3 *profano*; 8 *flagitium*; 10 *polluo*; 11 *profanus*; 13 *profano*

C.Th. 16.7.5.2 *caeco*; 2 *devius*; 5 *feralis*; 5 *infandus*

C.Th. 16.7.6.2 *maculo*; 2 *impius*; 2 *superstitio*

C.Th. 16.7.7.2 *apostata*; 4 *devio*; 10 *profanus*; 11 *error*; 13 *perfidia*

C.Th. 16.8.1.2 *feralis*; 3 *furor*; 4 *audeo*; 5 *nefarius*

C.Th. 16.8.5.2 *inquieto*

C.Th. 16.8.6.3 *flagitium*

C.Th. 16.8.8.4 *superstitio*; 5 *subreptio*

C.Th. 16.8.9.4 *praesumo*; 5 *conor*

C.Th. 16.8.10.4 *audeo*

C.Th. 16.8.11.1 *audeo*

C.Th. 16.8.14.1 *superstitio*; 7 *depraedatio*; 9 *violator*

C.Th. 16.8.19.1 *Caelicola*; 3 *superstitio*; 4 *perversitas*; 5 *haereticus*; 10 *audeo*; 10 *foedus*; 16 *tempto*; 20 *polluo*; 4^2 *tempto*

C.Th. 16.8.20.2 *audeo*; 2 *violo*; 8 *violo*

C.Th. 16.8.21.4 *scelus*

C.Th. 16.8.22.2^2 *seditio*; 7^2 *foedo*; 7^2 *tempto*

C.Th. 16.8.24.1 *superstitio*; 6 *perversitas*

C.Th. 16.8.26.2 *abomino*; 2 *paganus*; 3 *audacia*; 3 *haereticus*

C.Th. 16.8.28.3 *superstitio*

C.Th. 16.9.3.4 *insolentia*; 5 *subreptio*

C.Th. 16.9.4.3 *petulanter*; 6 *nefandus*; 6 *superstitio*; 8 *caenum*; 1^2 *scelus*; 1^2 *violo*

C.Th. 16.9.5.2 *audeo*; 2 *impius*

C.Th. 16.10.1.3 *haruspex*

C.Th. 16.10.2.2 *insania*; 2 *superstitio*; 3 *audeo*

C.Th. 16.10.3.1 *superstitio*

C.Th. 16.10.5.2 *nefarius*

C.Th. 16.10.7.2 *vesanus*; 3 *scelus*; 6 *dirus*; 6 *profano*
C.Th. 16.10.9.2 *audacia*; 3 *execrabilis*; 5 *tempto*
C.Th. 16.10.10.1 *polluo*; 4 *profanus*
C.Th. 16.10.11.3 *profanus*; 5 *pollutus*; 6 *temerator*
C.Th. 16.10.12.5 *piaculum*; 7 *audeo*; 10 *tempto*; 15 *tempto*; 15 *violo*; 16 *gentilicius*; 16 *superstitio*; 21 *scelus*
C.Th. 16.10.13.2 *abomino*; 4 *devio*; 5 *audeo*; 5 *haereticus*; 5 *paganus*; 9 *haereticus*; 11 *tempto*
C.Th. 16.10.15.1^2 *conor*
C.Th. 16.10.16.2 *tumultus*; 2 *superstitio*; 2 *turba*
C.Th. 16.10.17.1 *profanus*; 3 *damnabilis*; 3 *superstitio*
C.Th. 16.10.18.2 *conor*; 5 *superstitio*
C.Th. 16.10.19.2^2 *paganus*; 7^2 *funestus*
C.Th. 16.10.20.1 *paganus*; 1 *superstitio*; 6 *error*; 8 *superstitio*; 17 *superstitio*; 19 *gentilicius*; 20 *error*; 2^2 *praesumptio*; 2^2 *invidia*
C.Th. 16.10.21.1 *paganus*; 1 *profanus*; 2 *polluo*; 2 *error*; 2 *gentilis*
C.Th. 16.10.22.1 *paganus*
C.Th. 16.10.23.1 *paganus*; 2 *execror*
C.Th. 16.10.24.1 *Manichaeus*; 2 *haereticus*; 2 *Pepyzita*; 3 *amentia*; 6 *turbulentus* (2×); 6 *paganus*; 6 *tempto*; 7 *audeo*; 8 *violentus*; 9 *rapio*
C.Th. 16.10.25.2 *execror*; 2 *paganus*; 2 *sceleratus*
C.Th. 16.11.3.3 *superstitio*
Const. Sirm. 1.8^2 *cupiditas*; 8^2 *improbus*
Const. Sirm. 2.2 *inquietus*; 2^2 *error*; 7^2 *turbator*; 7^2 *turba*; 8^2 *tumultus*
Const. Sirm. 3.2^2 *improbus*; 2^2 *temeritas*
Const. Sirm. 4.4^2 *inquietudo*
Const. Sirm. 5.5 *audeo*
Const. Sirm. 6.4 *invideo*; 4 *tyrannus*; 3^2 *audeo*; 3^2 *praesumptio*; 6^2 *praesumptor*; 6^2 *infaustus*; 14^2 *Caelestianus*; 14^2 *nefarius*; 14^2 *Pelagianus*; 15^2 *error*; 19^2 *macula*; 19^2 *error*; 20^2 *superstitio*; 21^2 *depravo*; 21^2 *haereticus*; 21^2 *Manichaeus*; 21^2 *mathematicus*; 21^2 *schismaticus*; 22^2 *inimicus*; 23^2 *contagio*; 23^2 *foedo*; 24^2 *paganus*; 26^2 *error*; 26^2 *error*; 26^2 *infaustus*
Const. Sirm. 7.5^2 *audeo*; 6^2 *immanitas*
Const. Sirm. 8.16 *feraliter*; 18 *pius*; 21 *feralis*; 21 *scelus*; 23 *scelus*; 24 *scelus*; 26 *magus*
Const. Sirm. 9.4 *subrepo*; 7 *pertinacia*; 17 *foedus*; 18 *improbus*
Const. Sirm. 10.7 *pravus*; 8 *contamino*; 7^2 *scaevus*; 13^2 *raptor*
Const. Sirm. 11.4 *temerarius*; 9 *ausus*; 4^2 *praesumptio*; 4^2 *temerarius*; 5^2 *tempto*
Const. Sirm. 12.1 *haereticus*; 1 *profanus*; 2 *gentilis*; 2 *superstitio*; 5 *devio*; 7 *pravus*; 9 *furor*; 9 *Donatista*; 9 *gentilis*; 9 *pertinacia*; 10 *desidia*; 12 *Donatista*;

12 *Manichaeus*; 12 *Montenses*; 13 *gentilis*; 13 *Priscillianista*; 16 *Caelicola*; 19 *Donatista*; 20 *scaevus*; 25 *paganus*; 1^2 *funestus*; 6^2 *Donatista*; 6^2 *haereticus*; 6^2 *Manichaeus*; 7^2 *gentilis*
Const. Sirm. 13.15 *feralis*
Const. Sirm. 14.2 *culpabilis*; 3 *turbo*; 6 *temeritas*; 7 *rapio*; 9 *foedo*; 11 *flagitium*; 11 *immanis*; 11 *nefas*; 11 *scelus*; 24 *audacia*; 5^2 *audacia*; 6^2 *violentus*; 11^2 *Donatista*; 12^2 *haereticus*; 14^2 *gentilis*; 14^2 *paganus*
Const. Sirm. 15.5 *inimicitia*; 1^2 *maculo*; 9^2 *pollutus*; 13^2 *polluo*; 14^2 *vesania*
Const. Sirm. 16.7 *barbaricus*; 7 *discursus*; 7 *feritas*; 12 *maculo*; 12 *avarus*; 17 *barbarus*; 18^2 *temeritas*; 18^2 *conor*; 23^2 *tempto*
Nov. Theod. 1.28 *invidia*
Nov. Theod. 3.6 *mente captus*; 6 *feritas*; 7 *immanitas*; 11 *audeo*; 11 *haereticus*; 11 *paganus*; 13 *piaculum*; 13 *obstinatus*; 15 *feralis*; 22 *inimicus*; 23 *subreptivus*; 35 *nefandus*; 45 *ausus*; 47 *perversus*; 62 *gentilis*; 62 *immanitas*; 62 *paganus*; 63 *vesania*; 63 *nefarius*; 63 *pertinax*; 64 *error*; 64 *funestus*; 64 *superstitio*; 66 *scelus*; 68 *furor*; 69 *audacia*; 69 *improbus*; 71 *dementia*; 71 *paganus*; 72 *contamino*; 72 *polluo*; 76 *paganus*; 76 *perfidia*; 79 *impietas*; 81 *Manichaeus*; 82 *Eunomianus*; 82 *haereticus*; 82 *Montanista*; 83 *Ascodrogi*; 83 *Borborita*; 83 *Fotinus*; 83 *Fryga*; 83 *Hydroparastata*; 83 *Ofita*; 83 *Priscillianista*; 84 *desidia*
Nov. Theod. 4.9 *barbaricus*; 9 *excursio*; 27 *avaritia*; 27 *cupiditas*; 30 *audax*
Nov. Theod. 5.1.25 *temerarius*; 25 *tempto*
Nov. Theod. 5.2.5 *libido*; 12 *temerator*
Nov. Theod. 5.3.18 *tempto*; 19 *audeo*
Nov. Theod. 6.28 *tempto*
Nov. Theod. 7.1.14 *tempto*
Nov. Theod. 7.2.11 *audacia*; 31 *pertinaciter*
Nov. Theod. 8.3 *temerator*; 15 *subreptio*
Nov. Theod. 9.6 *scaevus*
Nov. Theod. 10.1.3 *cupiditas*; 37 *temero*; 37 *tempto*
Nov. Theod. 15.2.2 *improbus*; 2 *temeritas*; 3 *audacia*; 4 *serpo*; 6 *subreptio*; 7 *barbarus*; 8 *audeo*; 10 *vastus*; 11 *scelus*; 14 vesania; 23 *subreptio*
Nov. Theod. 16.2 *barbarus*; 12 *praesumptio*
Nov. Theod. 17.1.18 *audeo*; 21 *subreptio*
Nov. Theod. 17.2.20 *audeo*; 27 *temeritas*; 44 *implacabilis*; 44 *tempto*
Nov. Theod. 18.7 *labes*; 8 *damnabilis*; 19 *temeritas*; 19 *tempto*; 20 *impius*; 21 *nefas*
Nov. Theod. 19.5 *cupiditas*; 6 *subreptio*
Nov. Theod. 20.24 *temerator*
Nov. Theod. 21.16 *temerator*; 20 *barbarus*?; 28 *tempto*
Nov. Theod. 22.2.28 *invideo*; 36 *inhumanus*; 37 *invidia*
Nov. Theod. 23.24 *aviditas*

Nov. Theod. 24.10 *libido*; 23 *audeo*; 23 *violator*; 24 *flagitium*; 35 *nefandus*; 36 *tempto*; 51 *tempto*; 52 *aviditas*; 53 *audeo*; 62 *desidia*; 65 *hostis*; 65 *tempto*
Nov. Theod. 25.50 *conor*
Nov. Theod. 26.9 *inquietudo*; 57 *conor*; 60 *subrepticus*
Nov. Valent. 1.1.16 *inquieto*
Nov. Valent. 1.2.1 *vastitas*; 7 *barbaricus*; 7 *vastitas*
Nov. Valent. 1.3.9 *subreptio*; 9 *invidus*; 10 *improbus*; 17 *avaritia*; 23 *depraedor*; 24 *improbus*; 26 *crudelitas* (2×); 27 *turbulentus*; 28 *hostis*; 28 *pertinax*; 48 *audeo*; 51 *cupiditas*
Nov. Valent. 2.3.4 *feralis*; 6 *hostilis*
Nov. Valent. 5.6 *invidia*
Nov. Valent. 6.1.2 *temeritas*; 2 *inexcusabilis*; 4 *tempto*; 14 *desertor*; 14 *hostilis*
Nov. Valent. 7.1.3 *obstinatio*; 4 *praesumptio*; 4 *scelus*; 8 *avaritia*; 16 *aviditas*; 21 *cupiditas*; 22 *rapina*; 32 *ausus*; 32 *improbus*
Nov. Valent. 7.2.2 *avaritia*; 5 *desidia*; 12 *segnities*; 14 *aviditas*; 17 *depraedatio*; 23 *cupiditas*
Nov. Valent. 7.3.2 *temerarius*; 3 *desidia*; 3 *segnis*; 4 *audeo*
Nov. Valent. 8.1.2 *temeritas*; 3 *praesumptio*; 15 *invasor*; 16 *ausus*; 27 *invado*; 33 *invasio*; 33 *temeritas*
Nov. Valent. 8.2.8 *invidia*
Nov. Valent. 9.4 *hostis*; 4 *praedo*; 5 *excursus*; 6 *depraedatio*; 12 *hostis*; 14 *hostis*; 17 *hostis*
Nov. Valent. 10.37 *pravus*
Nov. Valent. 12.2 *acerbus*; 5 *improbus*; 7 *acerbitas*; 11 *intolerabilis*; 12 *immanitas*; 13 *hostilis*; 14 *conor*; 20 *inquieto*; 33 *tempto*; 34 *cupiditas*; 34 *depravo*
Nov. Valent. 13.47 *barbaricus*; 47 *incursus*; 58 *barbarus*; 58 *discursus*; 63 *hostis*; 65 *hostis*
Nov. Valent. 14.3 *improbus*
Nov. Valent. 15.15 *intolerabilis*
Nov. Valent. 16.2 *ausus*; 2 *temerarius*
Nov. Valent. 17.7 *praesumptio*; 10 *ausus*; 10 *praesumo*; 10 *tempto*; 11 *abominabilis*; 11 *tumultus*; 11 *invado*; 13 *temeritas*; 13 *invado*; 16 *hostilis*; 24 *ausus*; 25 *violo*; 26 *turba*; 29 *tempto*; 36 *violo*
Nov. Valent. 18.2 *hostis*; 2 *paganus*; 2 *superstitio*; 2 *inimica*; 3 *Manichaeus*; 4 *execrabilis*; 8 *scelus*; 10 *scelus*; 11 *inexpiabiliter*; 11 *polluo*; 14 *Manichaeus*; 19 *Manichaeus*; 24 *polluo*; 24 *superstitio*; 25 *perversitas*
Nov. Valent. 19.2 *audacia*; 2 *polluo*; 5 *subreptio*; 15 *nefarius*
Nov. Valent. 21.2.11 *praesumo*; 11 *cupiditas*
Nov. Valent. 22.4 *invidia*

Nov. Valent. 23.3 *violo*; 4 *caecus*; 4 furor; 4 *rapio*; 6 *ausus*; 6 *funestus*; 6 *violentia*; 7 *cinis*; 8 *praesumptio*; 17 *vesanus*; 17 *barbarus*; 17 *crudelitas*; 17 *invideo*; 18 *inexpiabilis*; 19 *nefandus*; 19 *scelus*; 21 *cinis*; 21 *contagio*; 21 *polluo*; 23 *audeo*; 25 *foeditas*; 25 *maculo*; 26 *hostis*; 26 *violator*; 29 *temeritas*; 31 *praesumptio*; 33 *dirus*; 35 *scelus*; 36 *execrabilis*; 37 *violator*; 44 *rebellis*; 46 *violator*; 49 *violator*; 50 *improbus*
Nov. Valent. 24.5 *turba*
Nov. Valent. 25.17 *cupiditas*; 25 *scaevus*
Nov. Valent. 27.9 *improbus*; 31 *pravus*; 51 *subreptio*; 51 *temeritas*; 51 *temero*; 52 *audacia*; 52 *praesumo*
Nov. Valent. 28.14 *avaritia*
Nov. Valent. 29.4 *temeritas*
Nov. Valent. 31.20 *impius*; 21 *pravus*; 22 *obstinatio*
Nov. Valent. 32.16 *violentia*; 43 *improbus*; 44 *turbo*; 44 *hostis*
Nov. Valent. 33.23 *barbarus*
Nov. Valent. 34.6 *hostilis*; 6 *vastatio*; 15 *hostilis*; 15 *vastitas*; 18 *vastatio*; 21 *barbarus*; 22 *barbaries*; 24 *hostis*
Nov. Valent. 35.72 *hostilitas*
Nov. Valent. 36.41 *praesumptio*
Nov. Majo. 1.15 *hostis*
Nov. Majo. 2.27 *feralis*; 28 *acerbitas*; 30 *discurro*; 31 *depraedatio*; 32 *avidus*; 36 *acerbe*; 37 *depraedatio*; 44 *depraedatio*; 44 *saevio*; 47 *saevus*; 48 *crudelitas*; 49 *cupiditas*; 49 *improbitas*; 72 *rebellis*
Nov. Majo. 3.3 *improbitas*; 3 *insolens*; 10 *insolentia*
Nov. Majo. 4.8 *praesumo*; 15 *temero*; 16 *subreptio*
Nov. Majo. 5.4 *scelus*
Nov. Majo. 6.5 *pius*; 14 *cupiditas*; 17 *cupiditas*; 19 *impietas*; 25 *perfidus*; 48 *cupiditas*; 48 *improbus*; 48 *profanus*; 48 *rapio*; 48 *tempto*; 48 *violo*; 50 *polluo*; 50 *scelus*; 53 *tempto*; 54 *obstinatio*; 84 *subrepo*; 93 *macula*; 94 *cupiditas*; 98 *perfidia*; 102 *aviditas*; 104 *depravo*; 106 *pravus*; 107 *cupiditas*; 113 *improbitas*; 116 *impius*
Nov. Majo. 7.6 *polluo*; 8 *contagio*; 9 *praesumptio*; 19 *polluo*; 52 *depraedatio*; 54 *sceleratus*; 76 *praesumo*
Nov. Majo. 9.3 *nefarius*; 5 *macula*; 7 *temero*; 12 *nefandus*; 16 *incursus*; 17 *flagitium*; 18 *luxuria*; 19 *libido*; 19 *protervitas*; 20 *violo*
Nov. Majo. 11.6 *praesumptio*; 6 *pius*; [13] *ausus*; 15 *praesumptio*; 19 *violo*
Nov. Marc. 1.11 *flagitium*; 54 *invidia*; 67 *avaritia*; 67 *invidia*; 68 *perturbo*; 68 *conor*; 73 *petulans*
Nov. Marc. 2.3 *hostilis*
Nov. Marc. 3.2 *avaritia*

Nov. Marc. 4.26 *contamino*; 26 *polluo*; 31 *macula*; 31 *polluo*; 31 *sordeo*
Nov. Sev. 1.8 *pravus*
Nov. Sev. 2.5 *conor*
Nov. Anth. 1.34 *foeditas*; 40 *execrabiliter*

Bibliography

Primary sources

Acta conciliorum oecumenicorum, ed. E. Schwartz, I.1.3, I.1.4, Berolini 1927–1928.

Acta synodalia, vol. 1 ann. 50–381, ed. A. Baron, H. Pietras, Kraków 2006.

Aeschinis Orationes, ed. F. Blass, Lipsiae 1908.

Ambrosius, *De Iacob, De Ioseph, De patriarchi, De fuga saeculi, De interpellatione Iob et David, De apologia prophetae David, De Helia, De Nabuthae, De Tobia, CSEL* 32.2, rec. C. Schenkl, Vindobonae 1897.

Ambrosius, *Epistulae et acta, CSEL* 82.1–3, rec. O. Faller, M. Zelzer, Vindobonae 1968–1990.

Ambrosius, *Hexameron, De paradiso, De Cain, De Noe, De Abraham, De Isaac, De bono mortis, CSEL* 32.1, rec. C. Schenkl, Vindobonae 1897.

Ammiani Marcellini rerum gestarum libri qui supersunt, rec. W. Seyfarth, vol. I–III, Lipsiae 1999.

Anaximenis Ars rhetorica, quae vulgo fertur Aristotelis ad Alexandrum, ed. M. Fuhrmann, Lipsiae 1966.

Aristophanes, *Comoedias*, rec. Th. Bergk, t. 1, Lipsiae 1897.

Aristoteles, *Ars rhetorica*, rec. A. Roemer, Lipsiae 1898.

Aristoteles, *De arte poetica*, rec. R. Kassel, Oxonii 1965.

Augustinus, *Contra secundam Iuliani responsionem opus imperfectum, CSEL* 85.1–2, rec. M. Zelzer, Vindobonae 2004.

Augustinus, *De moribus ecclesiae catholicae et de moribus Manicheorum, CSEL* 90, rec. J.B. Bauer, Vindobonae 1992.

Augustinus, *De unico baptismo, Breviculus collationis cum Donatistis, Contra partem Donati post gesta, Sermo ad Caesarensis ecclesiae plebem, Gesta cum Emerito Donatistarum episcopo, Contra Gaudentium Donatistarum episcopum, CSEL* 53, rec. M. Petschening, Vindobonae 1910.

Augustinus, *Epistulae 124–184, CSEL* 44, rec. A. Goldbacher, Vindobonae 1904.

Augustinus, der Lehrer der Gnade 4.1 *Schriften gegen die Pelagianer. Gegen Julian*, Hrsg. Th. G. Ring, Übers. R. Habitzky, Würzburg 2005.

Sancti Aurelii Augustini *De civitate Dei*, *CCSL* 47–48, Turnholti 1955.
Sancti Aurelii Augustini *Enarrationes in psalmos*, *CCSL* 38, rec. E. Dekkers, Turnholti 1956.
C. Iuli Caesaris *Commentarii belli civilis*, rec. A. Klotz, Lipsiae 1950.
Magni Aurelii Cassiodori *Variarum Libri XII*, *CCSL* 96, rec. A.J. Fridh, Turnholti 1973.
M. Tulli Ciceronis *De officiis*, rec. C. Atzert, Lipsiae 1963.
M. Tulli Ciceronis *Epistualae ad Atticum*, rec. D.R. Shackleton Bailey, Stuttgardi 1987.
M. Tulli Ciceronis *Scripta quae mansuerunt omnia* 2. *Rhetorici libri 2 qui vocatur de inventione*, ed. E. Stroebel, Stuttgardi 1965.
M. Tulli Ciceronis *Scripta quae mansuerunt omnia* 5. *In Q. Caecilium divinatio, In C. Verrem actio I et II*, rec. A. Klotz, Lipsiae 1923.
M. Tulli Ciceronis *Scripta quae mansuerunt omnia* 6. *In L. Sergium Catilinam orationes*, rec. P. Reis, Lipsiae 1933.
M. Tulli Ciceronis *Scripta quae mansuerunt omnia* 18. *Oratio pro L. Murena*, rec. H. Kasten, Lipsiae 1961.
M. Tulli Ciceronis *Scripta quae mansuerunt omnia* 19. *Oratio pro P. Cornelio Sulla*, rec. H. Kasten, Lipsiae 1966.
M. Tulli Ciceronis *Scripta quae mansuerunt omnia* 21. *Orationes cum senatui gratias egit, cum populo gratias egit, de domo sua, de haruspicum responsis*, ed. T. Maslowski, Lipsiae 1981.
M. Tulli Ciceronis *Scripta quae mansuerunt omnia* 28. *In M. Antonium orationes Philippicae XIV*, rec. P. Fedeli, Lipsiae 1986.
M. Tulli Ciceronis *Scripta quae mansuerunt omnia* 45. *De natura deorum*, rec. V. Ax, Lipsiae 1933.
Claudii Claudiani *Carmina*, rec. J.B. Hall, Lipsiae 1985.
Corpus Inscriptionum Latinarum, Berolini 1862–
Corpus Iuris Civilis, vol. I: *Institutiones, Digesta*, rec. P. Krüger, Th. Mommsen, Berlolini 1963.
Corpus Iuris Civilis, vol. II: *Codex Iustinianus*, rec. P. Krüger, Berolini 1954.
Sancti Cypriani Episcopi *Epistularium*, ed. G.F. Diercks, *CCSL* 3B–C, Turnholti 1994–1996.
Demosthenes, *Oratio pro Corona*, rec. E.C.F. Wunderlich, Göttingae 1925.
Diokletians Preisedikt, Hrsg. S. Lauffer, Berlin 1971.
Epiphanius, *Ancoratus und Panarion*, Bd. 1, *GCS* 25, Hrsg. K. Holl, Lipsiae 1915.
Epistulae imperatorum pontificum aliorum, *CSEL* 35, rec. O. Guenther, Vindobonae 1895.
Eusebius, *Die Kirchengeschichte*, [in:] Eusebius, *Werke*, t. 2, *GCS* 9, ed. E. Schwartz, Th. Mommsen, Lipsiae 1902–1909.
Eusebius, *Vita Constantini*, [in:] Eusebius, *Werke*, t. 1, *GCS*, ed. I.A. Heikel, Lipsiae 1902.
Firmicus Maternus, *L'erreur de religions païennes*, ed. R. Turcan, Paris 1982.
Fontes Iuris Romani Anteiustiniani, t. 1–3, ed. S. Riccobono, Florentiae 1940–1943.
The Greek New Testament, ed. B. Aland, K. Aland, J. Karavidopoulos, C.M. Martini, B.E. Metzger, Nördlingen 2008.
Hieronymus, *Epistulae 71–120*, *CSEL* 55, rec. I. Hilberg, Vindobonae 1910.
Homer, *Ilias*, rec. A. Ludwich, Lipsiae 1902.
Q. Horatii Flacci *Opera*, rec. D.C. Shackleton Bailey, Stuttgardiae 1985.

Isidori Hispalensis Etymologiarum sive Originum libri XX, ed. W.M. Lindsay, Oxonii 1987.
Isocrates, *Orationes*, rec. F. Blass, Lipsiae 1898.
Lactantius, *De mortibus persecutorum*, ed. J.L. Creed, Oxonii 1984.
Libanius, *Opera*, rec. R. Förster, Lipsiae 1903–1927.
Titi Livii *Ab urbe Condita libri XXXVI–XXXVII*, rec. P.G. Walsh, Stutgardiae 1982.
G. Marius Victorinus, *Explanationes in Ciceronis rhetoricam*, *CCSL* 132, ed. A. Ippolito, Turnholti 2006.
Notitia dignitatum accedunt notitia urbis Constantinopolitanae et Latercula provinciarum, ed. O. Seeck, Berolini 1876.
XII Panegyrici Latini, rec. A. Mynors, Oxonii 1964.
Plato, *Epistulae*, rec. J. Moore-Blunt, Lipsiae 1985.
Plato, *Gorgias*, ed. E.R. Dodds, Oxonii 1959.
Plato, *Laches*, ed. J. Kral, Vindobonae 1888.
Plato, *Politeia*, ed. J. Adam, Cambridge 1969.
Platonis legum libri duodecim, rec. C.F. Hermann, Lipsiae 1877.
T. Macci Plauti Comoediae 3. *Cistellariam, Curculionem, Epidicum completens*, rec. G. Goetz, F. Schoell, Lipsiae 1895.
T. Macci Plauti Comoediae 6. *Pseudolum, Rudentem, Stichum completens*, rec. G. Goetz, F. Schoell, Lipsiae 1896.
C. Plini Caecili Secundi Epistularum Libri 9. *Epistularum ad Traianum liber, Panegyricus*, ed. M. Schuster, Lipsiae 1958.
Procopius, *Historia Arcana*, ed. J. Haury, Lipsiae 1963.
M. Fabi Quintiliani institutionis oratoriae libri XII, ed. L. Radermacher, Lipsiae 1971.
Rhetores Graeci, rec. L. Spengel, 1–3, Lipsiae 1853–1856.
Rhétorique à Herennius, ed. G. Achard, Paris 1989.
The Theodosian Code and Novels and the Sirmondian Constitutions. A Translation with Commentary, Glossary and Bibliography by C. Pharr, Princeton 1952.
Theodosiani Libri XVI cum Constitutionibus Sirmondianis et Leges Novellae ad Theodosianum Pertinentes, ed. Th. Mommsen, P.M. Meyer, Berolini 1905.
Tyranni Rufini opera, rec. M. Simonetti, Turnholti 1961.
C. Sallusti Crispi Catilina, Iugurtha, fragmenta ampliora, ed. A. Kurfess, Lipsiae 1957.
Salvien de Marseille, *Du gouverment de Dieu*, SChr 220, ed. G. Lagarrigue, Paris 1975.
Sokrates Kirchengeschichte, *GCS* NF 1, Hrsg. G.Ch. Hansen, mit Beiträgen von M. Sirinjan, Berolini 1995.
Sozomenus, *Kirchengeschichte*, *GCS* 68, Hrsg. J. Bidez, G.Ch. Hansen, Berolini 1960.
C. Suetonii Tranquilli opera 1. De Vita Caesarum libri XII, rec. M. Ihm, Stutgardiae 1964.
Quinti Septimi Florentii Tertulliani Opera Catholica, *CCSL* 1, Turnholti 1954.
Quinti Septimi Florentii Tertulliani Opera Montanistica, *CCSL* 2, Turnholti 1954.
Vellei Paterculi Historiarum ad M. Vinicium consulem libri duo, rec. W.S. Watt, Lipsiae 1988.
P. Vergilii Maronis Aeneis, rec. O. Ribbeck, Lipsiae 1907.

Xenophonotis qui inscribitur libellus Athēnaiōn politeia, ed. E. Kalinka, Stutgardiae 1961.
Zosimi Comitis et exadvocati fisci, Historia Nova, ed. L. Mendelssohn, Lipsiae 1887.

Secondary works

Abbott K.M. (1979): Satira and Satiricus in Late Latin, *ICS* 4: 192–199.

Achard G. (1981): *Pratique rhétorique et idéologie politique dans les discours « optimates » de Cicéron*, Leiden.

Adamik T. (1977–1978): Bemerkungen zur Invectiva, *AUB(class)* 5–6: 89–100.

Adamik T. (1995): *Cicero's Theory of Three Kinds of Style, ACD* 31: 3–9.

Adkin N. (1992): *Hieronymus Ciceronianus*. The *Catilinarians* in Jerome, *Latomus* 51: 408–420.

Agosti G. (2001): Late Antique Iambics and *Iambikè Idéa*, [in:] *Iambic Ideas. Essays on a Poetic Tradition from Archaic Greece to the Late Roman Empire*, eds. A. Carvarzere, A. Aloni, A. Barchiesi, Lanham–Boulder–New York–Oxford: 219–255.

Albaladejo T. (2003): The Three Types of Speeches in Quintilian, Book III, [in:] *Quintilian and the Law. The Art of Persuasion in Law and Politics*, ed. O. Tellegen-Couperus, Leuven: 51–58.

Ankum H. (1985): La captiva adultera, *RIDA* 32: 153–205.

Archi G.G. (1976): *Teodosio II e la sua codificazione*, Napoli.

Arjava A. (1996): *Women and Law in Late Antiquity*, Oxford.

Awianowicz B. (2004a): Progymnasmata w rzymskiej teorii i praktyce retorycznej od pierwszych świadectw do *Institutio oratoria* Kwintyliana, [in:] Sapere aude. *Księga pamiątkowa ofiarowana profesorowi dr hab. Marianowi Szarmachowi z okazji 65 rocznicy urodzin*, Toruń: 31–45.

Awianowicz B. (2004b): Pochwała – enkomion – panegiryk. Glosa terminologiczna na marginesie książki Jakuba Niedźwiedzia *Nieśmiertelne Teatra Sławy, Barok. Historia – Literatura – Sztuka* XI/1 (21): 185–193.

Baccari M.P. (1991): Comunione e cittadinanza (a proposito della posizione giuridica di eretici, apostati, giudei e pagani secondo i Codici di Teodosio II e Giustiniano I), *SDHI* 57: 264–286.

Baccari M.P. (1996): *Cittadini popoli e comunione nella legislazione dei secoli IV–VI*, Torino.

Badian E. (1975): Manius Acilius Glabrio and the Audacissimi, *AJPh* 96: 67–75.

Barnes T.D. (1984): Constantine's Prohibition of Pagan Sacrifice, *AJPh* 105: 69–72.

Barnes T.D. (1996): Oppressor, Persecutor, Usurper. The Meaning of 'Tyrannus' in the Fourth Century, [in:] *Historiae Augustae Colloquium Barcionense*, a cura di G. Bonamente, M. Mayer, Bari: 55–65.

Barone-Adesi G. (1986): Eresie "sociali" ed inquisizione teodosiana, *AARC* VI: 119–166.

Barr W. (1979): Claudian's *In Rufinum*. An Invective?, [in:] *Papers of the Liverpool Latin Seminar*, II vol., ed. F. Cairns, Liverpool.

Bassanelli Sommariva G. (1988): Brevi considerazioni su *C.Th.* 9.7.1, *AARC* VII, Napoli: 309–323.
Benner M. (1975): *The Emperor Says. Studies in Rhetorical Style in Edicts of the Early Empire*, Göteborg.
Benveniste E. (1960): *Profanus* et *profanare*, [in:] *Hommages à G. Dumézil*, Bruxelles: 46–53.
Berger A. (1953): *Encyclopedic Dictionary of Roman Law*, Philadelphia.
Berger A. (1955): La concezione di eretico nelle fonti giustinianee, *Rendiconti dell'Accademia Nazionale dei Lincei* 352 (serie 8, vol. 10): 353–368.
Berno F.R. (2007): La Furia di Clodio in Cicerone, *BStudLat* 37: 69–91.
Beskow P. (1988): The Theodosian Laws against Manichaeism, [in:] *Manichean Studies. Proceedings of the First International Conference on Manichaeism*, ed. P. Bryder, Lund: 1–11.
Bettini M., Borghini A. (1983): La guerra e lo scambio: hostis, perduellis, inimicus, [in:] *Linguistica e antropologia. Atti del XIV Congresso Internazionali di Studi, Lecco 23–25 maggio 1980*, a cura di gruppo di Lecce, Roma: 305–312.
Bianchini M. (1988): Ancora in tema di unioni fra barbari e Romani, [in:] *AARC* VII, Napoli: 225–249.
Birley A.R. (1983–1984): Magnus Maximus and the Persecution of Heresy, *BRL* 66: 13–43.
Bolonyai G. (2000): A Classification of Kinds of Speech in Aphthonius' Commentaries, *AAntHung* 40: 25–33.
Botta F. (2004): "Per vim inferre". *Studi sul* stuprum *violento e* raptus *nel diritto romano e bizantino*, Cagliari.
Bradbury S. (1994): Constantine and the Problem of Anti-Pagan Legislation in the Fourth Century, *CPh* 1994: 120–139.
Brandt H. (2004): Erneute Überlegungen zum Preisedikt Diokletians, [in:] *Diokletian und die Tetrarchie. Aspekte einer Zeitwende*, Hrsgg. A. Demandt, A. Goltz, H. Schlange-Schöningen, Berlin–New York: 47–55.
Brennecke H.Ch. (1988): *Studien zur Geschichte der Homöer. Der Osten bis zum Ende der homöischer Reichskirche*, Tübingen.
Bruggiser Ph. (2002): *Audacia* in Sallust "Verschwörung des Catilina", *Hermes* 130: 265–287.
Bucci O. (1986): Intolleranza ellenica e libertà romana nel libro XVI del Codice Teodosiano, [in:] *AARC* 6, Perugia: 363–417.
Burian J. (1982): Latrones. Ein Begriff im Römischen literarischen und juristischen Quellen, *Eirene* 19: 17–23.
Calderone S. (1972): Superstitio, [in:] *ANRW*, Hrsg. H. Temporini, I.2: 377–396.
Cameron Al. (1970): *Claudian. Poetry and Propaganda in the Court of Honorius*, Oxford.
Cameron Av. (1985): *Procopius and the Sixth Century*, London.
Cañizar Palacios J.L. (1998): Posibles causas de deserción en el ejército Romano vistas a través del Codex Theodosianus. Problemática bajo Constantino y problemática a partir de la segunda mitad del siglo IV D.C., *SHHA* 16: 217–232.
Cañizar Palacios J.L. (2005): *Propaganda y Codex Theodosianus*, Madrid.

Cañizar Palacios J.L. (2006): El uso propagandistico del *hostis publicus* en el *Codex Theodosianus*, *Latomus* 65: 130–144.
Cañizar Palacios J.L. (2009): La utilidad política y social del vocabulario religioso en la legislación del *Teodosiano*, [in:] *Droit, Religion et Société dans le* Code Théodosien. *Troisièmes Journées d'Etude sur le* Code Théodosien. *Neuchâtel, 15–17 février 2007*, eds. J.J. Aubert, Ph. Blanchard, Genève: 129–146.
Cantarella E. (1999): *Secondo natura. La bisessualità nel mondo antico*, Milano.
Caseau B. (2008): L'Adjectif *profanus* dans la livre XVI du *Code Théodosien*, [in:] *Empire Chrétien et Église au IV*e *et V*e *siècles. Intégration ou « concordat » ? Le témoignage du* Code Théodosien. *Actes du Colloque international (Lyon, 6, 7 et 8 octobre 2005)*, eds. J.N. Guinot, F. Richard, Paris: 195–210.
Centola D.A. (1999): *Il crimen calumniae. Contributo allo studio del processo criminale romano*, Napoli.
Champeaux J. (1989): « Pietas »: piété personnelle et piété collective à Rome, *BAGB* 3: 263–279.
Chastagnol A. (1992): *Le sénat romaine à l'époque impériale*, Paris.
Chauvot A. (1998): *Opinions romains face au barbares au IVe siècle ap. J.-C.*, Paris.
Classen C.J. (2002): *Virtutes* und *vitia* in Claudians Gedichten, [in:] *Humana sapit – Mélanges en l'honneur de L. Cracco Ruggini*, a cura di J.M. Carrié, R. Lizzi Testa, Turnhout: 157–167.
Classen P. (1955): Kaiserreskript und Königsurkunde. Diplomatische Studien zum römisch-germanischen Kontinuitätsproblem, Erster Teil, *Archiv für Diplomatik* 1: 1–87.
Conley Th. (2010): *Toward a Rhetoric of Insult*, Chicago–London.
Corcoran S. (1993): Hidden from History. The legislation of Licinius, [in:] *The Theodosian Code. Studies in the Imperial Law of Late Antiquity*, eds. J. Harries, I. Wood, London: 97–119.
Coyle J.K. (2004): Foreign and Insane: Labelling Manichaeism in the Roman Empire, *SR* 33: 217–234.
Craig Ch. (2004): Audience Expectations, Invective, and Proof, [in:] *Cicero the Advocate*, eds. J. Powell, J. Paterson, Oxford: 187–213.
Cribiore R. (2007): *The School of Libanius in Late Antique Antioch*, Princeton–Oxford.
Crogiez-Pétrequin S., Jaillette P. (2009): Images de la désertion et des déserteurs dans le *Code Théodosien*, [in:] *Droit, Religion et Société dans le* Code Théodosien. *Troisièmes Journées d'Etude sur le* Code Théodosien. *Neuchâtel, 15–17 février 2007*, eds. J.J. Aubert, Ph. Blanchard, Genève: 229–243.
Dagron G. (1974): *Naissance d'une capitale. Constantinople et ses institutions de 330* à *451*, Paris.
Dalla D. (1987): *"Ubi Venus mutatur". Omosessualità e diritto nel mondo romano*, Milano.
Danvoye S. (2007): Contacts pacifiques et violents entre les Barbares et les Romains dans les panégyriques de Claudien, *Latomus* 66: 132–149.
Dauge Y.A. (1981): *Le barbare: Recherches sur la conception romaine de la barbarie et de la civilsation*, Brussels.
Davies M. (1985): Coventional Topics of Invective in Alceus, *Prometheus* 11: 31–39.
De wonfils G. (1981): *Il comes et questor nell'età di dinastia costantiniana*, Napoli.

De Dominicis M.A. (1953): Registro delle alterazioni (glossemi ed interpolazioni) nelle costituzioni del Codice Teodosiano e nelle Novelle Postteodosiane segnalate dalla critica, *BIDR* 16–17: 383–442.

De Dominicis M.A. (1964): Indice delle glosse e interpolazioni ed omissioni nelle costituzioni del Codice Teodosiano (Supplemento), *Iura* 15: 117–136.

De Giovanni L. (1980): *Chiesa e Stato nel Codice Teodosiano. Saggio sul libro XVI*, Napoli.

De Visscher F. (1963): *Le droit des tombeaux romains*, Milano.

Dębiński A. (1990): *Ustawodawstwo karne rzymskich cesarzy chrześcijańskich w sprawach religijnych*, Lublin.

Dębiński A. (1992): Ustawodawstwo chrześcijańskich cesarzy rzymskich przeciw manichejczykom, *Kościół i Prawo* 8: 195–211.

Dębiński A. (1995): Sacrilegium *w prawie rzymskim*, Lublin.

Delmaire R. (1995): *Les institutions du Bas-empire romain de Constantin à Justinien. I. Les institutions civiles palatines*, Paris.

Delmaire R. (1997): Les usurpateurs du Bas-Empire et le recrutement des fonctionnaires (essai de reflexion sur les assises du puvoir et leur limites), [in:] *Usurpation in der Spätantike*, Hrsgg. F. Paschoud, J. Szidat, Stuttgart: 111–126.

Delmaire R. (2012): Du *Code Théodosien* au *Code Justinien*. L'adaptation de lois anciennes à des situations nouvelles, [in:] *Société, Économie, Administration dans le* Code Théodosien, eds. S. Crogiez-Pétrequin, P. Jaillette, Lille: 165–182.

Demandt A. (1989a): *Die Spätantike. Römische Geschichte von Diocletian bis Justinian 284–565 n.Chr.*, München.

Demandt A. (1989b): The Osmosis of Late Roman and Germanic Aristocracies, [in:] *Das Reich und die Barbaren*, Hrsgg. E.K. Chrysos, A. Schwarcz, Wien–Köln: 75–86.

Desanti L. (1990): Sileat omnibus perpetuo divinandi curiositas. *Indovini e sanzioni nel diritto romano*, Milano.

Desanti L. (1995): Astrologi: Eretici o pagani? Un problema esegetico, [in:] *AARC* 10, Napoli: 687–696.

Dewar M. (1990): The Fall of Eutropius, *CQ* 40: 582–584.

Di Berardino A. (2003): Tempo cristiano e la prima amnistia pasquale di Valentiniano I, [in:] *"Munera amicitiae" studi di storia e cultura sulla tarda antichità offerti a S. Pricoco*, a cura di R. Barcellona, T. Sardella, Rubettino: 131–150.

Di Mauro Todini A. (1990): *Aspetti della legislazione religiosa del IV secolo*, Roma.

Dölger F., Karayannopoulos J. (1968): *Byzantinische Urkundenlehre. Erster Abschnitt: Die Kaiserurkunden*, München.

Dreher M. (2006): Die Ursprünge des Kirchenasyls und die Gesetzgebung Theodosius' II, [in:] *Staatlichkeit und politisches Handeln in der römischen Kaiserzeit*, Hrsg. H.U. Wiemer, Berlin–New York: 151–174.

Dunkle J.R. (1967): The Greek Tyrant and Roman Political Invective of the Late Republic, *TAPhA* 98: 151–171.

Dunkle J.R. (1971): The Rhetorical Tyrant in Roman Historiography. Sallust, Livy and Tacitus, *CW* 65: 12–20.

Dzielska M. (2004): Antychrześcijańska ideologia neoplatoników późnego hellenizmu, [in:] *Ideologia i propaganda w starożytności. Materiały konferencji Komisji Historii Starożytnej PTH, Rzeszów, 12–14 września 2000*, red. L. Morawiecki, P. Berdowski, Rzeszów: 479–487.

Ehlers W. (1941): Piaculum, *RE* 20: 1179–1185.

Elbern S. (1984): *Usurpationen in spätrömischen Reich*, Bonn.

Errington R.M. (1988): Constantine and the Pagans, *GRBS* 29: 309–318.

Errington R.M. (1997): Christian Accounts of the Religious Legislation of Theodosius I, *Klio* 79: 398–443.

Erskine A. (1991): Hellenistic Monarchy and Roman Political Invective, *CQ* 41: 106–120.

Escribano M.V. (1997): La ilegitimidad política en los textos historiográficos y jurídicos tardíos (Historia Auguta, Orosius, Codex Theodosianus), *RIDA* 44: 85–120.

Escribano Paño M.V. (2008): La construction de l'image de l'hérétique dans le *Code Théodosien* XVI, [in:] *Empire Chrétien et Église au IVe et Ve siècles. Intégration ou* « concordat » ? Le témoignage du Code Théodosien. *Actes du Colloque international (Lyon, 6, 7 et 8 octobre 2005)*, eds. J.N. Guinot, F. Richard, Paris: 389–412.

Escribano Paño M.V. (2009): The Social Exclusion of Heretics in *Codex Theodosianus* XVI, [in:] *Droit, Religion et Société dans le Code Théodosien. Troisièmes Journées d'Etude sur le* Code Théodosien. *Neuchâtel, 15–17 février 2007*, eds. J.J. Aubert, Ph. Blanchard, Genève: 39–66.

Evans-Grubbs J. (1989): Abduction Marriage in Antiquity. A Law of Constantine (*CTh* IX.24.1) and Its Social Context, *JRS* 79: 59–83.

Evans-Grubbs J. (1993): "Marriage More Shameful Than Adultery". Slave-Mistress Relationships, "Mixed Marriages," and Late Roman Law, *Phoenix* 47: 125–154.

Evans-Grubbs J. (1995): *Law and Family in Late Antiquity. The Emperor Constantine's Marriage Legislation*, Oxford.

Falchi G.L. (1986): Legislazione e politica ecclesiastica nell'impero romano dal 380 d.C. al Codice Teodosiano, [in:] *AARC* 6, Perugia: 179–212.

Feissel D. (2007): Cesarz i administracja cesarska, [in:] Świat Bizancjum, t. 1: *Cesarstwo wschodniorzymskie*, red. C. Morrison, tłum. A. Graboń, Kraków: 97–132.

Feld K. (2005): *Barbarische Bürger. Die Isaurier und das Römische Reich*, Berlin–New York.

Ferrini C. (1976): *Diritto penale romano. Esposizione storica e dottrinale. Estratto dall'Enciclopedia del Diritto Penale Italiano diretta dal Prof. E. Pessina*, Roma.

Fichtenau H. (1957): *Arenga. Spätantike und Mittelalter im Spiegel der Urkundenformen*, Graz–Köln.

Flower R. (2013): *Emperors and Bishops in Late Roman Invective*, Cambridge.

Fögen M.Th. (1993): *Die Enteignung der Wahrsager. Studien zur kaiserlichen Wissensmonopol in der Spätantike*, Frankfurt am Main.

Fögen M.Th. (1998): Massenmord an Texten, *RJ* 17: 6–11.

Formigoni Candini W. (1990): *Ne lenones sunt in ullo loco reipublice romanae*, *AUFG* 4: 97–127.

Fournet J.L. (2004): Entre document et littérature: la pétition dans l'Antiquité Tardive, [in:] *La pétition à Byzance*, éds. D. Feissel, J. Gascou, Paris: 61–74.

Fraschetti A. (2005): Principi cristiani, templi e sacrifici nel Codice Teodosiano e in altre testimonianze parallele, [in:] *Diritto romano e identità cristiana. Definizioni storico-religiose e confronti interdisciplinari*, a cura di A. Saggioro, Roma: 123–140.

Frezza P. (1989): L'esperienza della tolleranza religiosa fra pagani e cristiani dal IV al V secolo d.C. nell'Oriente ellenistico, *SDHI* 55: 41–97.

Fridh A.J. (1956): *Terminologie et formules dans les Variae de Cassiodore. Études sur les développement du style administratif aux derniers siècles de l'antiquité*, Stockholm.

Fusco S.A. (1974): Constitutiones principum und Kodifikation in der Spätantike, *Chiron* 4: 609–628.

Garambois-Vasquez F. (2007): *Les invectives de Claudien. Une poétique de la violence*, Bruxelles.

Garnsey P. (1970): *Social Status and Legal Privilege in the Roman Empire*, Oxford.

Gaudemet J. (1976): Aspects politiques de la codification théodosienne, [in:] *Istituzioni giuridiche e realtà politiche nel Tardo Impero (III–V sec.d.C.). Atti di un incontro tra storici e giuristi*, a cura di G.G. Archi, Milano: 261–279.

Gaudemet J. (1990): La législation anti-païenne de Constantin à Justinien, *CrSt* 11: 449–468.

Gaudemet J. (1997): L'Édit de Thessalonique. Police locale ou déclaration de principe?, [in:] *Aspects of the Fourth Century A.D. Proceedings of the Symposion Power & Posession. State, Society and Church in the Fourth Century A.D., Leiden 3-5.06.1993*, eds. H.W. Pleket, A.M.F.W. Verhoogt, Leiden: 43–51.

Gaudemet J. (2000): La politique religieuse impériale au IVe siècle (envers les païennes, les juifs, les héretiques, les donatistes), [in:] *Legislazione imperiale e religiosa nel IV secolo*, Roma: 7–66.

Gertrude Emilie S. (1944): Cicero and the Roman Pietas, *CJ* 39: 536–542.

Giaro T. (2009): Historia i tradycja prawa rzymskiego, [in:] W. Dajczak, T. Giaro, F. Longchamps de Bérier, *Prawo rzymskie. U podstaw prawa prywatnego*, Warszawa: 31–116.

Gibel K. (2006): Antymanichejskie przepisy prawne w teorii i praktyce (IV–VI w.), [in:] *Cesarstwo Bizantyńskie. Dzieje, religia, kultura. Studia ofiarowane Profesorowi W. Ceranowi przez uczniów na 70-lecie Jego urodzin*, red. P. Krupczyński, M.J. Leszka, Łódź: 71–85.

Gildenhard I. (2006): Reckoning with Tyranny. Greek Thoughts on Caesar in Cicero's *Letters to Atticus* in Early 49, [in:] *Ancient Tyranny*, ed. S. Lewis, Edinburgh: 197–209.

Gildenhard I. (2007): Greek Auxiliaries: Tragedy and Philosophy in Ciceronian Invective, [in:] *Cicero on the Attack. Invective and Subversion in the Orations and Beyond*, ed. J. Booth, Swansea: 149–182.

Giuffrè V. (1981): Latrones desertoresque, *Labeo* 27: 214–218.

Gnoli F. (1979): *Ricerche sul crimen peculatus*, Milano.

Gradenwitz O. (1925): *Heidelberger Index zum Theodosianus mit Ergänzungsband*, hergestellt unter Leitung von O. Gradenwitz, Berlin (Nachdruck Hildesheim 1999).

Grillmeier A. (2004): *Jesus der Christus im Glauben der Kirche*, Freiburg–Basel–Wien[2].

Grodzynski D. (1974): Superstitio, *REA* 76: 36–60.

Grout-Gerletti D. (1998): Le vocabulaire de la contagion chez l'évêque Cyprien de Carthage (249–258): de l'idée à l'utilisation, [in:] *Maladie et maladies dans le textes latins antiques et médiévaux*, éd. C. Deroux, Bruxelles.

Grünewald Th. (2004): *Bandits in the Roman Empire. Myth and Reality*, transl. J. Drinkwater, London.

Grzegorczykowa R. (1991): Obelga jako akt mowy, *Poradnik językowy* 5-6: 193–201.

Guichard L. (2008): Le style de Valentinien Ier dans ses lois religieuses du *Code Théodosien* et dans ses lettres de la *Collectio Avellana*, [in:] *Empire Chrétien et Église au IVe et Ve siècles. Intégration ou « concordat » ? Le témoignage du* Code Théodosien. *Actes du Colloque international (Lyon, 6, 7 et 8 octobre 2005)*, eds. J.N. Guinot, F. Richard, Paris: 155–172.

Günther O. (1896): *Avellana Studien, Sitzungsberichte des philosophisch-historischen Classe der Kaiserlichen Akademie der Wissenschaften 134, V Abhandlung*, Wien.

Haack M.L. (2003): *Haruspices dans le monde romain*, Bordeaux.

Haase R. (1994): Justinian I und der Frauenraub (*raptus*), *ZRG* 111: 458–470.

Hagemann M. (1998): *Iniuria. Von den XII Tafeln bis zur Justinianischen Kodifikation*, Köln.

Hagendahl H. (1983): *Von Tertullian zu Cassiodor. Die profane literarische Tradition in dem lateinischen christlichen Schrifttum*, Göteborg.

Hano M. (2005): La Témoignage des textes législatifs du IVe siècle sur les haruspices et la divination, [in:] *La divination dans le monde etrusco-italique 9. Les ecrivans du IVe siècle. L'etrusca disciplina dans une monde en mutation. Actes de Table Ronde de Clermont-Ferrand 17 et 18 septembre 1999*, Paris: 4–26.

Hanson R.P.C. (1988): *The Search for the Christian Doctrine of God. The Arian Controversy 318–381*, Edinburgh.

Harmening D. (1979): Superstitio. Überlieferungs- und theoriegeschichtliche Untersuchungen zur kirchlich-theologischen Aberglaubensliteratur des Mittelalters, Berlin.

Harries B. (2007): Acting the Part. Techniques of the Comic Stage in Cicero's Early Speeches, [in:] *Cicero on the Attack. Invective and Subversion in the Orations and beyond*, ed. J. Booth, Swansea: 129–148.

Harries J. (1988): The Roman Imperial Quaestor from Constantine to Theodosius II, *JRS* 78: 148–172.

Harries J. (1999a): *Law and Empire in Late Antiquity*, Cambridge.

Harries J. (1999b): Constructing the Judge: Judicial Accountability and the Culture of Criticism in Late Antiquity, [in:] *Constructing Identities in Late Antiquity*, ed. R. Miles, London: 214–233.

Harries J. (2006): Violence, Victims and the Legal Tradition in Late Antiquity, [in:] *Violence in Late Antiquity: Perceptions and Practices*, ed. H.A. Drake, Aldershot–Burlington: 85–102.

Harries J. (2007): *Law and Crime in the Roman World*, Cambridge.

Hellegouarc'h (1963): *Le vocabulaire latin des relations et des partis politiques sous la République*, Paris.

Herrera R.M. (1993): Concepto de religión en las *Etimologías* de san Isidoro de Sevilla, *Helmantica* 44: 527–534.

Herz P. (1988): *Latrocinium* und Viehdiebstal. Soziale Spannungen und Strafrecht in römischer Zeit, [in:] *Soziale Randgruppen und Außenseiter im Altertum*, Hrsg. I. Weiler, Graz: 221–241.

Heumann H.G., Seckel E. (1914): *Heumanns Handlexikon zu den Quellen des römischen Recht*, 9 Aufl. neu bearbeitet von E. Seckel, Jena.

Hiltbrunner O. (1968): Die Heiligkeit des Kaisers (zur Geschichte des Begriffs *sacer*), *Frühmittelalterliche Studien* 2: 1–30.

Hobsbawn E.J. (1969): *Bandits*, London.

Hoffmann G. (1892): *Schimpfwörter der Griechen und Römer*, Berlin.

Holman S.R. (1999): Healing the Social Leper in Gregory of Nyssa and Gregory of Nazianzus's *Peri philoptochias*, *HThR* 92: 283–309.

Holtzedorff F. von (1859): *Die Deportationsstrafe im Römischen Altertum. Hinsichtlich ihrer Entstehung und Rechtsgeschichtlichen Entwicklung dargestellt*, Leipzig (Neudruck Aalen 1975).

Honig R.M. (1960): *Humanitas und Rhetorik in spätrömischen Kaisergesetzen (Studien zur Gesinnungsgrundlage des Dominats)*, Göttingen.

Honoré T. (1986): The Making of the Theodosian Code, *ZRG* 103: 133–222.

Honoré T. (1998): *Law in the Crisis of Empire 379–455 AD. The Theodosian Dynasty and Its Quaestors*, Oxford.

Huck O. (2003): Encore à propos des Sirmondiennes... Arguments présentés à l'appui de la thèse de l'authenticité en réponse à une mise en cause récente, *AntTard* 11: 181–196.

Hughes J.J. (1998): Invective and Comedic Allusion. Cicero, *In Pisonem*, fragment 9 (Nisbet), *Latomus* 57: 570–577.

Humfress C. (2007): *Orthodoxy and the Courts in Late Antiquity*, Oxford.

Humphries M. (1998): Savage Humour. Christian Anti-Panegyric in Hilary of Poitiers' *Against Constantius*, [in:] *The Propaganda of Power. The Role of Panegyric in Late Antiquity*, ed. M. Whitby, Leiden: 201–223.

Hunger H. (1964): *Prooimion. Elemente der Byzantinischen Kaiseridee in der Arengen und Urkunden*, Wien.

Hunt D. (1993): Christianising the Roman Empire, [in:] *The Theodosian Code. Studies in the Imperial Law of Late Antiquity*, eds. J. Harries, I. Wood, London: 143–158.

James P. (1998): *Taceat superata vetustas*. Living Legends in Claudian's *In Rufinum* 1, [in:] *The Propaganda of Power. The Role of Panegyric in Late Antiquity*, ed. M. Whitby, Leiden: 151–175.

Janssen L.F. (1975): Die Bedeutungsentwicklung von *supestitio/superstes*, *Mnemosyne* 28: 135–188.

Janssen L.F. (1979): 'Superstitio' and the Persecution of the Christians, *VChr* 33: 131–159.

Jońca M. (2008): Parricidium *w prawie rzymskim*, Lublin.

Jones A.H.M. (1986): *The Later Roman Empire 284-602. A Social, Economic and Administrative Survey*, Oxford.

Jones A.H.M., Martindale J.R., Morris J. (1971): *The Prosopography of the Later Roman Empire*, vol. 1, Cambridge.

Jürgasch Th. (2016): Christians and the Invention of Paganism in the Late Roman Empire, [in:] *Pagans and Christians in Late Antique Rome. Conflict, Competition and Coexistence in the Fourth Century*, eds. M.R. Salzman, M. Sághy, R.L. Testa, Cambridge: 115–138.

Kaden E.H. (1953): Die Edikte gegen die Manichäer von Diokletian bis Justinian, [in:] *Festschrift H. Levald bei Vollendung der vierzigsten Amtsjahres als Ordentliche Professor im Oktober 1953*, Basel: 55–68.

Kahlos M. (2007a): *Debate and Dialogue. Christian and Pagan Cultures c. 360–430*, Aldershot–Burlington.

Kahlos M. (2007b): *Religio* and *superstitio*. Retortions and Phases of a Binary Opposition in Late Antiquity, *Athaeneum* 95: 389–408.

Kahlos M. (2009): *Forbearance and Compulsion. The Rhetoric of Religious Tolerance and Intolerance in Late Antiquity*, London.

Kamińska-Szmaj I. (2007): *Agresja językowa w życiu publicznym. Leksykon inwektyw politycznych 1918-2000*, Wrocław.

Karayannopoulos J. (1958): *Das Finanzwesen des frühbyzantinischen Staates*, München.

Kelly J.N.D. (1988): *Początki doktryny chrześcijańskiej*, tłum. J. Mrukówna, Warszawa.

Kennedy G.A. (1983): *Greek Rhetoric under Christian Emperors*, Princeton.

King N.Q. (1961): *The Emperor Theodosius and the Establishment of Christianity*, London.

Koch C. (1954): Praetor, *RE* 22.2, Stuttgart: 1581–1607.

Kołodko P. (2006): Rzymska terminologia stosowana na określenie narzędzi używanych podczas chłosty, *Zeszyty Prawnicze UKSW* 6.1: 121–143.

Kołodziejek E. (1994): Językowe środki zwalczania przeciwnika, czyli o inwektywach we współczesnych tekstach politycznych, [in:] Język a kultura. 11. Język polityki, red. J. Anusiewicz, B. Siciński, Wrocław.

Kopecek Th.A. (1979): *A History of Neo-Arianism*, Philadelphia.

Korpanty J. (1979): *Rzeczpospolita potomków Romulusa. Ludzie – wydarzenia – idee*, Warszawa.

Korpanty J. (1985): *Furor* in der augusteischen Literatur, *Klio* 67: 248–257.

Koster S. (1980): *Die Invektive in der griechischen und römischen Literatur*, Meisenheim am Glan.

Kowalski H. (2002): *Impietas* w religii rzymskiej w okresie schyłku Republiki, *Res Historica 14. Graecorum et Romanorum memoria II*, red. J. Morawiecki, Lublin: 103–123.

Krause J.U. (1987): *Spätantike Patronatsformen im Westen des Römischen Reiches*, München.

Krüger H. (1898): Die *humanitas* und die *pietas* nach den Quellen des römischen Rechts, *ZRG* 19: 6–57.

Kubiak D.P. (1989): Piso's Madness (Cic. *In Pis.* 21 and 47), *AJPh* 110: 237–245.

Kuhoff W. (1983): Studien zur zivilen und senatorischen Laufbahn im 4 Jahrhundert n.Chr., Frankfurt.

Kussmaul P. (1981): *Pragmaticum und Lex. Formen spätrömischen Gesetzgebung 408–457*, Göttingen.

Lanza C. (1990): *Ricerche su 'furiosus' in diritto romano*. 1, Roma.

Lassandro D. (1981): La demonizzazione del nemico politico nei Panegyrici Latini, [in:] *Religione e politica nel mondo antico*, a cura di M. Sordi, Milano: 237–249.

Lassandro D. (2000): Sacratissimus imperator. *L'immagine del* princeps *nell'oratoria tardoantica*, Bari.

Lausberg H. (1960): *Handbuch der literarischen Rhetorik. Eine Grundlegung der Literaturwissenschaft*, München.

Lazzarini C. (1982): Audax/fortis: due opposti paradigmi eroici (a proposito di Aen. 10,284), *MD* 9: 157–166.

Lemosse M. (1967): *Le régime des relations internationales dans le Haut-Empire romain*, Paris.

Lenski N. (1999): Assimilation and Revolt in the Territory of Isauria, from 1st Century BC to the 6th Century AD, *JESHO* 42: 413–465

Lenski N. (2002): *Failure of Empire. Valens and the Roman State in the Fourth Century A.D.*, Berkeley–Los Angeles–London.

Lepore E. (1954): *Il principe ciceroniano e gli ideali politici della tarda repubblica*, Napoli.

Leszka M.J. (1999): *Uzurpacje w cesarstwie bizantyńskim w okresie od IV do połowy IX wieku*, Łódź.

Levy H.L. (1946): Claudian's *In Rufinum* and Rhetorical Ψόγος, *TAPhA* 77: 57–65.

Levy H.L. (1958): Themes of Encomium and Invective in Claudian, *TAPhA* 89: 336–347.

Liebs D. (1968): *Damnum, damnare* und *damnas*. Zur Bedeutungsgeschichte einiger lateinischer Rechtswörter, *ZRG* 85: 173–252.

Liebs D. (1985): Unverhohlene Brutalität in den Gesetzen der ersten Christlichen Kaiser, [in:] *Römisches Recht in der europäischen Tradition. Symposion aus Anlaß des 75. Geburtstages von F. Wieacker*, Hrsgg. O. Behrends, M. Diesselhorst, W.E. Voss, Ebelsbach: 89–116.

Liebs D. (1986): Juristen als Sekretäre des römischen Kaisers, *ZRG* 100: 485–509.

Liebs D. (1992): Das Gesetz im spätrömischen Recht, [in:] *Das Gesetz in Spätantike und frühen Mittelalter. 4. Symposion „Die Funktion des Gesetzes in Geschichte und Gegenwart"*, Hrsg. W. Sellert, Göttingen: 11–27.

Liebs D. (2006): Konstantin als Gesetzgeber, [in:] *Konstantin der Grosse. Geschichte – Archäologie – Rezeption. Internationales Kolloquium von 10–15. Oktober 2005 an Universität Trier zur Landesaustellung Rheinland-Pfalz 2007 „Konstantin der Grosse"*, Hrsgg. A. Demandt, J. Engemann, Trier: 97–107.

Lieu S.N.C. (1985): *Manichaeism in the Later Roman Empire and Medieval China. A Historical Survey*, Manchester.

Linder A. (1987): *The Jews in Roman Imperial Legislation*, Michigan–Jerusalem.

Linkomies E. (1931): Superstitio, *Arctos* 2: 73–88.

Litewski W. (2003): *Rzymski proces karny*, Kraków.

Long J. (1996): *Claudian's* In Eutropium. *Or, How, When, and Why to Slander a Eunuch*, Chapel Hill–London.

Longosz S. (1971): Inwektywa chrześcijańska, [in:] *Słownik wczesnochrześcijańskiego piśmiennictwa*, red. J.M. Szymusiak, M. Starowieyski, Poznań: 530–537.

Lyman R. (1993): A Topography of Heresy: Mapping the Rhetorical Creation of Arianism, [in:] *Arianism after Arius. Essays on the Development of the Fourth Century Trinitarian Conflicts*, eds. M.R. Barnes, D.H. Williams, Edinburgh: 45–62.

Maceratini R. (1994): *Ricerche sullo status giuridico dell'eretico nel ditto romano-cristiano e nel diritto canonico (da Graziano ad Uguccione)*, Milano.

MacMullen (1963a): *Soldier and Civilian in the Later Roman Empire*, Cambridge, MA.

MacMullen R. (1963b): The Roman Concept Robber = Pretender, *RIDA* 10: 221–225.

MacMullen R. (1966): *Enemies of Roman Order. Treason, Unrest and Alienation in the Empire*, Cambridge, MA.

MacMullen R. (1986): Judicial Savagery in the Roman Empire, *Chiron* 16: 147–166.

MacMullen R. (1988): *Corruption and the Decline of Rome*, New Haven–London.

Maiuri A. (2005): Il "Codex Theodosianus" come "Romani iuris rifusio" nella dimensione religiosa cristiana; alcuni esempi testuali, [in:] *Diritto romano e identità cristiana. Definizioni storico-religiose e confronti interdisciplinari*, a cura di A. Saggioro, Roma: 141–160.

Manfredini D. (1985): Qui commutant cum feminis vestem, *RIDA* 32: 257–271.

Mano M. (2005): Le témoignage des textes législatifs du IV siècle sur les haruspices et la divination, [in:] *La divination dans le monde* étrusco-*italique. 9 Les écrivains du IVe s.: l'Etrusca disciplina dans une monde en mutation. Actes de Table Ronde de Clermont-Ferrand 17–18.09.1999*, Tours: 4–26.

Martin C., Namo-Pekelman C. (2008): Les Juifs et la cité. Pour une clarification du statut personnel des juifs de l'antiquité tardive à la fin du royaume de Tolède (IVe–VIIe siècles), *AntTard* 16: 223–246.

Martin D.B. (2004): *Inventing Superstition. From the Hippocratic to the Christians*, Cambridge–London.

Martindale J.R. (1980): *The Prosopography of the Later Roman Empire*, vol. 2, Cambridge.

Mathisen R.W. (2004): *Adnotatio* and *Petitio*: The Emperor's Favor and Special Exceptions in the Early Byzantine Empire, [in:] *La pétition à Byzance*, éds. D. Feissel, J. Gascou, Paris: 23–32.

Mathisen R.W. (2006): Violent Behavior and the Construction of Barbarian Identity in Late Antiquity, [in:] *Violence in Late Antiquity. Perceptions and Practices*, ed. H.A. Drake, Aldershot–Burlington: 27–35.

Matthews J.F. (1993): The Making of the Text, [in:] *The Theodosian Code. Studies in the Imperial Law of Late Antiquity*, eds. J. Harries, I. Wood, London: 19–44.

Matthews J.F. (2000): *Laying Down the Law. A Study of the Theodosian Code*, New Haven.

Mentxalca R. (1998): Delitos contra la moral sexual en las 'etimologias' de Isidoro, Labeo 44: 77–85.

Michelini A.N. (1998): Isocrates' Civic Invective: *Acharnanians* and *On the Peace*, *TAPhA* 128: 115–133.

Millar F. (2006): *A Greek Roman Empire. Power and Belief under Theodosius II. 408–450*, Berkeley–Los Angeles–London.

Miniconi P.J. (1958): Les termes d'injure dans le théatre comique, *REL* 36: 159–175.

Misztal-Konecka J. (2007): *Incestum w prawie rzymskim*, Lublin.

Mitchell S. (1988): Maximinus and the Christians in A.D. 312: A New Latin Inscription, *JRS* 78: 105–124.

Mommsen Th. (1899): *Römisches Strafrecht*, Leipzig.

Mommsen Th. (1900): Das theodosische Gesetzbuch, *ZRG* 21: 179–190.

Mommsen Th. (1905): Th. Mommsen, P.M. Meyer (eds.), *Theodosiani Libri XVI cum Constitutionibus Sirmondianis et Leges Novellae ad Theodosianum Pertinentes*, I.1 *Prologomena*, Berolini 1905.

Mordek H. (1987): Das kirchliche Recht im Übergang von der Antike zum Mittelalter, [in:] *Akten des 26. Deutschen Rechtshistorikertages*, Hrsg. D. Simon, Frankfurt am Main: 455–466.

Mossé C. (2006): Plutarch and the Sicilian Tyrants, [in:] *Ancient Tyranny*, ed. S. Lewis, Edinburgh: 188–196.

Müller A. (1913): Die Schimpfwörter in der römischen Komödie, *Philologus* 72: 492–502.

Müller-Graupa E. (1931): Primitiae II,4 superstitio, *Glotta* 19: 62–64.

Muñoz Llamosas V. (2008): Insultos e invectiva entre Demóstenes y Esquines, *Minerva* 21: 33–49.

Murphy J.M.J. (1997): *Hubris* and *Superbia*. Different Greek and Roman Attitudes Concerning "Arrogant Pride", *AncW* 28: 73–81.

Myszor W. (2007): Walka z manicheizmem w świetle *Kodeksu Justyniana*, [in:] *Byzantina Europaea. Księga jubileuszowa ofiarowana Profesorowi Waldemarowi Ceranowi*, red. M. Kokoszko, M.J. Leszka, Łódź: 417–424.

Nagy G. (1976): Iambos. Typologies of Invective and Praise, *Arethusa* 9: 191–205.

Neri V. (1997): L'usurpatore come tiranno nel lessico politico della tarda antichità, [in:] *Usurpationen in der Spätantike*, Hrsgg. F. Paschoud, J. Szidat, Stuttgart: 71–86.

Neri V. (1998): *I marginali nell'Occidente tardoantico: poveri, 'infames' e criminali nella nascente società cristiana*, Bari.

Nesselhauf H. (1938): *Die spätrömische Verwaltung der gallisch-germanischen Länder*, Berlin.

Neumann U. (1998): Invektive, [in:] *Historisches Wörtebuch der Rhetorik*, Bd. IV, red. G. Ueding, Tübingen: 549–561.

Noethlichs K.L. (1971): *Die Gesetzgeberischen Maßnahmen der christlichen Kaiser des vierten Jahrhunderts gegen Häretiker, Heiden und Juden*, Köln.

Noethlichs K.L. (1981): *Beamtentum und Dienstvergehen. Zur Staatsverwaltung in der Spätantike*, Wiesbaden.

Noethlichs K.L. (2006): Revolution from the Top? "Orthodoxy" and the Persecution of Heretics in Imperial Legislation from Constantine to Justinian, [in:] *Religion and Law in Classical and Christian Rome*, eds. C. Ando, J. Rüpke, Stuttgart: 115–125.

Ohnacker E. (2003): *Die spätantike und frühmittelalterliche Entwicklung des Begriffs* barbarus. *Ein interdisziplinärer Versuch der Beschreibung distinktiver und integrativer gesellschaftlicher Konzepte*, Münster–Hamburg–London.

Olszaniec S. (2007): *Comites Consistoriani w wieku IV. Studium prozopograficzne elity dworskiej Cesarstwa Rzymskiego 320–395 n.e.*, Toruń.

Oost S.I. (1962): Count Gildo and Theodosius the Great, *CPh* 57: 27–30.

Oost S.I. (1966): The Revolt of Heraclian, *CPh* 61: 236–242.

Opelt I. (1965a): *Die lateinischen Schimpfwörter und verwandte sprachliche Erscheinungen. Eine Typologie*, Heidelberg.

Opelt I. (1965b): Griechische und lateinische Bezeichnungen der Nichtchristen. Ein Terminologischer Versuch, *VChr* 19: 1–22.

Opelt I. (1967): Der Christenverfolger bei Prudentius, *Philologus* 111: 242–257.

Opelt I. (1972): Formen der Polemik bei Lucifer von Calaris, *VChr* 26: 200–226.

Opelt I. (1973): Hilarius von Poitiers als Polemiker, *VChr* 27: 203–217.

Opelt I. (1974): Schimpfwörter in der Apologie De errore profanarum religionum des Firmicus Maternus, *Glotta* 52: 114–126.

Opelt I. (1980): *Die Polemik in der christlichen lateinischen Literatur von Tertullian bis Augustin*, Heidelberg.

Osthoff G. (1952): *Tumultus – seditio. Untersuchungen zum römischen Staatsrecht und zur politischen Terminologie der Römer*, Köln.

Otto W.F. (1909, 1911): Religio und Superstitio, *Archiv für Religionswissenschaft* 12: 533–554, 14: 406–422.

Owen G.E.L. (1983): Philosophical Invective, *OSAPh* 1: 1–25.

Palma A. (1992): *Humanior interpretatio: Humanitas nell'interpretazione e nella normazione da Adriano ai Severi*, Torino.

Palme B. (1999): Die *officia* der Statthalter in der Spätantike. Forschungsstand und Perspektiven, *AntTard* 7: 85–133.

Palmieri R. (1996): *Laudatio* e *vituperatio* nell'*exordium* dell'XI *Filippica* di Cicerone, *Euphrosyne* 24: 119–204.

Parker R. (1983): *Miasma: Pollution and Purification in Early Greek Religion*, Oxford.

Pernot L. (1993): *La Rhétorique de l'éloge dans le monde gréco-romain*, t. I: *Histoire et technique*, Paris.

Pfaff G. (1925): Latrones, *RE* 12: 978–980.

Pharr C. (1952): *The Theodosian Code and Novels and the Sirmondian Constitutions. A Translation with Commentary, Glossary and Bibliography*, Princeton.

Pieler P.E. (1978): Rechtsliteratur, [in:] H. Hunger, *Die Hochsprachliche Profane Literatur der Byzantiner* 2 (*Handbuch der Altertumswissenschaft* 5.2), München: 343–480.

Pottier B. (2012): La politique de prohibition et de prévention de la violence des empereurs du IVe siècle [in:] *Société, Économie, Administration dans le* Code Théodosien, eds. S. Crogiez-Pétrequin, P. Jaillette, Lille: 201–232.

Powell J.G.F. (2007): Invective and the Orator. Ciceronian Theory and Practice, [in:] *Cicero on the Attack. Invective and Subversion in the Orations and beyond*, ed. J. Booth, Swansea: 1–24.

Preisert M. (2004): *Formy i funkcje agresji werbalnej. Próba typologii*, Wrocław.

Prostko-Prostyński J. (2008): Iudicium quinquevirale. *Sąd senatorski w Rzymie i Konstantynopolu od Gracjana do Justyniana*, Poznań.

Puliatti S. (1995): La dicotomia *vir-mulier* e la disciplina del ratto nelle fonti legislative tardo-imperiali, *SDHI* 61: 471–529.

Rabello A.M. (1980): The Legal Condition of the Jews in the Roman Empire, *ANRW* II.13, Berlin–New York: 662–762.

Rees R. (1998): The Private Lives of Public Figures in Latin Prose Panegyric, [in:] *The Propaganda of Power. The Role of Panegyric in Late Antiquity*, ed. M. Whitby, Leiden: 77–101.

Renier D. (1950): Observations sur la terminologie de l'aliénation mentale, *RIDA* 5: 429–455.

Ries G. (1983): *Prolog und Epilog in Gesetzen des Altertums*, München.

Riess W. (2001): *Apuleius und die Räuber. Ein Beitrag zur historischen Kriminalitätsforschung*, Heidelberger Althistorische Beiträge und Epigraphische Studien 35, Stuttgart.

Rilinger R. (1985): Die Interpretation des späten Imperium Romanum als „Zwangsstaat", *GWU 36*: 321–340.

Rilinger R. (1988): Humiliores - Honestiores. *Zu einer sozialen Dichotomie im Strafrecht der römischen Kaiserzeit*, München.

Ritter A.M. (1965): *Das Konzil von Konstantinopel und sein Symbol*, Göttingen.

Rives J.B. (2006): Magic, Religion and Law. The Case of the Lex Cornelia *de sicariis et veneficis*, [in:] *Religion and Law in Classical and Christian Rome*, eds. C. Ando, J. Rüpke, Stuttgart: 47–67.

Rivière Y. (2002): *Les délateurs sous l'empire romain*, Rome.

Rizzelli G. (1990): Il *crimen lenocinii*, *AG* 210: 459–464.

Rizzelli G. (1997): Lex Iulia de adulteriis: *studi sulla disciplina di adulterium, lenocinium, stuprum*, Lecce.

Rizzelli G. (2014): *Modeli di « follia » nella cultura di giuristi Romani*, Lecce.

Robinson O. (1995): *The Criminal Law of Ancient Rome*, Baltimore.

Robinson O. (2000): Roman Criminal Law: Rhetoric and Reality. Some Forms of Rhetoric in the Theodosian Code, [in:] *Au-delà frontières. Mélanges de droit romain offerts à W. Wołodkiewicz*, éds. M. Zabłocka, J. Krzynówek, J. Urbanik, Warszawa: 765–785.

Robinson O. (2001): Unpardonable Crimes. Fourth Century Attitudes, [in:] *Critical Studies in Ancient Law, Comparative Law and Legal History*, eds. J.W. Cairns, O. Robinson, Oxford–Portland Oregon: 117–126.

Rodziewicz A. (2006): *Ustrój Ateńczyków* i jego nieznany autor, *Meander* 61: 195–212.

Rollin J.P. (1979): *Untersuchungen zu Rechtsfragen römischer Bildnisse*, Bonn.

Rosen K. (1990): Iudex und Officium: Kollektivstrafe, Kontrolle und Effizienz in der spätantiken Provinzialverwaltung, *AncSoc* 21: 273–292.

Rosen R.M. (1988): *Old Comedy and the Iambographic Tradition*, Atlanta.

Rountree C. (2001): The (Almost) Blamless Genre of Classical Greek Epideictic, *Rhetorica* 19: 293–305.

Rowe G.O. (1966): The Portrait of Aeschines in the *Oration on the Crown*, *TAPhA* 97: 397–406.

Rugullis S. (1992): *Die Barbaren in spätrömischen Gesetzen. Eine Untersuchung des Terminus* barbarus, Frankfurt am Main–Bern–New York–Paris.

Sachot M. (1991): « Religio/superstitio ». Histoire d'une subversion et d'un retournement, *RHR* 208: 355–394.

Saffrey H.D. (1992): Le thème du malheur des temps chez les derniers philosophes néoplatoniciens, [in:] ΣΟΦΙΗΣ ΜΑΙΗΤΟΡΕΣ « Chercheurs de sagesse » Hommage à J. Pépin, éds. M.-O. Goulet Cazé, G. Madec, D. O'Brien, Paris : 421–431.

Salvemini R. (2000): Empietà e follia nella caratterizzazione degli eretici. Alle origini del lessico di Fozio, *Nicolaus* 27: 355–389.

Salzman M.R. (1987): 'Superstitio' in the Codex Theodosianus and the Persecution of Pagans, *VChr* 41: 172–188.

Salzman M.R. (1993): The Evidence for the Conversion of the Roman Empire to Christianity in Book 16 of the *Theodosian Code*, *Historia* 42: 362–378.

Sanchez Leon J.C. (1996): *Los bagaudas, rebeles, demonios, mártires: revueltas campesinas en Galia e Hispania durante el bajo imperio*, Jaén.

Sargenti M. (1986): Contributi alla palingenesi delle costituzioni tardo-imperiali. II. Momenti della normativa religiosa da Teodosio I a Teodosio II, *AARC* 6, Perugia: 341–362.

Sargenti M. (1995): Il Codice Teodosiano fra mito e realtà, *SDHI* 61: 373–398.

Schadenwaldt W. (1973): Humanitas Romana, [in:] *Aufstieg und Niedergang der Römischen Welt* 1.4, Hrsg. H. Temporini, Berlin: 43–62.

Scheithauer A. (2004): Gildo und seine Revolte im Spiegel der Dichtungen Claudians, [in:] Studia Humanitatis ac Litterarum Trifolio Heidelbergensi dedicata. *Festschrift für E. Christmann, W. Edelmaier, R. Kettemann*, Hrsgg. A. Horning, Ch. Jäkel, W. Schubert, Frankfurt am Main–Berlin–Bern–Bruxelles–New York–Oxford–Wien: 309–327.

Schlinkert D. (1996): Ordo senatorius *und* nobilitas. *Die Konstitution des Senatsadels in der Spätantike. Mit einem Appendix über den* praepositus sacri cubiculi, *den „allmächtigen" Eunuchen am kaiserlichen Hof*, Stuttgart.

Schlinkert D. (2002): Between Emperor, Court and Senatorial Order. The Codification of *Codex Theodosianus*, *AncSoc* 32: 283–294.

Schmidt-Hofner S. (2008a): *Reagieren und Gestalten. Der Regierungsstil des spätrömischen Kaisers am Beispiel der Gesetzgebungs Valentinians I*, München.

Schmidt-Hofner S. (2008b): Regesten der Kaiser Valentinian und Valens, *ZRG* 125: 498–602.

Scholten H. (1995): *Der Eunuch in der Kaisernähe - Zur politischen und sozialen Bedeutung der praepositus sacri cubiculi im 4. und 5. Jahrhundert n. Chr.*, Frankfurt am Main.

Schubart W. (1941): Zum Edikt über das aurum coronarium, *APF* 14: 44–59.

Schubert W. (1969): Die rechtliche Sonderstellung der Dekurionen in der Kaisergesetzgebung des 4. Jhs., *ZRG* 86: 287–333.

Schulz F. (1961): *Geschichte der römischen Rechtswissenschaft*, Weimar.

Seager R. (2007): Ciceronian Invective. Themes and Variations, [in:] *Cicero on the Attack. Invective and Subversion in the Orations and Beyond*, ed. J. Booth, Swansea: 25–46.

Seeck O. (1909): *Exactor*, [in:] *RE* 6, Stuttgart: 1540–1547.

Seeck O. (1919): *Regesten der Kaiser und Päpste*, Stuttgart.

Shaw B. (1984): Bandits in the Roman Empire, *P&P* 105: 3–52.

Shaw B. (1990): Bandit Highlands and Lowland Peace. The Mountains of Isauria-Cilicia, *JESHO* 33: 199–233, 237–270.

Simon D.V. (1977): *Konstantinisches Kaiserrecht. Studien anhand der Reskriptenpraxis und der Schenkungsrecht*, Frankfurt am Main.

Simonetti M. (1975): *La crisi ariana nel IV secolo*, Roma.

Sirks A.J.B. (1986): From the Theodosian to the Justinian Code, *AARC* VI, Perugia: 265–302.

Sirks A.J.B. (1993a): Did the Late Roman Government Try to Tie People to Their Profession or Status?, *Tyche* 8: 159–175.

Sirks A.J.B. (1993b): The Sources of the Code, [in:] *The Theodosian Code. Studies in the Imperial Law of Late Antiquity*, eds. J. Harries, I. Wood, London: 45–67.

Sirks A.J.B. (2007): *The Theodosian Code. A Study*, Friedrichsdorf.

Sivan H.S. (1996): Why Not Marry a Barbarian? Marital Frontiers in Late Antiquity (The Example of *C.Th.* 3.14.1), [in:] *Shifting Frontiers in Late Antiquity*, eds. R.W. Mathisen, H.S. Sivan, Aldershot: 136–145.

Skorupka S. (red.) (1988): *Słownik wyrazów bliskoznacznych*, Warszawa.

Śnieżewski S. (2003): *Salustiusz i historia Rzymu*, Kraków.

Speyer W. (1969): 'Fluch', *RAC* 7: 1160–1287.

Speyer W., Opelt I. (1967): Barbar. Nachträge zur Reallexikon für Antike und Christentum, *JbAC* 10: 251–290.

Stachura M. (2000a): *Heretycy, schizmatycy i manichejczycy wobec cesarstwa rzymskiego*, Kraków.

Stachura M. (2000b): Pojęcie „heretycy" w ustawodawstwie Konstantyna Wielkiego i jego następców, *Historyka* 30: 59–72.

Stachura M. (2003): Zur Motivation der Häretikerverfolgung im Spiegel von Gesetztestexten der Theodosianischen Dynastie, [in:] *Freedom and Its Limits in the Ancient World. Proceedings of a Colloquium Held at the Jagiellonian University, Kraków, September 2003*, (*Electrum* 9), eds. D. Brodka, J. Janik, S. Sprawski, Kraków: 249–262.

Stachura M. (2004): W poszukiwaniu istoty przestępstwa innowieców, [in:] *Chrześcijaństwo u schyłku starożytności. Studia Źródłoznawcze t. 5*, eds. T. Derda, E. Wipszycka, Kraków: 219–269.

Stachura M. (2006a): Eunomian Rights to Draw Testaments in the Legislation of 389–399, *ZSS KA* 92: 45–62.

Stachura M. (2006b): Kodeks Teodozjusza – nowo odkrywane źródło historyczne, *PHist* 97: 311–331.

Stachura M. (2006c): Stadt und Peripherie in der Häretikerpolitik der frühbyzantinischen Kaiser (ca. 325 bis 455), *Palamedes* 1: 133–152.

Stachura M. (2007a): Kritik der *superstitio* und Affirmation der Orthodoxie in den Gesetzen des *Codex Theodosianus*, [in:] *Studies on the Late Roman History*, (*Electrum* 12), ed. E. Dąbrowa, Kraków: 33–61.

Stachura M. (2007b): Idea wykluczenia z rzymskiej społeczności obywatelskiej w antymanichejskim ustawodawstwie cesarzy późnorzymskich, [in:] Byzantina Europaea. *Księga jubileuszowa ofiarowana Profesorowi Waldemarowi Ceranowi*, red. M. Kokoszko, M.J. Leszka, Łódź: 533–542.

Stachura M. (2008): Pogańska ofiara i heretyckie nabożeństwo w ujęciu praw Kodeksu Teodozjusza, [in:] *Sympozja Kazimierskie poświęcone kulturze świata późnego antyku i wczesnego chrześcijaństwa*, t. VI: *Ofiara - kapłan - ołtarz w świecie późnego antyku*, red. B. Iwaszkiewicz-Wronikowska, D. Próchniak, Lublin: 179–192.

Stein E. (1922): *Untersuchungen über das Officium der Prätorianerpräfektur seit Diokletian*, Wien.

Steinwenter A. (1916): Iniuria, *RE* 9.2, Stuttgart: 1555–1558.

Stemberger G. (2002): Die Verbindung von Juden mit Häretikern in den spätantiken römischen Gesetzgebung, [in:] *Hairesis. Festschrift für K. Hoheisel, JbAC Ergänzungsband* 34, Hrsgg. M. Hutter, W. Klein, U. Vollmer, Münster: 203–214.

Stępień T. (2000): O inwektywie, [in:] *Językowy obraz świata i kultura* (*Acta Universitatis Wratislawiensis. Język a Kultura*, t. 13), red. A. Dąbrowska, J. Ankiewicz, Wrocław: 311–325.

Stolte B. (2008): The Use of Greek in the Theodosian Code, [in:] *Aspects of Law in Late Antiquity. Dedicated to A.M. Honoré on the Occasion of the Sixtieth Year of His Teaching in Oxford*, ed. B. Sirks, Oxford: 77–94.

Sussman L.A. (1998): Antony the *Meretrix Audax*: Cicero's Novel Invective in *Philippic* 2: 44–46, *Eranos* 96: 114–128.

Taldone A. (1993): Su insania e furor in Cicerone, *BStudLat* 23: 3–19.

Tellegen J.W. (1979): *Captatio* and *crimen*, *RIDA* 26: 387–397.

Thesaurus Linguae Latinae, Lipsiae 1900–

Thomas J.D. (1959): The Office of Exactor in Egypt, *CE* 34: 124–140.

Thome G. (1992): Crime and Punishment, Guilt and Expiation. Roman Thought and Vocabulary, *AClass* 35: 73–98.

Thome G. (1993): *Vorstellungen von Bösen in der lateinischen Literatur. Begriffe, Motive, Gestalten*, Stuttgart.

Thome G. (2000): *Zentrale Wertvorstellungen der Römer II. Texte - Bilder - Interpretationen*, Bamberg.

Thraede K. (1969): Exorcismus, *RAC* 7: 43–117.

Trombley F.R. (1993): *Hellenic Religion and Christianization C. 370–529*, vol. I, Leiden–New York–Köln.

Turpin W. (1985): The Law Codes and Late Roman Law, *RIDA* 32: 339–353.

Turpin W. (1988): *Adnotatio* and Imperial Rescript in Roman Legal Procedure, *RIDA* 35: 285–307.

Turpin W. (1991): Imperial Subscriptions and the Administration of Justice, *JRS* 81: 101–118.

Ulrich Th. (1930): *Pietas (pius) als politischer Begriff im römischen Staate bis zum Tode des Kaisers Commodus*, Breslau.

Uría J. (2007): The Semantics and Pragmatics of Ciceronian Invective, [in:] *Cicero on the Attack. Invective and Subversion in the Orations and Beyond*, ed. J. Booth, Swansea: 47–70.

Vaggione R.P. (2000): *Eunomius of Cyzicus and the Nicene Revolution*, Oxford.

Vallar S. (2016): Folie et droi romain – Quelques observations, *Criminocorpus revue hypermédia*, [http://journals.openedition.org/3146 access data 5.09.2018]

Van der Wal N. (1980): Die Textfassung der spätrömischen Kaisergesetze in den Codices, *BIDR* 83: 1–27.

Van der Wal N. (1981): *Edictum* und *lex edictalis*. Form und Inhalt der Kaisergesetze im spätrömischen Reich, *RIDA* 28: 277–313.

Venturini C. (1988): Accusatio adulterii e politica costantiniana (per riesame di *C.Th.* 9.7.2), *SDHI* 54: 66–109.

Vera D. (1986): Alcune note sul quaestor sacri palatii, [in:] *Hestíasis. Studi di tarda antichità offerti a S. Calderone I (Studi tardoantichi No 1)*, Messina: 27–53.

Vernay E. (1913): Note sur le changement de style dans les constitutions impériales de Dioclétien a Constantin, [in:] Études d'histoire juridiques offertes à P.F. Girard, 2, Paris: 263–274.

Vessey M. (1993): The Origins of the *Collectio Sirmondiana*. A New Look at the Evidence, [in:] *The Theodosian Code. Studies in the Imperial Law of Late Antiquity*, eds. J. Harries, I. Wood, London: 178–199.

Veyne P. (1981): Clientèle et corruption au service de l'état: la vénalité des offices dans le Bas Empire, *Annales (ESC)*: 339–360.

Vincenti U. (1995): La legislazione contro gli apostati data a Concordia nell'anno 391 (*C.Th.* 16.7.4–5), *SDHI* 61: 399–412.

Vismara G. (1947): Limitazioni al commercio intenazionale nell'impero romano e nella comunità cristiana medioevale, [in:] *Scritti in onore di C. Ferrini*, t. 1, Milano: 443–470.

Voci P. (1953): Diritto sacro romano in età arcaica, *SDHI* 19: 38–103.

Volterra E. (1959): Quelques remarques sur le style des constitutions de Constantin, [in:] *Droits de l'Antiquité et Sociologie Juridique. Mélanges H. Lévy-Bruhl*, Paris: 325–334.

Voß W.E. (1982): *Recht und Rhetorik in den Kaisergesetzen der Spätantike: Eine Untersuchung zum nachklassischen Kauf- und Übereignungsrecht* (Forschungen zur Byzantinischen Rechtsgeschichte 9), Frankfurt am Main.

Voß W.E. (1989): (recensione) Materiali per una palingenesi delle costituzioni tardo-imperiali, 2: O. Seeck, Die Zeitfolge der Gesetze Konstantins. Ristampa anastatica con introduzione e tavole di raffronto a cura di M. Sargenti, *ZSS* 106: 632–645.

Wagenvoort H. (1980a): Pietas, [in:] H. Wagenvoort, *Pietas, Selected Studies in Roman Religion*, Leiden: 1–20.

Wagenvoort H. (1980b): Profanus, profanare, [in:] H. Wagenvoort, *Pietas, Selected Studies in Roman Religion*, Leiden: 25–38.

Waldstein W. (1964): *Untersuchungen zum römischen Begnadigungsrecht*, Innsbruck.

Wardman A.E. (1984): Usurpers and Internal Conflicts in the 4th Century A.D., *Historia* 33: 220–237.

Ware C. (2004): Gildo *tyrannus*: Accusation and Allusion in the Speeches of Roma and Africa, [in:] Aetas Claudianea. *Eine Tagung an der Freier Universität Berlin 28–30.06.2002*, Hrsgg. W.-W. Ehlers, F. Felgentreu, M. Wheeler, Leipzig: 96–103.

Weische A. (1966): *Studien zur politischen Sprache der römischen Republik*, Münster.

Wenger L. (1953): *Die Quellen des Römischen Recht*, Wien.

Wilken R.L. (1983): *John Chrysostom and the Jews. Rhetoric and Reality in the Late 4th Century*, Berkeley–Los Angeles–London.

Wipszycka E. (1999): Źródła normatywne świeckie, [in:] *Vademecum historyka starożytnej Grecji i Rzymu. Źródłoznawstwo czasów późnego antyku*, red. E. Wipszycka, Warszawa: 585–617.

Wirszubski Ch. (1961): *Audaces*: A Study in Political Phraseology, *JRS* 51: 12–22.

Wissemann M. (1992): *Schimpfwörter in der Bibelübersetzung des Hieronymus*, Heidelberg.

Wolf J.G. (2009): Das Stigma Ignominia, *ZRG* 126: 55–113.

Wood N. (1986): *Populares* and *circumcelliones*. The Vocabulary of the 'Fallen Man' in Cicero and St. Augustine, *HPTh* 7: 33–51.

Wood I. (1993): The Code in Merovingian Gaul, [in:] *The Theodosian Code. Studies in the Imperial Law of Late Antiquity*, eds. J. Harries, I. Wood, London: 161–177.

Zanetto G. (2001): Iambic Patterns in Aristophanic Comedy, [in:] *Iambic Ideas. Essays on a Poetic Tradition from Archaic Greece to the Late Roman Empire*, eds. A. Carvarzere, A. Aloni, A. Barchiesi, Lanham–Boulder–New York–Oxford: 65–76.

Zeddies N. (2003): *Religio et sacrilegium. Studien zur Inkriminierung von Magie, Häresie und Heidentum (4.–7. Jahrhundert)*, Frankfurt am Main.

Ziegler J. (1970): *Zur religiösen Haltung der Gegenkaiser im 4. Jh. n. Chr.*, Kallmünz.

Zinser H. (2002): Religio, secta, hairesis in den Häresiegesetzen des Codex Theodosianus (16,5,1/66) von 438, [in:] *Hairesis. Festschrift für K. Hoheisel, JbAC Ergänzungsband* 34, Hrsgg. M. Hutter, W. Klein, U. Vollmer, Münster: 215-219.

Zuccotti F. (1992): *Furor Haereticorum. Studi sul trattamento giuridico della follia e sulla persecuzione della eterodossia religiosa nella legislazione del tardo impero Romano*, Milano.

Index of Latin terms

abomino 206–208, 255
acerbitas 106, 176, 179, 239 n. 31
adulterium 92–94, 147 n. 15, 180, 188, 190–193, 195, 200, 203, 212–214, 236 n. 12, 253, 255, 259
adversarius 121, 123–124
amentia 152 n. 47, 163, 165 n. 69, 166 n. 76, 168–172, 170 n. 109
Apollinarianus 137, 138
apostata 121 n. 20, 134, 140–142, 169, 177, 179, 194, 195, 197, 198, 227, 247
Apotactita 135 n. 99, 138
Arrianus 27, 46 n. 19, 100–102, 134 n. 91, 138
Ascodrogus 140
attingo 202–204
audacia 44 n. 6, 64 n. 5, 80, 87, 91, 100, 104, 105, 109, 123 n. 28, 129, 145, 149–170, 172, 184, 206, 213, 236, 237, 240, 241, 247 n. 117, 249–251, 253–255, 259 n. 16, 260, 263
Audianus 138
augur 143, 226 n. 27, 228
avaritia 145–147, 249, 251, 251 n. 163
avaritia 81, 83, 145–147, 184, 249, 251

barbarus 21, 60 n. 78, 64 n. 5, 105, 108 n. 73, 117, 119, 124–128, 141, 146 n. 1, 147, 168, 176–180, 191, 192, 210–212, 221, 238, 239, 241, 253, 261, 263
Borborianus 138

Caelestianus 138
Caelicola 138, 224 n. 16, 226, 244 n. 80, 258
Chaldeus 142
conor 104, 153, 162
contagium 60 n. 78, 91, 93–98, 103, 121, 178, 187, 189 n. 10, 195–206, 213, 219, 222, 226, 228, 240, 241, 244–247, 250, 253–255, 262
contaminatio 27, 100, 102, 196, 198, 200, 202, 203, 205 n. 76, 259 n. 17
crimen 27, 100–103, 106, 110, 170, 183, 187–193, 201, 214, 215, 223, 224, 226, 228, 235, 242, 243, 252–256
crimen vis 154, 159, 209, 212–214, 255, 256
crudelitas 146, 168, 175, 179, 184, 238, 239, 251 n. 163, 254
culpabilis 206, 208
cupiditas 55 n. 59, 146, 147, 152 n. 43, 165, 197, 249, 251

damnabilis 206, 208, 226 n. 26
delictum 188, 190 n. 14
dementia 100, 104, 163, 168–171
depraedatio 81, 83, 124 n. 30, 127, 211, 212, 238 n. 28, 249, 251
depravatio 226–228, 244 n. 81, 246 n. 83
desertor 132, 155, 159, 191, 192, 211, 241
detestor, detestabilis 110, 114, 122 n. 24, 204, 208

desidia 146, 148
devasto 211
devio 226–228
dirus 178, 203, 205, 244 n. 83, 253, 254 n. 188
discursus 211, 212
Donatista 134 n. 91, 135 n. 98, 138, 169, 170 n. 109, 243

Encratita 135 n. 99, 138
Enthusiasta 138
error 98, 143 n. 123, 124, 169, 170, 172 n. 114, 199 n. 39, 226, 227, 244, 246 n. 103, 252
Euchita 138
Eunomianus 27, 100–103, 138, 169, 171, 243 n. 74
excursus 211, 212
execror 110, 114, 207, 208, 224, 244, 254, 255
expiatio 196

facinus 64, 143, 188–190, 191 n. 18, 193 n. 23
feritas 126, 175–179, 238, 241
fides 145, 165, 180–182, 214, 236 n. 20
flagitium 91, 179, 188, 191 n. 18, 193, 194, 251, 259 n. 17
Fotinianus 27, 100–103, 139, 200 n. 50, 205 n. 76
Fryga 135, 139
funestus 199 n. 39, 200 n. 50, 203, 204, 205 n. 76, 250
furor 64 n. 5, 81, 84–85, 91, 94, 98, 104, 119, 126 n. 42, 129, 145, 153 n. 51, 163–173, 176, 215, 219, 222, 226, 238, 240–242, 244, 246, 247 n. 116, 118, 250, 254–256

gentilis 141–142, 169, 171
haereticus, *haeresis* 21, 34, 38, 39 n. 81, 58, 74 n. 43, 81, 100–105, 112, 117, 120, 134–140, 142, 152, 153 n. 52, 157, 159, 160, 167, 169–174, 176–179, 182, 185, 190, 191, 193–198, 200 n. 50, 202–207, 214, 216–218, 223–228, 235, 242–246, 248, 251, 253, 258, 261
hariolus 143
haruspex 18 n. 16, 142, 143, 224, 225
homicidium 48 n. 26, 91–93, 130 n. 63, 159, 190, 195, 200, 213, 253, 256, 261
hostis 75, 84, 85, 110, 114, 117–124, 126, 130, 142 n. 122, 169, 171, 178 n. 144, 200, 201, 212, 237–241, 253, 260
humanitas 19, 44, 57, 60 n. 79, 80, 73, 91, 124, 145, 174–179, 221, 238
Hydroparastata 135 n. 99, 139

immanitas 134–137, 221, 238, 254, 259 n. 17
impietas 170, 182, 183, 192, 193
implacabilis 206, 207
improbitas 152, 184, 185
incursus 127, 212
inexcusabilis 206, 207
inexpiabilis 110, 115, 196, 206, 254 n. 191
infandus 130, 194, 195, 240
infaustus 205, 244 n. 83
inhumanus 175, 178
inimicus 89, 110, 114, 117–123, 142 n. 122, 237, 223 n. 15, 242, 244, 253, 261
inquietudo 209–211, 216, 217, 250, 251
insania 84–85, 132, 163, 168–172, 176 n. 137
insolentia 84, 88, 154, 162, 163, 184, 185, 250
intolerabilis 206, 207
invasio 91, 94, 185, 212, 213, 256, 259
invidia 129, 148, 149, 240
Iudeus 112, 123, 134, 157, 161, 163, 167, 169, 171, 172, 179, 182, 193, 195,

210, 211, 214, 215, 217, 223–228, 243 n. 189, 247, 248, 258

labes 94, 96–98 n. 44, 102, 129, 153 n. 51, 203, 205, 206, 240, 241, 253
latro, latrocinium 15, 81, 83, 109, 117, 130–133, 155, 159, 167–169, 171, 176 n. 137, 177, 179, 190–192, 194, 211, 213, 215, 217, 241, 251, 259, 262
libido 145–148
luxuria 147, 165

macula 91, 93, 98 n. 44, 198, 199 n. 39, 201–203, 205 n. 76
magus, magia 15, 22, 89–93, 99 n. 47, 121–123, 136, 142, 143, 147 n. 15, 155, 159, 177, 190, 195, 200, 203, 205, 206, 217, 220 n. 3, 222 n. 8, 252, 253, 255, 256, 259, 262, 263
maiestas 87, 91–93, 99 n. 47, 154, 188, 190–192, 204, 214, 236, 253, 261
maleficus 91, 92, 142, 143, 190, 200 n. 52, 205 n. 76
Manicheus 22, 110–115, 120, 121 n. 20, 135 n. 99, 136, 139, 167, 169, 170 n. 109, 172 n. 114, 190, 191, 196, 197, 235, 242, 243 n. 74, 253 n. 175
Marcellianus 139
Marcianista 139
mathematicus 142, 143, 226, 227, 252
mente caecitas 91, 94, 168, 170 n. 110, 171
mente captus 170, 171, 176 n. 137
Messalianus 139
Montanista 139

nefas, nefarius, nefandus 27, 81, 83, 91, 93, 100, 103, 188, 194, 195, 251
notabilis 206, 207
Novatianus 135, 139, 243

obstinatio 100, 169, 170, 172, 173, 247 n. 116, 249
Ofita 139

paganus 21, 33, 34, 39 n. 81, 62, 110, 112, 114, 120, 125 n. 38, 128 n. 52, 134, 136, 140–142, 157, 160, 167–171, 173, 180, 182, 185, 193, 196–199, 201–204, 207, 213–217, 222–226, 228, 235, 243–247, 253, 258, 262
parricidium 64, 91–93, 169, 171, 189, 191, 203, 215, 236 n. 12, 254 n. 196
Paulianus 135, 139
peculatus 191, 193 n. 23, 200 n. 50, 204, 215, 251, 260 n. 22
perfidia 27, 100, 103, 180, 182, 244, 246
pertinacia 49, 100, 168, 170 n. 107, 172, 173, 244, 246 n. 104, 249, 250
perversitas 55, 111, 115, 226–228, 244, 247 n. 116, 248, 250 n. 150
pestis 89, 90, 177, 179, 200, 203–206, 244 n. 83, 250, 253
petulans 154, 163
piaculum 169, 187, 188, 193 n. 26, 195–196, 254
pietas 145, 146, 165, 182–184
plectibilis 206, 208
Pneumatomachus 140
polluo 94–98, 110, 111, 114, 115, 143 n. 124, 198–206, 254
Porfyrianus 136, 137, 139
praedo 130, 131, 133, 211, 212 n. 89
praesumptio 84, 86, 87, 129, 130, 153, 157–162, 172, 199 n. 39, 236
pravitas 167, 169, 173, 180, 222, 223, 226, 227, 244, 246 n. 103, 251
Priscillianista 140
procacitas 154, 163
profanus, profanatio 91, 93, 104, 105, 185, 187, 195–198, 227, 244, 246, 247, 255 n. 198

praetervitas 154, 163
Protopaschita 140

rabies 95, 98, 168, 171
rapacitas 27, 81, 83, 215, 216, 251
raptus 93, 154, 159, 189–193, 195, 197, 200, 203, 208, 209, 213, 215, 255–256, 259
rebellis 132, 133
repetundae 203
reprehensibilis 206, 208

Sabbatianus 139, 243
Saccoforus 135 n. 99, 140
sacrilegium 27, 91, 100, 103, 110, 113, 170 n. 111, 188, 195, 213–215, 202 n. 64, 226 n. 29, 233–237, 255
saevitia, *saevitas* 175, 177, 178, 181, 238, 239 n. 31
scaevitas 94, 96, 224, 226, 228, 229, 244
scelus 64, 106, 110, 115, 165, 188–193, 195, 196, 199 n. 38, 201, 243, 246, 247 n. 119, 251, 252–255, 259 n. 16
seditio 92 n. 29, 151, 210, 216–218, 248
segnitia 148
serpo 105, 109, 174, 257 n. 1
Simonianus 136, 137, 139
sordes 94, 98, 201–204
subreptio 105, 106, 109, 173, 174
superbia 91, 93, 151, 152, 164 n. 62, 172 n. 116
superstitio 18 n. 16, 21, 64 n. 5, 110, 111, 113, 114, 120, 123, 141, 143 n. 124, 164, 166, 167, 169 n. 102, 170, 198, 201, 204, 219–226, 243, 244, 246, 247, 253, 254, 262

Tascodrogita 140
temeritas 84–87, 99, 100, 105, 152, 153, 157–162, 165, 166, 184, 185, 206 n. 79, 212 n. 89, 236, 259 n. 16
tempto 84, 100, 103, 104, 142 n. 119, 153, 156–162, 259 n. 16
tumultus 211, 212, 216–218
turba, *turbare* 100, 102, 216–218, 244
turbare 89, 91, 142 n. 119, 216–218
tyrannus 31, 33 n. 45, 38, 98, 117, 119, 126, 128–130, 149, 150, 152, 155, 159, 165, 167, 169, 171, 176, 192, 194, 195, 203–206, 228–229, 240, 241, 263

Valentinianus 135, 140
vastatio 106, 127, 210, 211, 238
vates 143, 226 n. 27, 228
venenum 27, 100, 103, 173
vesania 106, 110, 154 n. 53, 163, 168, 170–171, 176, 254
violentia, *violatio* 84, 91, 94, 100, 103, 202, 203, 209, 212–214, 235 n. 10, 236, 253, 255, 256, 263
violatio sepulchri 81, 91, 93, 96, 120, 121, 126, 128, 147 n. 14, 149, 155, 159, 168, 169, 171, 176, 179, 180, 183, 185, 190, 192, 195, 196, 199, 200, 203, 205, 207, 208, 213–215, 234 n. 1, 252–254, 256, 259, 263
virus 173

PROOFREADERS
Jadwiga Makowiec
Małgorzata Szul

TYPESETTER
Magdalena Warzecha

Jagiellonian University Press
Editorial Offices: Michałowskiego 9/2, 31-126 Kraków
Phone: +48 12 663 23 80, Fax: +48 12 663 23 83